Table of Contents

The Official
CompTIA
A+ Core 1
Study Guide
(Exam 220-1101)

Course Edition: 1.0

Acknowledgments

CompTIA.

James Pengelly, Author
Becky Mann, Director, Product Development
James Chesterfield, Senior Manager, User Experience and Design
Danielle Andries, Manager, Product Development

Notices

Disclaimer

Trademark Notice

Copyright Notice

About This Course

CompTIA is a not-for-profit trade association with the purpose of advancing the interests of information technology (IT) professionals and IT channel organizations; its industry-leading IT certifications are an important part of that mission. CompTIA's A+ certification is a foundation-level certification designed for professionals with 12 months hands-on experience in a help desk support technician, desk support technician, or field service technician job role.

CompTIA A+ certified professionals are proven problem solvers. They support today's core technologies from security to cloud to data management and more. CompTIA A+ is the industry standard for launching IT careers into today's digital world. It is trusted by employers around the world to identify the go-to person in end-point management and technical support roles. CompTIA A+ is regularly re-invented by IT experts to ensure that it validates core skills and abilities demanded in the workplace.

Course Description

Course Objectives

This course can benefit you in two ways. If you intend to pass the CompTIA A+ Core 1 (Exam 220-1101) certification examination, this course can be a significant part of your preparation. But certification is not the only key to professional success in the field of IT support. Today's job market demands individuals with demonstrable skills, and the information and activities in this course can help you build your skill set so that you can confidently perform your duties in any entry-level PC support role.

On course completion, you will be able to do the following:

- Install, configure, and troubleshoot PC motherboards, system components, and peripheral devices.

- Compare networking hardware types and configure local addressing and Internet connections.

- Summarize uses for network services, virtualization, and cloud computing.

- Support the use of mobile devices and print devices.

Target Student

The Official CompTIA A+ Core 1 (Exam 220-1101) is the primary course you will need to take if your job responsibilities include supporting the use of PCs, mobile devices, and printers within a corporate or small office home office (SOHO) network. You can take this course to prepare for the CompTIA A+ Core 1 (Exam 220-1101) certification examination.

 Please note that in order to become A+ certified, a candidate must pass both Exams 220-1101 and 220-1102.

Prerequisites

To ensure your success in this course, you should have 12 months of hands-on experience working in a help desk technician, desktop support technician, or field service technician job role. CompTIA ITF+ certification, or the equivalent knowledge, is strongly recommended.

 The prerequisites for this course might differ significantly from the prerequisites for the CompTIA certification exams. For the most up-to-date information about the exam prerequisites, complete the form on this page: www.comptia.org/training/resources/ exam-objectives

How to Use the Study Notes

The following notes will help you understand how the course structure and components are designed to support mastery of the competencies and tasks associated with the target job roles and will help you prepare to take the certification exam.

As You Learn

At the top level, this course is divided into **lessons,** each representing an area of competency within the target job roles. Each lesson is composed of a number of topics. A **topic** contains subjects that are related to a discrete job task, mapped to objectives and content examples in the CompTIA exam objectives document. Rather than follow the exam domains and objectives sequence, lessons and topics are arranged in order of increasing proficiency. Each topic is intended to be studied within a short period (typically 30 minutes at most). Each topic is concluded by one or more activities designed to help you apply your understanding of the study notes to practical scenarios and tasks.

In addition to the study content in the lessons, there is a glossary of the terms and concepts used throughout the course. There is also an index to assist in locating particular terminology, concepts, technologies, and tasks within the lesson and topic content.

 In many electronic versions of the book, you can click links on key words in the topic content to move to the associated glossary definition, and you can click page references in the index to move to that term in the content. To return to the previous location in the document after clicking a link, use the appropriate functionality in your eBook viewing software.

Watch throughout the material for the following visual cues.

Student Icon	Student Icon Descriptive Text
	A **Note** provides additional information, guidance, or hints about a topic or task.
	A **Caution** note makes you aware of places where you need to be particularly careful with your actions, settings, or decisions so that you can be sure to get the desired results of an activity or task.

As You Review

Any method of instruction is only as effective as the time and effort you, the student, are willing to invest in it. In addition, some of the information that you learn in class may not be important to you immediately, but it may become important later. For this reason, we encourage you to spend some time reviewing the content of the course after your time in the classroom.

Following the lesson content, you will find a table mapping the lessons and topics to the exam domains, objectives, and content examples. You can use this as a checklist as you prepare to take the exam, and review any content that you are uncertain about.

As a Reference

The organization and layout of this book make it an easy-to-use resource for future reference. Guidelines can be used during class and as after-class references when you're back on the job and need to refresh your understanding. Taking advantage of the glossary, index, and table of contents, you can use this book as a first source of definitions, background information, and summaries.

Lesson 1

Installing Motherboards and Connectors

LESSON INTRODUCTION

One of the main roles for a CompTIA A+ technician is to install and configure personal computer (PC) hardware. This hands-on part of the job is what draws many people to a career in information technology (IT) support. As an IT professional, you will set up desktop computers and help end users to select a system configuration and peripheral devices that are appropriate to their work. You will often have to connect peripheral devices using the correct cables and connectors and install plug-in adapter cards.

To complete these tasks, you must understand how the peripheral devices and internal PC components are connected via the motherboard. As you may encounter many different environments in your work, you must also be able to distinguish and support both modern and legacy connection interfaces.

Lesson Objectives

In this lesson, you will:

- Explain cable types and connectors.

- Install and configure motherboards.

- Explain legacy cable types.

Topic 1A

Explain Cable Types and Connectors

CORE 1 EXAM OBJECTIVES COVERED
3.1 Explain basic cable types and their connectors, features, and purposes.

A PC is made up of many different components. All these components need to be able to communicate with each other so that the computer can function properly. If you can distinguish connection interfaces and connectors quickly, you will be able to support users by installing, upgrading, and replacing PC peripherals efficiently.

Personal Computers

The components of a personal computer (PC) are divided between those that are designed to be handled by the user—peripheral devices—and those that would be damaged or dangerous if exposed. Peripheral devices typically perform the function of input (keyboard, mouse, microphone, and camera), output (monitor and speakers), or external storage.

The system case/chassis houses the internal components. These include the motherboard, central processing unit (CPU), system memory modules, adapter cards, fixed disks, and power supply unit. Most cases use a tower form factor that is designed to be oriented vertically and can be placed on a desk or on the floor.

PCs can also be purchased as all-in-one units. All-in-one means that the internal components are contained within a case that is also a monitor.

To perform PC maintenance, you must understand how to open a desktop computer's case.

- A tower case has a side cover that can be removed by sliding the panel from its housing. Cases might be secured by screws or retaining clips and might have anti-tamper security mechanisms. Always refer to the system documentation, and follow the recommended steps.

- The front panel provides access to the removable media drives, a power on/off switch, and light- emitting diodes (LEDs) to indicate drive operation. The front cover can be removed but may require the side panel to be removed first to access the screws or clips that secure it.

Features on the front of a typical PC case. (Image © 123RF.com)

The rear panel provides access to the power supply unit (PSU) sockets. The PSU has an integral fan exhaust. Care should be taken that it is not obstructed, as this will adversely affect cooling. There may be an additional case fan.

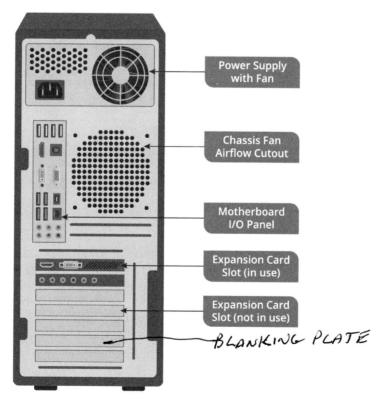

Features on the rear panel of a typical PC case. (Image © 123RF.com)

Below the PSU, there is a cutout aligned with the motherboard's input/output (I/O) ports. These allow for the connection of peripheral devices.

At the bottom of the rear panel there are cutout slots aligned with the position of adapter card slots to allow cables to be connected to any I/O ports on the cards. These slots should either be covered by an adapter card or a metal strip known as a blanking plate. Uncovered slots can disrupt the proper flow of air around components in the PC and cause overheating and increase the amount of dust in the system.

Peripheral Devices

An input/output (I/O) port allows a device to be connected to the PC via a **peripheral cable**. Some ports are designed for a particular type of device, such as a graphics port to connect a monitor. Other ports support a variety of device types. External ports are positioned at the rear or front of the PC through cutouts in the case. They can be provided on the motherboard or as an expansion card.

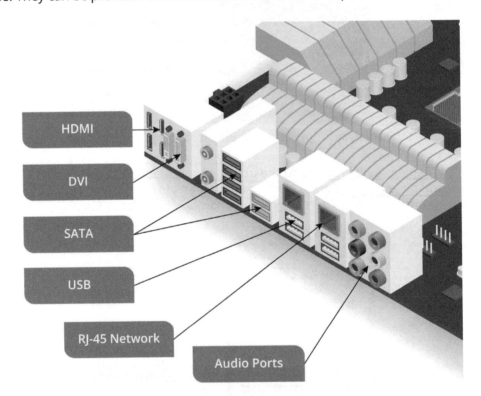

I/O ports on a motherboard. (Image © 123RF.com)

Interfaces, Ports, and Connectors

A hardware port is the external connection point for a particular type of bus interface. A bus allows the transfer of data to and from devices. The connector is the part of a peripheral cable that can be inserted into a port with the same shape or form factor. Each bus interface type might use multiple connector form factors. Most connectors and ports now use edge contacts and either have an asymmetric design called *keying* to prevent them from being inserted the wrong way around or are reversible.

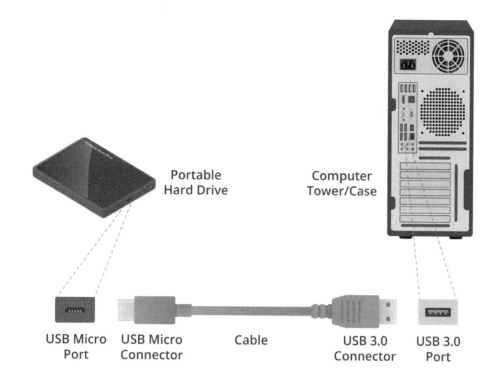

A peripheral cable for the Universal Serial Bus (USB) interface with different connector types being used to connect a portable hard drive and a desktop computer. (Image © 123RF.com)

Binary Data Storage and Transfer Units

When comparing bus interfaces, it is important to use appropriate units. Computers process binary data. Each binary digit or bit (b) can have the value one or zero. Storage is often measured in multiples of eight bits, referred to as a byte (B). A lowercase "b" unit refers to a bit, while uppercase means a byte.

Transfer rates are expressed in units per second of the following multiples of bits and bytes:

- 1000—Kilobits (Kb/s or Kbps) and kilobytes (KB/s and KBps).

- 1000x1000—Megabits (Mb/s) or megabytes (MB/s).

- 1000x1000x1000—Gigabits (Gb/s) and gigabytes (GB/s).

Universal Serial Bus Cables

The Universal Serial Bus (USB) is the standard means of connecting most types of peripheral device to a computer. USB peripheral device functions are divided into classes, such as human interface (keyboards and mice), mass storage (disk drives), printer, audio device, and so on.

A USB is managed by a host controller. Each host controller supports multiple ports attached to the same bus. In theory, there could be up to 127 connected devices per controller, but to overcome the limitations of sharing bandwidth, most PC motherboards provision multiple USB controllers, each of which has three or four ports.

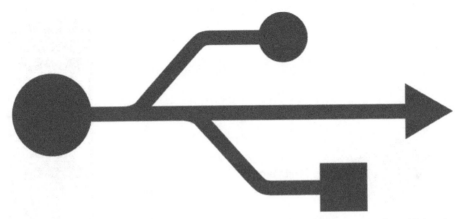

USB port symbol. Variations on this basic icon identify supported features, such as higher transfer rates and power delivery. Wikimedia Commons (commons.wikimedia.org/wiki/File:USB_icon.png)

USB Standards

There have been several iterations of the USB standard. Each version introduces better data rates. A version update may also define new connector form factors and other improvements. The **USB 2.0** HighSpeed standard specifies a data rate of 480 Mbps shared between all devices attached to the same host controller. The bus is half-duplex, meaning that each device can send or receive, but not at the same time.

Iterations of USB 3.x introduced new connector form factors and upgraded transfer rates, each of which are full-duplex, so a device can send and receive simultaneously. USB 3.2 deprecated some of the older terms used to describe the supported transfer rate:

Standard	Speed	Connectors	Legacy Designation
USB 3.2 Gen 1 SuperSpeed USB	5 Gbps	USB-A, USB-C, USB Micro	USB 3.0
USB 3.2 Gen 2x1 SuperSpeed USB 10 Gbps	10 Gbps	USB-A, USB-C, USB Micro	USB 3.1 SuperSpeed+
USB 3.2 Gen 2x2 SuperSpeed USB 20 Gbps	2 x 10 Gbps	USB-C	

USB 3 controllers feature two sub-controllers. One controller handles SuperSpeed-capable devices, while the other supports legacy HighSpeed, FullSpeed, and LowSpeed USB v1.1 and v2.0 devices. Consequently, legacy devices will not slow down SuperSpeed-capable devices.

USB Connector Types

The connector form factors specified in USB 2 are as follows:

- Type A—For connection to the host and some types of peripheral device. The connector and port are shaped like flat rectangles. The connector should be inserted with the USB symbol facing up.

- Type B—For connection to large devices such as printers. The connector and port are square, with a beveled top.

- Type B **Mini**—A smaller peripheral device connector. This type of connector was seen on early digital cameras but is no longer widely used.

- Type B **Micro**—An updated connector for smaller devices, such as smartphones and tablets. The micro connector is distinctively flatter than the older mini type of connector.

USB 2 ports and connectors. (Image © 123RF.com)

A USB cable can feature Type A to Type A connectors or can convert from one type to another (Type A to Type B or Type A to Micro Type B, for instance).

In USB 3, there are new versions of the Type A, Type B, and Type B Micro connectors with additional signaling pins and wires. USB 3 receptacles and connectors often have a blue connector tab or housing to distinguish them. USB 3 Type A connections are physically compatible with USB 1.1 and 2.0 connections, but the Type B/Type B Micro connections are not. So, for example, you could plug a USB 2 Type A cable into a USB 3 Type A port, but you could not plug a USB 3 Type B cable into a USB 2 Type B port.

USB 3.0 and 3.1

Type A   Type B   Type B Micro   Type C

USB 3 connectors and ports (from left to right): Type A, Type B, Micro Type B, Type C.
(Image ©123RF.com)

USB 3.1 defines the USB-C connector type. This compact form factor is intended to provide a single, consistent hardware interface for the standard. The connector is reversible, meaning it can be inserted either way up. The connector design is also more robust than the earlier miniB and microB types. USB-C can use the same type of connector at both ends, or you can obtain USB-C to USB Type A or Type B converter cables.

Cable Length

The maximum cable length for LowSpeed devices is 3 m, while for FullSpeed and HighSpeed the limit is 5 m. Vendors may provide longer cables, however. Although SuperSpeed-capable cables do not have an official maximum length, up to about 3 m is recommended.

Power

As well as a data signal, the bus can supply power to the connected device. Most USB Type A and Type C ports can be used to charge the battery in a connected device.

 Basic USB ports can supply up to about 4.5 watts, depending on the version. A power delivery (PD)–capable port can supply up to 100 watts, given suitable connectors and cabling.

HDMI and DisplayPort Video Cables

The USB interface supports many types of devices, but it has not traditionally been used for video. As video has high bandwidth demands, it is typically provisioned over a dedicated interface.

Video cable bandwidth is determined by two main factors:

- The resolution of the image, measured in horizontal pixels by vertical pixels. For example, 1920x1200 is the typical format of high-definition (HD) video and 3840x2160 is typical of 4K video.

- The speed at which the image is redrawn, measured in hertz (Hz) or frames per second (fps).

As examples, uncompressed HD video at 60 fps requires 4.5 Gbps, while 4K at 60 fps requires 8.91 Gbps.

The frame rate in fps is used to describe the video source, while hertz is the refresh rate of the display device and video interface. To avoid display artefacts such as ghosting and tearing, the refresh rate should match the frame rate or be evenly divisible by it. For example, if the frame rate is 60 fps and the refresh rate is 120 Hz, the video should play smoothly.

Computer displays are typically of the liquid crystal display (LCD) thin film transistor (TFT) type. Each pixel in a color LCD comprises cells with filters to generate the three additive primary colors red, green, and blue (RGB). Each pixel is addressed by a transistor to vary the intensity of each cell, therefore creating the gamut (range of colors) that the display can generate. The panel is illuminated by a light-emitting diode (LED) array or backlight.

An LCD/TFT is often just referred to as a flat-panel display. They are also called LED displays after the backlight technology (older flat panels use fluorescent tube backlights). Premium flat-panel monitors are of the organic LED (OLED) type. This means that each pixel is its own light source. This allows for much better contrast and color fidelity.

High-Definition Multimedia Interface

The **High-Definition Multimedia Interface (HDMI)** is the most widely used video interface. It is ubiquitous on consumer electronics, such as televisions, games consoles, and Blu-ray players as well as on monitors designed for use with PCs. HDMI supports both video and audio, plus remote control and digital content protection (HDCP). Updates to the original HDMI specification have introduced support for high resolutions, such as 4K and 8K, and gaming features, such as the ability to vary the monitor refresh rate to match the frame rate of the video source.

Support for audio is useful because most TVs and monitors have built-in speakers. The video card must have an audio chipset for this to work, however.

There are full-size (Type A), mini (Type C), and micro (Type D) connectors, all of which are beveled to ensure correct orientation.

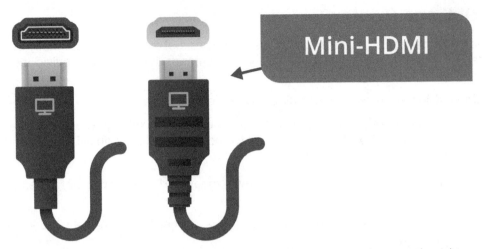

*HDMI connector and port on the left and mini-HDMI connector and port on the right.
(Image ©123RF.com)*

HDMI cable is rated as either Standard (Category 1) or High Speed (Category 2). High Speed cable supports greater lengths and is required for v1.4 features, such as 4K and refresh rates over 60 Hz. HDMI versions 2.0 and 2.1 specify Premium High Speed (up to 18 Gbps) and Ultra High Speed (up to 48 Gbps) cable ratings.

DisplayPort Interface

HDMI was developed by consumer electronics companies and requires a royalty to use. **DisplayPort** was developed as a royalty-free standard by the Video Electronics Standards Association (VESA), which is an organization that represents PC graphics adapter and display technology companies. DisplayPort supports similar features to HDMI, such as 4K, audio, and content protection. There are full-size DP++ and MiniDP/mDP port and connector types, which are keyed against incorrect orientation.

A DP++ DisplayPort port and connector. (Image ©123RF.com)

Bandwidth can be allocated in bonded lanes (up to four). The bitrate of each lane was originally 2.7 Gbps but is now (with version 2.0) up to 20 Gbps.

One of the main advantages of DisplayPort over HDMI is support for daisy-chaining multiple monitors to the same video source. Using multiple monitors with HDMI requires one video card port for each monitor.

Thunderbolt and Lightning Cables

Although the Thunderbolt and Lightning interfaces are most closely associated with Apple computers and mobile devices, Thunderbolt is increasingly implemented on Windows and Linux PCs too.

Thunderbolt Interface

Thunderbolt can be used as a display interface like DisplayPort or HDMI and as a general peripheral interface like USB. Thunderbolt versions 1 and 2 use the same physical interface as MiniDP and are compatible with DisplayPort so that a monitor with a DisplayPort port can be connected to a computer via a Thunderbolt port and a suitable adapter cable. Thunderbolt ports are distinguished from MiniDP by a lightning bolt/flash icon. Version 2 of the standard supports links of up to 20 Gbps. Like DisplayPort multiple monitors can be connected to a single port by daisy-chaining.

The USB-C form factor adopted for Thunderbolt 3. (Image © 123RF.com)

Thunderbolt version 3 changes the physical interface to use the same port, connector, and cabling as USB-C. Converter cables are available to connect Thunderbolt 1 or 2 devices to Thunderbolt 3 ports. A USB device plugged into a Thunderbolt 3 port will function normally, but Thunderbolt devices will not work if connected to a USB port that is not Thunderbolt-enabled. Thunderbolt 3 supports up to 40 Gbps over a short, high-quality cable (up to 0.5 m/1.6 ft.).

 Not all USB-C ports support Thunderbolt 3. Look for the flash icon on the port or confirm using the system documentation. At the time of writing, converged USB 4 and Thunderbolt 4 standards have been developed, and products are starting to appear on the market.

Lightning Interface

Apple's iPhone and iPad mobile devices use a proprietary **Lightning** port and connector. The Lightning connector is reversible.

Apple Lightning connector and port. (Image ©123RF.com)

The Lightning port is found only on Apple's mobile devices. To connect such a device to a PC, you need a suitable adapter cable, such as Lightning-to-USB A or Lightning-to-USB C.

SATA Hard Drive Cables

As well as external cabling for peripheral devices, some types of internal components use cabling to attach to a motherboard port.

Serial Advanced Technology Attachment Interface

Serial Advanced Technology Attachment (SATA) is the standard means of connecting internal storage drives within a desktop PC. SATA uses cables of up to 1 m (39 in.) terminated with compact 7-pin connectors. Each SATA host adapter port supports a single device.

SATA connectors and ports (from left to right): SATA data, SATA power (with 3.3V orange wire). (Image ©123RF.com)

The 7-pin data connector does not supply power. A separate 15-pin SATA power connector is used to connect the device to the PC's power supply.

The first commercially available SATA standard supported speeds of up to 150 MBps. This standard was quickly augmented by SATA revision 2 (300 MBps) and then SATA revision 3 (600 MBps).

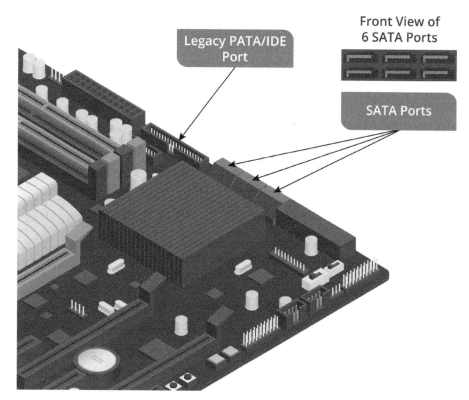

Motherboard SATA and legacy PATA/IDE ports. (Image ©123RF.com)

Molex Power Connectors

Internal storage device data cables are unpowered. While the SATA power connector is the best option for new devices, legacy components connect to the power supply unit (PSU) via a **Molex connector**. A Molex connector is usually white or clear plastic and has 4 pins. The color coding of the wire insulation represents the DC voltage: red (5 VDC), yellow (12 VDC), and black (ground).

A Molex connector. (Image © 123RF.com)

  Some devices might have both SATA and Molex power connectors.

External SATA

There is also an **external SATA (eSATA)** standard for the attachment of peripheral drives, with a 2 m (78 in.) cable. You must use an eSATA cable to connect to an external eSATA port; you cannot use an internal SATA cable. eSATAp is a nonstandard powered port used by some vendors that is compatible with both USB and SATA (with an eSATAp cable). The USB interface dominates the external drive market, however.

Review Activity:

Cable Types and Connectors

Answer the following questions:

1. **A technician has removed an adapter card from a PC. Should the technician obtain and install a blanking plate to complete the service operation?**

2. **You are labelling spare parts for inventory. What type of USB connector is shown in the exhibit?**

(Image ©123RF.com)

3. **What is the nominal data rate of a USB port supporting Gen 3.2 2x1?**

4. **True or false? USB-C ports and connectors are compatible with Apple Lightning connectors and ports.**

5. **A technician connects a single port on a graphics card to two monitors using two cables. What type of interface is being used?**

6. A technician is completing a storage upgrade on an older computer. Examining the power supply, the technician notices that only two of the five plugs of the type shown in the exhibit are connected to devices. What is the purpose of these plugs, and can some be left unconnected?

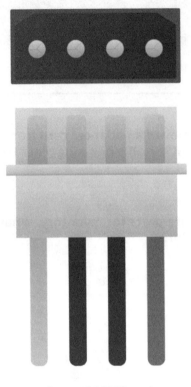

(Image ©123RF.com)

Topic 1B

Install and Configure Motherboards

 CORE 1 EXAM OBJECTIVES COVERED
3.4 Given a scenario, install and configure motherboards, central processing units (CPUs), and add-on cards.

The motherboard houses sockets for the devices that implement the core system functions of a personal computer: compute, storage, and networking. Knowledge of motherboard types and capabilities plus the different connector types will enable you to perform component upgrades and repairs efficiently.

Motherboard Functions

All computer software and data are processed by using the ones and zeroes of binary code. Software works by running instructions in the central processing unit (CPU). This can be referred to as the compute or processing function of a PC.

Instructions and data also require storage. The CPU can only store a limited number of instructions internally at any one time. Additional storage for running programs and open data files is provided through system memory. This random-access memory (RAM) storage technology is nonpersistent. *Nonpersistent* means that the RAM devices can only hold data when the PC is powered on. Mass storage devices are used to preserve data when the computer is turned off.

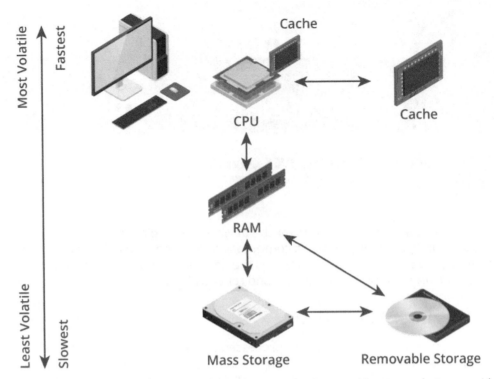

CPU, cache, and RAM are fast but volatile. Mass storage and removable storage devices provide slower but permanent data retrieval. (Image ©123RF.com)

These processing and storage components are connected by bus interfaces implemented on the motherboard. The instructions and data are stored using transistors and capacitors and transmitted between components over the bus using electrical signals.

The motherboard's system clock synchronizes the operation of all parts of the PC and provides the basic timing signal for the CPU. Clock speeds are measured in megahertz (MHz) or gigahertz (GHz). Clock multipliers take the timing signal produced by the generator and apply a multiplication factor to produce different timing signals for different types of buses. This means that one type of bus can work at a different speed (or frequency) to another type of bus.

The type of motherboard influences system speed and the range of system devices and adapter cards that can be installed or upgraded. There are many motherboard manufacturers, including AOpen (Acer), ASRock, ASUSTek, Biostar, EVGA Corporation, Gigabyte, Intel, and MSI. Each motherboard is designed to support a particular range of CPUs. PC CPUs are principally manufactured by Intel and Advanced Micro Devices (AMD).

Electrical Safety and ESD

When you open the case to perform upgrades or troubleshooting, you must follow proper operational procedures to ensure your safety and minimize the risk of damaging components.

Electrical Safety

When working with a PC, you must ensure your own safety. This means that the PC must be disconnected from the power supply before opening the case. Additionally, hold the power button for a few seconds after disconnecting the power cord to ensure that all internal components are drained of charge. Do not attempt to disassemble components that are not field repairable, such as the power supply.

Electrostatic Discharge

You need to use tools and procedures that minimize the risk of damage to the sensitive electronic components used inside the PC. Components such as the CPU, system RAM, adapter cards, and the motherboard itself are vulnerable to electrostatic discharge (ESD). This is where a static charge stored on your clothes or body is suddenly released into a circuit by touching it. Handle components by their edges or plastic parts, and ideally, use an anti-ESD wrist strap and other protective equipment and procedures.

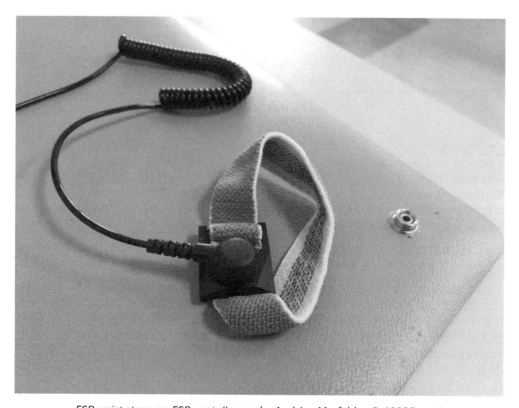

ESD wrist strap on ESD mat. (Image by Audrius Merfeldas © 123RF.com)

Operational procedures covering personal safety and the use of anti-ESD equipment are covered in more detail in the Core 2 course.

Motherboard CPU and System Memory Connectors

All motherboards have a variety of **connector types** and socket types for the system devices: CPU, memory, fixed disk drives, and adapter cards.

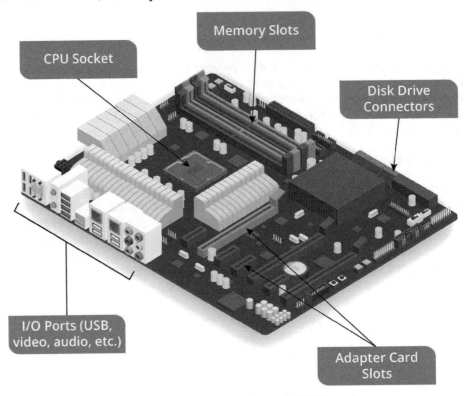

Motherboard connectors. (Image © 123RF.com)

CPU Sockets

New motherboards are generally released to support the latest CPU models. Most PC CPUs are manufactured by Intel and AMD, and these vendors use different socket designs. Because CPU technology changes rapidly, a given motherboard will only support a limited number of processor models.

The CPU socket has a distinctive square shape. When the CPU has been installed, it is covered by a heat sink and fan.

The function of the CPU is supported by the motherboard's chipset. This consists of controllers that handle the transfer of data between the CPU and various devices. The chipset is soldered onto the motherboard and cannot be upgraded. The type of chipset on the motherboard determines the choice of processor; the type and maximum amount of RAM; and support for integrated interfaces/ports, such as video, sound, and networking. Interfaces that are not supported by the chipset can be installed or upgraded as an adapter card.

System Memory Slots

System memory uses a type of memory technology called random-access memory (RAM). Program code is loaded into RAM so that it can be accessed and executed by the processor. RAM also holds data, such as the contents of a spreadsheet or document, while it is being modified. System RAM is volatile; it loses its contents when power is removed.

System RAM is normally packaged as a dual inline memory module (DIMM) fitted to a motherboard slot. A DIMM slot has catches at either end, is located close to the CPU socket, and is numbered and often color-coded. There are successive generations of RAM technologies, such as DDR3, DDR4, and DDR5. A DIMM form factor is specific to a particular DDR version. A label next to the slots should identify the type of DIMMs supported.

The capabilities of the memory controller and number of physical slots determine how much memory can be fitted.

Motherboard Storage Connectors

One or more fixed disks installed inside the PC case provide persistent storage for the operating system, software programs, and data files. Fixed disks use either solid state drive (SSD) or hard disk drive (HDD) technology.

Serial Advanced Technology Attachment Interface

The motherboard will contain several Serial Advanced Technology Attachment (SATA) ports to connect one or more fixed drives. SATA can also be used to connect removable drives, such as tape drives and optical drives (DVD/Blu-ray). SATA devices are installed to a drive bay in the chassis and then connected to a data port via a cable and to the power supply via a SATA power or Molex connector.

M.2 Interface

An SSD can be provisioned in an adapter card form factor. These often use an M.2 interface. An M.2 port is oriented horizontally. The adapter card is inserted at an angle and then pushed into place and secured with a screw. M.2 adapters can be different lengths (42 mm, 60 mm, 80 mm, or 110 mm), so you should check that any given adapter will fit on your motherboard. Labels indicate the adapter sizes supported. M.2 supplies power over the bus, so there is no need for a separate power cable.

M.2 form factor SSD being inserted into a motherboard connector. (Image ©123RF.com)

External SATA Interface

There is also an **external SATA (eSATA)** standard for the attachment of external drives, with a 2 m (78 in.) cable. You must use an eSATA cable to connect to an external eSATA port; you cannot use an internal SATA cable. eSATAp is a nonstandard powered port used by some vendors that is compatible with both USB and SATA (with an eSATAp cable).

 The main drawback of eSATA compared to USB or Thunderbolt external drives is that power is not supplied over the cable. This is not so much of an issue for 3.5-inch drives, which require a separate power supply, but it limits the usefulness of eSATA for 2.5-inch portable drives.

Motherboard Adapter Connectors

Expansion slots accept plug-in adapter cards to extend the range of functions the computer can perform. There are two main types of expansion slot interface.

Peripheral Component Interconnect Express Interface

The **Peripheral Component Interconnect Express (PCIe)** bus is the mainstream interface for modern adapter cards. It uses point-to-point serial communications, meaning that each component can have a dedicated link to any other component.

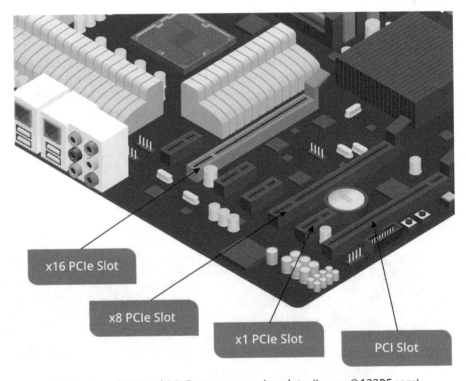

Motherboard PCI and PCI Express expansion slots. (Image ©123RF.com)

Each point-to-point connection is referred to as a link. Each link can make use of one or more lanes. The raw transfer rate of each lane depends on the PCIe version supported. Transfer rates are measured in gigatransfers per second (GT/s). Throughput in GB/s is the rate achieved after loss through encoding is accounted for.

Version	GT/s	GB/s for x1	GB/s for x16
2	5	0.5	8
3	8	0.985	15.754
4	16	1.969	31.508
5	32	3.938	63.015

Adapter slots with more lanes are physically longer. Each PCIe adapter card supports a specific number of lanes, typically x1, x4, x8, or x16. Ideally, the card should be plugged into a port that supports the same number of lanes. However, if insufficient slots are available, a card will fit in any port with an equal or greater number of lanes. This is referred to as up-plugging. For example, a x8 card will fit in a x8 or x16 socket. The card should work at x8 but in some circumstances may only work at x1.

It may also be possible to fit a longer card into a shorter slot, referred to as down-plugging, so long as the card is not obstructed by other features in the case.

A slot may support a lower number of lanes than its physical size suggests. The number of lanes supported by each slot is indicated by a label on the motherboard. For example, a slot that is physically x16 but supports only x8 operation will be labelled x16/x8 or x16 @ x8.

All PCIe versions are backwards-compatible. For example, you can connect a PCIe version 2 adapter to a version 4 motherboard or install a version 3 adapter into a version 2 motherboard. The bus works at the speed of the lowest version component.

PCIe can supply up to 75W to a graphics card via a dedicated graphics adapter slot and up to 25W over other slots. An extra 75W power can be supplied via a PCIe power connector.

Peripheral Component Interconnect Interface

Computers can support more than one expansion bus, often to support older technologies. **Peripheral Component Interconnect (PCI)** is a legacy bus type, having been superseded by PCI Express. PCIe is software compatible with PCI, meaning that PCI ports can be included on a PCIe motherboard to support legacy adapter cards, but PCI cards cannot be fitted into PCIe slots.

As with many legacy technologies, PCI uses parallel communications. Most types of PCI are 32-bit and work at 33.3 MHz, achieving a transfer rate of up to 133 MBps (that is, 32 bits divided by 8 to get 4 bytes, then multiplied by the clock rate of 33.3). The earliest PCI cards were designed for 5V signaling, but 3.3V and dual voltage cards became more prevalent. To prevent an incompatible PCI card from being inserted into a motherboard slot (for example, a 3.3V card in a 5V PCI slot), the keying for the three types of cards is different.

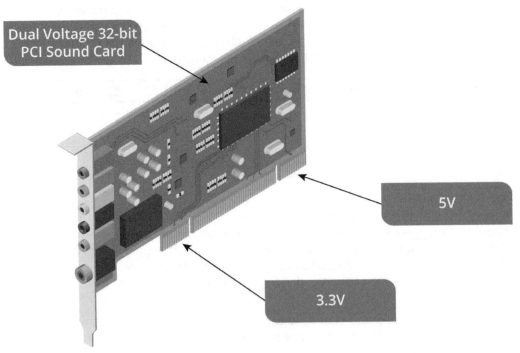

32-bit PCI sound card with dual voltage. (Image ©123RF.com)

Motherboard Form Factors

The **motherboard form factor** describes its shape, layout, and the type of case and power supply that can be used, plus the number of adapter cards that can be installed.

Advanced Technology eXtended Form Factor

The **Advanced Technology Extended (ATX)** specification is the standard form factor for most desktop PC motherboards and cases. Full-size ATX boards are 12 inches wide by 9.6 inches deep (or 305 mm x 244 mm). An ATX board can contain up to seven expansion slots.

The Micro-ATX (mATX) standard specifies a 9.6-inch (244 mm x 244 mm) square board. mATX boards can have a maximum of four expansion slots.

 Most mATX boards can be mounted in ATX cases.

Information Technology eXtended Form Factor

Small form factor (SFF) PCs are popular as home machines and for use as mini servers. SFF PCs often use Via's Mini-ITX (**Information Technology Extended**) form factor.

Mini-ITX is 6.7 inches (170 mm x 170 mm) square with one expansion slot. These are designed for small cases, but do note that most mini-ITX boards can be mounted in ATX cases. There are also smaller nano-, pico-, and mobile-ITX form factors, but these are used for embedded systems and portables, rather than PCs.

 No commercial motherboards were ever produced from the original plain ITX specification.

Motherboard Installation

The motherboard is attached to the case by using standoffs. These hold the motherboard firmly and ensure no other part of it touches the case. The standoffs are positioned in holes that line up in the same position in the case and the motherboard if they use compatible form factors

The general procedure for installing a motherboard is as follows:

1. Use the motherboard documentation to familiarize yourself with the specific installation procedure. Check whether any jumper clips need to be adjusted. A jumper is placed over header pins in a particular orientation. For example, there might be a jumper that enables recovery mode.

 The motherboard is vulnerable to electrostatic discharge (ESD). Always take anti-ESD precautions when handling and storing these devices.

2. Orient the board to the oblong I/O cutout at the rear of the case. Prepare the motherboard I/O blanking plate in the correct orientation by removing caps so that USB, audio, and video ports will be uncovered when the board is fitted. Fit the blanking plate to the case by snapping it into the cutout.

3. Insert standoffs into the case to match the hole locations on the motherboard. Standoffs are usually threaded, though older cases might use push-down pegs. There might be a guide standoff attached to the case or all standoffs might come preinstalled. Make sure that corners, long edges, and the center of the board will be supported. Do not add standoffs where there is no corresponding hole in the motherboard.

4. Optionally, add the CPU and memory modules to the motherboard before installing the board in the case.

5. Check the alignment and standoff location again and verify that each standoff is secure. If everything is correct, place the motherboard on the standoffs.

Align the board with the I/O cutout (top left) and ensure that it is supported by standoffs at the edges and in the center. (Image courtesy of CompTIA.)

6. Secure each standoff using the appropriate screw type. Make sure that the board is firm and stable, but do not overtighten the screws or you risk cracking the board.

7. To complete PC installation, add the power and disk devices to the case, install any addon adapter cards to the motherboard, and install the data and power connectors.

 Selection and installation of power, disk, system memory, and CPU devices are covered in detail in the next lesson.

Motherboard Headers and Power Connectors

In addition to slots and sockets for system devices, motherboards also include connectors for components such as case buttons, speakers, and fans.

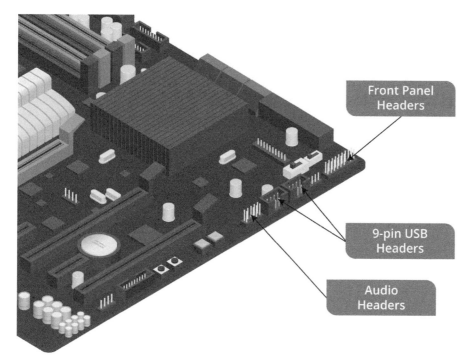

Motherboard front panel, USB, and audio headers. (Image ©123RF.com)

Headers

Components on the front and rear panels of the case connect to **headers** on the motherboard:

- **Power button (soft power)**—Sends a signal that can be interpreted by the OS as a command to shut down rather than switching the PC off. Holding down the power button for a few seconds will cut the power, however.

- **Drive (HDD) activity lights**—Show when an internal hard disk is being accessed.

- **Audio ports**—Allow speakers and/or headphones and a microphone to be connected to the computer.

- **USB ports**—Internal USB 2 connections are made via 9-pin headers, which accept up to two 4-pin port connections (the 9th pin is to orient the cable correctly). USB 3 headers use a 2x10 format and can be cabled to two ports.

When disassembling the system, you should make a diagram of the position and orientation of header connectors. If you do not have a diagram, you will have to refer to the motherboard documentation or go by any labels printed on the wires and headers. These are not always very easy to follow, however.

Power Connectors

The motherboard also contains various connection points for the power supply and fans.

- The main P1 motherboard **power connector** is a distinctive 2-pin x 12-pin block with square pin receptacles.

- Fan connectors are 3- or 4-pin Molex KK format. There will be one for the CPU and one or more for the case fans and components such as memory and video adapters. 4-pin fan connectors support precise fan-speed control via a pulse width modulation (PWM) signal carried by the blue wire. 3-pin fans are controlled by varying the voltage.

 Fans with a 3-pin connector can usually be used with 4-pin headers, but the system may not be able to vary the fan speed (or may need special configuration to be able to do so). A fan with a 4-pin connector will usually work with a 3-pin header but will not be able to use PWM.

Video Cards and Capture Cards

An **expansion card** adds functions or ports that are not supported by the integrated features of the motherboard. An expansion card can be fitted to an appropriate PCIe or PCI slot. Some of the main types of expansion card are sound, video, capture, and network.

Video Cards

The **video card** (or graphics adapter) generates the signal to drive a monitor or projector. Low-end graphics adapters are likely to be included with the motherboard chipset or as part of the CPU itself. This is also referred to as an onboard adapter or onboard graphics. If a computer is to be used for 3-D gaming, computer-aided design (CAD), or digital artwork, a more powerful video adapter is required. This can be installed as an add-on card via a PCIe slot. Most graphics adapters are based on chipsets by ATI/AMD, NVIDIA, and Intel. Video cards are distinguished by the following features:

- **Graphics Processing Unit (GPU)**—A microprocessor designed and optimized for processing instructions that render 2-D and 3-D images and effects on-screen. The basic test for a GPU is the frame rate it can produce for a particular game or application. Other performance characteristics include support for levels of texture and lighting effects.

- **Graphics memory**—3-D cards need a substantial amount of memory for processing and texture effects. A dedicated card may be fitted with up to 12 GB GDDR RAM at the high end; around 4–6 GB would be more typical of current mid-range performance cards. Low-end cards use shared memory (that is, the adapter uses the system RAM). Some cards may use a mix of dedicated and shared memory.

- **Video ports**—The type and number of connectors, such as HDMI, DisplayPort, and Thunderbolt.

 Graphics Double Data Rate (GDDR) memory technology is similar to the DDR modules used for system RAM.

Most modern cards use a PCIe x16 interface. Dual cards, using two (or more) slots, are also available.

A video/graphics card with DisplayPort, HDMI, and DVI-I ports. (Image ©123RF.com)

Capture Cards

Where a graphics card generates an output video signal to drive a monitor, a **capture card** is used to record video input and save it as a type of movie or streaming media file. Many capture cards are designed to record footage from computer games. Some are designed to work with PC games, while others record from game console HDMI sources or from a live camera HDMI source, such as a camcorder or security camera. Another class of capture card can act as a TV tuner and record video from broadcast TV sources.

A capture card can be fitted as an internal PCIe or as an external unit connected via USB/Thunderbolt.

Sound Cards

Audio playback is achieved via speakers or headphones, which are connected to a **sound card** via an audio jack. Sound cards are also used to record input from a microphone. Most audio jacks are 3.5 mm (⅛ inch) mono or stereo jacks. These are also referred to as phone plugs or mini tip, ring, sleeve (TRS) connectors.

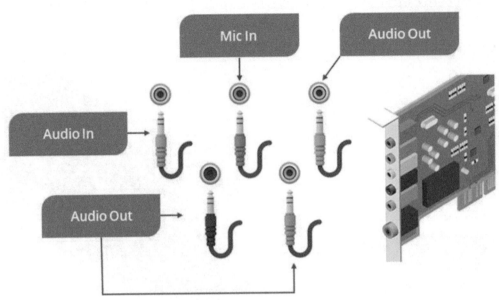

Audio jacks on a sound card. (Image ©123RF.com)

Sound cards supporting multiple output channels with an appropriate speaker system can provide various levels of playback, from mono (on legacy systems) or stereo to some type of surround sound. Surround sound uses multiple speakers positioned around the listener to provide a "cinematic" audio experience.

A basic sound chip may be provided as part of the motherboard chipset, but better-quality audio functions can be provided as a PCIe or PCI expansion card. Pro-level cards may also feature onboard memory, flash memory storing sound samples (wavetables), and additional jack types for different input sources.

 Audio hardware built into a computer may be susceptible to noise from other internal components when using recording functionality. Consequently, most audio interfaces designed for professional use are external units connected via USB or Thunderbolt.

Network Interface Cards

Most computers have an Ethernet network adapter already installed as part of the motherboard chipset. However, there may be occasions when you need to install an add-on **network interface card (NIC)** or need to upgrade an adapter to use a different type of network or cabling/connector, such as copper cable versus fiber optic. A dedicated NIC may also provision multiple ports. These can be bonded into a single higher bandwidth link.

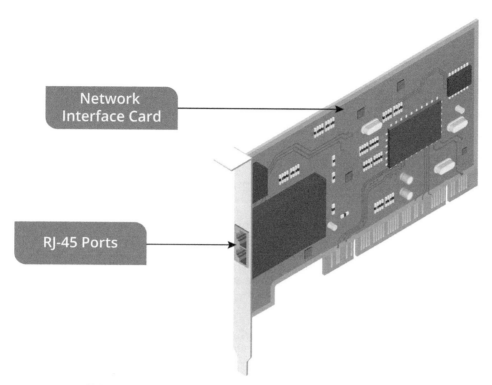

RJ45 ports on a Network Interface Card (NIC). (Image ©123RF.com)

A Wi-Fi adapter can be added to connect to a wireless network. Wi-Fi adapters are developed to different 802.11 standards. There are also cards that can connect to cellular data networks.

Review Activity:

Motherboards

Answer the following questions:

1. **What type of motherboard socket is used to install system memory?**

2. **How many storage devices can be attached to a single SATA port?**

3. **What is the bandwidth of a PCIe v2.0 x16 graphics adapter?**

4. **You have a x8 PCIe storage adapter card—can you fit this in a x16 slot?**

5. **You are labelling spare parts for inventory. What type of motherboard is displayed here?**

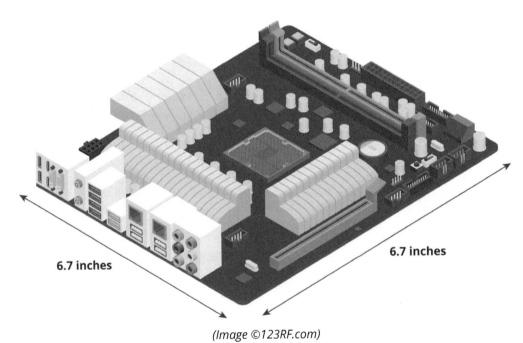

6.7 inches

6.7 inches

(Image ©123RF.com)

6. **You have another part to label for inventory. What category of adapter card is shown in the exhibit?**

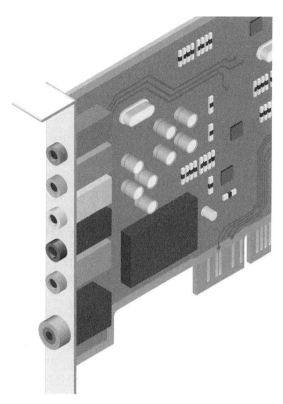

(Image ©123RF.com)

Topic 1C

Explain Legacy Cable Types

CORE 1 EXAM OBJECTIVES COVERED
3.1 Explain basic cable types and their connectors, features, and purposes.

As PC designs have evolved over the years, many types of bus interface have been implemented as connectivity solutions for computer components that maximize the performance and functionality at the time. There can be many reasons why computer systems using these older bus types remain in use in the workplace. As you are likely to work in diverse environments over the course of your career, it is important that you be able to support older technologies alongside modern ones.

DVI and VGA Video Cables

The HDMI and DisplayPort video interfaces only support digital flat-panel displays. Older video interfaces were used when computer monitors and projectors were predominantly of the cathode ray tube (CRT) type, driven by an analog signal.

Digital Visual Interface

Digital Visual Interface (DVI) is designed to support both analog and digital outputs. While popular for a period after its introduction in 1999, DVI is no longer in active development. You are only likely to encounter DVI on older display devices and video cards.

There are five types of DVI, supporting different configurations for single and dual link (extra bandwidth) and analog/digital output signaling. The pin configuration of the connectors identifies what type of DVI is supported by a particular port.

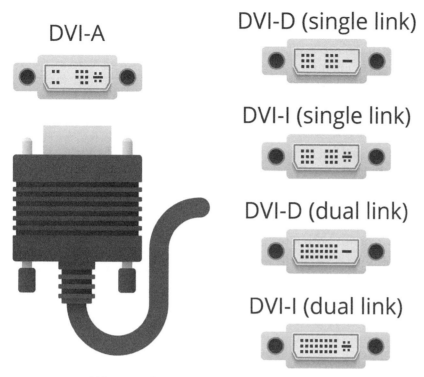

DVI port and connector types. (Image ©123RF.com)

DVI-I supports both analog equipment and digital outputs. DVI-A supports only analog output and DVI-D supports only digital.

Video Graphics Array Interface

The 15-pin **Video Graphics Array (VGA)** port was the standard analog video interface for PC devices for a very long time. Up until a few years ago, most video cards and monitors included a VGA port, though it is starting to be phased out completely now. VGA will usually support resolutions up to HD (1920x1080), depending on cable quality. The connector is a D-shell type with screws to secure it to the port.

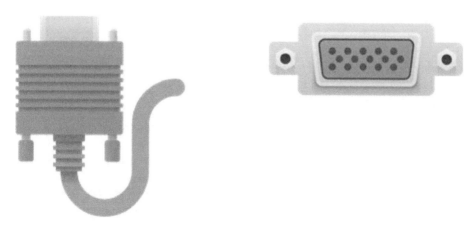

A VGA connector and port. (Image ©123RF.com)

Small Computer System Interface

Modern bus interfaces such as USB and Thunderbolt use serial communications. These serial links can achieve Mbps and Gbps speeds through the use of improved signaling and encoding methods. Back when serial interfaces were much slower, PC vendors used parallel data transmission to support better transfer rates. While a serial interface essentially transfers 1 bit at a time, a parallel interface transfers 8 bits (1 byte) or more. This requires more wires in the cable and more pins in the connectors, meaning parallel interfaces are bulky.

Small computer system interface (SCSI) is one example of a legacy parallel bus. One SCSI host bus adapter (HBA) can control multiple devices attached by internal ribbon cables or external SCSI cables. The SCSI standard also defines a command language that allows the host adapter to identify which devices are connected to the bus and how they are accessed.

SCSI could be used for both internal devices and external peripherals, such as scanners and printers, but you are now unlikely to find it used for any purpose other than the connection of internal hard disk drives. SCSI could support data rates up to 320 MBps. There have been numerous versions of SCSI with many different physical connectors, but you are only likely to come across high density (HD) 68-pin connectors or single connector attachment (SCA) 80-pin connectors. SCA incorporates a power connector, while HD-68 is used with Molex power connectors.

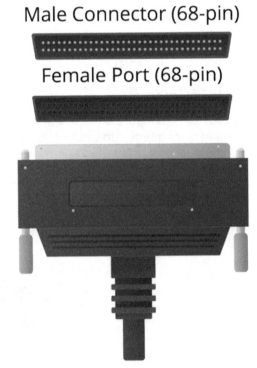

Internal and external male HD connectors. (Image ©123RF.com)

Each device on a wide SCSI bus must be configured with a unique ID, from 0 to 15. The host adapter is usually set to 7 or 15. A bootable hard disk is usually allocated ID 0. The first and last devices on a SCSI bus must be terminated. Termination may either be enabled internally on the device by setting a switch or by physically connecting a terminator pack to a device or the host adapter.

Additionally, you should note that while parallel SCSI as a physical interface has almost completely disappeared, the software interface and command set are used in many other storage technologies, including serial attached SCSI (SAS). SAS is a dominant interface for enterprise-class storage devices in the PC workstation and server market.

Integrated Drive Electronics Interface

The **integrated drive electronics (IDE)** interface was the principal mass storage interface for desktop PCs for many years. The interface is also referred to as parallel advanced technology attachment (PATA). The extended IDE (EIDE) bus interface uses 16-bit parallel data transfers.

A motherboard supporting IDE may come with one or two host adapters, called the IDE1 channel and the IDE2 channel. These may also be labelled primary (PRI IDE) and secondary (SEC IDE). A single IDE channel is now more typical if the motherboard also supports SATA. Each IDE channel supports two devices, 0 and 1.

An EIDE cable typically has three color-coded connectors. The blue connector is for the motherboard port. The black (end) and grey (middle) connectors attach to devices 0 and 1 respectively. When inserting a connector, pin 1 on the cable must be oriented with pin 1 on the port. On the cable, pin 1 is identified with a red stripe. The connectors are also keyed to prevent them from being inserted the wrong way around.

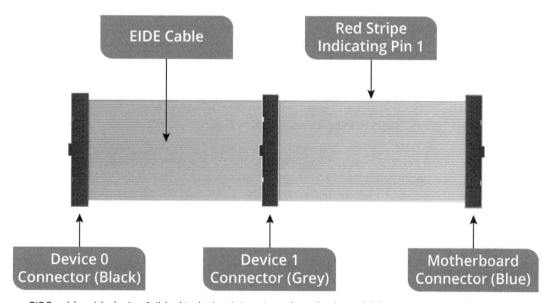

EIDE cable with device 0 (black), device 1 (grey), and motherboard (blue) connectors. The red strip indicates pin 1 on the cable. (Image ©123RF.com)

 Unfortunately, the terms master and slave were used to distinguish device 0 and device 1. CompTIA and the computing industry generally are working to eliminate this type of non-inclusive terminology, but you will often still see it used in historical support documentation.

Serial Cables

The **serial** port is a legacy connection interface where data is transmitted over one wire one bit at a time. Start, stop, and parity bits are used to format and verify data transmission. This interface is also referred to as Recommended Standard #232 (RS-232). While modern interfaces like USB are also serial, an RS-232 interface uses much less sophisticated signaling methods. Consequently, an RS-232 serial port supports data rates up to about 115 Kbps only.

9-pin serial connector and port. (Image ©123RF.com)

Serial ports are generally associated with connecting external modems, used to establish dial-up Internet connections, though even this function has largely been superseded by USB. You may also come across serial ports on network equipment, where a serial connection can be used to manage the device.

RS-232 specifies a 25-pin hardware interface, but in practice, PC manufacturers used the cheaper 9-pin D-subminiature (**DB-9**) female port shown above.

In Windows, the serial port is referred to as a Communications (COM) port.

 You might also come across PS/2 serial ports. PS/2 i used to attach mice and keyboards. PS/2 ports use a 6-pin mini-DIN format. The green color-coded port is used to attach a mouse, and the purple one is for a keyboard.

Adapter Cables

Given the numerous cable types and connector types, it will often be the case that a basic peripheral cable will not provide a connection between a port available on the PC and the port used on the peripheral device. An adapter cable can often be used to overcome this issue. An **adapter cable** has connectors for two different cable types at each end. An active adapter uses circuitry to convert the signal, while a passive adapter simply converts between two connector form factors.

The following types of adapter cable are typical:

- Video adapters convert between signaling types, such as HDMI to VGA, HDMI to DisplayPort, or HDMI to DVI.

- USB adapters to convert connector types, such as USB-C to USB-A. There are also USB hubs that provide additional ports.

- USB adapters to various kinds of output, including Lightning and HDMI.

Review Activity:

Legacy Cable Types

Answer the following questions:

1. **You are labelling systems for inventory. What two types of display cabling can be connected to this laptop?**

2. **Which ports are present on the graphics card shown below?**

3.   Which interfaces does the adapter cable shown below support?

Lesson 1

Summary

You should be able to identify and install types of interfaces and their physical connectors on the motherboard and on peripheral devices.

Guidelines for Installing and Configuring Motherboards and Connectors

Follow these guidelines to support the installation and configuration of motherboards, peripheral devices, and connectors:

- Make support documentation available so that technicians can easily identify the features of system cases and motherboards—especially ATX/ITX form factor, CPU socket type, and header configuration—and perform maintenance and upgrades efficiently.

- Identify requirements for peripheral cables and connector types so that missing or faulty cables can be replaced quickly. Consider stocking adapter cables so that use can be made of devices even if the connector type is not directly supported by the motherboard.

- Identify opportunities to upgrade devices that use legacy interfaces—VGA, DVI, PCI, EIDE/PATA, SCSI, and RS-232 serial—with faster and more reliable modern versions—USB/Thunderbolt, HDMI, DisplayPort, PCIe, SATA, and M.2.

- Identify systems that have additional requirements to the controllers and ports provided on the motherboard and research the best model of video, capture, sound, or network card to meet the requirement.

Lesson 2
Installing System Devices

LESSON INTRODUCTION

The market for the system components of a personal computer is a complex one. Processors, memory modules, disk drives, and power supplies are advertised with a bewildering range of technology improvements and performance differentiators. As a CompTIA A+ technician, you need to interpret these performance characteristics and understand how processing, storage, and power components contribute to a PC specification that is appropriate for a given usage scenario. You must be able to resolve compatibility issues and be confident about the manual installation and removal procedures for these often expensive and delicate devices.

Lesson Objectives

In this lesson, you will:

- Install and configure power supplies and cooling.

- Select and install storage devices.

- Install and configure system memory.

- Install and configure CPUs.

Topic 2A

Install and Configure Power Supplies and Cooling

 CORE 1 EXAM OBJECTIVES COVERED
3.4 Given a scenario, install and configure motherboards, central processing units (CPUs), and add-on cards.
3.5 Given a scenario, install or replace the appropriate power supply.

Understanding the power requirements of all the components and the maximum power output is crucial in managing new builds, upgrades, and repairs. Along with power, all PC components generate heat. Managing heat by installing and maintaining cooling systems makes for a more reliable computing environment. A computer that runs too hot risks damaging its own components and is likely to run at reduced performance levels.

Power Supply Units

The power supply unit (PSU) delivers direct current (DC) low voltage power to the PC components. A PSU contains a rectifier to convert alternating current (AC) building power to DC voltage output, transformers to step down to lower voltages, and filters and regulators to ensure consistent output voltage levels. The other important component in the PSU is the fan, which dissipates the heat generated.

The power supply's size and shape determine its compatibility with the system case, in terms of available room plus screw and fan locations. The form factor also determines compatibility with the motherboard, in terms of power connectors. Most PSUs designed for use with desktop PCs are based on the ATX form factor.

A PSU is plugged into an electrical outlet using a suitable power cord. Before doing this, you must ensure that the PSU is compatible with the **input voltage** from the outlet. A PSU designed only for use in North America, where the input voltage for most homes and offices is 120 VAC (low-line), will not work in the UK, where the voltage is 230 VAC (high-line). Also, facilities such as data centers typically use high-line voltage because it is more efficient. Most PSUs are dual voltage and are auto-switching; some have a manual switch to select the correct voltage; fixed voltage types can only accept either low-line or high-line. The input operating voltages should be clearly marked on the unit and accompanying documentation.

 AC voltage supply varies by country and by the nature of AC distribution circuits. Consequently, PSUs have quite a wide tolerance in each band. The low-line range is **100-127 VAC**, *while the high-line range is* **220-240 VAC**.

*Autoswitching PSU (left) and PSU with manual voltage selector
(between the power points). (Image © 123RF.com)*

Wattage Rating

Power is the rate at which things generate or use energy. Power is measured in
in watts (W), calculated for electrical components as voltage multiplied by current
(V*I). A PSU must be able to meet the combined power requirements of the PC's
components. The PSU's output capability is measured as its **wattage rating**. A PSU
designed for use in a standard desktop PC is typically rated at around 200–300 W.
Enterprise workstation PCs and servers often have units rated over 300 W to meet
the demands of multiple CPUs, additional memory modules, disk drives, and tape
units. Gaming PCs might require 500 W or better power supplies to cope with the
high specification CPU and graphics card(s).

*The power requirement of different components varies widely. For example, CPUs
can range from 17 W to over 100 W, depending on the model. If you are building or
upgrading a system, the simplest way to work out the power requirement is to use
an online calculator. Examples of these tools include enermax.outervision.com and
coolermaster.com/power-supply-calculator.*

*The power output is not the same as the power the PSU draws from grid power. If a PSU
works at around 75% efficiency, a 300 W supply would draw 400 W from the outlet. The
extra energy is lost mainly as heat. As energy becomes more expensive both in terms
of cost and in terms of the climate, power efficiency is an important criterion to use
when selecting a PSU. An ENERGY STAR 80 PLUS compliant PSU must be 80% efficient at
20–100% of load.*

When specifying a PSU for a system with high power requirements, it is also important to assess the power distribution for its **output voltages (3.3 VDC, 5 VDC, and 12 VDC)**. Distribution refers to how much power is supplied over each rail. A rail is a wire providing current at a particular voltage. The following table shows an example of how power distribution for a PSU might be configured:

Output Rail (VDC)	Maximum Load (A)	Maximum Output (W)
+3.3	20	130
+5	20	130
+12	33	396
-12	0.8	9.6
+5 (standby)	2.5	12.5

Note that the output of +3.3 V and +5 V has a combined limit. For a modern computer, the output rating of the +12 VDC rail (or rails) is the most important factor, as +12 VDC is the most heavily used.

Power Supply Connectors

Each PSU has a number of power connectors attached. The power connectors supply DC voltage to the motherboard and devices at 3.3 VDC, 5 VDC, and 12 VDC. Not all components use power at precisely these voltages. Voltage regulators are used to correct the voltage supplied from the PSU to the voltage required by the component. The motherboard's power port is referred to as the P1 connector. A PSU will also have a number of Molex and/or SATA device power connectors and 4/6/8-pin connectors for use with CPU and PCIe adapter card power ports.

20-pin to 24-pin Motherboard Adapter

The ATX PSU standard has gone through several revisions, specifying different connector form factors. In the original ATX specification, the P1 connector is 20-pin (2x10). Wires with black insulation are ground, yellow are +12 V, red are +5 V, and orange are +3.3 V.

Most systems are now based on the ATX12V version 2 specification. This defines a 24-pin (2x12) P1 form factor to replace the 20-pin one. Some PSUs have a **20+4-pin P1 adapter cable** for compatibility with older motherboards with a 20-pin port.

A 24-pin main motherboard power cable and port. (Image ©123RF.com)

Modular Power Supplies

A **modular PSU** has power connector cables that are detachable from the unit. Reducing the number of cables to the minimum required minimizes clutter within the chassis, improving air flow and cooling. For example, a non-modular PSU might have four or five Molex or SATA device power connectors, but the PC might only require two of them. With a modular PSU, the unnecessary cables can be removed.

Modular power supply with pluggable cables. (Image ©123RF.com)

Redundant Power Supplies

A computer system may be fitted with two PSUs, with one acting as a failover **redundant power supply**. This could also be connected to a different grid power circuit. A redundant PSU configuration requires a compatible motherboard. This configuration is more commonly found on server systems than on desktop PCs. On a server, typically each PSU plugs into a backplane and is hot-swappable. This allows a faulty unit to be removed and replaced without having to open the case and without the server ever losing power.

Fan Cooling Systems

Components in a computer system emit heat because of some degree of resistance when electrical current passes through them. Without a cooling solution, this heat will raise the temperature of each component and increase the ambient temperature inside the case. Excessive temperatures can cause the components to malfunction or even damage them. This issue particularly affects CPUs. While Intel and AMD are both focusing on making new CPU designs more thermally efficient, all CPUs require **cooling** to keep the temperature within an acceptable operational range.

 As well as the CPU, components such as memory cards, graphics adapters, and SSDs also require cooling solutions.

Heat Sinks and Thermal Paste

A **heat sink** is a block of copper or aluminum with fins. The fins expose a larger surface area to the air around the component to achieve a cooling effect by convection. The heat sink is "glued" to the surface of the chip using **thermal paste** to ensure the best transfer of heat by eliminating small air gaps. A **thermal pad** performs a similar function. The pad is a compound that is solid at room temperature but softens when heated. This can be easier to apply but does not always perform as reliably.

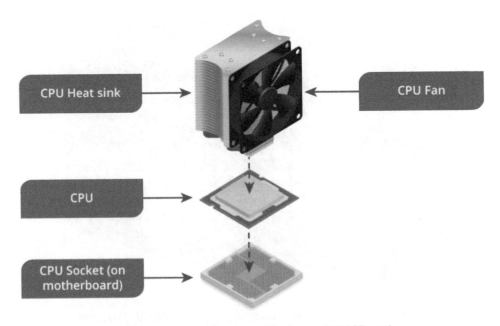

CPU heat sink and fan assembly. (Image ©123RF.com)

There are various mechanisms for clamping a CPU heat sink to the motherboard. There may be a retaining clip or push pins. Push pins can be released and reset for insertion by making a half turn with a screwdriver.

Fans

A heat sink is a passive cooling device. Passive cooling means that it does not require extra energy (electricity) to work. To work well, a heat sink requires good airflow around the PC. It is important to try to keep "cable clutter" to a minimum and to ensure that spare adapter slots are covered by blanking plates.

Many PCs have components that generate more heat than can be removed by passive cooling. A **fan** improves airflow, which helps to dissipate heat. Fans are used for the power supply and chassis exhaust points. The fan system will be designed to draw cool air from the low vents in the front of the case over the motherboard and expel warmed air from the fan positioned at the top of the back of the case. Most heat sinks are fitted with fans to improve their cooling performance. The fan's power connector must be plugged into a motherboard fan power port.

Thermometer sensors are used at each fan location to set an appropriate speed and to detect whether a fan has failed.

Some chassis designs incorporate a plastic shroud or system of baffles to cover the CPU and channel the flow of air. The shroud is usually attached to the case using plastic clips.

Both fans and heat sinks become less effective if dust is allowed to build up. These components and any air vents should be cleaned periodically, either manually with a soft brush and/or compressed air or using a vacuum cleaner approved for use with PCs.

Liquid Cooling Systems

PCs used for high-end gaming may generate more heat than basic thermal management can cope with. PCs used where the ambient temperature is very high may also require exceptional cooling measures.

A liquid-cooled PC. (Image © 123RF.com.)

A **liquid-based cooling system** refers to a system of pumping water around the chassis. Water is a more effective coolant than air convection, and a good pump can run more quietly than numerous fans.

An open-loop, liquid-based cooling system uses the following components:

- The water loop/tubing and pump push the coolant added via the reservoir around the system.

- Water blocks and brackets are attached to each device to remove heat by convection. These are attached in a similar way to heat sink/fan assemblies and then connected to the water loop.

- Radiators and fans are positioned at air vents to dispel the excess heat.

 There are also simpler closed-loop systems that install to a single component (CPU or GPU) only.

An open-loop system will usually need draining, cleaning, and refilling periodically. It is also important to keep the fans and radiators dust-free. The system should also be drained prior to moving the PC to a different location.

Review Activity:

Power Supplies and Cooling

Answer the following questions:

1. What is the significance of a PSU's wattage rating when you are designing a custom-build PC?

2. Your company has recently closed a foreign branch office, and you are repurposing some PCs that were shipped from the old location. What feature of the PSUs must you check before powering the systems on?

3. One of the PCs has a faulty CPU, and one has a faulty power supply. You can use the CPU from one machine in the other. You have opened the case and taken anti-static precautions. What steps must you perform to access the CPU?

4. The repurposed PC is put into service, but later that day the PC's user contacts you to say that the system has been displaying numerous alerts about high temperature. What do you think might be the cause?

Topic 2B

Select and Install Storage Devices

CORE 1 EXAM OBJECTIVES COVERED
3.3 Given a scenario, select and install storage devices.

A PC is often much less valuable than the data that it stores and processes. This means that the reliability and performance of the devices used to store system files and user files is of critical importance. If these storage devices fail, the PC will not work, and valuable information may be lost. By identifying the types and characteristics of storage devices, you will be prepared to select, install, and maintain them to ensure a reliable computing environment for users.

Mass Storage Devices

Non-volatile storage devices hold data when the system is powered off. These devices are also referred to as mass storage. Mass storage devices use magnetic, optical, or solid-state technology to store data.

A mass storage device installed as an internal component is referred to as a fixed disk. Storage devices are produced in a number of standard widths: 5.25 inches, 3.5 inches, and 2.5 inches. The computer chassis has several drive bays to fit these form factors. Form factor bays with a 5.25-inch width are provided with removable panels so that they can be used with devices that have removable media, such as DVD drives and smart card readers.

A fixed disk is typically installed to a drive bay using a caddy. You screw the drive into the caddy, then screw the caddy into the drive bay. A caddy can also allow you to fit a drive of a different size to the bay. For example, you can fit a 2.5-inch drive in a 3.5-inch bay or a 3.5-inch drive in a 5.25-inch bay by using an adapter caddy. Some caddies use rails so that you can pull the drive out without having to open the case.

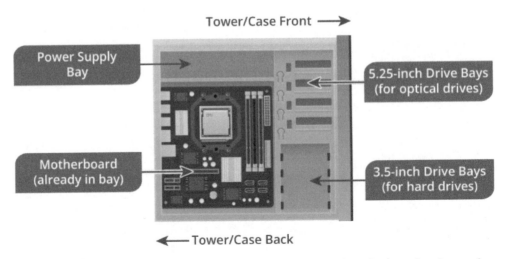

Computer tower with main panel removed showing an attached motherboard and areas for optical disc drives, 3.5-inch drive bays, and a power supply bay. (Image ©123RF.com)

Removable mass storage devices and removable media allow data to be archived from the PC and transferred between PCs. External storage devices are also used for backup and data transfer or to provide a drive type not available as an internal unit. A device such as an external hard drive would typically be connected to the computer via a USB or Thunderbolt port.

Apart from cost, several factors impact the choice of mass storage device:

- **Reliability**—This concerns both the risk of total device failure and the risk of partial data corruption. Reliability and expected lifespan are rated by various statistics that are different for each technology type.

- **Performance**—When comparing different types of storage technology, you need to evaluate performance for the type of data transfer that the device will use predominantly. For example, read and write performance have different characteristics. There are also differences between sequential access (reading data from the same "block" as might happen when transferring a large file) and random access (reading data from different locations on the drive or transferring lots of small files). Along with the data throughput measured in MB/s or GB/s, you may need to consider the number of input/output operations per second (IOPS) that can be achieved by a device for different kinds of data transfer operations.

- **Use**—Reliability and performance factors can only be properly evaluated when considering use. Examples of how storage is used include running an OS, hosting a database application, streaming audio/video data, as removable media, and for data backup and archiving. These use cases have different cost, reliability, and performance considerations.

Some of the mass storage drive vendors include Seagate, Western Digital, Hitachi, Fujitsu, Toshiba, and Samsung.

Solid-State Drives

A **solid-state drive (SSD)** uses flash memory technology to implement persistent mass storage. Flash memory performs much better than the mechanical components used in hard disk drives, especially in terms of read performance. Risks from total failure of the device due to mechanical shock and wear are generally lower. Costs per gigabyte have fallen rapidly in the last few years.

A 2.5-inch form factor solid state drive with SATA interface. (Image ©123RF.com)

SSDs normally outperform HDDs, but there are situations where they can perform worse than HDDs (when serving multi-gigabyte file sizes, for example).

Flash chips are also susceptible to a type of degradation over the course of many write operations. The drive firmware and operating system use wear leveling routines that evenly distribute writing on all blocks of an SSD to optimize the life of the device.

 The NOT AND (NAND) flash memory used in SSDs comes in different types. Single level cell (SLC) is more reliable and more expensive than multi-level cell (MLC) and triple level cell (TLC) types.

On a typical modern desktop PC, an SSD might be installed as the computer's only internal drive or as a boot drive for use with an additional hard drive. In the second scenario, the SSD would be used to install the OS and software applications, while the HDD would be used for user data files.

In terms of the **communications interface**, an SSD might be packaged in a 2.5-inch caddy and installed to a **SATA** port using the normal SATA data and power connectors. Alternatively, the **mSATA** form factor allows an SSD packaged as an adapter card to be plugged into a combined data and power port on the motherboard. With both form factors, the main drawback is that the 600 MBps SATA interface can be a bottleneck to the best performing SSDs, which can achieve transfer rates of up to 6.7 GB/s.

mSATA SSD form factor. (Image ©123RF.com)

Consequently, modern SSDs often use the **PCI Express (PCIe)** bus directly. Where SATA uses the advanced host controller interface (AHCI) logical interface to communicate with the bus, PCIe-based SSDs use the non-volatile memory host controller interface specification (NVMHCI) or **NVM Express (NVMe)**.

An NVMe SSD can either be packaged for installation to a PCIe slot as an expansion card or to an **M.2** slot. The M.2 adapter card form factor is considerably smaller than a PCIe adapter and oriented horizontally rather than vertically, so the interface is often used on laptops as well as PC motherboards. M.2 supplies power over the bus so there is no need for a separate power cable. M.2 adapters can be different widths and lengths so you should check that any given adapter will fit on your motherboard. Labels indicate the adapter sizes supported. For example, an M.2 2280 adapter is 22mm wide and 80mm long.

 M.2 is a physical form factor. You can obtain M.2 SSDs that use the SATA/AHCI bus. These will typically not perform as well as NVMe-based M.2 SSDs. On the motherboard, an M.2 socket may be able to support both types of drive or only one; check the documentation. SATA interface SSDs are usually B keyed, 2-lane PCIe SSDs are usually B/M keyed, and 4-lane SSDs are usually M keyed.

 SSDs are vulnerable to electrostatic discharge (ESD). Always take anti-ESD precautions when handling and storing these devices.

Hard Disk Drives

A **hard disk drive (HDD)** stores data on metal or glass platters that are coated with a magnetic substance. The top and bottom of each platter is accessed by its own read/write head, moved by an actuator mechanism. The platters are mounted on a spindle and spun at high speed. Each side of each platter is divided into circular tracks, and a track contains several sectors, each with a capacity of 512 bytes. This low-level formatting is also referred to as the drive geometry.

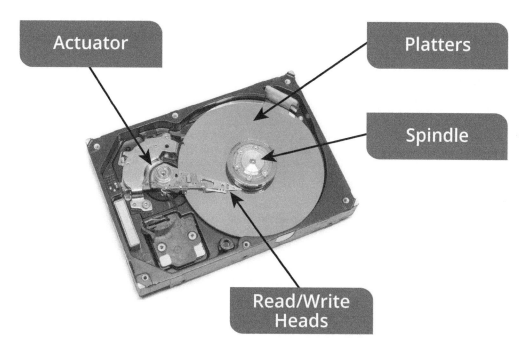

HDD with drive circuitry and casing removed showing 1) Platters; 2) Spindle; 3) Read/Write Heads; 4) Actuator. (Image by mkphotoshu @123RF.com)

This technology means that the performance of an HDD is determined by the speed at which the disks spin, measured in revolutions per minute (RPM). High performance drives are rated at **15,000** or **10,000** rpm; average performance is **7,200** or **5,400** rpm. RPM is one factor determining access time, measured in milliseconds. Access time is the delay that occurs as the read/write head locates a particular track position, which is known as seek time. Access time is also impacted by the sector location process (rotational latency) on the drive. A high-performance drive will have an access time below 3 ms; a typical drive might have an access time of around 6 ms.

The internal transfer rate (or data or disk transfer rate) of a drive is a measure of how fast read/write operations are performed on the disk platters. A 15 K drive should support an internal transfer rate of up to about 180 MBps, while 7.2 K drives will be around 110 MBps.

Most HDDs use a SATA interface, though you may come across legacy devices using EIDE/PATA or SCSI interfaces. There are two main **form factors** for HDDs. The mainstream type used in desktop PCs are 3.5-inch units. The **2.5-inch** form factor is used for laptops and as portable external drives. Devices with 2.5-inch form factors can also vary in height, with 15 mm, 9.5 mm, 7 mm, and 5 mm form factors available.

Redundant Array of Independent Disks

Whether it is the system files required to run the OS or data files generated by users, an HDD or SSD stores critical data. If a boot drive fails, the system will crash. If a data drive fails, users will lose access to files and there may be permanent data loss if those files have not been backed up. To mitigate these risks, the disks that underpin the mass storage system can be provisioned as a **redundant array of independent disks (RAID)**. Redundancy sacrifices some disk capacity but provides fault tolerance. To the OS, the RAID array appears as a single storage resource, or volume, and can be partitioned and formatted like any other drive.

 RAID can also be said to stand for "Redundant Array of Inexpensive Disks," and the "D" can also stand for "devices."

A RAID level represents a **drive configuration** with a given type of fault tolerance. Basic RAID levels are numbered from 0 to 6. There are also nested RAID solutions, such as RAID 10 (RAID 1 + RAID 0).

RAID can be implemented using features of the operating system, referred to as software RAID. Hardware RAID uses a dedicated controller, installed as an adapter card. The RAID disks are connected to SATA ports on the RAID controller adapter card, rather than to the motherboard.

 As another option, some motherboards implement integrated RAID functionality as part of the chipset.

Hardware solutions are principally differentiated by their support for a range of RAID levels. Entry-level controllers might support only RAID 0 or RAID 1, whereas mid-level controllers might add support for RAID 5 and RAID 10. In addition, hardware RAID is often able to hot swap a damaged disk. Hot swap means that the failed device can be replaced without shutting down the operating system.

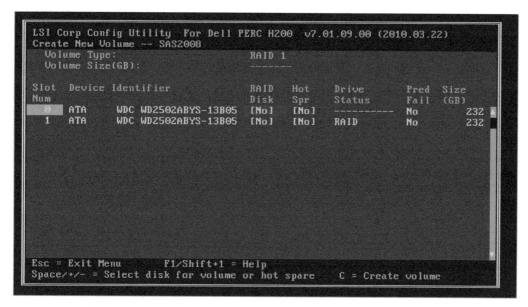

Configuring a volume using RAID controller firmware.

RAID 0 and RAID 1

When implementing RAID, it is important to select the appropriate RAID level. The factors influencing this decision include the required level of fault tolerance, read/write performance characteristics, required capacity, and cost.

When building a RAID array, all the disks should normally be identical in terms of capacity and ideally in terms of type and performance. If disks are different sizes, the size of the smallest disk in the array determines the maximum amount of space that can be used on the larger drives.

RAID 0 (Striping without Parity)

Disk striping divides data into blocks and spreads the blocks in a fixed order among all the disks in the array. This improves performance as multiple disks are available to service requests in parallel. **RAID 0** requires at least two disks. The logical volume size is the combined total of the smallest capacity physical disk in the array.

However, RAID 0 provides no redundancy at all. If any physical disk in the array fails, the whole logical volume will fail, causing the computer to crash and requiring data to be recovered from backup. Consequently, RAID 0 only has specialist uses—typically as some type of non-critical cache store.

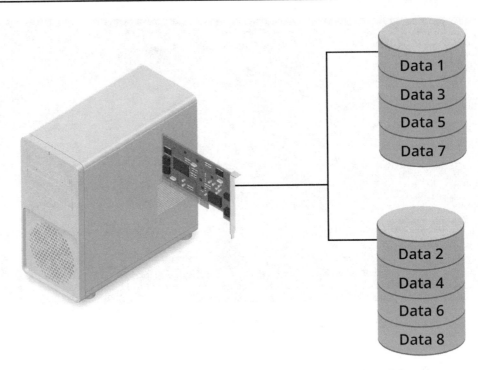

RAID 0 (striping)—Data is spread across the array. (Image ©123RF.com)

RAID 1 (Mirroring)

RAID 1 is a mirrored drive configuration using two disks. Each write operation is duplicated on the second disk in the set, introducing a small performance overhead. A read operation can use either disk, boosting performance somewhat. This strategy is the simplest way of protecting a single disk against failure. If one disk fails, the other takes over. There is little impact on performance during this, so availability remains good, but the failed disk should be replaced as quickly as possible as there is no longer any redundancy. When the disk is replaced, it must be populated with data from the other disk. Performance while rebuilding is reduced, though RAID 1 is better than other levels in that respect and the rebuilding process is generally shorter than for parity-based RAID.

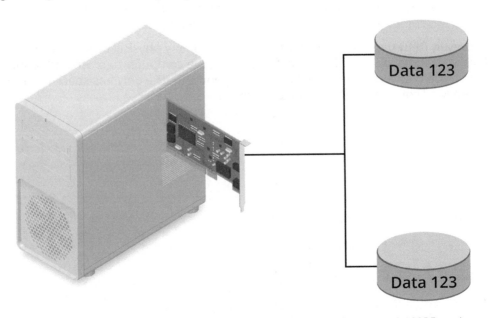

RAID 1 (mirroring)—Data is written to both disks simultaneously. (Image ©123RF.com)

In terms of cost per gigabyte, disk mirroring is more expensive than other forms of fault tolerance because disk space utilization is only 50%.

RAID 5 and RAID 10

RAID 5 and RAID 10 have performance, disk utilization, and fault tolerance characteristics that can make them better choices than basic mirroring.

RAID 5 (Striping with Distributed Parity)

RAID 5 uses striping (like RAID 0) but with distributed parity. Distributed parity means that error correction information is spread across all the disks in the array. The data and parity information are managed so that the two are always on different disks. If a single disk fails, enough information is spread across the remaining disks to allow the data to be reconstructed. Stripe sets with parity offer the best performance for read operations. However, when a disk has failed, the read performance is degraded by the need to recover the data using the parity information. Also, all normal write operations suffer reduced performance due to the parity calculation.

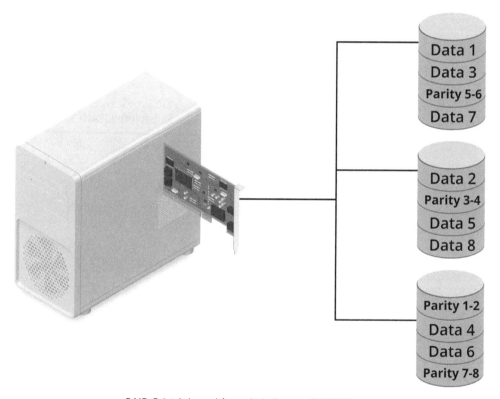

RAID 5 (striping with parity). (Image ©123RF.com)

RAID 5 requires a minimum of three drives but can be configured with more. This allows more flexibility in determining the overall capacity of the array than is possible with RAID 1. A "hard" maximum number of devices is set by the controller or OS support, but the number of drives used is more likely to be determined by practicalities such as cost and risk. Adding more disks increases the chance of failure. If more than one disk fails, the volume will be unavailable.

The level of fault tolerance and available disk space is inverse. As you add disks to the set, fault tolerance decreases but usable disk space increases. If you configure a RAID 5 set using three disks, a third of each disk is set aside for parity. If four are used, one-quarter is reserved on each disk. Using a three 80 GB disk configuration, you would have a 160 GB usable volume.

RAID 10 (Stripe of Mirrors)

A nested RAID configuration combines features of two basic RAID levels. **RAID 10** is a logical striped volume (RAID 0) configured with two mirrored arrays (RAID 1). This configuration offers excellent fault tolerance, as one disk in each mirror can fail, and the volume will still be available.

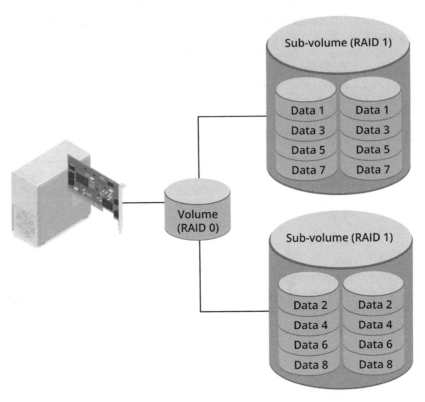

RAID 10—Either disk in each of the sub-volumes can fail without bringing down the main volume. (Image ©123RF.com)

This configuration requires at least four disks, and there must be an even number of disks. It carries the same 50% disk overhead as mirroring.

Removable Storage Drives

Removable storage can refer either to a storage device that can be moved from computer to computer without having to open the case or to storage media that is removable from its drive.

Drive Enclosures

HDDs and SSDs can be provisioned as removable storage in an enclosure. The enclosure provides a data interface (USB, Thunderbolt, or eSATA), a power connector (if necessary), and protection for the disk.

External storage device. (Image ©123RF.com)

Some enclosures can be connected directly to a network rather than to a PC. This is referred to as network attached storage (NAS). Advanced enclosures can host multiple disk units configured as a RAID array.

Flash Drives and Memory Cards

The flash memory underpinning SSDs can also be provisioned in the flash drive and memory card form factors. A **flash drive**—also called a USB drive, thumb drive, or pen drive—is simply a flash memory board with a USB connector and protective cover. This type of drive plugs into any spare USB port.

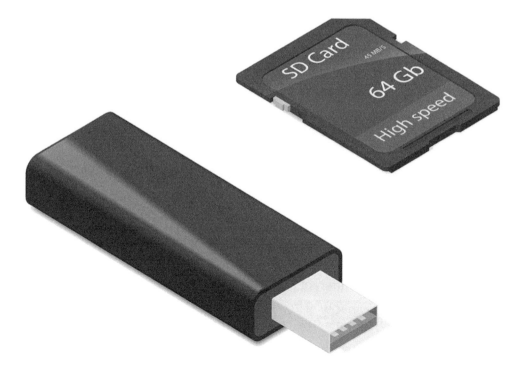

USB thumb drive (left) and SD memory card (right). (Image ©123RF.com)

The **memory card** form factor is used in consumer digital imaging products, such as digital still and video cameras, and to expand smartphone and tablet storage. A PC can be fitted with a memory card reader device. These are usually designed to fit in a front-facing drive bay. The reader then needs to be connected to a USB controller. Most motherboards have at least one spare USB header for making internal connections. Alternatively, the reader may come with an expansion card.

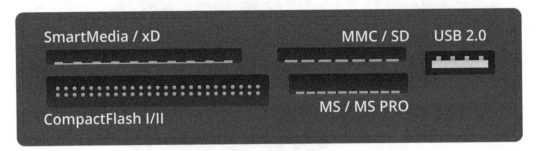

Multi-card reader. (Image ©123RF.com)

There are several proprietary types of memory card, each of which also has different sizes and performance ratings. Most memory card readers work with multiple card types. As an example, Secure Digital (SD) cards are available in three capacity variants. The original SD cards have a 2 GB maximum capacity, whereas SDHC is up to 32 GB and SDXC is up to 2 TB. There are also four speed variants. The original specification is up to 25 MBps, UHS allows up to 108 MBps, UHS-II is rated at up to 156 MBps full-duplex or 312 MBps half-duplex, while UHS-III specifies two full-duplex rates of 312 MBps (FD312) and 624 MBps (FD624). Smaller form factor microSD, microSDHC, and microSDXC cards are also available.

 The smaller form factors can be used with regular size readers using a caddy to hold the card.

Optical Drives

Compact Discs (CDs), Digital Versatile Discs (DVDs), and Blu-ray Discs (BDs) are mainstream storage formats for music and video retail. All types of optical media use a laser to read the data encoded on the disc surface. The discs are marketed as being hard-wearing, but scratches can render them unreadable.

These discs can also be used as storage media for PC data. Each disc type is available in recordable and rewritable formats:

- Basic recordable media can be written to once only in a single session.

- Multisession recordable media can be written to in more than one session, but data cannot be erased.

- Rewritable media can be written and erased in multiple sessions, up to a given number of write cycles.

Each optical disc type has different capacity and transfer rate:

- CD has a maximum capacity of 700 MB and is available in recordable (CD-R) and rewritable (CD-RW) formats. The base transfer rate of a CD is 150 KBps.

- DVD has a capacity of 4.7 GB for a single layer, single-sided disc up to about 17 GB for a dual-layer, double-sided disc. At launch, there were competing DVD+R/RW and DVD-R/RW recordable and rewritable formats, but most drives can use either, designated by the ± symbol. The base transfer rate for DVD is 1.32 MBps, equivalent to 9x CD speed.

- Blu-ray has a capacity of 25 GB per layer. The base speed for Blu-ray is 4.5 MBps, and the maximum theoretical rate is 16x (72 MBps).

An internal **optical drive** can be installed to a 5.25-inch drive bay and connected to the motherboard via SATA data and power connectors. An external unit would be connected via USB (or possibly eSATA or Thunderbolt). External optical drives typically require their own power supply, provided via a supplied AC adapter. Some drives use a tray-based mechanism, while other use a slot-loading mechanism.

Optical drive unit. (Image ©123RF.com)

 Drives also feature a small hole that accesses a disc eject mechanism (insert a paper clip to activate the mechanism). This is useful if the standard eject button will not work or if the drive does not have power.

Optical drives are rated according to their data transfer speed. An optical drive that can perform recording/rewriting is marketed with three speeds, always expressed as the record/rewrite/read speed (for example, 24x/16x/52x). New drives are generally multi-format, but you may come across older drives with no Blu-ray support.

Consumer DVDs and Blu-rays feature digital rights management (DRM) and region-coding copy-protection mechanisms. Region coding, if enforced, means that a disc can only be used on a player from the same region. On a PC, the region can usually be set using device properties. The firmware normally prevents this from being changed more than a couple of times.

Review Activity:

Storage Devices

Answer the following questions:

1. True or false? A solid-state drive (SSD) attached to an M.2 port must be using the non-volatile memory host controller interface specification (NVMHCI) or NVM Express (NVMe).

2. What basic factor might you look at in selecting a high-performance hard disk drive?

3. If you have a computer with three hard disks, what type of RAID fault-tolerant configuration will make best use of them?

4. You are configuring four 120 GB drives in a RAID 5 array. How much space will be available?

5. What is the minimum number of disks required to implement RAID 10, and how much of the disks' total capacity will be available for the volume?

6. True or false? A memory card reader is needed to attach a thumb drive to a PC.

Topic 2C
Install and Configure System Memory

CORE 1 EXAM OBJECTIVES COVERED
3.2 Given a scenario, install the appropriate RAM.

The fixed disk provides persistent storage when the computer is turned off, but a PC also requires fast random access memory (RAM) to load applications and files. Adding system RAM is one of the simplest and most cost-effective ways to increase a computer's performance, but there are many types of RAM and ways of configuring the memory subsystem that you must be able to choose between for given scenarios.

System RAM and Virtual Memory

The CPU works by processing the instructions generated by software (processes) in a pipeline. Instructions that are at the top of the pipeline are stored in the CPU's registers and cache. The CPU only has a small amount of cache, however. Consequently, the operation of the CPU must be supported by additional storage technologies.

When a process is executed or a data file opened, the image is loaded from the fixed disk into system memory. Instructions are fetched from system memory and into the CPU's cache and registers as required. This process is handled by a memory controller.

System memory is implemented as random-access memory (RAM) devices. RAM is faster than the flash memory used for SSDs and much faster than an HDD, but it is volatile. Volatile means that the memory device can only store data when it is powered on.

System memory is measure in gigabytes (GB). The amount of system RAM determines the PC's ability to work with multiple applications at the same time and to process large files efficiently.

Virtual RAM/Virtual Memory

If there is not enough system RAM, the memory space can be extended by using disk storage. This is referred to as a pagefile or swap space. The total amount of addressable memory (system RAM plus swap space) is referred to as virtual memory or **virtual RAM**. With virtual memory, the OS assigns memory locations to processes in 4 kilobyte chunks called pages. The memory controller moves inactive pages of memory to the swap space to free up physical RAM and retrieves pages from the swap space to physical RAM when required by process execution. An excessive amount of such paging activity will slow the computer down because disk transfer rates are slower than RAM transfer rates.

Virtual memory is not just used to supplement RAM with swap space. It serves an important function in protecting the operation and integrity of the PC. Multiple processes can share the RAM device resource as a virtual memory space that is mediated by the operating system. This is more secure and reliable than allowing each process to use physical RAM devices.

Address Space

The bus between the CPU, memory controller, and memory devices consists of a data pathway and an address pathway:

- The width of the data pathway determines how much information can be transferred per clock cycle. In a single channel memory controller configuration, the data bus is usually 64 bits wide.

- The width of the address bus determines how many memory locations the CPU can keep track of and consequently limits to the maximum possible amount of physical and virtual memory. A 32-bit CPU with a 32-bit address bus can access a 4 GB address space. In theory, a 64-bit CPU could implement a 64-bit address space (16 exabytes), but most 64-bit CPUs actually use a 48-bit address bus, allowing up to 256 terabytes of memory.

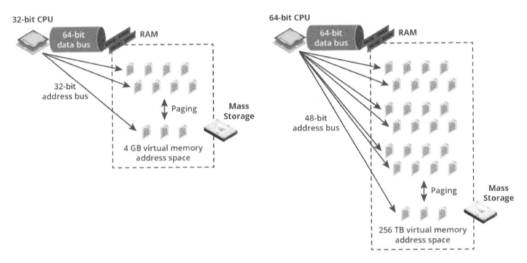

A 64-bit CPU can address more memory locations than a 32-bit CPU. The 64-bit data bus is the amount of memory that can be transferred between the CPU and RAM per cycle.
(Image ©123RF.com)

RAM Types

Modern system RAM is implemented as a type called Double Data Rate Synchronous Dynamic Random Access Memory (DDR SDRAM). Unpacking that name reveals a history of PC system memory implementations from the 1990s to today:

- Dynamic RAM stores each data bit as an electrical charge within a single bit cell. A bit cell consists of a capacitor to hold a charge (the cell represents 1 if there is a charge and 0 if there is not) and a transistor to read the contents of the capacitor.

- Synchronous DRAM (SDRAM) is so-called because its speed is synchronized to the motherboard system clock.

- **Double Data Rate SDRAM (DDR SDRAM)** makes two data transfers per clock cycle.

DDR memory modules are labeled using the maximum theoretical bandwidth, such as PC1600, PC2100, and so on. As an example of how this value is derived, consider DDR-200 PC-1600 memory:

- The internal memory device clock speed and memory bus speed (between the memory devices and memory controller) are both 100 MHz.

- The data rate is double this as there are two operations per clock "tick." This is expressed in units called megatransfers per second (200 MT/s). This gives the DDR-200 designation.

- The peak transfer rate is 1600 MBps (200 MT/s multiplied by 8 bytes (64 bits) per transfer). This gives the "PC-1600" designation. 1600 MBps is equivalent to 1.6 GBps.

Subsequent generations of DDR technology—DDR2, DDR3, DDR4, and DDR5—increase bandwidth by multiplying the bus speed, as opposed to the speed at which the actual memory devices work. This produces scalable speed improvements without making the memory modules too unreliable or too hot. Design improvements also increase the maximum possible capacity of each memory module.

RAM Type	Data Rate	Transfer Rate	Maximum Size
DDR3	800 to 2133 MT/s	6.4 to 17.066 GB/s	8 GB
DDR4	1600 to 3200 MT/s	12.8 to 25.6 GB/s	32 GB
DDR5	4800 to 6400 MT/s	38.4 to 51.2 GB/s	128 GB

The transfer rate is the speed at which data can be moved by the memory controller. Memory modules also have internal timing characteristics, expressed as values, such as 14-15-15-35 CAS 14. These timings can be used to differentiate performance of RAM modules that are an identical DDR type and speed. Lower values are better.

Memory Modules

A memory module is a printed circuit board that holds a group of RAM devices that act as a single unit. Memory modules are produced in different capacities. Each DDR generation sets an upper limit on the maximum possible capacity. DDR for desktop system memory is packaged in a form factor called dual inline memory module (DIMM). The notches (keys) on the module's edge connector identify the DDR generation (DDR3/DDR4/DDR5) and prevent it from being inserted into an incompatible slot or inserted the wrong way around. DDR DIMMs typically feature heat sinks, due to the use of high clock speeds.

DDR SDRAM packaged in DIMMs. (Image © 123RF.com)

Memory slots look similar to expansion slots but with catches on each end to secure the memory modules. Memory modules are vulnerable to electrostatic discharge (ESD). Always take anti-ESD precautions when handling and storing these devices.

The DIMM's DDR type must match the motherboard. You cannot install DDR5 modules in DDR4 slots, for instance. For best performance, the modules should be rated at the same bus speed as the motherboard. It is possible to add modules that are faster or slower than the motherboard slots or mix modules of different speeds. However, the system will operate only at a speed that is supported by all installed components (memory modules and controller), so this is not generally a good idea.

Laptop RAM is packaged in a smaller form factor called **Small Outline DIMM (SODIMM)**. The memory is typically fitted into slots that pop-up at a 45° angle to allow the chips to be inserted or removed.

SODIMM (Image ©123RF.com)

Multi-channel System Memory

In the 2000s, the increasing speed and architectural improvements of CPU technologies led to memory becoming a bottleneck to system performance. To address this, Intel and AMD developed a dual-channel architecture for DDR memory controllers. Dual-channel was originally used primarily on server-level hardware but is now a common feature of desktop systems and laptops.

Single-channel memory means that there is one 64-bit data bus between the CPU, memory controller, and RAM devices. With a **dual-channel** memory controller, there are effectively two 64-bit pathways through the bus to the CPU, meaning that 128 bits of data can be sent per transfer rather than 64 bits. This feature requires support from the CPU, memory controller, and motherboard but not from the RAM devices. Ordinary RAM modules are used. There are no "dual-channel" DDR memory modules.

 DDRx memory is sold in "kits" for dual-channel use, but there is nothing special about the modules themselves other than being identical.

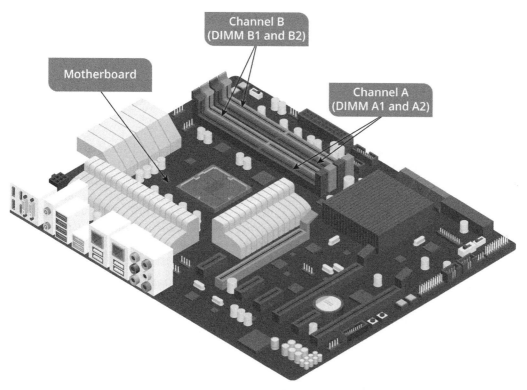

Motherboard DIMM slots (dual channel). Slots 1 and 3 (black slots) make up one channel, while slots 2 and 4 (grey slots) make up a separate channel. (Image ©123RF.com)

When configuring a dual-channel system, you will need to consult the system documentation to identify the appropriate slots to use. As a generic example, a dual-channel motherboard might have four DIMM slots arranged in color-coded pairs. Each pair represents one channel. For example, channel A might be color-coded orange and channel B color-coded blue. Each slot in a pair represents one of the two sockets in the channel (A1 and A2, for instance).

If only two 4 GB modules are available, to enable dual-channel, the modules must be installed in socket 1 of each channel (A1 and B1, for instance). This pair of modules should be identical in terms of clock speed and capacity. Ideally other characteristics, such as timings and latency, should be identical too. If they are not, the lowest (worst performing) values are used. Dual-channel mode may also need to be enabled via the PC firmware's system setup program.

There is no consistent approach to this labelling and color-coding. Some vendors use the same color for each channel, and some use the same color for each socket number. Some motherboards might require socket 1 to be populated first; others might recommend using socket 2 first. Consult the system documentation before proceeding.

Depending on the motherboard and firmware settings, adding an odd number of modules or adding DIMMs that are not the same clock speed and size will have different outcomes. A configuration with mismatched modules may cause the system to operate in single-channel mode, in a dual-channel mode with the spare module disabled, or in flex mode. Flex mode means that if A1 contains a 2 GB module and B1 contains a 6 GB module, dual-channel mode will be enabled for 2 GB of memory and the remaining 4 GB from the module in B1 will work in single-channel mode.

Some CPUs and supporting chipsets have **triple-** or **quadruple-channel** memory controllers. In these architectures, if the full complement of modules is not installed, the system will revert to as many channels as are populated.

DDR5 introduces a different type of data bus. Each memory module has two channels of 32 bits. When installed in a dual channel memory controller configuration, this becomes four 32-bit channels. This architecture distributes the load on each RAM device better. This supports better density (more gigabytes per module) and reduces latency. It also works better with the multi-core features of modern CPUs.

ECC RAM

Error correcting code (ECC) RAM is used for workstations and servers that require a high level of reliability. For each transfer, ECC RAM performs a hash calculation on the data value and stores it as an 8-bit checksum. This checksum requires an extra processor chip on the module and a 72-bit data bus rather than the regular 64 bits. The memory controller performs the same calculation and should derive the same checksum. This system can detect and correct single-bit errors and allow the PC to continue functioning normally. ECC can also detect errors of 2, 3, or 4 bits but cannot correct them. Instead, it will generate an error message and halt the system.

Most types of ECC are supplied as registered DIMMs (RDIMMs). A registered DIMM uses an extra component to reduce electrical load on the memory controller. This has a slight performance penalty, but makes the system more reliable, especially if large amounts of memory are installed. Most types of non-ECC memory are unbuffered DIMMs (UDIMMs). Some types of ECC RAM are packaged in UDIMMs, though this is rarer.

All these factors must be considered when selecting memory for a system:

- Both the motherboard and CPU must support ECC operation for it to be enabled.

- Most motherboards support either UDIMMs or RDIMMs, but not both.

- If a motherboard does support both, UDIMM and RDIMM modules cannot be mixed on the same motherboard. The system will not boot if there are different types.

- Mixing non-ECC UDIMMs and ECC UDIMMs is unlikely to work.

DDR5 implements a form of error checking that is internal to the module. This is not the same as ECC implemented by the memory controller, where the error information is communicated to the CPU. There are still non-ECC and ECC types of DDR5 RAM.

Review Activity:

System Memory

Answer the following questions:

1. **What type of memory technology supports paging?**

2. **You need to upgrade the system RAM on a PC. The motherboard has two 8 GB modules of DDR3 RAM installed and two free slots. You have two spare 16 GB DDR4 modules in your stores. Can these be used for this upgrade?**

3. **You are configuring a different workstation with dual-channel memory. You have two modules and there are four slots. How would you determine which slots to use?**

4. **Consulting the vendor documentation, you find that this system uses DDR4 error-correcting code (ECC) RDIMMs. The spares you have are DDR4 ECC UDIMMs. Can they be used for the upgrade?**

Topic 2D

Install and Configure CPUs

CORE 1 EXAM OBJECTIVES COVERED
3.4 Given a scenario, install and configure motherboards, central processing units (CPUs), and add-on cards.

The central processing unit (CPU) is the principal system controller and has the greatest overall impact on system performance. On most of today's systems, opportunities to improve the performance of a computer by upgrading the CPU are limited. However, you must still understand the features of CPU architecture and packaging to assist users with selecting appropriate systems, to perform upgrades and replacements where necessary, and to help when troubleshooting various issues.

CPU Architecture

The central processing unit (CPU), or simply the processor, executes program instruction code. When a software program runs (whether it be system firmware, an operating system, anti-virus utility, or word-processing application), it is assembled into instructions utilizing the fundamental instruction set of the CPU platform and loaded into system memory. The CPU then performs the following basic operations on each instruction:

1. The control unit fetches the next instruction in sequence from system memory to the pipeline.

2. The control unit decodes each instruction in turn and either executes it itself or passes it to the arithmetic logic unit (ALU) or floating-point unit (FPU) for execution.

3. The result of the executed instruction is written back to a register, to cache, or to system memory.

    *   A register is a temporary storage area available to the different units within the CPU working at the same clock speed as the CPU.

    *   Cache is a small block of memory that works at the speed of the CPU or close to it, depending on the cache level. Cache enhances performance by storing instructions and data that the CPU is using regularly.

x86 CPU Architecture

Over the years, many different internal **CPU architectures** have been developed to optimize the process of fetch, decode, execute, and writeback, while retaining compatibility with the **x86**-32 or IA-32 (Intel Architecture) instruction set. This x86 instruction set defines a CPU as IBM PC compatible. x86 PC processors are designed and manufactured by **Intel** and **Advanced Micro Devices (AMD)**.

x64 CPU Architecture

x86 is a 32-bit instruction set. 32-bit means that each instruction can be up to 32-bits wide. However, since the early 2000s most CPUs have been capable of running 64-bit code. The x86 instruction set has been extended for 64-bit operation as the **x64** instruction set, developed initially by AMD as AMD64 or x86-64. Intel refers to it as EM64T or Intel 64.

All firmware and software—operating system, device drivers, and applications— must be specifically designed and compiled to run as 64-bit software. No 32-bit CPU can run 64-bit software. However, a 64-bit CPU can run 32-bit software.

A device driver is code that provides support for a specific model of hardware component for a given operating system.

ARM CPU Architecture

The principal alternative to the standard x86/x64 CPU architecture is one devised by **Advanced RISC Machines (ARM)**. Unlike AMD and Intel, ARM do not manufacture CPUs. Instead, they produce designs that hardware vendors customize and manufacture. ARM designs are used in the current generation of Apple hardware, in most Android smartphones and tablets (notably by the vendors Qualcomm, Nvidia, and Samsung), in many Chromebooks, and in some Windows tablets and laptops. A typical ARM design implements a system-on-chip (SoC). SoC means that all the controllers—video, sound, networking, and storage—are part of the CPU. ARM designs use fewer, less complex instructions than is typical of x86. These features allow much better power and thermal efficiency, meaning longer battery life and the use of passive (fanless) cooling.

An x86/x64 platform is complex instruction set computing (CISC), meaning that it uses a larger number (say around 1,000) of relatively more complex instructions. A single complex instruction might generate multiple operations across the CPU's registers and take multiple clock cycles to complete. Reduced ISC (RISC) uses a small number of simpler instructions (say 100). This means that tasks require the execution of more instructions than with CISC, but each takes precisely one clock cycle. Because there are fewer instructions overall, RISC can make better use of the CPU registers and cache.

For an operating system and hardware drivers to run on an ARM-based device, they must be redesigned and compiled to use the ARM instruction set. While this task is typically within the reach of operating system developers, converting existing x86/x64 software applications to run on a different instruction set is an onerous task. Another option is support for emulation. This means that the ARM device runs a facsimile of an x86 or x64 environment. Windows 10 ARM-based devices use emulation to run x86 and x64 software apps. Emulation typically imposes a significant performance penalty, however.

CPU Features

Given the architectural features just discussed, the speed at which the CPU runs is generally seen as a key indicator of performance. This is certainly true when comparing CPUs with the same architecture but is not necessarily the case otherwise.

Thermal and power performance impose limits to running the CPU faster and faster. Another way to make execution more efficient is to improve the operation of the instruction pipeline. The basic approach is to do the most amount of work possible in a single clock cycle. This can be achieved through simultaneous **multithreading** (SMT), referred to as HyperThreading by Intel. A thread is a stream of instructions generated by a software application. Most applications run a single process in a single thread; software that runs multiple parallel threads within a process is said to be multithreaded. SMT allows the threads to run through the CPU at the same time. This reduces the amount of "idle time" the CPU spends waiting for new instructions to process. To the OS, it seems as though there are two or more CPUs installed.

Another approach is to use two or more physical CPUs, referred to as symmetric multiprocessing (SMP). An SMP-aware OS can then make efficient use of the processing resources available to run application processes on whichever CPU is "available." This approach is not dependent on software applications being multithreaded to deliver performance benefits. However, a **multi-socket** motherboard is significantly more costly and so is implemented more often on servers and high-end workstations than on desktops. The CPUs used in each socket must be identical models and specifications and must be models that support SMP.

Improvements in CPU fabrication techniques led to the ability to expand compute resources by fabricating multiple CPU cores on a single package. A **single-core** CPU has a single execution unit and set of registers implemented on a single package. A dual-core CPU is essentially two processors combined in the same package. This means that there are two execution units and sets of registers. Each core will also have its own cache plus access to a shared cache. This is referred to as chip level multiprocessing (CMP).

The market has quickly moved beyond dual-core CPUs to **multicore** packages with eight or more processors. Multicore and multithreading features are designated by *n*C/*n*T notation. For example, an 8C/16T CPU with multithreading support has eight cores but processes double that number of simultaneous threads.

Finally, a computer can be made more efficient and useful by configuring it to run multiple operating systems at the same time. This is achieved through virtualization software. Each OS is referred to as a virtual machine (VM). Intel's Virtualization Technology (VT) and AMD's AMD-V provide processor extensions to **support virtualization**, also referred to as hardware-assisted virtualization. This makes the VMs run much more quickly. These extensions are usually features of premium models in each processor range.

There is also a second generation of virtualization extensions to support Second Level Address Translation (SLAT), a feature of virtualization software designed to improve the management of virtual memory. These extensions are referred to as Extended Page Table (EPT) by Intel and Rapid Virtualization Indexing (RVI) by AMD.

CPU Socket Types

CPU packaging refers to the CPU's form factor and how it is connected to the motherboard. Intel and AMD use different **socket types**, so you will not be able to install an AMD CPU in a motherboard designed for an Intel CPU (and vice versa). All CPU sockets use a zero insertion force (ZIF) mechanism. This means that no pressure is required to insert the CPU, reducing the risk of bending or breaking the fragile pin contacts.

 CPUs are vulnerable to electrostatic discharge (ESD). Always take anti-ESD precautions when handling and storing these devices.

Intel uses land grid array (LGA) socket form factor CPUs. The LGA form factor positions the pins that connect the CPU on the socket. The CPU is placed on a hinged plate and then secured to the socket using a locking lever.

GIGA-BYTE Z590 Gaming motherboard with Intel Socket 1200 LGA form factor CPU socket. (Image used with permission from Gigabyte Technology.)

AMD uses pin grid array (PGA) form factor chips predominantly. The PGA form factor positions the pins on the underside of the processor package. The CPU is placed gently into the socket and then secured using a locking lever. Care must be taken to orient pin 1 on the CPU correctly with pin 1 on the socket so as not to bend or break any of the pins.

GIGA-BYTE X570S Gaming X motherboard with AMD Socket AM4 PGA form factor CPU socket. (Image used with permission from Gigabyte Technology.)

When removing a CPU with a heat sink and fan assembly, use a gentle twist to remove the heat sink to avoid it sticking to the CPU. Release the latch securing the CPU before attempting to remove it. If reinstalling the same heat sink, clean old thermal grease from the surfaces and apply a small amount of new grease in an X pattern. Do not apply too much—if it overruns, the excess could damage the socket.

CPU Types and Motherboard Compatibility

The nature of the current CPU market means that there is rapid turnover of models. Each vendor releases a CPU design with a number of architectural improvements and quite often with a new socket design. This is referred to as a CPU's generation. In each generation, the manufacturer releases several models.

Motherboards are specific to either Intel or AMD CPUs. Typically, **motherboard compatibility** is limited to the same generation of CPUs. The CPU must be supported by both the physical form factor of the motherboard's **CPU socket** and by the motherboard's chipset. There are limited opportunities to upgrade the CPU model while keeping the same motherboard, and such upgrades rarely offer much value.

Within each generation, CPU brands and models target different market segments, such as desktop, server, and mobile.

Desktops

Desktop is shorthand for a basic PC as used at home or in the office. The term *desktop* derives from a time when computer cases were designed to sit horizontally on a desk, rather than the vertical tower or all-in-one configurations used today. The desktop segment covers a wide range of performance levels, from budget to gaming PC. These performance levels are reflected in the CPU manufacturer's ranges, with multiple models of Intel Core (i3/i5/i7/i9) and AMD Ryzen (A and 1 up to 9) CPUs at price points ranging from tens of dollars (i3 or Ryzen 1 series) to thousands (Ryzen Threadripper Pro). Intel also uses its historic brands, such as Pentium and Celeron, to market budget chips.

Current Intel desktop socket designs include LGA 2011, LGA 1151, LGA 2066, LGA 1200, and LGA 1700. Most current AMD CPUs use the PGA form factor socket AM4.

Workstations

The term *workstation* can be used in the same way as desktop to refer to any type of business PC or network client. However, in the context of PC sales, most vendors use the term *workstation* to mean a high-performance PC, such as one used for software development or graphics/video editing. Workstation-class PCs often use similar components to server-class computers.

Servers

Server-class computers must manage more demanding workloads than most types of desktops and operate to greater reliability standards. Server motherboards are often **multi-socket**, meaning that multiple CPU packages can be installed. Each of these CPUs will have multiple cores and support for multithreading, giving the server the raw processing power it needs to service requests from hundreds or thousands of client systems.

Other features of server-class motherboards include support for tens of gigabytes of ECC RAM and additional levels and amounts of cache memory. There are dedicated CPU ranges for servers, such as Intel's Xeon and AMD's Epyc brands. These ranges are also usually tied to specific supporting motherboards. A motherboard for an Intel Xeon CPU is unlikely to be compatible with an Intel Core CPU.

Intel's recent Xeon models use LGA 1150, LGA 1151, and LGA 2011 sockets. AMD's Epyc CPU uses the LGA Socket SP3 form factor.

Mobiles

Smartphones, tablets, and laptops need to prioritize power and thermal efficiency plus weight over pure performance. Many **mobiles** use ARM-based CPUs for this reason, and both Intel and AMD have separate mobile CPU models within each generation of their platforms. Mobile CPUs tend to use different socket form factors to desktops. Many are soldered to the motherboard and not replaceable or upgradeable.

Review Activity:

CPUs

Answer the following questions:

1. **Why can cache improve performance?**

2. **A workstation has a multi-socket motherboard but only a single LGA 1150 socket is populated. The installed CPU is a Xeon E3-1220. You have a Xeon E3-1231 CPU in store that also uses the LGA 1150. Should this be used to enable symmetric multiprocessing and upgrade system performance?**

3. **You are specifying a computer for use as a software development workstation. This will be required to run multiple virtual machines (VMs). Can any x64-compatible CPU with sufficient clock speed be used?**

4. **What must you check when inserting a PGA form factor CPU?**

Lesson 2

Summary

You should be able to install power supplies, cooling systems, storage devices, system memory, and CPUs.

Guidelines for Installing System Devices

Follow these guidelines to support the installation and configuration of motherboards, peripheral devices, and connectors:

- When provisioning PSUs, check the input voltage and wattage rating (output) requirements. Consider provisioning modular connectors to reduce cable clutter.

- Ensure that the passive, fan-based, or liquid-based cooling system is sufficient to keep the computer operating within an acceptable temperature range. Perform regular maintenance to ensure that the computer is dust-free and that heat transfer is optimized through the correct application of thermal paste.

- When upgrading memory, assess motherboard requirements, especially when using RDIMMs and ECC memory. Match motherboard and DDR module clock speeds for best performance, and use matched modules installed according to the system documentation to enable multi-channel modes.

- When provisioning a new computer or upgrading the processor, match CPU features such as high clock speed, multiprocessor support, multithreading support, core count, and virtualization support to the computer role (basic desktop, workstation, gaming PC, server, or mobile).

Lesson 3

Troubleshooting PC Hardware

LESSON INTRODUCTION

Troubleshooting is a core competency for the role of CompTIA A+ service technician. Whether it is trying to identify a fault in a new build system or assisting a user with a computer that has just stopped working, you will typically be required to demonstrate your troubleshooting skills on each and every day of your job.

To become an effective troubleshooter, you need a wide range of knowledge, the ability to pay attention to details, and the readiness to be open and flexible in your approach to diagnosing issues. It is also important to learn and apply best practices and a structured methodology to give yourself the best chance of success when diagnosing complex troubleshooting scenarios.

Along with best practices, you also need to build knowledge of and experience with the common symptoms that affect PC system components and peripheral devices.

Lesson Objectives

In this lesson, you will:

- Apply troubleshooting methodology.

- Configure BIOS/UEFI.

- Troubleshoot power and disk issues.

- Troubleshoot system and display issues.

Topic 3A
Apply Troubleshooting Methodology

 CORE 1 EXAM OBJECTIVES COVERED
5.1 Given a scenario, apply the best practice methodology to resolve problems.

Before you can begin to troubleshoot a problem with some component or system error, you need to understand best practices for problem-solving and management. Even experienced technicians can sometimes overlook obvious symptoms or causes. Troubleshooting can be challenging, but if you follow a standard methodology and use a best practice approach, you will often be able to achieve successful outcomes to the issues you are presented with.

Best Practice Methodology

To some extent, being an effective troubleshooter simply involves having a detailed knowledge of how something is supposed to work and of the sort of things that typically go wrong. However, the more complex a system is, the less likely it is that this sort of information will be at hand. Consequently, it is important to develop general troubleshooting skills to approach new and unexpected situations confidently.

Troubleshooting starts with a process of problem-solving. It is important to realize that problems have causes, symptoms, and consequences. For example:

- A computer system has a fault in the hard disk drive (cause).

- Because the disk drive is faulty, the operating system is displaying a "blue screen" (symptom).

- Because of the fault, the user cannot do any work (consequence).

From a business point-of-view, resolving the consequences or impact of the problem is more important than solving the original cause. For example, the most effective solution might be to provide the user with another workstation, then get the drive replaced.

Problems also need to be dealt with according to priority and severity. The disk issue affects a single user and cannot take priority over issues with wider impact, such as the data center suddenly losing power.

It is also important to realize that the cause of a specific problem might be the symptom of a larger problem. This is particularly true if the same problem recurs. For example, you might ask why the disk drive is faulty—is it a one-off error or are there problems in the environment, supply chain, and so on?

These issues mean that the troubleshooting procedures should be developed in the context of best practice methodologies and approaches. One such best practice framework is the CompTIA's A+ troubleshooting model. The steps in this model are as follows:

1.   Identify the problem:

     a)   Gather information from the user, identify user changes, and, if applicable, perform backups before making changes.

     b)   Inquire regarding environmental or infrastructure changes.

2.   Establish a theory of probable cause (question the obvious):

     a)   If necessary, conduct external or internal research based on symptoms.

3.   Test the theory to determine the cause:

     a)   Once the theory is confirmed, determine the next steps to resolve the problem.

     b)   If the theory is not confirmed, re-establish a new theory or escalate.

4.   Establish a plan of action to resolve the problem and implement the solution:

     a)   Refer to the vendor's instructions for guidance.

5.   Verify full-system functionality and, if applicable, implement preventive measures.

6.   Document the findings, actions, and outcomes.

Identify the Problem

The troubleshooting process starts by **identifying the problem**. Identifying the problem means establishing the consequence or impact of the issue and listing symptoms. The consequence can be used to prioritize each support case within the overall process of problem management.

Gather Information from the User

The first report of a problem will typically come from a user or another technician, and this person will be one of the best sources of information, if you can ask the right questions. Before you begin examining settings in Windows or taking the PC apart, spend some time **gathering information from the user** about the problem. Ensure you ask the user to describe *all* the circumstances and symptoms. Some good questions to ask include:

*   What are the exact error messages appearing on the screen or coming from the speaker?

*   Is anyone else experiencing the same problem?

*   How long has the problem been occurring?

*   What changes have been made recently to the system? Were these changes initiated by you or via another support request?

*   The latest **change** to a system is very often the cause of the problem. If something worked previously, then excepting mechanical failures, it is likely that the problem has arisen because of some user-initiated change or some **environmental or infrastructure change**. If something has never worked, a different approach is required.

*   Has anything been tried to solve the problem?

Perform Backups

Consider the importance of data stored on the local computer when you open a support case. Check when a **backup** was last made. If a backup has not been made, perform one before changing the system configuration, if possible.

Establish and Test a Theory

If you obtain accurate answers to your initial questions, you will have determined the severity of the problem (how many are affected), a rough idea of what to investigate (hardware or OS, for instance), and whether to consider the cause as deriving from a recent change, an oversight in the initial configuration, or some unexpected environmental or mechanical event.

You diagnose a problem by identifying the symptoms. From knowing what causes such symptoms, you can consider *possible* causes to determine the **probable cause** and then devise tests to show whether it is the cause or not. If you switch your television on and the screen remains dark, you could ask yourself, "Is the problem in the television? Has the fuse blown? Is there a problem at the broadcasting station rather than with my television?" With all problems we run through a list of possibilities before deciding. The trick is to do this methodically (so that possible causes are not overlooked) and efficiently (so that the problem can be solved quickly).

Conduct Research

You cannot always rely on the user to describe the problem accurately or comprehensively. You may need to use **research** techniques to identify or clarify symptoms and possible causes. One of the most useful troubleshooting skills is being able to perform research to find information quickly. Learn to use web and database search tools so that you can locate information that is relevant and useful. Identify different knowledge sources available to you. When you research a problem, be aware of both internal documentation and information and external support resources, such as vendor support or forums.

- Make a physical inspection—look and listen. You may be able to see or hear a fault (scorched motherboard, "sick"-sounding disk drive, no fan noise, and so on).

- If the symptoms of the problem are no longer apparent, a basic technique is to reproduce the problem—that is, repeat the exact circumstances that produced the failure or error. Some problems are intermittent, though, which means that they cannot be repeated reliably. Issues that are transitory or difficult to reproduce are often the hardest to troubleshoot.

- Check the system documentation, installation and event logs, and diagnostic tools for useful information.

- Consult other technicians who might have worked on the system recently or might be working now on some related issue. Consider that environmental or infrastructure changes might have been instigated by a different group within the company. Perhaps you are responsible for application support and the network infrastructure group has made some changes without issuing proper notice.

- Consult vendor documentation and use web search and forum resources to see if the issue is well-known and has an existing fix.

Question the Obvious

As you identify symptoms and diagnose causes, take care not to overlook the **obvious**—sometimes seemingly intractable problems are caused by the simplest things. Diagnosis requires both attention to detail and a willingness to be systematic.

One way to consider a computer problem systematically is to step through what should happen, either by performing the steps yourself or by observing the user. Hopefully, this will identify the exact point at which there is a failure or error.

If this approach does not work, break the troubleshooting process into compartments or categories, such as power, hardware components, drivers/ firmware, software, network, and user actions. If you can isolate your investigation to a particular subsystem by eliminating "non-causes," you can troubleshoot the problem more quickly. For example, when troubleshooting a PC, you might work as follows:

1. Decide whether the problem is hardware or software related (Hardware).

2. Decide which hardware subsystem is affected (Disk).

3. Decide whether the problem is in the disk unit or connectors and cabling (Connectors).

4. Test your theory.

 A basic technique when troubleshooting a cable, connector, or device is to have a "known good" duplicate on hand. This is another copy of the same cable or device that you know works that you can use to test by substitution.

Establish a New Theory or Escalate

If your theory is not proven by the tests you make or the research you undertake, you must **establish a new theory**. If one does not suggest itself from what you have discovered so far, there may be more lengthy procedures you can use to diagnose a cause. Remember to assess business needs before embarking on very lengthy and possibly disruptive tests. Is there a simpler workaround that you are overlooking?

If a problem is particularly intractable, you can take the system down to its base configuration (the minimum needed to run). When (if) this is working, you can then add peripherals and devices or software subsystems one by one, testing after each, until eventually the problem is located. This is time-consuming but may be necessary if nothing else is providing a solution.

If you cannot solve a problem yourself, it is better to **escalate** it than to waste a lot of time trying to come up with an answer. Formal escalation routes depend on the type of support service you are operating and the terms of any warranties or service contracts that apply. Some generic escalation routes include:

*   Senior technical and administrative staff, subject matter experts (SMEs), and developers/programmers within your company.

*   Suppliers and manufacturers via warranty and support contracts and helplines or web contact portals.

*   Other support contractors/consultants, websites, and social media.

Obtain authorization to use social media or public forums. Do not disclose proprietary, confidential, or personal information when discussing an issue publicly.

Choosing whether to escalate a problem is complex because you must balance the need to resolve a problem in a timely fashion against the possibility of incurring additional costs or adding to the burdens/priorities that senior staff are already coping with. You should be guided by policies and practices in the company you work for. When you escalate a problem, make sure that what you have found out or attempted so far is documented. Failing that, describe the problem clearly to whoever is taking over or providing you with assistance.

Implement a Plan of Action

When you have a reliable theory of probable cause, you then need to determine the **next steps to solve the problem**.

Troubleshooting is not just a diagnostic process. Devising and implementing a plan to solve the problem requires effective decision-making. Sometimes there is no simple solution. There may be several solutions, and which is best might not be obvious. An apparent solution might solve the symptoms of the problem but not the cause. A solution might be impractical or too costly. Finally, a solution might be the cause of further problems, which could be even worse than the original problem.

There are typically three generic approaches to resolving an IT problem:

- **Repair**—You need to determine whether the cost of repair makes this the best option.

- **Replace**—Often more expensive and may be time-consuming if a part is not available. There may also be an opportunity to upgrade the part or software.

- **Workaround**—Not all problems are critical. If neither repair nor replacement is cost-effective, it may be best either to find a workaround or just to document the issue and move on.

If a part or system is under warranty, you can return the broken part for a replacement. To do this, you normally need to obtain a returned materials authorization (RMA) ticket from the vendor.

Establish a Plan of Action

When you determined the best solution, you must devise a **plan of action** to put the solution in place. You have to assess the resources, time, and cost required. Another consideration is potential **impacts** on the rest of the system that your plan of action may have. A typical example is applying a software patch, which might fix a given problem but cause other programs not to work.

An effective change and configuration management system will help you to understand how different systems are interconnected. You must seek the proper authorization for your plan and conduct all remedial activities within the constraints of **corporate policies and procedures**.

Implement the Solution

If you do not have authorization to implement a solution, you will need to escalate the problem to more senior personnel. If applying the solution is disruptive to the wider network or business, you also need to consider the most appropriate time to schedule the reconfiguration work and plan how to notify other network users.

When you make a change to the system as part of **implementing a solution**, test after each change. If the change does not fix the problem, reverse it, and then try something else. If you make a series of changes without recording what you have done, you could find yourself in a tricky position.

 Remember that troubleshooting may involve more than fixing a particular problem; it is about maintaining the resources that users need to do their work.

Refer to Vendor Instructions

If you are completing troubleshooting steps **under instruction** from another technician—the vendor's support service, for instance—make sure you properly understand the steps you are being asked to take, especially if it requires disassembly of a component or reconfiguration of software that you are not familiar with.

Verify and Document

When you apply a solution, test that it fixes the reported problem and that the **system as a whole continues to function normally**. Tests could involve any of the following:

- Trying to use a component or performing the activity that prompted the problem report.

- Inspecting a component to see whether it is properly connected or damaged or whether any status or indicator lights show a problem.

- Disabling or uninstalling the component (if it might be the cause of a wider problem).

- Consulting logs and software tools to confirm a component is configured properly.

- Updating software or a device driver.

Before you can consider a problem closed, you should both be satisfied in your own mind that you have resolved it and get the customer's acceptance that it has been fixed. Restate what the problem was and how it was resolved, and then confirm with the customer that the incident log can be closed.

Implement Preventive Measures

To fully solve a problem, you should implement **preventive measures**. This means eliminating any factors that could cause the problem to reoccur. For example, if the power cable on a PC blows a fuse, you should not only replace the fuse, but also check to see if there are any power problems in the building that may have caused the fuse to blow in the first place. If a computer is infected with a virus, ensure that the anti-virus software is updating itself regularly and users are trained to avoid malware risks.

Document Findings, Actions, and Outcomes

Most troubleshooting takes place within the context of a ticket system. This shows who is responsible for any particular problem and what its status is. This gives you the opportunity to add a complete description of the problem and its solution (**findings, actions, and outcomes**).

This is very useful for future troubleshooting, as problems fitting into the same category can be reviewed to see if the same solution applies. Troubleshooting steps can be gathered into a "Knowledge Base" or Frequently Asked Questions (FAQ) of support articles. It also helps to analyze IT infrastructure by gathering statistics on what types of problems occur and how frequently.

The other value of a log is that it demonstrates what the support department is doing to help the business. This is particularly important for third-party support companies, who need to prove the value achieved in service contracts. When you complete a problem log, remember that people other than you may come to rely on it. Also, logs may be presented to customers as proof of troubleshooting activity. Write clearly and concisely, checking for spelling and grammar errors.

Review Activity:

Troubleshooting Methodology

Answer the following questions:

1. **You are dealing with a support request and think that you have identified the probable cause of the reported problem. What should be your next troubleshooting step?**

2. **If you must open the system case to troubleshoot a computer, what should you check before proceeding?**

3. **What should you do if you cannot determine the cause of a problem?**

4. **You think you have discovered the solution to a problem in a product Knowledge Base, and the solution involves installing a software patch. What should be your next troubleshooting step?**

5. **After applying a troubleshooting repair, replacement, or upgrade, what should you do next?**

Topic 3B

Configure BIOS/UEFI

 CORE 1 EXAM OBJECTIVES COVERED
3.4 Given a scenario, install and configure motherboards, central processing units (CPUs), and add-on cards.

The motherboard firmware provides a low-level interface for configuring PC devices. It verifies that the components required to run an operating system are present and working correctly and provisions a trusted environment for various security functions. You will often need to use the system setup program when troubleshooting to check or modify firmware settings.

BIOS and UEFI

Firmware is specialized program code stored in flash memory. Firmware is distinct from software because it is very closely tied to the basic functions of a specific hardware device type and model. PC or system firmware provides low-level code to allow PC components installed on a particular motherboard to be initialized so that they can load the main operating system software.

For many years, the system firmware for a PC was a type called the **Basic Input/Output System (BIOS)**. BIOS only supports 32-bit operation and limited functionality. Newer motherboards may use a different kind of firmware called **Unified Extensible Firmware Interface (UEFI)**. UEFI provides support for 64-bit CPU operation at boot, a full GUI and mouse operation at boot, networking functionality at boot, and better boot security. A computer with UEFI may also support booting in a legacy BIOS mode.

System **settings** can be configured via the system firmware setup program. The system setup program is accessed via a keystroke during the power-on (boot) process, typically when the PC vendor's logo is displayed. The key combination used will vary from system to system; typical examples are **Esc**, **Del**, **F1**, **F2**, **F10**, or **F12**.

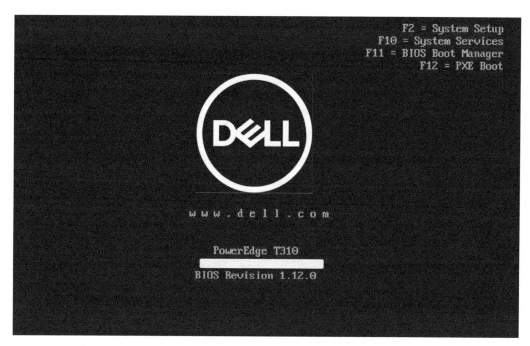

Bootup access to system firmware setup. (Reproduced with permission of Dell Copyright © Dell 2022 (2022). ALL Rights Reserved.)

 *One issue with modern computers is that the boot process can be very quick. If this is the case, you can **Shift**-click the **Restart** button from the Windows logon screen to access UEFI boot options.*

You navigate a legacy BIOS setup program using the keyboard arrow keys. Pressing **Esc** generally returns to the previous screen. When closing setup, there will be an option to exit and discard changes or exit and save changes. Sometimes this is done with a key (**Esc** versus **F10**, for instance), but more often there is a prompt. There will also be an option for reloading the default settings in case you want to discard any customizations you have made.

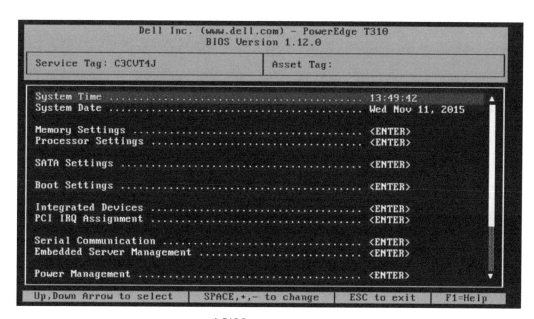

A BIOS setup program.

UEFI setup programs use a graphical interface and have mouse support, though advanced menus may still require keyboard navigation.

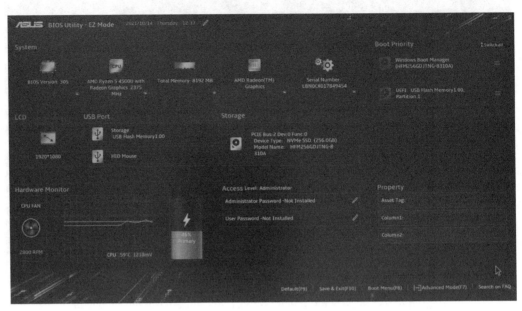

A UEFI setup program. (Screenshot used with permission from ASUSTek Computer Inc.)

Boot and Device Options

One of the most important parameters in system setup is the **boot options** sequence or boot device priority. This defines the order in which the system firmware searches devices for a boot manager.

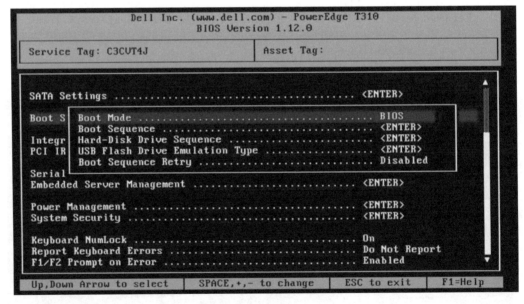

Boot parameters.

Typical choices include:

- **Fixed disk (HDD or SSD)**—A SATA boot disk should generally be connected to the lowest numbered port, but it is usually possible to select the hard drive sequence if multiple fixed drives are installed. An SSD attached using SATA will be listed with SATA/AHCI devices; an SSD installed as a PCIe Add-in Card (AIC) or on the M.2 interface will be listed under NVMe.

- **Optical drive (CD/DVD/Blu-ray)**—If you are performing a repair install from optical media, you might need to make this device the highest priority.

- **USB**—Most modern systems can boot from a USB drive that has been formatted as a boot device. This option is often used for OS installs and repair utility boot disks that are too large to fit on optical media.

- **Network/PXE**—Uses the network adapter to obtain boot settings from a specially configured server.

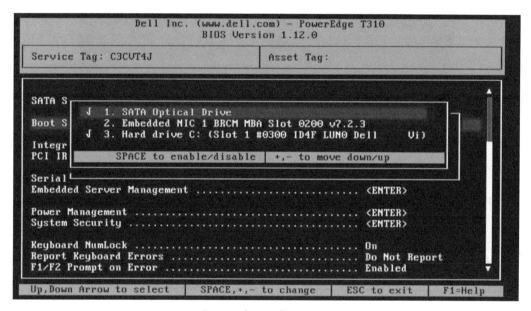

Boot order configuration.

USB Permissions

As well as boot device configuration, there will be options for enabling/disabling and configuring controllers and adapters provided on the motherboard. This provides a way of enforcing **USB permissions**. On many systems, allowing the connection of USB devices is a security risk. The setup program might allow individual ports to be enabled or disabled.

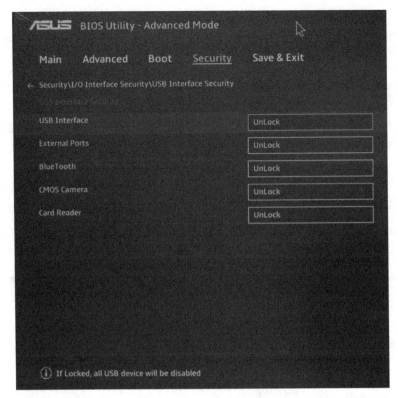

Using UEFI setup to configure permissions for USB and other external interfaces.
(Screenshot used with permission from ASUSTek Computer Inc.)

Fan Considerations

Most cooling **fans** can be controlled via system settings, typically under a menu such as Cooling, Power, or Advanced. The menu will present options such as balanced, cool (run fans harder), quiet (reduce fan speed and allow higher temperatures), fanless, and custom. There will also be settings for minimum temperature, which is the value at which fans will be started to cool the system. Duty cycle settings are used to control the frequency of power pulses to keep the fan running. A high percentage makes the fan run faster.

The setup program will also report the current temperature of the probes located near each fan connector.

There are many third-party utilities that can access these settings and monitors from within the OS.

Boot Passwords and Secure Boot

A **boot password** requires the user to authenticate before the operating system is loaded. Different system software will provide different support for authentication methods. There are usually at least two passwords, though some systems may allow for more:

- **Supervisor/Administrator/Setup**—Protect access to the system setup program.

- **User/System**—Lock access to the whole computer. This is a very secure way of protecting an entire PC as nothing can be done until the firmware has initialized the system.

You must tell everyone who uses the PC the password, which weakens the security considerably. This option would be used only on workstations and servers that aren't used for interactive logon, such as computers running monitoring or management software.

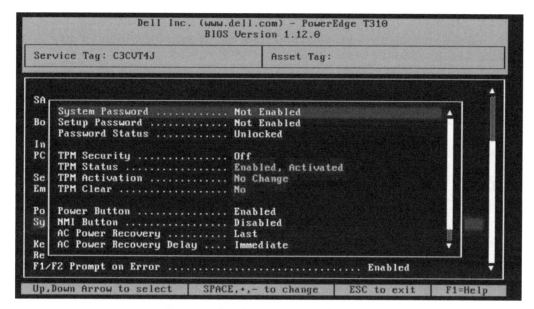

Configuring system security.

Secure boot is a UEFI feature designed to prevent a computer from being hijacked by malware. Under secure boot, the computer firmware is configured with cryptographic keys that can identify trusted code. The system firmware checks the operating system boot loader using the stored keys to ensure that it has been digitally signed by the OS vendor. This prevents a boot loader that has been modified by malware or an OS installed without authorization from being used.

 Keys from vendors such as Microsoft (Windows and Windows Server) and Linux distributions (Fedora, openSUSE, and Ubuntu) will be pre-loaded. Additional keys for other boot loaders can be installed (or the pre-loaded ones removed) via the system setup software. It is also possible to disable secure boot.

Trusted Platform Modules

Encryption products make data secure by scrambling it in such a way that it can only subsequently be read if the user has the correct decryption key. This security system is only strong as long as access to the key is protected. UEFI-based systems provide built-in secure storage for cryptographic keys.

 Encryption encodes data using a key to give it the property of confidentiality. Many cryptographic processes also make use of hashing. A secure hash is a unique code that could only have been generated from the input. Hashes can be used to compare two copies of data to verify that they are the same. Unlike encryption, the original data cannot be recovered from the hash code.

Trusted Platform Module

Trusted platform module (TPM) is a specification for hardware-based storage of digital certificates, cryptographic keys, and hashed passwords.

The TPM establishes a root of trust. Each TPM microprocessor is hard coded with a unique, unchangeable key, referred to as the endorsement key. During the boot process, the TPM compares hashes of key system state data (system firmware, boot loader, and OS kernel) to ensure they have not been tampered with. The TPM chip has a secure storage area that a disk encryption program such as Windows BitLocker can write its keys to.

The TPM can be enabled or disabled and reset via the system setup program, though it is also possible to manage it from the OS as well.

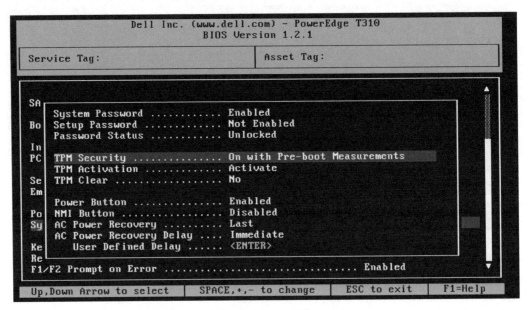

Configuring a TPM.

Hardware Security Module

It is also possible to use a removable USB thumb drive to store keys. This is useful if the computer does not support TPM, as a recovery mechanism in case the TPM is damaged, or if a disk needs to be moved to another computer. A secure USB key or thumb drive used to store cryptographic material can be referred to as a **hardware security module (HSM)**. Secure means that the user must authenticate with a password, personal identification number (PIN), or fingerprint before he or she is able to access the keys stored on the module.

Review Activity:

BIOS/UEFI

Answer the following questions:

1. **Name three keys commonly used to run a PC's BIOS/UEFI system setup program.**

2. **What widely supported boot method is missing from the following list? HDD, Optical, USB.**

3. **When you are configuring firmware-enforced security, what is the difference between a supervisor password and a user password?**

4. **True or false? A TPM provides secure removable storage so that encryption keys can be used with different computers.**

Topic 3C

Troubleshoot Power and Disk Issues

CORE 1 EXAM OBJECTIVES COVERED
5.2 Given a scenario, troubleshoot problems related to motherboards, RAM, CPU, and power.
5.3 Given a scenario, troubleshoot and diagnose problems with storage drives and RAID arrays.

Troubleshooting a PC that will not boot is one of the most common tasks for a PC technician to undertake. You need to diagnose causes relating to power, motherboard components, or disk issues from common symptoms.

Problems with disks and storage systems can have impacts beyond just booting the computer. End users rely on the storage devices in their PCs to store important system information and personal or professional data and files. Without a storage device that works properly, the computer system is essentially worthless. As a CompTIA A+ technician, you will likely be called upon to fix or troubleshoot common problems with HDDs, SSDs, and other storage devices.

Troubleshoot Power Issues

PC components need a constant, stable supply of power to run. If the computer will not start, it is likely to be due to a power problem. If the PC suddenly turns off or restarts, power is a common cause.

When a computer is switched on, the power supply unit (PSU) converts the AC input voltage (VAC) to DC voltages (VDC). DC voltage is used to power the motherboard components and peripheral devices. The PSU supplies 12 V power immediately, and the fans and hard disks should spin up. The PSU then tests its 5 V and 3.3 V supplies. When it is sure that it is providing a stable supply, it sends a power good signal to the processor.

To diagnose **no power** symptoms, check if the LEDs on the front panel of the system case are lit up and whether you can hear the fans. A power issue might arise due to a fault in the PSU, incoming electricity supply, power cables/connectors, or fuses. To isolate the cause of no power, try the following tests:

1. Check that other equipment in the area is working—There may be a fault in the power circuit or a wider complete failure of power (a blackout).

2. Try plugging another piece of known-good basic electrical equipment, such as a lamp, into the wall socket. If it does not work, the wall socket is faulty. Get an electrician to investigate the fault.

3. Check that the PSU cabling is connected to the PC and the wall socket correctly and that all switches are in the "on" position.

4. Try another power cable—There may be a problem with the plug or fuse. Check that all the wires are connected to the correct terminals in the plug. Check the fuse resistance with a multimeter or swap with a known good fuse.

5. Try disconnecting extra devices, such as a plug-in graphics card. If this solves the problem, either the PSU is underpowered and you need to fit one with a higher wattage rating, or one of the devices is faulty.

6. If you can ensure a safe working environment, test the PSU using a multimeter or power supply tester.

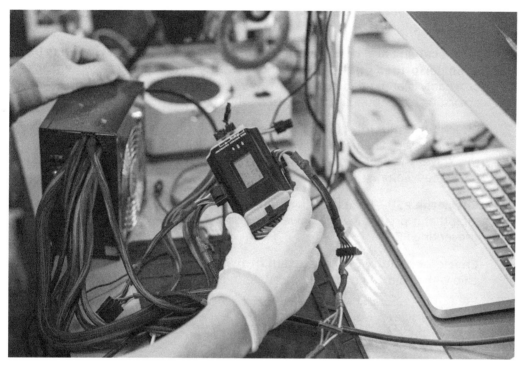

Technician working with a power supply tester. (Image by Konstantin Malkov @123RF.com)

You must take appropriate safety measures before testing a live power supply. PC power supplies are NOT user serviceable. Never remove the cover of a power supply.

If you still cannot identify the fault, then the problem is likely to be a faulty motherboard or power supply. If you suspect that a power supply is faulty, do not leave it turned on for longer than necessary and do not leave it unattended. Keep an eye out for external signs of a problem (for example, smoke or fire). Turn off immediately if there are any unusual sights, smells, or noises.

Troubleshoot POST Issues

Once the CPU has been given the power good signal, the system firmware performs a **power-on self-test (POST)**. The POST is a diagnostic program implemented in the system firmware that checks the hardware to ensure the components required to boot the PC are present and functioning correctly.

On modern computers the POST happens very quickly to improve boot times, so you are unlikely to see any POST messages. Also, the PC is likely to be configured to show a logo screen and will only display messages under error conditions.

If power is present—you can hear the fans spinning, for instance—but the computer does not start, there is a **black screen**, and there are no beeps from the internal speaker, it is likely either that the display is faulty or that the POST procedure is not executing. Assuming you can rule out an issue with the display, to troubleshoot POST, try the following tests and solutions:

1.   **Ask what has changed**—If the system firmware has been updated and the PC has not booted since, the system firmware update may have failed. Use the reset procedure.

2.   **Check cabling and connections, especially if maintenance work has just been performed on the PC**—An incorrectly oriented storage adapter cable or a badly seated adapter card can stop the POST from running. Correct any errors, reset adapter cards, and then reboot the PC.

3.   **Check for faulty interfaces and devices**—It is possible that a faulty adapter card or device is halting the POST. Try removing one device at a time to see if this solves the problem (or remove all non-essential devices, then add them back one by one).

4.   **Check the PSU**—Even though the fans are receiving power, there may be a fault that is preventing the power good signal from being sent to the CPU, preventing POST.

5.   **Check for a faulty CPU or system firmware**—If possible, replace the CPU chip with a known good one or update the system firmware.

 Some motherboards have jumpers to configure modes (such as firmware recovery) or processor settings. If the jumpers are set incorrectly, it could cause the computer not to boot. If a computer will not work after being serviced, check that the jumpers have not been changed.

If POST runs but detects a problem, it generates an error message. As the fault may prevent the computer from displaying anything on the screen, the error is often indicated by a **beep code**. Use resources such as the manufacturer's website to determine the meaning of the beep code.

The codes for the original IBM PC are listed in this table.

Code	Meaning
1 short beep	Normal POST—system is OK. Most modern PCs are configured to boot silently, however.
2 short beeps	POST error—error code shown on screen.
No beep	Power supply, motherboard problem, or faulty onboard speaker.
Continuous beep	Problem with system memory modules or memory controller.
Repeating short beeps	Power supply fault or motherboard problem.
1 long, 1 short beep	Motherboard problem.
1 long, 2 or 3 short beeps	Video adapter error.
3 long beeps	Keyboard issue (check that a key is not depressed).

Some PCs will not boot if a key is stuck. Check that nothing is resting on the keyboard. If the board is clogged with dust or sticky liquid, clean it using approved products, such as swabs and compressed air blowers.

Troubleshoot Boot Issues

Once the POST tests are complete, the firmware searches for devices as specified in the boot sequence. If the first device in the sequence is not found, the system attempts to boot from the next device. For example, if there is no fixed disk, the boot sequence checks for a USB-attached drive. If no disk-based boot device is found, the system might attempt to boot from the network. If no boot device is found, the system displays an error message and halts the boot process.

If the system attempts to boot from an incorrect device, check that the removable drives do not contain media that are interfering with the boot process and that the boot device order is correctly configured.

If a fixed disk is not detected at boot, try to check that it is powering up. Drive activity is usually indicated by an LED on the front panel of the system unit case. If this is inactive, check that the drive has a power connector attached. If the PC has no LEDs, or you suspect that they may be faulty, it is usually possible to hear a hard disk spinning up. Once you have determined that the drive is powering up, try the following:

- Check that data cables are not damaged and that they are correctly connected to the drive.

- If the drives are connected to a motherboard port, check that it has not been disabled by a jumper or via system setup.

Troubleshoot Boot Sector Issues

If you can rule out issues with power and cabling, suspect an issue with the device's boot sector and files. Corruption due to faults in the disk unit, power failure, incorrect installation of multiple operating systems, or malware will prevent the disk from working as a boot device. There are two ways of formatting the boot information: MBR and GPT.

- In the legacy master boot record (MBR) scheme, the MBR is in the first sector of the first partition. Partitions allow a single disk device to be divided into multiple logical drives. The first sector contains information about the partitions on the disk plus some code that points to the location of the active boot sector. The boot sector is located either on the sector after the MBR or the first sector of each other partition. It describes the partition file system and contains the code that points to the method of booting the OS. Typically, this will be the Boot Configuration Data (BCD) store for a Windows system or GRUB or LILO Linux boot managers. Each primary partition can contain a boot sector, but only one of them can be marked active.

- With the modern globally unique ID (GUID) partition table (GPT) boot scheme, the boot information is not restricted to a single sector but still serves the same basic purpose of identifying partitions and OS boot loaders.

Whether the disk is using an MBR or GPT partitioning scheme, damage to these records results in boot errors such as "**Boot device not found**," "OS not found," or "Invalid drive specification." If this problem has been caused by malware, the best way to resolve it is to use the boot disk option in your anti-virus software. This will include a scanner that may detect the malware that caused the problem in the first place and contain tools to repair the boot sector.

If you don't have the option of using a recovery disk created by the anti-virus software, you can try to use the repair options that come with the OS setup disk.

Troubleshoot OS Errors and Crash Screens

If a boot device is located, the code from the boot sector on the selected device is loaded into memory and takes over from the system firmware. The boot sector code loads the rest of the operating system files into system memory. Error messages received after this point can usually be attributed to software or device driver problems rather than physical issues with hardware devices.

If there is a serious fault, a Windows system will display a **blue screen of death (BSOD)**. This typically indicates that there is a system memory fault, a hardware device/driver fault, or corruption of operating system files. Use the error code displayed on the fault screen to look up the issue via online resources. The system will generate a memory dump that you can forward for analysis if you have a support contract.

Blue screen of death (BSOD) preventing a Windows PC from booting. (Screenshot courtesy of Microsoft.)

 *A blue screen is a Windows **proprietary crash screen**. A macOS system that suffers catastrophic process failure shows a spinning **pinwheel** (of death), also called a spinning wait cursor. Linux displays a kernel panic or "Something has gone wrong" message.*

Troubleshoot Drive Availability

A hard disk drive (HDD) is most likely to fail due to mechanical problems either in the first few months of operation or after a few years. A solid-state drive (SSD) is typically more reliable but also has a maximum expected lifetime. With any fixed disk, sudden loss of power can cause damage and/or file corruption, especially if power loss occurs in the middle of a write operation.

A fixed disk that is failing might display the following symptoms:

- Unusual noise (HDD only)—A healthy hard disk makes a certain low-level noise when accessing the platters. A loud or **grinding noise**, or any sort of **clicking sound**, is a sign of a mechanical problem.

- No **LED status indicator** activity—If disk activity lights are not active, the whole system might not be receiving power, or the individual disk unit could be faulty.

- **Constant LED activity**—Constant activity, often referred to as disk thrashing, can be a sign that there is not enough system RAM so that the disk is being used continually for paging (virtual memory). It could also be a sign of a faulty software process or that the system is infected with malware.

- **Bootable device not found**—If the PC fails to boot from the fixed disk, it is either faulty or there is file corruption.

- **Missing drives in OS**—If the system boots, but a second fixed disk or removable drive does not appear in tools such as File Explorer or cannot be accessed via the command-line, first check that it has been initialized and formatted with a partition structure and file system. If the disk is not detected by a configuration tool such as Windows Disk Management, suspect that it has a hardware or cable/connector fault.

- **Read/write failure**—This means that when you are trying to open or save a file, an error message such as "Cannot read from the source disk" is displayed. On an HDD, this is typically caused by **bad sectors**. A sector can be damaged through power failure or a mechanical fault. If you run a test utility, such as chkdsk, and more bad sectors are located each time the test is run, it is a sign that the disk is about to fail. On an SSD, the cause will be one or more bad blocks. SSD circuitry degrades over the course of many write operations. An SSD is manufactured with "spare" blocks and uses wear leveling routines to compensate for this. If the spare blocks are all used up, the drive firmware will no longer be able to compensate for ones that have failed.

- **Blue screen of death (BSOD)**—A failing fixed disk and file corruption may cause a particularly severe read/write failure, resulting in a system stop error (a crash screen).

When experiencing any of these symptoms, try to make a data backup and replace the disk as soon as possible to minimize the risk of data loss.

Troubleshoot Drive Reliability and Performance

In addition to symptoms that you can detect by observing system operation, most fixed disks have a self-diagnostic program called **Self-Monitoring, Analysis, and Reporting Technology (SMART)**. SMART can alert the operating system if a **failure** is detected. If you suspect that a drive is failing or if you experience performance issues such as **extended read/write times**, you should try to run more advanced diagnostic tests on the drive. Most fixed disk vendors supply utilities for testing drives, or there may be a system diagnostics program supplied with the computer system.

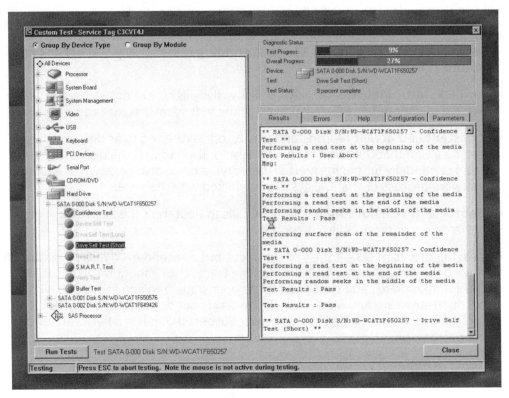

Using system diagnostics software to test a hard drive.

You can also use Windows utilities to query SMART and run manual tests.

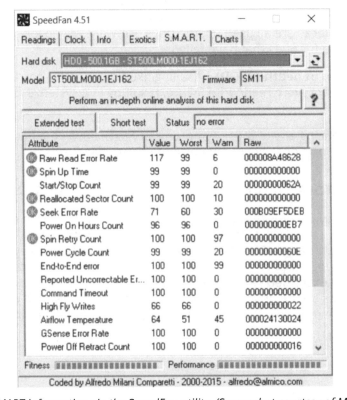

Viewing SMART information via the SpeedFan utility. (Screenshot courtesy of Microsoft.)

These tests can detect whether there is any damage to the device's storage mechanisms. In the case of performance, they can report statistics such as **input/output operations per second (IOPS)**. If performance is reduced from the vendor's baseline measurements under test conditions, it is likely that the device itself is faulty. If performance metrics are similar to the device's benchmark under test conditions, any slow read/write access observed during operation is likely to be due to a more complex system performance issue. Possible causes include application load and general system resource issues, file fragmentation (on hard disks), and limited remaining capacity.

Extended read/write times can also occur because particular sectors (HDDs) or blocks (SSDs) fail (go "bad"). **Data loss/corruption** means that files stored in these locations cannot be opened or simply disappear. When bad sectors or blocks are detected, the disk firmware marks them as unavailable for use.

If there is file corruption on a hard disk and no backup, you can attempt to recover data from the device using a recovery utility.

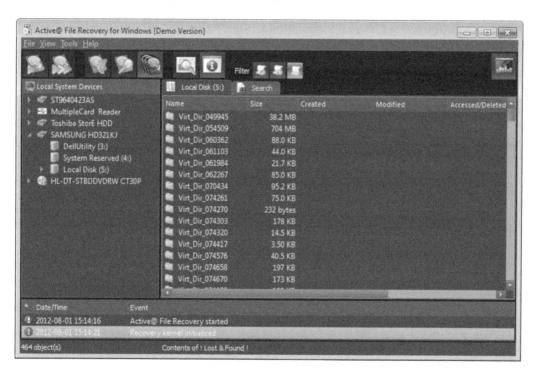

Using file recovery software to scan a disk. (Screenshot courtesy of Microsoft.)

File recovery from an SSD is not usually possible without highly specialized tools.

Troubleshoot RAID Failure

Redundant Array of Independent Disks (RAID) is usually configured as a means of protecting data against the risk of a single fixed disk failing. The data is either copied to a second drive (mirroring) or additional information is recorded on multiple drives to enable them to recover from a device failure (parity). RAID can be implemented using hardware controllers or features of the operating system.

The redundant storage is made available as a volume, which can be partitioned and formatted in the OS as one or more drives.

There are two main scenarios for **RAID failure**: failure of a device within the array and failure of the whole array or volume.

If one of the underlying devices fails, the volume will be listed as "degraded," but the data on the volume will still be accessible and it should continue to function as a boot device, if so configured.

 RAID 0 has no redundancy, so if one of the disks fails, the volume will stop working. RAID 0 only has specialist uses where speed is more important than reliability.

Most desktop-level RAID solutions can tolerate the loss of only one disk, so it should be replaced as soon as possible. If the array supports hot swapping, then the new disk can simply be inserted into the chassis of the computer or into a disk chassis. Once this is done, the array can be rebuilt using the RAID configuration utility (if a hardware RAID controller is used) or an OS utility (if you are using software RAID). Note that the rebuilding process is likely to severely affect performance as the controller is probably writing multiple gigabytes of data to the new disk.

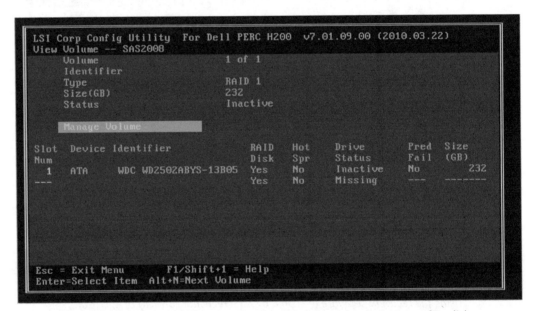

RAID errors using the configuration utility. This volume is missing one of its disks.

 When hot swapping a faulty disk out, take extreme caution not to remove a healthy disk from the array as making a mistake could cause the array to fail, depending on the configuration. Disk failure is normally indicated by a red LED. Always make a backup beforehand.

If a volume is not available, either more than the tolerated number of disks has failed, or the controller has failed. If the boot volume is affected, then the operating system will not start. If too many disks have failed, you will have to turn to the latest backup or try to use file recovery solutions. If the issue is controller failure, then data on the volume should be recoverable, though there may be file corruption if a write operation was interrupted by the failure. Either install a new controller or import the disks into another system.

If the failure affects the boot process, use the RAID configuration utility to verify its status. If you cannot access the configuration utility, then the controller itself is likely to have failed.

```
                                           F10 = System Services
                                           F11 = BIOS Boot Manager
                                                 F12 = PXE Boot
One 2.40 GHz Quad-core Processor, Bus Speed:4.80 GT/s, L2/L3 Cache:1 MB/8 MB

System Memory Size: 4.0 GB, System Memory Speed: 1067 MHz



Broadcom NetXtreme II Ethernet Boot Agent v5.0.5
Copyright (C) 2000-2009 Broadcom Corporation
All rights reserved.
Press Ctrl-S to Configure Device (MAC Address - 842B2B19E291)



Dell PERC H200/6Gbps SAS HBA BIOS
MPT2BIOS-7.01.09.00 (2010.03.22)
Copyright 2000-2009 LSI Corporation.

Integrated RAID exception detected:
   Volume (Hd1:079) is currently in state INACTIVE/OPTIMAL
Enter the Dell PERC H200/HBA Configuration Utility to investigate!

Press Ctrl-C to start Dell PERC H200/HBA Configuration Utility..
```

Boot message indicating a problem with the RAID volume. PressCtrl+C to start the utility and troubleshoot.

Review Activity:

Power and Disk Issues

Answer the following questions:

1. You have been servicing a computer, but when you have finished you find that it will not turn on. There was no power problem before, and you have verified that the computer is connected to a working electrical outlet. What is the most likely explanation?

2. Additional memory was installed in a user's system, and now it will not boot. What steps would you take to resolve this job ticket?

3. You are trying to install Windows from the setup disc, but the computer will not boot from the DVD. What should you do?

4. Following a power cut, a user reports that their computer will not boot. The message "BCD missing" is shown on the screen. The computer does not store data that needs to be backed up. What is the best first step to try to resolve the issue?

5. A user reports that there is a loud clicking noise when she tries to save a file. What should be your first troubleshooting step?

6. You receive a support call from a user of one of the company's computer-aided design (CAD) workstations. The user reports that a notification "RAID utility reports that the volume is degraded" is being displayed. A recent backup has been made. What should you do to try to restore the array?

7. A user reports hearing noises from the hard disk—does this indicate it is failing and should be replaced?

Topic 3D

Troubleshoot System and Display Issues

CORE 1 EXAM OBJECTIVES COVERED
5.2 Given a scenario, troubleshoot problems related to motherboards, RAM, CPU, and power.
5.4 Given a scenario, troubleshoot video, projector, and display issues.

As a CompTIA A+ technician, many of the service calls that you respond to will involve troubleshooting a wide range of issues and scenarios, including intermittent faults, performance problems, and display errors. Your ability to quickly and effectively diagnose and solve the problems across a range of scenarios will be essential in maintaining an optimal environment for the users you support.

Troubleshoot Component Issues

Symptoms such as the system locking up, **intermittent shutdowns**, continuous rebooting, OS blue screen/Kernel panic errors, and **application crashes** are difficult to diagnose with a specific cause, especially if you are not able to witness the events directly. The most likely causes are software, disk/file corruption problems, or malware.

If you can discount these, try to establish whether the problem is truly intermittent or whether there is a pattern to the errors. If they occur when the PC has been running for some time, it could be a thermal problem.

Next, check that the power supply is providing good, stable voltages to the system. If you can discount the power supply, you must start to suspect a problem with memory, CPU, or motherboard. The vendor may supply a diagnostic test program that can identify hardware-level errors. These programs are often run from the firmware setup utility rather than from the OS.

If no diagnostic utilities are available, you might be able to identify motherboard, RAM, or CPU hardware issues by observing physical symptoms.

Overheating

Excessive heat can easily damage the sensitive circuitry of a computer. If a system feels hot to the touch, you should check for **overheating** issues. Unusual odors, such as a **burning smell** or smoke, will almost always indicate something (probably the power supply) is overheating. The system should be shut down immediately and the problem investigated. A burning smell may also arise because the case and/ or fan vents are clogged with dust.

CPUs and other system components heat up while running. Take care not to burn yourself when handling internal components.

Other techniques for diagnosing and correcting overheating issues include the following:

- Most systems come with internal temperature sensors that you can check via driver or management software. Use the vendor documentation to confirm that the system is operating within acceptable limits.

- Ensure that the CPU fan is working. Proper cooling is vital to the lifespan and performance of the processor. If the processor is running too hot, it can decrease performance. A processor that is overheating can cause crashes or reboot the machine. Is the fan's power cable properly connected? Is the fan jammed, clogged, or too small? If a processor upgrade is installed, the fan from the original CPU may not be suitable for the new device.

- Make sure the heat sink is properly fitted. It should be snug against the processor. It might be necessary to clean away old thermal paste and replace it to help the processor to run at a lower temperature.

- Always use blanking plates to cover up holes in the back or front of the PC. Holes can disrupt the airflow and decrease the effectiveness of the cooling systems.

- Verify whether the room in which the PC is installed is unusually warm or dusty or whether the PC is positioned near a radiator or in direct sunlight.

Thermal problems may also affect system operation by causing loose connectors to drift apart, components to move in their sockets, or circuit board defects such as hairline cracks to widen and break connections. Some of these faults can be detected by visual inspection.

Physical Damage

Actual physical damage to a computer system is usually caused to peripherals, ports, and cables. Damage to other components is only likely if the unit has been in transit somewhere. Inspect a unit closely for damage to the case; even a small crack or dent may indicate a fall or knock that could have caused worse damage to the internal components than is obvious from outside.

If a peripheral device does not work, examine the port and the end of the cable closely for bent, broken, or dirty pins and connectors. Examine the length of the cable for damage.

Few problems are actually caused by the motherboard itself, but there are a few things to be aware of.

- The motherboard's soldered chips and components could be damaged by electrostatic discharge (ESD), electrical spikes, or overheating.

- The pins on integrated connectors can also be damaged by careless insertion of plugs and adapter cards.

- In some cases, errors may be caused by dirt (clean the contacts on connectors) or chip creep, where an adapter works loose from its socket over time, perhaps because of temperature changes.

- If a system has had liquid spilled on it or if fans or the keyboard are clogged by dust or dirt, there may be visible signs of this.

- If a component has "blown," it can leave scorch marks. You could also look for **capacitor swelling**. The capacitors are barrel-like components that regulate the flow of electricity to the system chips. If they are swollen or bulging or emitting any kind of residue, they could have been damaged or could have failed due to a manufacturing defect.

If there is physical damage to the motherboard, you will almost certainly need diagnostic software to run tests that confirm whether there is a problem. Testing by substituting "known good" components would be too time consuming and expensive. It is worth investigating any environmental problems or maintenance procedures that could be the "root cause" of the error.

Troubleshoot Performance Issues

Performance issues are one of the hardest types of problem to diagnose and troubleshoot because the symptoms of poor performance have a wide variety of causes. Use a structured approach to try to compartmentalize the source of the performance issue:

1. **Check for overheating**—If the temperature is too high, the CPU and other components are likely to reduce the performance level to avoid overheating. This is referred to as throttling. Check temperature sensors and fan speeds. If these are high, check whether the computer needs cleaning or if cooling systems need to be replaced or upgraded.

2. **Check for misconfigurations**—If the symptom of sluggish performance is found on a new build or after an upgrade or maintenance, verify the compatibility of new components with the motherboard. For example, a memory upgrade might result in the computer no longer using dual-channel mode, reducing performance. Remember to ask the question "What has changed?" when a problem is reported.

3. **Verify the problem**—A PC has compute, storage, and networking functions. Any three of these may be the source of sluggish performance. If possible, use diagnostic tests to compare performance of the CPU, system memory, fixed disk, and network adapter to known performance baselines. Quantifying what "sluggish" really means and isolating the issue to a particular subsystem will help to identify the probable cause. If the system performance is not sufficient, one or more subsystems can be upgraded.

 A bottleneck is an underpowered component that slows down the whole system. For example, a PC might have a fast CPU, dedicated graphics, and lots of system memory, but if the fixed disk is an HDD, then performance will be very slow.

4. **Rule out operating system/app/configuration/networking issues**—Users might describe a computer's performance as sluggish when in fact there is a configuration problem. For example, a computer might seem to be unresponsive and lead the user to say, "My computer is slow," but the issue is caused by a faulty network login script, and the fault does not actually lie in the computer. Try to rule out issues with the operating system and apps before assuming that there is a hardware issue. You can use a built-in or third-party diagnostic suite to verify the performance of individual components. If the diagnostic tool does not indicate a problem, suspect a software/configuration issue.

Troubleshoot Inaccurate System Date/Time

It is important for computers to keep time accurately. If the date and time are not correctly synchronized with other computers on the network or on the Internet, security systems such as authentication will not work and utilities such as backup programs and schedulers will be unreliable.

The real time clock (RTC) is a part of the chipset that keeps track of the calendar date and time. This component runs on battery power when the computer is turned off. The RTC battery is a coin cell lithium battery.

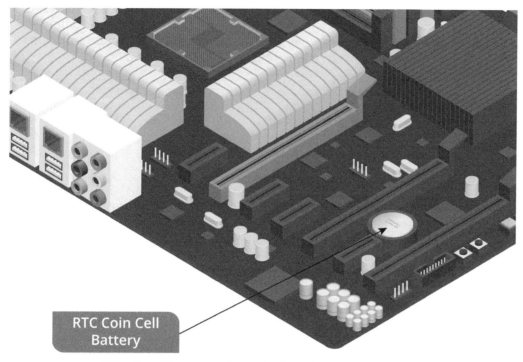

RTC coin cell battery on the motherboard. (Image ©123RF.com)

If the date or time displayed in the system firmware setup program is inaccurate, it can be a sign that the RTC battery is failing. You should replace it with the same size and type. Typically, the coin cell type is CR2032, but check the motherboard documentation.

 The RTC battery is also often called the CMOS battery. On older computers, system firmware custom settings were saved to CMOS RAM. CMOS stands for complementary metal-oxide semiconductor, which describes the manufacturing process used to make the RAM chip. CMOS requires battery backup to save data. On current motherboards, configuration data is stored in a non-volatile RAM (NVRAM) chip (flash memory), rather than in CMOS RAM. Flash memory does not require battery backup.

Troubleshoot Missing Video Issues

If no image is displayed on the monitor or projector, first make sure that the display device is plugged in and turned on. Check that the monitor is not in standby mode (press a key or cycle the power to the monitor to activate it).

You may also need to use controls on the monitor itself to adjust the image or select the **appropriate data source** or input channel. For example, if there is no image on the screen, check that the monitor is set to use the HDMI port that the computer is connected to, rather than an empty DVI port. These on-screen display (OSD) menus are operated using buttons on the monitor case. As well as input control, you can usually find settings for brightness, color/contrast, and power saving.

Physical Cabling Issues

If the display is powered on and you can rule out a problem with the input source, check the **cable and connectors** between the video card and monitor. Make sure the cable is connected securely at both ends and is not loose. Make sure that the cable has not become stretched or crimped. Verify that the cable specification is valid for the application. For example, a basic HDMI cable might not be sufficient quality for 4K resolution, which requires High Speed rated cable.

To rule out cable problems, use the "known good" technique and substitute with another cable. Alternatively, try the monitor with a different PC to identify whether the problem is with the display unit or with the input source.

Burned-Out-Bulb Issues

A video projector is a large-format display, suitable for use in a presentation or at a meeting. The image is projected onto a screen or wall using a lens system. Like display monitors, projectors can use different imaging technologies, such as cathode ray tube (CRT), liquid crystal display (LCD), and digital light processing (DLP). Where a PC monitor display uses a small backlight or LED array, a projector uses a very strong bulb light source to project the image onto a screen or backdrop.

A DLP projector. (Image ©123RF.com)

Projector bulbs have a limited lifetime and will often need to be replaced. You might notice the image generated by the projector start to dim. There may also be a bulb health warning indicator light. A completely failed bulb is referred to as a **burned-out bulb**. You might hear the bulb "pop" and observe scorch marks on the inside or a broken filament.

Take care when handling projectors. During use, the bulb becomes very hot, and while it is hot, it will be very fragile. Allow a projector to cool completely before attempting to remove it.

Intermittent Projector Shutdown Issues

Intermittent projector shutdown is typically caused by overheating. Check that the projector's fan is working, that the vents are free from dust and are not obstructed, and that the ambient temperature is not too high. If you can rule out overheating, check for loose connector cables and verify that the bulb is secured properly.

Troubleshoot Video Quality Issues

There might be an image on the display unit, but it might exhibit unusual artefacts or glitches. These video quality issues might be due to a fault in the display itself or with the input source (the signal from the video card).

- **Dim image**—Use the OSD to check the brightness and contrast controls to make sure they are not turned all the way down. It is possible that a power-saving mode is dimming the display. It is also possible that an adaptive brightness, auto-brightness, or eye-saving feature of the device or operating system has been enabled. These reduce brightness and contrast and can use lower blue-light levels. This type of feature might activate automatically at a certain time of day or could use an ambient light sensor to trigger when the room is dark. If the image is almost invisible, the display's backlight has probably failed, and the unit will have to be repaired under warranty or replaced.

- **Fuzzy image**—If the output resolution does not match the display device's native resolution, the image will appear fuzzy. This typically happens if the video card's driver is faulty or incorrectly configured. For example, the TFT monitor's resolution might be 1920x1080, but the video card is set to 1024x768. Use the OS to change the output resolution or update the driver.

- **Flashing screen**—Check the video cable and connectors. If the connector is not securely inserted at both ends, this could cause flickering. A flickering or flashing image could also be caused by the display's backlight or circuitry starting to fail. Other symptoms of a failing display include bright or dim bands or lines and bright spots at the edge of the screen. Any of these symptoms will typically require the display to be repaired under warranty or replaced.

 A flashing screen could also be caused by a faulty or overheating video card. Attach the display device to a different computer to isolate the cause of the issue.

- **Dead pixels**—Defects in a flat-panel monitor may cause individual pixels to be "stuck" or "dead." If a digital display panel has stuck (constantly bright) pixels, and the panel cannot be replaced under warranty, there are software utilities available to cycle the pixel through a series of relatively extreme color states to try to reactivate it. Fixed pixels can also sometimes be reactivated by gently pressing or tapping the affected area of the screen with a stylus or pencil eraser, though there is the risk of causing further damage or scratching the screen. Dead pixels (solid black) cannot usually be fixed.

- **Burn-in**—When the same static image is displayed for an extended period, the monitor's picture elements can be damaged, and a ghost image is "burned" permanently onto the display. Devices such as plasma screens and organic LED (OLED) displays can be more vulnerable to burn-in than ordinary TFT/LED displays. Always ensure that a display is set to turn off, or use an animated screen saver when no user input is detected.

 A TFT/LED monitor uses an LED backlight to illuminate the image. In an OLED, each pixel provides its own illumination.

- **Incorrect color display**—If a computer is used to produce digital art, it is very important that the display be calibrated to scanning devices and print output. Color calibration (or workflow) refers to a process of adjusting screen and scanner settings so that color input and output are balanced. Color settings should be configured with the assistance of a color profile. You can use the Color Management applet in Control Panel along with test card color patterns and spectrophotometers to define a color profile and verify that the display matches it.

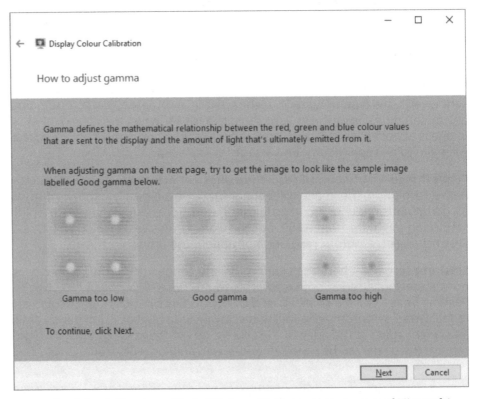

Display Color Calibration utility in Windows 10. (Screenshot courtesy of Microsoft.)

You may also come across color glitches, such as purple or green horizontal lines or colors changing unexpectedly. These are usually caused by a faulty or loose connector or cabling that is either faulty or insufficient quality for the current image resolution. Try replacing the cable. If this does not fix the issue, there could be a hardware fault in either the monitor or graphics adapter.

- **Audio issues**—HDMI and DisplayPort can deliver a combined video and audio signal if that is supported by the video card. DVI and VGA cannot carry a sound signal, so the speakers must be connected to the computer's audio ports using 3.5 mm jacks. If there is no sound from built-in or separate speakers, check power, cables/connectors, and any physical volume control on the speaker device. If you can discount these issues, use the OS to verify that the audio output is set to the correct device and check the OS volume control.

Review Activity:

System and Display Issues

Answer the following questions:

---

1. What cause might you suspect if a PC experiences intermittent lockups?

2. True or false? Running the fans continually at maximum speed is the best way to prevent overheating.

3. You receive a support call from a lecturer. A projector is only displaying a very dim image. Which component should you prioritize for investigation?

4. A user has been supplied with a monitor from stores as a temporary replacement. However, the user reports that the device is unusable because of a thick green band across the middle of the screen. What technique could you use to diagnose the cause?

Lesson 3
Summary

You should be able to apply the CompTIA A+ troubleshooting model to common scenarios and diagnose symptoms such as no power, POST error, boot device failure, storage device/RAID issue, or display device issue.

Guidelines for Troubleshooting PC Hardware

Follow these guidelines to support troubleshooting procedures:

- Establish documented support and troubleshooting procedures that embed the standard methodology of identifying symptoms; diagnosing and testing causes; planning, implementing, and verifying solutions; and documenting findings, actions, and outcomes.

- Ensure that vendor documentation for system BIOS/UEFI is available and that technicians are familiar with the system setup program and configure boot order, user/supervisor passwords, USB protection, and TPM settings.

- Develop a knowledge base for troubleshooting problems related to motherboards, RAM, CPU, and power, such as POST beeps, proprietary crash screens, no power/black screen, sluggish performance, overheating, intermittent shutdown, capacitor swelling, and inaccurate system date/time.

- Develop a knowledge base for troubleshooting problems with storage drives and RAID arrays, such as LED status indicators, grinding/clicking noises, bootable device not found errors, data loss/corruption, RAID failure, SMART failure, extended read/write times, and missing drives in OS.

- Develop a knowledge base for troubleshooting problems related to video, projector, and display issues, such as incorrect data source, physical cabling issues, burned-out bulb, fuzzy image, display burn-in, dead pixels, flashing screen, incorrect color display, audio issues, dim image, and intermittent projector shutdown.

Lesson 4

Comparing Local Networking Hardware

LESSON INTRODUCTION

Network support is a great competency for IT technicians at all levels to possess. In today's environment, standalone computing is a rarity. Just about every digital device on the planet today is connected to external resources via a network, whether it is a small office/home office (SOHO) network, a corporate WAN, or to the Internet directly.

The ability to connect, share, and communicate using a network is crucial for running a business and staying connected to everything in the world. As a CompTIA® A+® support technician, if you understand the technologies that underlie both local and global network communications, you can play an important role in ensuring that the organization you support stays connected.

This lesson will help you understand how different types of networks are categorized and how to compare and contrast network cabling, hardware, and wireless standards.

Lesson Objectives

In this lesson, you will:

- Compare network types.

- Compare networking hardware.

- Explain network cable types.

- Compare wireless networking types.

Topic 4A

Compare Network Types

CORE 1 EXAM OBJECTIVES COVERED
2.7 Compare and contrast Internet connection types, network types, and their features.

A network type categorizes the area over which the parts of the network are managed. Being able to use the correct terminology to classify the scope of a network and distinguish their specific requirements will enable you to assist with installation and support procedures.

LANs and WANs

A **local area network (LAN)** is a group of computers connected by cabling and one or more network switches that are all installed at a single geographical location. A LAN might span a single floor in a building, a whole building, or multiple nearby buildings (a campus). Any network where the nodes are within about 1 or 2 km (or about 1 mile) of one another can be thought of as "local." LAN cabling and devices are typically owned and managed by the organization that uses the network.

Most cabled LANs are based on the **802.3 Ethernet** standards maintained by the Institute of Electrical and Electronics Engineers (IEEE). The IEEE 802.3 standards are designated *x*BASE-*Y*, where *x* is the nominal data rate and *Y* is the cable type. For example:

- 100BASE-T refers to Fast Ethernet over copper twisted pair cabling. Fast Ethernet works at 100 Mbps.

- 1000BASE-T refers to Gigabit Ethernet over copper twisted pair cabling. Gigabit Ethernet works at 1000 Mbps (or 1 Gbps). 1000BASE-T is the mainstream choice of standard for most LANs.

- 10GBASE-T refers to a copper cabling standard working at 10 Gbps.

Copper cabling uses electrical signaling to communicate data. Other types of Ethernet work over fiber optic cabling. Fiber uses pulses of light to communicate data.

Wireless LANs

A **wireless local area network (WLAN)** uses radios and antennas for data transmission and reception. Most WLANs are based on the IEEE 802.11 series of standards. IEEE 802.11 is better known by its brand name, **Wi-Fi**. Wi-Fi and Ethernet technologies complement one another and are often used together as segments within the same local network. This allows computers with wired and wireless networking adapters to communicate with one another.

Wide Area Networks

Where a LAN operates at a single site, a **wide area network (WAN)** spans multiple geographic locations. One example of a WAN is the Internet, a global network of networks. A company dedicated to facilitating access to the Internet from local networks is called an Internet Service Provider (ISP).

Most private or enterprise WANs use cabling and equipment leased from an ISP to interconnect two or more LAN sites. For example, a company might use a WAN to connect branch office sites to the LAN at its head office.

Metropolitan Area Networks

Metropolitan area network (MAN) can be used to mean a specific network type covering an area equivalent to a city or other municipality. It could mean a company with multiple connected networks within the same metropolitan area—so, larger than a LAN but smaller than a WAN.

SOHO and Enterprise Networks

A **small office home office (SOHO)** LAN is a business-oriented network possibly using a centralized server, in addition to client devices and printers, but often using a single networking appliance to provide LAN and Internet connectivity. This is often referred to as a "SOHO router," "Internet router," or "broadband router."

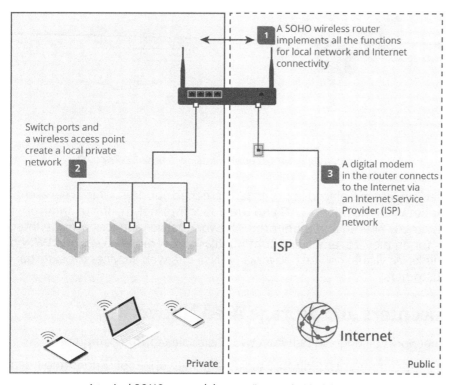

A typical SOHO network layout. (Image © 123RF.com.)

Networks supporting larger businesses or academic institutions networking appliances with the same basic functions as a SOHO router, but because they must support more clients with a greater degree of reliability, each function is performed by a separate network device.

The following graphic illustrates how an enterprise LAN might be implemented. Each segment of the network is designed as a modular function. Client computers and printers are located in work areas and connected to the network by cabling running through wall conduit. Laptops and mobile devices connect to the network via wireless access points (APs). Network servers are separated from client computers in a server room. Workgroup switches connect each of these blocks to core/distribution switches, routers, and firewalls. These network appliances allow authorized connections between the clients and servers.

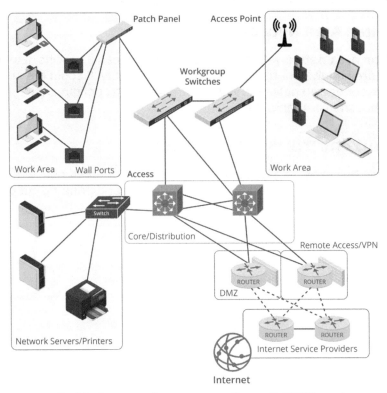

Positioning network components. (Image © 123RF.com.)

Internet services are placed in protected screened subnets, which represent a border between the private LAN and the public Internet. Traffic to and from this zone is strictly filtered and monitored. Network border services provide Internet access for employees, email and communications, remote access and WAN branch office links via virtual private networks (VPNs), and web services for external clients and customers.

Datacenters and Storage Area Networks

Most networks distinguish between two basic roles for the computers:

- A server computer is dedicated to running network applications and hosting shared resources.

- A client computer allows end users to access the applications and resources to do work.

On an enterprise LAN, server computers are hosted in a separate area, referred to as a "server room." A company with high server requirements might operate a datacenter, however. A **datacenter** is a whole site that is dedicated to provisioning server resources. Most datacenters are housed in purpose-built facilities. A datacenter has dedicated networking, power, climate control, and physical access control features all designed to provide a highly available environment for running critical applications.

Within an enterprise LAN or datacenter, a **storage area network (SAN)** provisions access to a configurable pool of storage devices that can be used by application servers. An SAN is isolated from the main network. It is only accessed by servers, not by client PCs and laptops. SAN clients are servers running databases or applications. Provisioning a shared storage pool as an SAN is more flexible and reliable than using local disks on each server machine. SANs use connectivity technologies such as Fiber Channel and Internet SCSI (iSCSI).

Personal Area Networks

A **personal area network (PAN)** refers to using wireless connectivity to connect to devices at a range of a few meters. A PAN can be used to share data between a PC and a mobile devices and wearable technology devices, such as smart watches. It can also connect PCs and mobiles to peripheral devices, such as printers, headsets, speakers, and video displays. As digital and network functionality continues to be embedded in more and more everyday objects, appliances (the IOT), and clothing, the use of PANs will only grow.

Review Activity:

Network Types

Answer the following questions:

1. A network uses an IEEE 802.11 standard to establish connections. What type of network is this?

2. What type of network has no specific geographical restrictions?

3. A network uses Fiber Channel adapters to implement connections. What type of network is this?

Topic 4B

Compare Networking Hardware

CORE 1 EXAM OBJECTIVES COVERED
2.2 Compare and contrast common networking hardware.

Networking hardware is the devices that allow computers to connect to a network over a certain type of network media and that forward data between computers. Network adapters, patch panels, and switches are used to implement local Ethernet networks. Understanding the functions and capabilities of Ethernet devices will prepare you to support a local office or SOHO network effectively.

Network Interface Cards

Ethernet communications are established by either electrical signaling over copper twisted pair cable or pulses of light transmitted over fiber optic cable. The physical connection to the cable is made using a transceiver port in the computer's network interface card (NIC). All PC motherboards have a built-in 1000BASE-T compatible adapter. You might use an NIC adapter card to support other types of Ethernet, such as fiber optic. You can also purchase cards with multiple ports of the same type—two or four 1000BASE-T ports, for instance. The multiple ports can be bonded to create a higher-speed link. Four Gigabit Ethernet ports could be bonded to give a nominal link speed of 4 Gbps.

For the NIC to be able to process the electrical or light signals as digital data, the signals must be divided into regular units with a consistent format. There must also be a means for each node on the local network to address communications to other nodes. Ethernet provides a data link protocol to perform these framing and addressing functions.

Each Ethernet NIC port has a unique hardware/physical address, called the "media access control" (MAC) address. Each frame of Ethernet data identifies the source MAC address and destination MAC address in fields in a header.

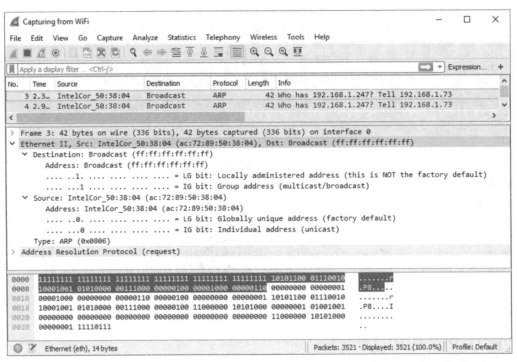

Captured Ethernet frame showing the destination and source MAC addresses. The destination address is a broadcast address. (Screenshot courtesy of Wireshark.)

A MAC address consists of 48 binary digits, making it six bytes in size. A MAC address is typically represented as 12 digits of hexadecimal. Hex is a numbering system often used to represent network addresses of different types. A hex digit can be one of sixteen values: 0–9 and then A, B, C, D, E, F. Each hex digit represents half a byte (or four bits or a nibble). The 12 digits of a MAC address might be written with colon or hyphen separators or no separators at all—for example, `00:60:8c:12:3a:bc` or `00608c123abc`.

Patch Panels

In most types of office cabling, the computer is connected to a wall port and—via cabling running through the walls—to a **patch panel**. The cables running through the walls are terminated to insulation displacement connector (IDC) punchdown blocks at the back of the panel.

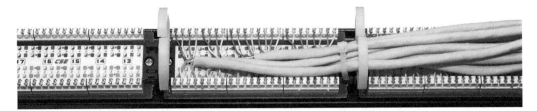

IDCs at the rear of a patch panel. (Image by plus69 © 123RF.com.)

The other side of the patch panel has prewired RJ45 ports. A patch cord is used to connect a port on the patch panel to a port on an Ethernet switch. This cabling design makes it easier to change how any given wall port location is connected to the network via switch ports.

Patch panel with prewired RJ45 ports. (Image by Svetlana Kurochkina © 123RF.com.)

 It is vital to use an effective labeling system when installing structured cabling so that you know which patch panel port is connected to which wall port.

Hubs

A **hub** is a legacy network hardware device that was used to implement the 10BASE-T and 100BASE-T Ethernet cabling designs. This design is referred to as a star topology" because each end system is cabled to a concentrator (the hub).

A hub has a number of ports—typically between four and 48—and each computer is cabled to one port. The circuitry in the hub repeats an incoming transmission from a computer attached to one port across all the other ports. In effect, the computers seem to be attached to the same cable. Each computer attached to a hub receives all the traffic sent by other connected devices. This is referred to as a "collision domain."

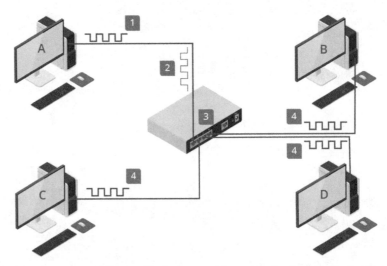

Using a hub to implement an Ethernet. Node A transmits a signal, which is received by the hub and forwarded out of each other port for reception by all the other nodes. (Image © 123RF.com.)

Each computer will ignore any frames that do not match its MAC address. However, when lots of computers are in the same collision domain, performance is reduced, as only one computer can send a frame at any one time. If two computers try to send at the same time, there is a collision, and they must wait for a random period before trying again. The more computers there are, the more collisions. The computers contend for a share of the media bandwidth and all communications are half-duplex. Half-duplex means that the computer can send or receive, but not at the same time.

As well as the effect of contention on performance, there are no hubs that are compatible with Gigabit Ethernet. These limitations mean that almost all networks are now based on Ethernet switching. You are only likely to encounter a hub being used in very specific circumstances, such as where legacy equipment must be kept in service.

Switches

A solution to the issue of collisions was first provided by inserting Ethernet bridges between hubs to break up collision domains. Ethernet bridges were quickly refined into the Ethernet **switch** appliances that underpin almost all modern office networks. Like a hub, an Ethernet switch provisions one port for each device that needs to connect to the network. Unlike a hub, an Ethernet switch can decode each frame and identify the source and destination MAC addresses. It can track which MAC source addresses are associated with each port. When it receives an incoming frame, the switch intelligently forwards it to the port that is a match for the destination MAC address.

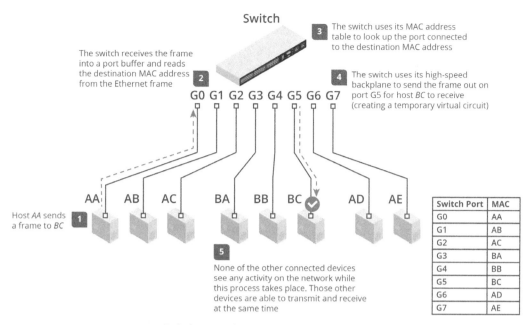

Switch operation. (Image © 123RF.com.)

This means that each switch port is a separate collision domain, and the negative effects of contention are eliminated. Each computer has a full duplex connection to the network and can send and receive simultaneously at the full speed supported by the network cabling and NIC.

When a computer sends a frame, the switch reads the source address and adds it to its MAC address table. If a destination MAC address is not yet known, the switch floods the frame out of all ports.

Unmanaged and Managed Switches

An **unmanaged** switch performs its function without requiring any sort of configuration. You just power it on and connect some hosts to it, and it establishes Ethernet connectivity between the network interfaces without any more intervention. You might find unmanaged switches with four or eight ports used in small networks. There is an unmanaged four-port switch embedded in most of the SOHO router/modems supplied by Internet Service Providers (ISPs) to connect to their networks.

On some older SOHO routers, the LAN interfaces are implemented as a hub. These do not support 1 Gbps operation.

Larger workgroups and corporate networks require additional functionality in their switches. Switches designed for larger LANs are **managed switches**. A managed switch will work as an unmanaged switch out of the box, but an administrator can connect to it over a management port, configure security settings, and then choose options for the switch's more advanced functionality. Most managed switches are designed to be bolted into standard network racks. A typical workgroup switch will come with 24 or 48 access ports for client PCs, servers, and printers. These switches have uplink ports allowing them to be connected to other switches.

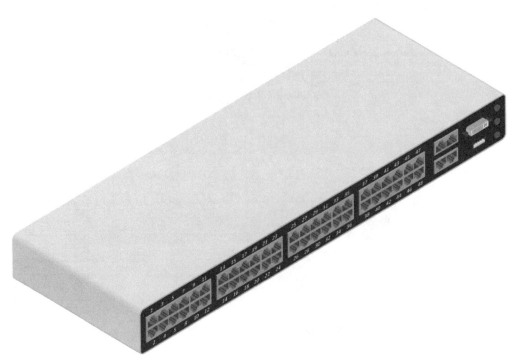

A workgroup switch. (Image © 123RF.com.)

An enterprise might also use modular switches. These provide a power supply and fast communications backplane to interconnect multiple switch units. This enables the provisioning of hundreds of access ports via a single compact appliance.

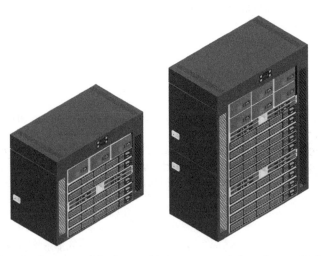

Modular chassis allows provisioning multiple access switches. (Image © 123RF.com.)

Configuring a managed switch can be performed over either a web or command line interface.

```
FastEthernet1/0/1 is up, line protocol is up (connected)
  Hardware is Fast Ethernet, address is f41f.c253.7103 (bia f41f.c253.7103)
  MTU 1500 bytes, BW 100000 Kbit/sec, DLY 100 usec,
     reliability 255/255, txload 1/255, rxload 1/255
  Encapsulation ARPA, loopback not set
  Keepalive set (10 sec)
  Full-duplex, 100Mb/s, media type is 10/100BaseTX
  input flow-control is off, output flow-control is unsupported
  ARP type: ARPA, ARP Timeout 04:00:00
  Last input 00:00:51, output 00:00:00, output hang never
  Last clearing of "show interface" counters never
  Input queue: 0/75/0/0 (size/max/drops/flushes); Total output drops: 0
  Queueing strategy: fifo
  Output queue: 0/40 (size/max)
  5 minute input rate 0 bits/sec, 0 packets/sec
  5 minute output rate 0 bits/sec, 0 packets/sec
     18 packets input, 1758 bytes, 0 no buffer
     Received 4 broadcasts (2 multicasts)
     0 runts, 0 giants, 0 throttles
     0 input errors, 0 CRC, 0 frame, 0 overrun, 0 ignored
     0 watchdog, 2 multicast, 0 pause input
     0 input packets with dribble condition detected
     111 packets output, 13828 bytes, 0 underruns
     0 output errors, 0 collisions, 1 interface resets
     0 unknown protocol drops
```

Viewing interface configuration on a Cisco switch.

Power over Ethernet

Power over Ethernet (PoE) is a means of supplying electrical power from a switch port over ordinary data cabling to a powered device (PD), such as a voice over IP (VoIP) handset, camera, or wireless access point. PoE is defined in several IEEE **standards**:

- **802.3af** allows powered devices to draw up to about 13 W. Power is supplied as 350mA@48V and limited to 15.4 W, but the voltage drop over the maximum 100 feet of cable results in usable power of around 13 W.

- **802.3at (PoE+)** allows powered devices to draw up to about 25 W, with a maximum current of 600 mA.

- **802.3bt (PoE++ or 4PPoE)** supplies up to about 51 W (Type 3) or 73 W (Type 4) usable power.

A **PoE-enabled switch** is referred to as endspan power sourcing equipment (PSE). When a device is connected to a port on a PoE switch, the switch goes through a detection phase to determine whether the device is PoE enabled. If so, it determines the device's power consumption and sets an appropriate supply voltage level. If not, it does not supply power over the port and, therefore, does not damage non-PoE devices.

Powering these devices through a switch is more efficient than using a wall-socket AC adapter for each appliance. It also allows network management software to control the devices and apply energy saving schemes, such as making unused devices go into sleep states and power capping.

If the switch does not support PoE, a device called a "power **injector**" (or "midspan") can be used. One port on the injector is connected to the switch port. The other port is connected to the device. The overall cable length cannot exceed 100 m.

Review Activity:

Networking Hardware

Answer the following questions:

1. True or false? A MAC address identifies the network to which a NIC is attached.

2. A workstation must be provisioned with a 4 Gbps network link. Is it possible to specify a single NIC to meet this requirement?

3. You are completing a network installation as part of a team. Another group has cabled wall ports to a patch panel. Is any additional infrastructure required?

4. You are planning to install a network of wireless access points with power supplied over data cabling. Each access point requires a 20W power supply. What version of PoE must the switch support to fulfill this requirement?

Topic 4C

Explain Network Cable Types

CORE 1 EXAM OBJECTIVES COVERED
2.8 Given a scenario, use networking tools.
3.1 Explain basic cable types and their connectors, features, and purposes.

Recognizing suitable cabling options for a given scenario will help you determine the best choice for a particular network location. As you gain knowledge and experience of the different cable installation and testing tools, you will be able to support highly reliable networks.

Unshielded Twisted Pair

The most popular type of **network cable** is of a **copper** wire construction called "**unshielded twisted pair**" **(UTP)**. UTP is made up of four copper conductor wire pairs. Each pair of insulated conductors is twisted at a different rate from the other pairs, which reduces interference. The electrical signals sent over each pair are balanced. This means that each wire carries an equal but opposite signal to its pair. This is another factor helping to identify the signal more strongly against any source of interference. However, the electrical signaling method is still only reliable over limited range. The signal suffers from attenuation, meaning that it loses strength over long ranges. Most UTP cable segments have a maximum recommended distance of 100 m (328 feet).

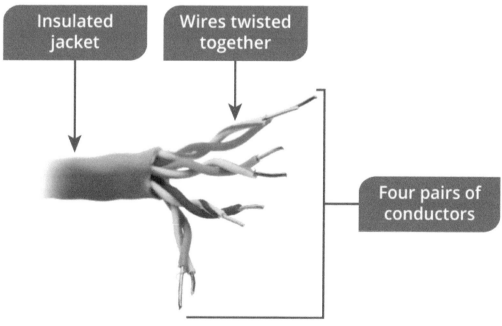

UTP cable. (Image © 123RF.com.)

Shielded Twisted Pair

Shielded twisted pair (STP) provides extra protection against interference. Shielded cable is often used for 10G Ethernet and higher within datacenter networks because it is more reliable than UTP. Shielding may also be a requirement in environments with high levels of external interference, such as cable that must be run in proximity to fluorescent lighting, power lines, motors, and generators.

Shielded cable can be referred to generically as "STP," but several types of shielding and screening exist:

- Screened cable has one thin outer foil shield around all pairs. Screened cable is usually designated as screened twisted pair (ScTP) or foiled/unshielded twisted pair (F/UTP), or sometimes just foiled twisted pair (FTP).

- Fully shielded cabling has a braided outer screen and foil-shielded pairs and is referred to as "shielded/foiled twisted pair" (S/FTP). There are also variants with a foil outer shield (F/FTP).

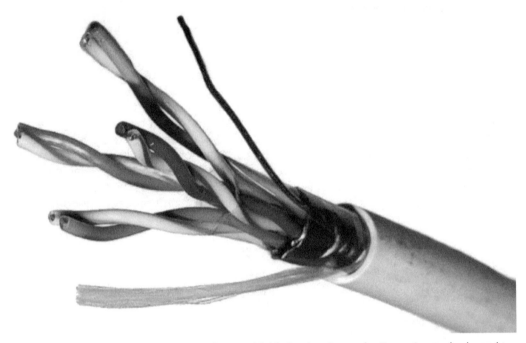

F/UTP cable with a foil screen surrounding unshielded pairs. (Image by Baran Ivo and released to public domain.)

The screening/shielding elements of shielded cable must be bonded to the connector to prevent the metal from acting as a large antenna and generating interference. Modern F/UTP and S/FTP solutions (using appropriate cable, connectors, and patch panels) facilitate this by incorporating bonding within the design of each element.

Cat Standards

A Cat specification is a particular **twisted pair cable** construction method rated for use with given Ethernet standards. Higher Cat specification cable is capable of higher data rates. Cat specifications are defined in the TIA/EIA-568-C Commercial Building Telecommunications Cabling Standards.

Cat	Max. Transfer Rate	Max. Distance	Ethernet Standard Support
5	100 Mbps	100 m (328 ft)	100BASE-TX (Fast Ethernet)
5e	1 Gbps	100 m (328 ft)	1000BASE-T (GB Ethernet)
6	1 Gbps	100 m (328 ft)	1000BASE-T (GB Ethernet)
	10 GBps	55 m (180 ft)	10GBASE-T (10 GB Ethernet)
6A	10 GBps	100 m (328 ft)	10GBASE-T (10 GB Ethernet)

The Cat specification is printed on the cable jacket along with the cable type (UTP or F/UTP, for instance). Cat 5 cable supports the older 100 Mbps Fast Ethernet standard. It is no longer commercially available. A network cabled with Cat 5 will probably need to be rewired to support Gigabit Ethernet.

Cat 5e would still be an acceptable choice for providing Gigabit Ethernet links for client computers, but most sites would now opt to install Cat 6 cable. The improved construction standards for Cat 6 mean that it is more reliable than Cat 5e for Gigabit Ethernet, and it can also support 10 Gbps, though over reduced range.

Cat 6A supports 10 Gbps over 100 m, but the cable is bulkier and heavier than Cat 5e and Cat 6, and the installation requirements more stringent, so fitting it within pathways designed for older cable can be problematic. TIA/EIA standards recommend Cat 6A for health care facilities, with Power over Ethernet (PoE) 802.3bt installations, and for running distribution system cable to wireless access points.

Copper Cabling Connectors

Twisted pair cabling for Ethernet can be terminated using modular **RJ45** connectors. RJ45 connectors are also referred to as "8P8C," standing for eight-position/eight-contact. Each conductor in four-pair Ethernet cable is color-coded. Each pair is assigned a color (orange, green, blue, and brown). The first conductor in each pair has a predominantly white insulator with stripes of the color; the second conductor has an insulator with the solid color.

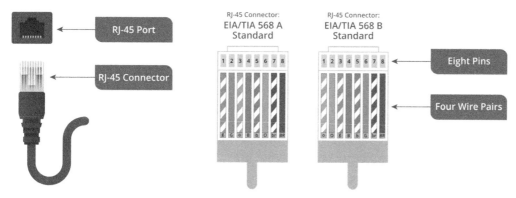

Twisted pair RJ45 connectors. (Image © 123RF.com.)

The TIA/EIA-568 standard defines two methods for terminating twisted pair: **T568A/T568B**. In T568A, pin 1 is wired to green/white, pin 2 is wired to green, pin 3 is wired to orange/white, and pin 6 is wired to orange. In T568B, the position of the green and orange pairs is swapped over, so that orange terminates to 1 and 2 and green to 3 and 6. When cabling a network, it is best to use the same termination method consistently. A straight through Ethernet cable is wired with the same type of termination at both ends.

 Using T568A at one end and T568B at the other creates a crossover cable. Crossover cables were once used to connect computers directly, but Gigabit Ethernet interfaces can perform the crossover automatically, even if standard cable is used.

Twisted-pair can also be used with **RJ11** connectors. Unlike the four-pair cable used with Ethernet, RJ11 is typically used to terminate two-pair cable, which is widely used in telephone systems and with broadband digital subscriber line (DSL) modems.

Copper Cabling Installation Tools

Data cable for a typical office is installed as a structured cabling system. With structured cabling, the network adapter port in each computer is connected to a wall port using a flexible **patch cord**. Behind the wall port, **permanent cable** is run through the wall and ceiling to an equipment room and connected to a patch panel. The port on the patch panel is then connected to a port on an Ethernet switch.

A structured cabling system uses two types of cable termination:

- Patch cords are terminated using RJ45 plugs crimped to the end of the cable.

- Permanent cable is terminated to wall ports and patch panels using insulation displacement connectors (IDC), also referred to as "**punchdown blocks**."

 The 100 m distance limitation is for the whole link, referred to as "channel link." Each patch cord can only be up to 5 m long. Permanent link use solid cable with thicker wires. Patch cords use stranded cable with thinner wires that is more flexible but also suffers more from attenuation.

Installing cable in this type of system involves the use of cable strippers, punchdown tools, and crimpers.

Cable Stripper and Snips

To terminate cable, a small section of outer jacket must be removed to expose the wire pairs. This must be done without damaging the insulation on the inner wire pairs. A **cable stripper** is designed to score the outer jacket just enough to allow it to be removed. Set the stripper to the correct diameter, and then place the cable in the stripper and rotate the tool once or twice. The score cut in the insulation should now allow you to remove the section of jacket.

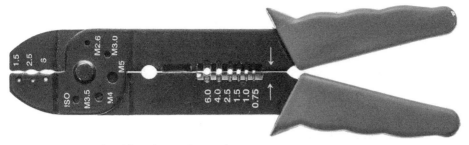

A cable stripper. (Image by gasparij © 123RF.com)

Most Cat 6 and all Cat 6A cable has a plastic star filler running through it that keeps the pairs separated. You need to use electrician's scissors (snips) to cut off the end of this before terminating the cable. There will also be a nylon thread called a "ripcord." This can be pulled down the jacket to open it up more if you damaged any of the wire pairs initially. Snip any excess ripcord before terminating the cable.

Punchdown Tool

A **punchdown tool** is used to fix each conductor into an IDC. First, untwist the wire pairs, and lay them in the color-coded terminals in the IDC in the appropriate termination order (T568A or T568B). To reduce the risk of interference, no more than ½" (13 mm) should be untwisted. Use the punchdown tool to press each wire into the terminal. Blades in the terminal cut through the insulation to make an electrical contact with the wire.

Connecting UTP cable to IDCs using a punchdown tool. (Image by dero2084 © 123RF.com.)

Crimper

A **crimper** is used to fix a jack to a patch cord. Orient the RJ45 plug so that the tab latch is underneath. Pin 1 is the first pin on the left. Arrange the wire pairs in the appropriate order (T568A or T568B), and then push them into the RJ45 plug. Place the plug in the crimper tool, and close it tightly to pierce the wire insulation at the pins and seal the jack to the outer cable jacket.

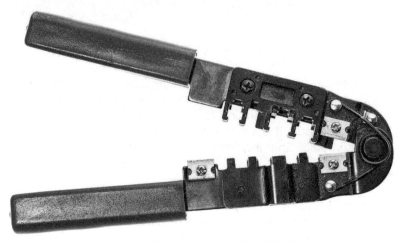

A wire crimper. (Image by gasparij © 123RF.com)

Copper Cabling Test Tools

Once you have terminated cable, you must test it to ensure that each wire makes a good electrical contact and is in the correct pin position. The best time to verify wiring installation and termination is just after you have made all the connections. This means you should still have access to the cable runs. Identifying and correcting errors at this point will be much simpler than when you are trying to set up end user devices.

You can use several cabling and infrastructure troubleshooting devices to assist with this process.

Cable Tester

A **cable tester** is a pair of devices designed to attach to each end of a cable. It can be used to test a patch cord or connected via patch cords to a wall port and patch panel port to test the permanent link. The tester energizes each wire in turn, with an LED indicating successful termination. If an LED does not activate, the wire is not conducting a signal, typically because the insulation is damaged or the wire isn't properly inserted into the plug or IDC. If the LEDs do not activate in the same sequence at each end, the wires have been terminated to different pins at each end. Use the same type of termination on both ends.

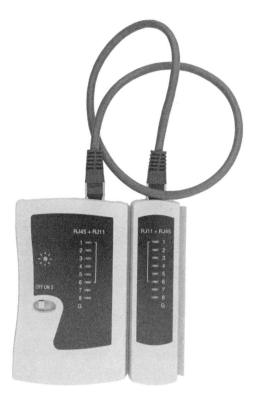

Basic cable tester. (Image by samum © 123RF.com)

Toner Probe

Many cable testers also incorporate the function of a **toner probe**, which is used to identify a cable from within a bundle. This may be necessary when the cables have not been labeled properly. The **tone generator** is connected to the cable using an RJ45 jack and applies a continuous audio signal on the cable. The probe is used to detect the signal and follow the cable over ceilings and through ducts or identify it from within the rest of the bundle.

 Disconnect the other end of the cable from any network equipment before activating the tone generator.

Loopback Plug

A **loopback plug** is used to test an NIC or switch port. You can make a basic loopback plug from a 6" cable stub where the wires connect pin 1 to pin 3 and pin 2 to pin 6. When you connect a loopback plug to a port, you should see a solid link LED showing that the port can send and receive.

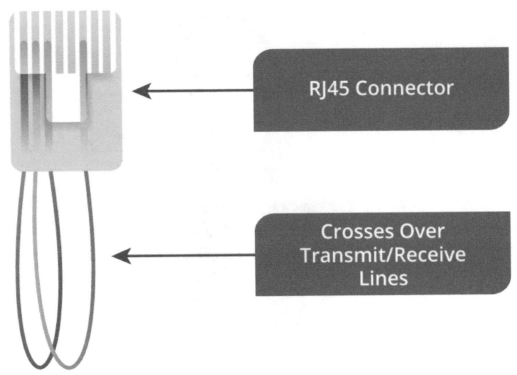

A loopback plug. (Image © 123RF.com)

 A loopback plug made from a cable stub is unlikely to work with Gigabit Ethernet ports. You can obtain manufactured Gigabit port loopback testers.

Network Taps

A **network tap** is used to intercept the signals passing over a cable and send them to a packet or protocol analyzer. Taps are either powered or unpowered:

- A **passive test access point** (TAP) is a box with ports for incoming and outgoing network cabling and an inductor or optical splitter that physically copies the signal from the cabling to a monitor port. No logic decisions are made, so the monitor port receives every frame—corrupt or malformed or not—and the copying is unaffected by load.

- An **active TAP** is a powered device that performs signal regeneration, which may be necessary in some circumstances. Gigabit signaling over copper wire is too complex for a passive tap to monitor, and some types of fiber links may be adversely affected by optical splitting. Because it performs an active function, the TAP becomes a point of failure for the links during power loss.

 *Network sniffing can also be facilitated using a **switched port analyzer (SPAN)**/ mirror port. This means that the sensor is attached to a specially configured port on a network switch. The mirror port receives copies of frames addressed to nominated access ports (or all the other ports).*

Copper Cabling Installation Considerations

Installation of cable must be compliant with local building regulations and fire codes. This means that specific cable types must be used in some installation scenarios.

Plenum Cable

A **plenum** space is a void in a building designed to carry heating, ventilation, and air conditioning (HVAC) systems. Plenum space is typically a false ceiling, though it could also be constructed as a raised floor. As it makes installation simpler, this space has also been used for communications wiring in some building designs. Plenum space is an effective conduit for fire, as there is plenty of airflow and no fire breaks. If the plenum space is used for heating, there may also be higher temperatures. Therefore, building regulations require the use of fire-retardant plenum cable in such spaces. Plenum cable must not emit large amounts of smoke when burned, be self-extinguishing, and meet other strict fire safety standards.

General purpose (non-plenum) cabling uses PVC jackets and insulation. Plenum-rated cable uses treated PVC or fluorinated ethylene polymer (FEP). This can make the cable less flexible, but the different materials used have no effect on bandwidth. Data cable rated for plenum use under the US National Electrical Code (NEC) is marked as CMP/MMP on the jacket. General purpose cables are marked CMG/MMG or CM/MP.

Direct Burial

Outside plant (OSP) is cable run on the external walls of a building or between two buildings. This makes the cable vulnerable to different types of weathering:

* Aerial cable is typically strung between two poles or anchors. The ultraviolet (UV) rays in sunlight plus exposure to more extreme and changing temperatures and damp will degrade regular PVC.

* Conduit can provide more protection for buried cable runs. Such cable can still be exposed to extreme temperatures and damp, however, so regular PVC cable should not be used.

* **Direct burial** cable is laid and then covered in earth or cement/concrete.

OSP cable types use special coatings to protect against UV and abrasion and are often gel filled to protect against temperature extremes and damp. Direct burial cable may also need to be armored to protect against chewing by rodents.

Optical Cabling

Copper wire carries electrical signals, which are sensitive to interference and attenuation. The light pulses generated by lasers and LEDs are not susceptible to interference and suffer less from attenuation. Consequently, **optical cabling** can support much higher bandwidth links, measured in multiple gigabits or terabits per second, and longer cable runs, measured in miles rather than feet.

A fiber optic strand. (Image by atrush © 123RF.com)

An **optical fiber** consists of an ultra-fine core of glass to convey the light pulses. The core is surrounded by glass or plastic cladding, which guides the light pulses along the core. The cladding has a protective coating called the "buffer." The **fiber optic cable** is contained in a protective jacket and terminated by a connector.

Fiber optic cables fall into two broad categories: single-mode and multi-mode:

- **Single-mode fiber (SMF)** has a small core (8–10 microns) and is designed to carry a long wavelength (1,310 or 1,550 nm) infrared signal, generated by a high-power, highly coherent laser diode. Single-mode cables support data rates up to 10 Gbps or better and cable runs of many kilometers, depending on the quality of the cable and optics.

- **Multi-mode fiber (MMF)** has a larger core (62.5 or 50 microns) and is designed to carry a shorter wavelength infrared light (850 nm or 1,300 nm). MMF uses less expensive and less coherent LEDs or vertical cavity surface emitting lasers (VCSELs) and consequently is less expensive to deploy than SMF. However, MMF does not support such high signaling speeds or long distances as single-mode and so is more suitable for LANs than WANs.

The core of a fiber optic connector is a ceramic or plastic ferrule that ensures continuous reception of the light signals. Several connector form factors are available:

- **Straight tip (ST)** is a bayonet-style connector that uses a push-and-twist locking mechanism; it is used mostly for multi-mode networks.

- **Subscriber connector (SC)** has a push/pull design that allows for simpler insertion and removal than fiber channel (FC) connector. There are simplex and duplex versions, though the duplex version is just two connectors clipped together. It can be used for single- or multi-mode.

- **Lucent connector (LC)** is a small form factor connector with a tabbed push/pull design. LC is similar to SC, but the smaller size allows for higher port density.

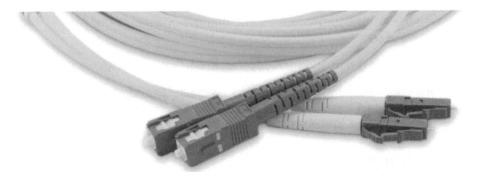

Patch cord with duplex SC format connectors (left) and LC connectors (right). (Image by YANAWUT SUNTORNKIJ © 123RF.com.)

Patch cords for fiber optic can come with the same connector on each end (ST-ST, for instance) or a mix of connectors (ST-SC, for instance). Fiber optic connectors are quite easy to damage and should not be repeatedly plugged in and unplugged. Unused ports and connectors should be covered by a dust cap to minimize the risk of contamination.

Coaxial Cabling

Coaxial (coax) cable is a different type of copper cabling, also carrying electrical signals. Where twisted pair uses balancing to cancel out interference, coax uses two conductors that share the same axis. The core signal conductor is enclosed by plastic insulation (dielectric), and then a second wire mesh conductor serves both as shielding from EMI and as a ground.

Detailed layers of a coaxial cable. (Image by destinacigdem © 123RF.com)

Coax is now mostly used for CCTV installations and as patch cable for Cable Access TV (CATV) and broadband **cable modems**. Coax for CATV installations is typically terminated using a screw-down **F-type connector**.

F-type coaxial connector. (Image © 123RF.com.)

Review Activity:

Network Cable Types

Answer the following questions:

1. You are performing a wiring job, but the company wants to purchase the media and components from another preferred supplier. The plan is to install a network using copper cabling that will support Gigabit Ethernet. The customer is about to purchase Cat 5e cable spools. What factors should they consider before committing to this decision?

2. A network consultant is recommending the use of S/FTP to extend a cable segment through a factory. Is this likely to be an appropriate cable choice?

3. You are reviewing network inventory and come across an undocumented cable reel with "CMP/MMP" marked on the jacket. What installation type is this cable most suitable for?

4. You need to connect permanent cable to the back of a patch panel. Which networking tool might help you?

5. Which fiber optic connector uses a small form factor design?

Topic 4D

Compare Wireless Networking Types

CORE 1 EXAM OBJECTIVES COVERED
2.2 Compare and contrast common networking hardware (Access point only).
2.3 Compare and contrast protocols for wireless networking.
2.8 Given a scenario, use networking tools (Wi-Fi analyzer only).

Wireless technologies can now achieve sufficient bandwidth to replace wired ports for many types of clients in a typical office. It is also more convenient for SOHO networks to use wireless as the primary access method for computers, laptops, smartphones, tablets, and smart home devices. Wireless can provide connectivity for desktops or even servers in places where it is difficult or expensive to run network cabling. As a CompTIA A+ technician, you will often be called upon to install, configure, and troubleshoot wireless technologies, so understanding the standards and types of devices that underpin a wireless network will help you to provide effective support to your users and customers.

Access Points

Wireless technologies use radio waves as transmission media. Radio systems use transmission and reception antennas tuned to a specific frequency for the transfer of signals. Most wireless LANs (WLANs) are based on the **IEEE 802.11 standards**, better known by the brand name Wi-Fi.

Most Wi-Fi networks are configured in what is technically referred to as "infrastructure mode." Infrastructure mode means that each client device (station) is configured to connect to the network via an **access point (AP)**. In 802.11 documentation, this is referred to as an infrastructure "Basic Service Set" (BSS). The MAC address of the AP's radio is used as the **Basic Service Set Identifier (BSSID)**.

An access point can establish a wireless-only network, but it can also work as a bridge to forward communications between the wireless stations and a wired network. The wired network is referred to as the "distribution system" (DS). The access point will be joined to the network in much the same way as a host computer is—via a wall port and cabling to an Ethernet switch. An enterprise network is likely to use Power over Ethernet (PoE) to power the AP over the data cabling.

An access point. (Image © 123RF.com)

802.11a and the 5 GHz Frequency Band

Every Wi-Fi device operates on a specific radio frequency range within an overall **frequency band**. Each frequency band is split into a series of smaller ranges referred to as "**channels.**"

Frequency Bands

It is important to understand the performance characteristics of the two main **frequency bands** used by the IEEE 802.11 standards:

- The 2.4 GHz standard is better at propagating through solid surfaces, giving it the longest signal range. However, the 2.4 GHz band does not support a high number of individual channels and is often congested, with both other Wi-Fi networks and other types of wireless technology, such as Bluetooth®. Also, microwave ovens work at frequencies in the 2.4 GHz band. Consequently, with the 2.4 GHz band, there is increased risk of interference, and the maximum achievable data rates are typically lower than with 5 GHz.

- The **5 GHz** standard is less effective at penetrating solid surfaces and so does not support the maximum ranges achieved with 2.4 GHz standards, but the band supports more individual channels and suffers less from congestion and interference, meaning it supports higher data rates at shorter ranges.

The nominal indoor range for Wi-Fi over 2.4 GHz is 45 m (150 feet) and 30 m (100 feet) over 5 GHz. Depending on the wireless standard used, building features that may block the signal, and interference from other radio sources, clients are only likely to connect at full speed from a third to a half of those distances.

IEEE 802.11a and 5 GHz Channel Layout

The **IEEE 802.11a** standard uses the 5 GHz frequency band only. The data encoding method allows a maximum data rate of 54 Mbps. The 5 GHz band is subdivided into 23 non-overlapping channels, each of which is 20 MHz wide.

The exact use of channels can be subject to different regulation in different countries. **Regulatory impacts** also include a limit on power output, constraining the range of Wi-Fi devices. Devices operating in the 5 GHz band must implement **dynamic frequency selection (DFS)** to prevent Wi-Fi signals from interfering with nearby radar and satellite installations.

U-NII-1	U-NII-2	U-NII-2 Extended	U-NII-3
20 MHz	36 40 44 48	52 56 60 64	100 104 108 112 116 120 124 128 132 136 140	149 153 157 161

Dynamic Frequency Selection (DFS) Range

Unlicensed National Information Infrastructure (U-NII) sub-bands form the 20 MHz channels used in the 5 GHz frequency band. Each sub-band is 5 MHz wide, so the Wi-Fi channels are spaced in intervals of four to allow 20 MHz bandwidth. Channels within the DFS range will be disabled if the access point detects radar signals.

802.11b/g and the 2.4 GHz Frequency Band

The **IEEE 802.11b** standard uses the **2.4 GHz** frequency band and was released in parallel with 802.11a. The signal encoding methods used by 802.11b are inferior to 802.11a and support a nominal data rate of just 11 Mbps.

The 2.4 GHz band is subdivided into up to 14 channels, spaced at 5 MHz intervals from 2,412 MHz up to 2,484 MHz. Because the spacing is only 5 MHz and Wi-Fi needs 20 MHz channel bandwidth, 802.11b channels overlap quite considerably. This means that interference is a real possibility unless widely spaced channels are chosen (1, 6, and 11, for instance). Also, in the Americas, regulations permit the use of channels 1–11 only, while in Europe, channels 1–13 are permitted, and in Japan, all 14 channels are permitted.

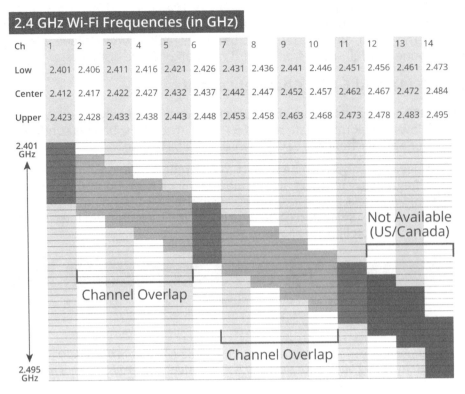

Channel overlap in the 2.4 GHz band.

The **IEEE 802.11g** standard offered a relatively straightforward upgrade path from 802.11b; uses the same encoding mechanism and 54 Mbps rate as 802.11a but in the 2.4 GHz band used by 802.11b and with the same channel layout. This made it straightforward for vendors to design 802.11g devices that could offer backwards support for legacy 802.11b clients.

802.11n

The **IEEE 802.11n** standard introduced several improvements to increase bandwidth. It can work over both 2.4 GHz and 5 GHz. Each band is implemented by a separate radio. An access point or adapter that can support simultaneous 2.4 GHz and 5 GHz operation is referred to as "dual band." Cheaper client adapters and many smartphone adapters support only a 2.4 GHz radio.

The 802.11n standard allows two adjacent 20 MHz channels to be combined into a single 40 MHz channel, referred to as "**channel bonding.**" Due to the restricted channel layout of 2.4 GHz, on a network with multiple APs, channel bonding is a practical option only in the 5 GHz band. However, note that 5 GHz channels are not necessarily contiguous and use of some channels may be blocked if the access point detects a radar signal.

	U-NII-1				U-NII-2				U-NII-2 Extended											U-NII-3			
20 MHz	36	40	44	48	52	56	60	64	100	104	108	112	116	120	124	128	132	136	140	149	153	157	161
40 MHz	38		46		54		62		102		110		118		126		134			151		159	
											Dynamic Frequency Selection (DFS) Range												

802.11n 40 MHz bonded channel options in the 5 GHz band. The center channel number is used to identify each bonded channel.

The other innovation introduced with 802.11n increases reliability and bandwidth by multiplexing signal streams from 2–3 separate antennas. This technology is referred to as **"multiple input multiple output" (MIMO).** The antenna configuration is represented as 1x1, 2x2, or 3x3 to indicate the number of transmit and receive antennas available to the radio.

The nominal data rate for 802.11n is 72 Mbps per stream or 150 Mbps per stream for a 40 MHz bonded channel, and 802.11n access points are marketed using Nxxx designations, where xxx is the nominal bandwidth. As an example, an N600 2x2 access point can allocate a bonded channel two streams for a data rate of 300 Mbps, and if it does this simultaneously on both its 2.4 GHz and 5 GHz radios, the bandwidth of the access point could be described as 600 Mbps.

In recent years, Wi-Fi standards have been renamed with simpler digit numbers; 802.11n is now officially designated as Wi-Fi 4.

Wi-Fi 5 and Wi-Fi 6

The Wi-Fi 5 (or **802.11ac**) and Wi-Fi 6 (**802.11ax**) standards continue the development of Wi-Fi technologies to increase bandwidth and support modern networks.

Wi-Fi 5 (802.11ac)

Wi-Fi 5 is designed to work only in the 5 GHz band. A dual band access point can use its 2.4 GHz radio to support clients on legacy standards (802.11g/n). A tri band access point has one 2.4 GHz radio and two 5 GHz radios. Wi-Fi 5 allows up eight streams, though in practice, most Wi-Fi 5 access points only support 4x4 streams. A single stream over an 80 MHz channel has a nominal rate of 433 Mbps.

Wi-Fi 5 also allows wider 80 and 160 MHz bonded channels.

	U-NII-1				U-NII-2				U-NII-2 Extended												U-NII-3			
20 MHz	36	40	44	48	52	56	60	64	100	104	108	112	116	120	124	128	132	136	140	149	153	157	161
40 MHz	38		46		54		62		102		110		118		126		134			151		159	
80 MHz	42				58				106				122							155			
160 MHz	50								114														

Dynamic Frequency Selection (DFS) Range

80 and 160 MHz bonded channel options for Wi-Fi 5.

Wi-Fi 5 access points are marketed using AC values, such as AC5300. The 5300 value is made up of the following:

- 1,000 Mbps over a 40 MHz channel with 2x2 streams on the 2.4 GHz radio.

- 2,166 Mbps over an 80 MHz bonded channel with 4x4 streams on the first 5 GHz radio.

- 2,166 Mbps on the second 5 GHz radio.

You'll notice that, given 802.11n 150 Mbps per stream (40 MHz channels) and 802.11ac 433 Mbps per stream (80 MHz channels), none of those values can be made to add up. The labels are only useful as relative performance indicators.

Multiuser MIMO

In basic 802.11 operation modes, bandwidth is shared between all stations. An AP can communicate with only one station at a time; multiple station requests go into a queue. This means that Wi-Fi networks experience the same sort of contention issues as legacy Ethernet hubs. Wi-Fi 5 products partially address this problem using **multiuser MIMO (MU-MIMO)**. In Wi-Fi 5, downlink MU-MIMO (DL MU-MIMO) allows the access point to use its multiple antennas to send data to up to four clients simultaneously.

Wi-Fi 6 (802.11ax)

Wi-Fi 6 improves the per-stream data rate over an 80 MHz channel to 600 Mbps. As with Wi-Fi 5, products are branded using the combined throughput of all radios. For example, AX6000 claims nominal rates of 1,148 Mbps on the 2.4 GHz radio and 4,804 Mbps over 5 GHz.

Wi-Fi 6 works in both the 2.4 GHz and 5 GHz bands. The Wi-Fi 6e standard adds support for a new 6 GHz frequency band. 6 GHz has less range, but more frequency space, making it easier to use 80 and 160 MHz channels.

Where Wi-Fi 5 supports up to four simultaneous clients over 5 GHz only, Wi-Fi 6 can support up to eight clients, giving it better performance in congested areas. Wi-Fi 6 also adds support for uplink MU-MIMO, which allows MU-MIMO-capable clients to send data to the access point simultaneously.

Wi-Fi 6 introduces another technology to improve simultaneous connectivity called **"orthogonal frequency division multiple access" (OFDMA)**. OFDMA can work alongside MU-MIMO to improve client density—sustaining high data rates when more stations are connected to the same access point.

Wireless LAN Installation Considerations

Clients identify an infrastructure WLAN through the network name or **service set identifier (SSID)** configured on the access point. An SSID can be up to 32 bytes in length and, for maximum compatibility, should only use ASCII letters and digits plus the hyphen and underscore characters.

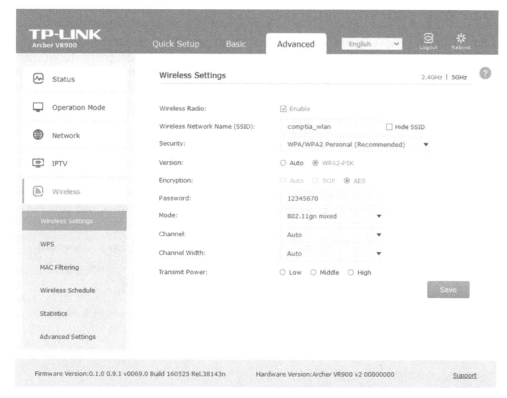

Configuring an access point. (Screenshot courtesy of TP-Link.)

When configuring an access point, you need to choose whether to use the same or different network names for both frequency bands. If you use the same SSID, the access point and client device will use a probe to select the band with the strongest signal. If you configure separate names, the user can choose which network and band to use.

For each frequency band, you also need to select the operation mode. This determines compatibility with older standards and support for legacy client devices. Supporting older devices can reduce performance for all stations.

Finally, for each frequency band, you need to configure the channel number and whether to use channel bonding. If there are multiple access points whose ranges overlap, they should be configured to use nonoverlapping channels to avoid interference. An access point can be left to autoconfigure the best channel, but this does not always work well. You can configure wide channels (bonding) for more bandwidth, but this has the risk of increased interference if there are multiple nearby wireless networks. Channel bonding may only be practical in the 5 GHz band, depending on the wireless site design.

 Along with the Wi-Fi frequency band and channel settings, you should also configure security parameters to control who is allowed to connect. Wi-Fi security is covered in the Core 2 course.

Wi-Fi Analyzers

To determine the best channel layout and troubleshoot wireless network performance, you need to measure the signal strength of the different networks using each channel. This can be accomplished using a **Wi-Fi analyzer**. This type of software can be installed to a laptop or smartphone. It will record statistics for the AP that the client is currently associated with and detect any other access points in the vicinity.

Wireless signal strength is measured in **decibel (dB)** units. Signal strength is represented as the ratio of a measurement to 1 milliwatt (mw), where 1 mW is equal to 0 dBm. Because 0 dBm is 1 mW, a negative value for dBm represents a fraction of a milliwatt. For example, -30 dBm is 0.001 mW; -60 dBm is 0.000001 mW. Wi-Fi devices are all constrained by regulations governing spectrum use and output only small amounts of power.

When you are measuring signal strength, dBm values closer to zero represent better performance. A value around -65 dBm represents a good signal, while anything over -80 dBm is likely to suffer packet loss or be dropped.

The dB units express the ratio between two values using a logarithmic scale. A logarithmic scale is nonlinear, so a small change in value represents a large change in the performance measured. For example, +3 dB means doubling, while -3 dB means halving.

The comparative strength of the data signal to the background noise is called the **signal-to-noise ratio (SNR)**. Noise is also measured in dBm, but here values closer to zero are less welcome, as they represent higher noise levels. For example, if signal is -65 dBm and noise is -90 dBm, the SNR is the difference between the two values, expressed in dB (25 dB). If noise is -80 dBm, the SNR is 15 dB and the connection will be much, much worse.

In the following screenshot, a Wi-Fi analyzer is being used to report nearby networks and channel configurations. The "hom" network is supported by two access points using the same SSID for both bands. They are configured to use channels 6 and 11 on the 2.4 GHz band, with the stronger signal on channel 6, indicating the closer access point. On the 5 GHz band, only the signal on channel 36 is detected by this client. This is because 5 GHz has less range than 2.4 GHz. The blurred networks belong to other owners and have much weaker signals. Also note from the status bar that the client adapter supports Wi-Fi 6 (ax), but the access points only support b/g/n/ac (shown in the mode column).

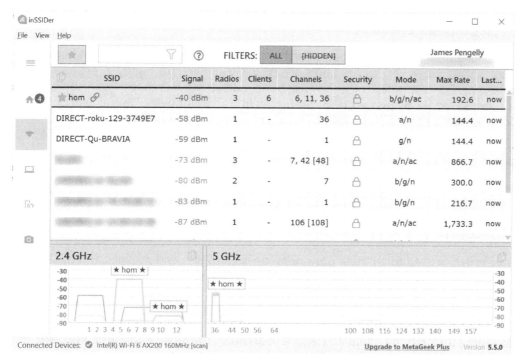

Metageek inSSIDer Wi-Fi analyzer software showing nearby access points. (MetaGeek, LLC. © Copyright 2005-2021)

Long-Range Fixed Wireless

Wireless technology can be used to configure a bridge between two networks. This can be a more cost-effective and practical solution than laying cable. However, regulation of the radio spectrum means that the transmitters required to cover long distances must be carefully configured. These solutions are referred to as **long-range fixed wireless**.

Point-to-point line of sight fixed wireless uses ground-based high-gain microwave antennas that must be precisely aligned with one another. "High-gain" means that the antenna is strongly directional. Each antenna is pointed directly at the other and can transmit signals at ranges of up to about 30 miles as long as they are unobstructed by physical objects. The antennas themselves are typically affixed to the top of tall buildings or mounted on tall poles to reduce the risk from obstructions.

Long-range fixed wireless can be implemented using licensed or unlicensed frequency spectrum. **Licensed** means that the network operator purchases the exclusive right to use a frequency band within a given geographical area from the regulator. The US regulator is the Federal Communications Commission (FCC). If any interference sources are discovered, the network operator has the legal right to get them shut down.

Unlicensed spectrum means the operator uses a public frequency band, such as 900 MHz, 2.4 GHz, and 5 GHz. Anyone can use these frequencies, meaning that interference is a risk. To minimize the potential for conflicts, **power** output is limited by **regulatory requirements**. A wireless signal's power has three main components:

- Transmit power is the basic strength of the radio, measured in dBm.

- Antenna gain is the amount that a signal is boosted by directionality—focusing the signal in a single direction rather than spreading it over a wide area. Gain is measured in **decibels isotropic (dBi)**.

- **Effective isotropic radiated power (EIRP)** is the sum of transmit power and gain, expressed in dBm.

Lower frequencies that propagate farther have stricter power limits than higher frequencies. However, higher EIRPs are typically allowed for highly directional antennas. For example, in the 2.4 GHz band, each 3 dBi increase in gain can be compensated for by just a 1 dBm reduction in transmit power. This allows point-to-point wireless antennas to work over longer ranges than Wi-Fi APs.

Bluetooth, RFID, and NFC

Wi-Fi is used for networking computer hosts together, but other types of wireless technology are used to implement personal area networking (PAN).

Bluetooth

Bluetooth is used to connect peripheral devices to PCs and mobiles and to share data between two systems. Many portable devices, such as smartphones, tablets, wearable tech, audio speakers, and headphones, now use Bluetooth connectivity. Bluetooth uses radio communications and supports speeds of up to 3 Mbps. Adapters supporting version 3 or 4 of the standard can achieve faster rates (up to 24 Mbps) through the ability to negotiate an 802.11 radio link for large file transfers.

The earliest Bluetooth version supports a maximum range of 10 m (30 feet), while newer versions support a range of over 100 feet, though signal strength will be weak at this distance. Bluetooth devices can use a pairing procedure to authenticate and exchange data securely.

Bluetooth pairing. (Image © 123RF.com)

Version 4 introduced a Bluetooth Low Energy (BLE) variant of the standard. BLE is designed for small battery-powered devices that transmit small amounts of data infrequently. A BLE device remains in a low power state until a monitor application initiates a connection. BLE is not backwards compatible with "classic" Bluetooth, though a device can support both standards simultaneously.

Radio Frequency Identification

Radio Frequency ID (RFID) is a means of identifying and tracking objects using specially encoded tags. When an RFID reader scans a tag, the tag responds with the information programmed into it. A tag can be either an unpowered, passive device that only responds when scanned at close range (up to about 25 m) or a powered, active device with a range of 100 m. Passive RFID tags can be embedded in stickers and labels to track parcels and equipment. RFID is also used to implement some types of access badge to operate electronic locks.

Near Field Communications

Near Field Communications (NFC) is a peer-to-peer version of RFID; that is, an NFC device can work as both tag and reader to exchange information with other NFC devices. NFC normally works at up to two inches (6 cm) at data rates of 106, 212, and 424 Kbps. NFC sensors and functionality are starting to be incorporated into smartphones. NFC is mostly used for contactless payment readers, security ID tags, and shop shelf-edge labels for stock control. It can also be used to configure other types of connection, such as pairing Bluetooth devices.

Review Activity:

Wireless Networking Types

Answer the following questions:

1. You are assessing standards compatibility for a Wi-Fi network. Most employees have mobile devices with single-band 2.4 GHz radios. Which Wi-Fi standards work in this band?

2. You are explaining your plan to use the 5 GHz band predominantly for an open plan office network. The business owner has heard that this is shorter range, so what are its advantages over the 2.4 GHz band?

3. Can 802.11ac achieve higher throughput to a single client by multiplexing the signals from both 2.4 and 5 GHz frequency bands? Why or why not?

4. You are setting up a Wi-Fi network. Do you need to configure the BSSID?

5. **True or false? Only a single network name can be configured on a single access point.**

6. **True or false? A long-range fixed wireless installation operating without a license is always illegal.**

Lesson 4

Summary

You should be able to compare network types (LAN, WLAN, WAN, MAN, SAN, and PAN), network hardware, cable types, and wireless protocols and use networking tools to install and verify local cabled and wireless networks.

Guidelines for Installing a SOHO Network

Follow these guidelines to install a SOHO network:

- Identify the number of wired ports that must be provisioned and whether Cat 6 cable for Gigabit Ethernet will suffice or Cat 6A for 10G Ethernet and/or high power PoE is required.

- Identify cable runs, and assess them for factors that might require special cable types, such as shielding against external interference, plenum-rated, or outdoor/ direct burial.

- Obtain patch panels matched to the cable type and switches with sufficient ports to meet the requirement. Determine whether the port requirement can be met with a single unmanaged switch or the network is large enough to require managed switches.

- Use cable stripper and punchdown tools to wire wall ports to patch panel IDCs using solid cable, taking care to label each port and validate each segment using a cable tester.

- Optionally, create RJ45 patch cords using stranded cable, testing each one.

- Use patch cords to connect each patch panel port to a switch port.

- Deploy one or more access points to provision a wireless network supporting a given range of protocols/standards (802.11abg or Wi-Fi 4/5/6) using a Wi-Fi analyzer to check signal strength. If multiple access points are required, configure nonoverlapping channels for them to use. Consider whether to use the same network for 2.4 and 5 GHz bands or create separate networks for each band.

- Consider whether there is any requirement for long-range fixed wireless to bridge two sites and the implications of using licensed or unlicensed spectrum to implement it.

- Assess requirements for Bluetooth, RFC, and NFC wireless products to implement PANs or inventory/access control systems.

- Assess requirements for SMF and/or MMF fiber optic cabling terminated using SC, ST, or LC connectors to implement high bandwidth LAN links or long distance WAN links.

Lesson 5

Configuring Network Addressing and Internet Connections

LESSON INTRODUCTION

Network cabling, wireless radios, and devices such as switches and APs are used to implement local networks at the hardware level. A local-only network has limited uses, however. The full functionality of networking is only realized when local networks join wide area networks, such as the Internet. This requires modem devices and radio antennas that can communicate over the cabling and wireless media types used by Internet service providers (ISPs). It also requires technologies that can identify each network and forward data between them. This network addressing and forwarding function is performed by router devices and the Internet Protocol (IP).

This lesson will help you to compare the technologies that underpin Internet access and to configure the main protocols in the Transport Control Protocol/Internet Protocol (TCP/IP) suite that enable communications over an internetwork.

Lesson Objectives

In this lesson, you will:

- Compare Internet connection types.

- Use basic TCP/IP concepts.

- Compare protocols and ports.

- Compare network configuration concepts.

Topic 5A

Compare Internet Connection Types

CORE 1 EXAM OBJECTIVES COVERED
2.2 Compare and contrast common networking hardware.
2.7 Compare and contrast Internet connection types, network types, and their features.

An LAN is of limited use. The full functionality of networking is only realized by connecting local networks to the Internet. Being able to compare the technologies used by ISPs to facilitate Internet connections will allow you to assist customers in selecting suitable options.

Internet Connection Types and Modems

The Internet is a global network of networks. The core of the Internet consists of high bandwidth fiber optic links connecting Internet exchange points (IXPs). These trunk links and IXPs are mostly created by telecommunications companies and academic institutions. Within the datacenter supporting any given IXP, **Internet service providers (ISPs)** establish high-speed links between their networks, using transit and peering arrangements to carry traffic to and from parts of the Internet they do not physically own. There is a tiered hierarchy of ISPs that reflects to what extent they depend on transit arrangements with other ISPs.

Customers connect to the Internet via an ISP's network. The connection to the ISP's network uses its nearest point of presence (PoP), such as a local telephone exchange. An **Internet connection type** is the media, hardware, and protocols used to link the local network at a domestic residence or small office to the ISP's PoP. This WAN interface is typically point-to-point. This means that there are only two devices connected to the media (unlike Ethernet). Where Ethernet connections are made using NICs and switches, the connection to a WAN interface is typically made by a type of digital modem.

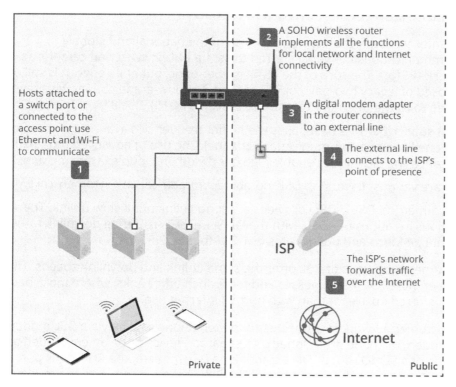

Role of a digital modem to connect a local network to an ISP's network for Internet access.

The modem establishes the physical connection to the WAN interface, but when interconnecting networks, there must also be a means of identifying each network and forwarding data between them. This function is performed by a router that implements the Internet Protocol (IP).

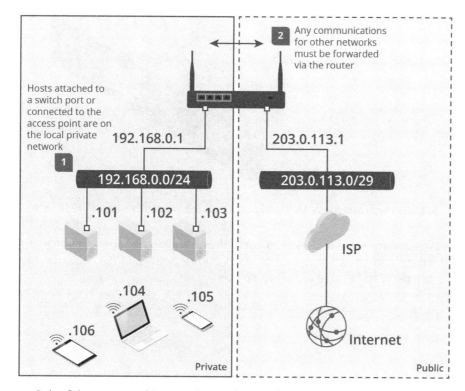

Role of the router and Internet Protocol (IP) in distinguishing logical networks.

Digital Subscriber Line Modems

Many internet connection types make use of the national and global telecommunications network referred to as the **public switched telephone network (PSTN)**. The core of the PSTN is fiber optic, but at its edge, it is still often composed of legacy two-pair copper cabling. This low-grade copper wire segment is referred to as the **plain old telephone system (POTS)**, "local loop," or "last mile."

Digital subscriber line (DSL) uses the higher frequencies available in these copper telephone lines as a communications channel. The use of advanced modulation and echo cancelling techniques enable high bandwidth, full duplex transmissions.

There are various "flavors" of DSL, notably asymmetrical and symmetrical types:

- Asymmetrical DSL (ADSL) provides a fast downlink but a slow uplink. There are various iterations of ADSL, with the latest (ADSL2+) offering downlink rates up to about 24 Mbps and uplink rates of 1.25 Mbps or 2.5 Mbps.

- Symmetric versions of DSL offer the same uplink and downlink speeds. These are of more use to businesses and for branch office links, where more data is transferred upstream than with normal Internet use.

The customer network is connected to the telephone cabling via a DSL modem. The DSL modem might be provisioned as a separate device or be an embedded as a function of a SOHO router. On a standalone DSL modem, the RJ11 WAN port on the modem connects to the phone point. The RJ45 interface connects the modem to the router.

RJ11 DSL (left) and RJ45 LAN (right) ports on a DSL modem. (Image © 123RF.com.)

A filter (splitter) must be installed to each phone socket to separate voice and data signals. These can be self-installed on each phone point by the customer. Modern sockets are likely to feature a built-in splitter.

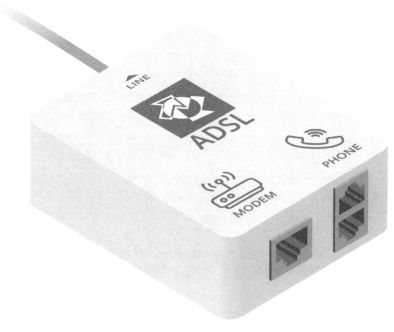

A self-installed DSL splitter. (Image © 123RF.com.)

Cable Modems

A cable Internet connection is usually available as part of a cable access TV (CATV) service. A CATV network is often described as hybrid fiber coax (HFC), as it combines a fiber optic core network with copper coaxial cable links to customer premises equipment. It can also be described as broadband cable or just as cable. Cable based on the Data Over Cable Service Interface Specification (DOCSIS) supports downlink speeds of up to 38 Mbps (North America) or 50 Mbps (Europe) and uplinks of up to 27 Mbps. DOCSIS version 3 allows the use of multiplexed channels to achieve higher bandwidth.

Installation of a **cable modem** follows the same general principles as for a DSL modem. The cable modem is interfaced to the local router via an RJ45 port and with the access provider's network by a short segment of coax terminated using threaded F-type connectors. More coax then links all the premises in a street with a cable modem termination system (CMTS), which forwards data traffic via the fiber backbone to the ISP's point of presence and from there to the internet.

A cable modem: The RJ45 port connects to the local network router, while the coax port connects to the service provider network. (Image © 123RF.com.)

A F-type connector is screwed down to secure it. Do not overtighten it.

Fiber to the Curb and Fiber to the Premises

The major obstacle to providing internet access that can perform like a LAN is bandwidth in the last mile, where the copper wiring infrastructure is often low grade. The projects to update this wiring to use **fiber** optic links are referred to by the umbrella term fiber to the X (FTTx).

Fiber to the Curb and VDSL

A fiber to the curb (FTTC) solution retains some sort of copper wiring to the customer premises while extending the fiber link from the point of presence to a communications cabinet servicing multiple subscribers. The service providers with their roots in telephone networks use very high-speed DSL (VDSL) to support FTTC. VDSL achieves higher bit rates than other DSL types at the expense of range. It allows for both symmetric and asymmetric modes. Over 300 m (1,000 feet), an asymmetric link supports 52 Mbps downstream and 6 Mbps upstream, while a symmetric link supports 26 Mbps in both directions. VDSL2 specifies a very short range (100 m/300 feet) rate of 100 Mbps (bi-directional).

DSL modems are not interchangeable. An ADSL modem is unlikely to support VDSL, though most VDSL modems support ADSL.

Fiber to the Premises and Optical Network Terminals

A **fiber to the premises (FTTP)** Internet connection means that the service provider's fiber optic cable is run all the way to the customer's building. This full fiber connection type is implemented as a passive optical network (PON). In a PON, a single fiber cable is run from the point of presence to an optical line terminal

(OLT) located in a street cabinet. From the OLT, splitters direct each subscriber's traffic over a shorter length of fiber to an **optical network terminal (ONT)** installed at the customer's premises. The ONT converts the optical signal to an electrical one. The ONT is connected to the customer's router using an RJ45 copper wire patch cord.

Optical network terminal—the PON port terminates the external fiber cable and the LAN ports connect to local routers or computers over RJ45 patch cords. (Image by artush © 123RF.com)

Fixed Wireless Internet Access

Wired broadband internet access is not always available, especially in rural areas or older building developments, where running new cable capable of supporting DSL or full fiber is problematic. In this scenario, some sort of fixed wireless internet access might be an option.

Geostationary Orbital Satellite Internet Access

A **satellite**-based microwave radio system provides far bigger areas of coverage than can be achieved using other technologies. The transfer rates available vary between providers and access packages, but 2 or 6 Mbps up and 30 Mbps down would be typical.

One drawback of satellites placed in a high geostationary orbit is increased latency. The signal must travel over thousands of miles more than terrestrial connections, introducing a delay of many times what might be expected over a land link. For example, if accessing an internet web server over DSL involves a 10–20 ms round trip time (RTT) delay on the link, accessing the same site over a satellite link could involve a 600–800 ms RTT delay. This is an issue for real-time applications, such as video conferencing, VoIP, and multiplayer gaming.

 RTT is the two-way latency, or the time taken for a probe to be sent and a response to be received.

To create a satellite internet connection, the ISP installs a very small aperture terminal (VSAT) satellite dish antenna at the customer's premises and aligns it with the orbital satellite. The satellites are in high geostationary orbit above the equator, so in the northern hemisphere, the dish will be pointing south. Because the satellite does not move relative to the dish, there should be no need for any realignment. The antenna is connected via coaxial cabling to a Digital Video Broadcast Satellite (DVB-S) modem.

Low Earth Orbital Satellite Internet Access

A different type of service uses an array of satellites positioned in low Earth orbit (LEO). LEO satellites support better bandwidth (around 70–100 Mbps at the time of writing) and are lower latency (100–200 ms RTT). The drawback is that the satellites move relative to the surface of the Earth. The customer's premises antenna must be provisioned with a motor so that it can periodically realign with the array. The dish construction uses a technology called "phased array" to connect to different satellites as they pass overhead and minimize the amount of mechanical realignment required. The antenna must have a clear view of the whole sky.

Wireless Internet Service Providers

A **wireless internet service provider (WISP)** uses ground-based long-range fixed access wireless technology. The WISP installs and maintains a directional antenna to work as a bridge between the customer's network and the service provider. A WISP might use Wi-Fi type networking or proprietary equipment and licensed or unlicensed frequency bands.A fixed access wireless link is often low latency, or at least, lower latency than satellite. A disadvantage of fixed access wireless is that the actual unobstructed line of sight between the two antennas can be difficult to maintain. If the provider uses unlicensed frequencies, there are risks of interference from other wireless networks and devices.

 All types of microwave radio link can be adversely affected by snow, rain, and high winds.

Cellular Radio Internet Connections

The 2.4 GHz and 5 GHz frequency bands used by Wi-Fi have limited range, while fixed wireless internet requires a large dish antenna. **Cellular radio** wireless networking facilitates communications over much larger distances using mobile devices. Cellular networking is also used by some Internet of Things (IoT) devices, such as smart energy meters.Cellular digital communications standards are described as belonging to a particular generation.

3G

A 3G cellular radio makes a connection to the closest base station. The area served by each base station is referred to as a "cell." Cells can have an effective range of up to 5 miles (8 km), though signals can be obstructed by building materials. A 3G cellular radio typically works in the 850 and 1,900 MHz frequency bands (mostly in the Americas) and the 900 and 1,800 MHz bands (rest of the world). These lower frequency waves do not need so much power to propagate over long distances.

With 3G cellular, there are two competing formats, established in different markets:

- **Global System for Mobile Communication (GSM)**-based phones. GSM allows subscribers to use a removable subscriber identity module (SIM) card to use an unlocked handset with their chosen network provider.

- **Code Division Multiple Access (CDMA)**-based handsets. With CDMA, the handset is directly managed by the provider and there is no removable SIM card.

4G

Long-Term Evolution (LTE) is a series of converged 4G standards supported by both the GSM and CDMA network providers. LTE devices must have a SIM card issued by the network provider installed.

5G

The 5G standard uses different spectrum bands from low (sub-6 GHz) to medium/high (20–60 GHz). Low bands have greater range and penetrating power; high bands, also referred to as millimeter wave (mmWave), require close range (a few hundred feet) and cannot penetrate walls or windows. Consequently, design and rollout of 5G services is relatively complex. Rather than a single large antenna serving a wide area wireless cell, 5G involves installing many smaller antennas to form an array that can take advantage of multipath and beamforming to overcome the propagation limitations of the spectrum. This technology is referred to as massive multiple input multiple output (MIMO).

As well as faster speeds for mobile device internet connections, 4G and 5G can be used as a fixed-access wireless broadband solution for homes and businesses and to support IoT networks.

Routers

The devices discussed so far enable physical links where the only type of addressing used identifies a host hardware interface:

Ethernet switches and Wi-Fi access points forward frames using MAC addresses. A network segment is where hosts can send frames to one another using their MAC addresses.

Digital modems, ONTs, and cellular radios transmit data over DSL, cable, fiber, satellite, and cellular links to connect a local network or device to an ISP. This is typically a point-to-point link and so does not require unique interface addressing.

These network segments use different media types and have no physical or logical means of communicating with one another. When you want to connect a local network to the internet, you need to use a protocol that can distinguish between the private LAN and public WAN and an intermediate system with interfaces in both networks. The protocol used to implement this is the Internet Protocol (IP), and the intermediate system is a **router**.

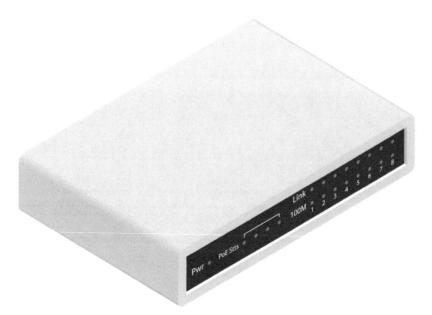

A router. (Image © 123RF.com.)

Where a switch forwards frames using MAC (hardware) addresses, a router forwards packets around an internetwork using IP addresses. A MAC address only identifies a hardware port. An IP address contains the identity of both the network and a single host within that network.

There are several types of routers and different uses for them. A SOHO router often simply routes between its local network interface and its WAN/Internet interface. An enterprise network is likely to use different router models to perform different routing tasks:

- A LAN router divides a single physical network into multiple logical subnetworks. Each logical network becomes a separate broadcast domain. Having too many hosts in the same broadcast domain reduces performance. There is also a security benefit because traffic passing from one logical network to another can be subject to filtering rules. This type of router generally has only Ethernet interfaces.

- A WAN or border router forwards traffic to and from the Internet or over a private WAN link. This type of router has an Ethernet interface for the local network and a digital modem interface for the WAN.

Firewalls

Once you have joined public and private networks using a router, you then need to control which computers are allowed to connect to them and which types of traffic you will accept. The role of filtering allowed and denied hosts and protocols is performed by a network **firewall**. A basic firewall is configured with rules, referred to as a network access control list (ACL). Each entry in the ACL lists source and/or destination network addresses and protocol types and whether to allow or block traffic that matches the rule.

Firewalls can also be deployed within a private network. For example, you might only want certain clients to connect to a particular group of servers. You could place the servers behind a local network firewall to enforce the relevant ACL.

Most routers can implement some level of firewall functionality. A firewall can be implemented as a standalone appliance. These dedicated appliances can perform deeper analysis of application protocol data and use more sophisticated rules to determine what traffic is allowed. They are often implemented as unified threat management (UTM) appliances to perform multiple other security functions.

Sample ruleset configured on the OPNsense open source firewall implementation.
(Screenshot used with permission from OPNsense.)

 There are also personal or software firewalls. These are installed to a single computer rather than working to protect a network segment.

Review Activity:

Internet Connection Types

Answer the following questions:

1. You are setting up an ADSL router/modem for a client; unfortunately, the contents of the box have become scattered. What type of cable do you need to locate to connect the router's WAN interface?

2. You are assisting another customer with a full fiber connection terminated to an optical network terminal (ONT). The customer's router was disconnected while some building work was being completed, and the patch cable is now missing. The customer thinks that the cable should be a fiber optic one because the service is "full fiber." What type of cable do you need to locate?

3. True or false? Both 4G and 5G cellular can be used for fixed access broadband as well as in mobile devices.

4. True or false? A SOHO router uses an embedded modem and Ethernet adapter to forward traffic between public and private network segments over a single hardware port.

Topic 5B

Use Basic TCP/IP Concepts

CORE 1 EXAM OBJECTIVES COVERED
2.5 Given a scenario, install and configure basic wired/wireless small office/home office (SOHO) networks.

The Transmission Control Protocol/Internet Protocol (TCP/IP) suite is used to perform logical addressing and data forwarding functions on most networks. As a CompTIA A+ technician, you must be able to configure these protocols on PCs and SOHO routers to implement fully functional local networks with Internet connectivity.

TCP/IP

A protocol is set of rules that allows networked hosts to communicate data in a structured format. Often, several protocols used are designed to work together as a protocol suite. Most networks have converged on the use of the **Transmission Control Protocol/Internet Protocol (TCP/IP)** suite. The function of each protocol can be better understood by dividing network functions into layers. Protocols operating at lower layers are said to encapsulate data from higher protocols. Each protocol adds its own header fields to data it is transporting from an upper layer protocol.

The TCP/IP suite uses a model with four distinct layers.

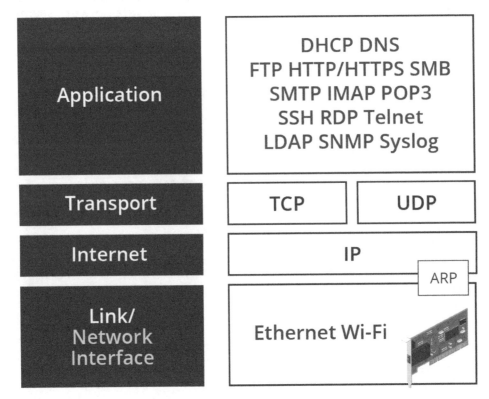

TCP/IP model.

Link or Network Interface layer

The Link layer is responsible for putting frames onto the physical network. This layer does not contain TCP/IP protocols as such. At this layer, different local networking products and media can be used, such as Ethernet or Wi-Fi. WAN interfaces, such as DSL and cable modems, also work at the Link layer.

Communications on this layer take place only on a local network segment and not between different networks. On an Ethernet or Wi-Fi segment, data at the link layer is packaged in a unit called a frame and node interfaces are identified by a MAC address.

Internet Layer

The **Internet Protocol (IP)** provides packet addressing and routing within a network of networks. A PC, laptop, mobile device, or server that can communicate on an IP network is generically referred to as an "end system host." For data to be sent from one IP network to another, it must be forwarded by an intermediate system (a router). When IP is being used with a physical/data link specification, such as Ethernet or Wi-Fi, there must be a mechanism to deliver messages from IP at the Internet layer to host interfaces addressed at the Link layer. This function is performed by the Address Resolution Protocol (ARP), which allows a host to query which MAC address is associated with an IP address.IP provides best effort delivery that is unreliable and connectionless. A packet might be lost, delivered out of sequence, duplicated, or delayed.

Transport Layer

Where the network layer deals with addressing, the Transport layer determines how each host manages multiple connections for different application layer protocols at the same time. The transport layer is implemented by one of two protocols: **Transmission Control Protocol (TCP)** guarantees connection-oriented forwarding of packets. TCP can identify and recover from lost or out-of-order packets, mitigating the inherent unreliability of IP. This is used by most TCP/IP application protocols, as failing to receive a packet or processing it incorrectly can cause serious data errors. **User Datagram Protocol (UDP)** provides unreliable, connectionless forwarding. UDP is faster and comes with less of a transmission overhead because it does not need to send extra information to establish reliable connections. It is used in time-sensitive applications, such as speech or video, where a few missing or out-of-order packets can be tolerated. Rather than causing the application to crash, they would just manifest as a glitch in video or a squeak in audio.

Application Layer

The Application layer contains protocols that perform some high-level function, rather than simply addressing hosts and transporting data. There are numerous application protocols in the TCP/IP suite. These used to configure and manage network hosts and to operate services, such as the web and email. Each application protocol uses a TCP or UDP port to allow a client to connect to a server.

TCP/IP was originally developed by the US Department of Defense but is now an open standard to which anyone may contribute. Developments are implemented through the Internet Engineering Task Force (IETF), which is split into working groups. Standards are published as Request For Comments (RFCs). The official repository for RFCs is at rfc-editor.org.

IPv4 Addressing

The core protocol in TCP/IP is the **Internet Protocol (IP)**, which provides network and host **addressing** and packet forwarding between networks. An IP packet adds some headers to whatever transport/application layer data it is carrying in its payload. Two of the most important header fields are the source and destination IP address fields.There are two versions of IP: **IPv4** and **IPv6**. An IPv4 address is 32 bits long. In its raw form it appears as 11000000101010000000000 000000001. The 32 bits can be arranged into four groups of eight bits (one byte) known as "octets." The above IP address could therefore be rearranged as 11000000 10101000 00000000 00000001. This representation of an IP address is difficult for a human to memorize or to enter correctly into configuration dialogs. To make IP addresses easier to use, they are used in dotted decimal notation. This notation requires each octet to be converted to a decimal value. The decimal numbers are separated using a period. Converting the previous number to this notation gives 192.168.0.1

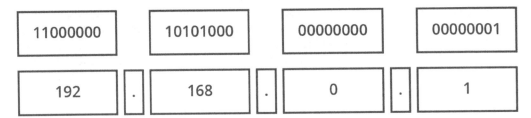

Dotted decimal notation.

If all the bits in an octet are set to 1, the number obtained is 255 (the maximum possible value). Similarly, if all the bits are set to 0, the number obtained is 0 (the minimum possible value). Therefore, theoretically an IPv4 address may be any value between 0.0.0.0 and 255.255.255.255. However, some addresses are not permitted or are reserved for special use.

Network Prefixes

An IPv4 address provides two pieces of information encoded within the same value:

- The network number (network ID) is common to all hosts on the same IP network.

- The host number (host ID) identifies a host within a particular IP network.

These two components within a single IP address are distinguished by combining the address with a network prefix. A prefix is a 32-bit value with a given number of contiguous bits all set to 1. For example, a prefix with 24 bits is the following binary value: 11111111 11111111 11111111 00000000.

This can be written in slash notation in the form /24. The prefix can also be expressed in dotted decimal as a **subnet mask**: 255.255.255.0

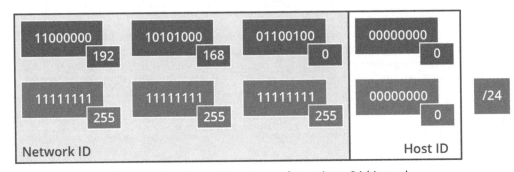

Network ID and host ID portions when using a 24-bit mask.

The name "subnet mask" comes about because a single IP network can be divided into multiple logical subnetworks (subnets) using this method.

When combined with an IP address, the prefix masks the host ID portion to reveal the network ID portion. Where there is a binary 1 in the prefix, the corresponding binary digit in the IP address is part of the network ID.

Slash notation is used to refer to network IDs, while the subnet mask is typically used in host configuration dialogs. For example, 192.168.0.0/24 refers to an IP network, while 192.168.0.1/255.255.255.0 refers to a host address on that IP network.

IPv4 Forwarding

When a host attempts to send a packet via IPv4, the protocol compares the source and destination IP address in the packet against the sending host's subnet mask. If the masked portions of the source and destination IP addresses match, then the destination interface is assumed to be on the same IP network or subnet. For example:

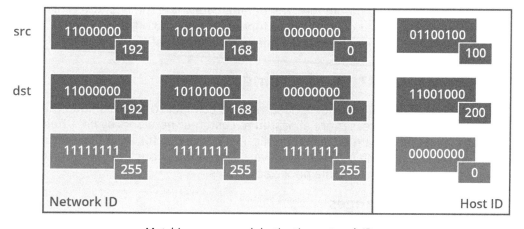

Matching source and destination network IDs.

In the example, the host will determine that the destination IPv4 address is on the same IP network (192.168.0.0/24) and try to deliver the packet locally. On Ethernet, the host would use the address resolution protocol (ARP) to identify the MAC address associated with the destination IP address.

If the masked portion does not match, the host assumes that the packet must be routed to another IP network. For example:

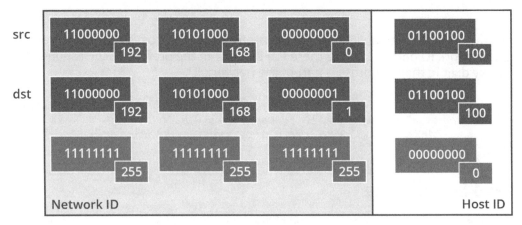

Different source and destination network IDs.

In this case, the source host 192.168.0.100 identifies that the destination IPv4 address is on a different IP network (192.168.1.0/24). Consequently, it forwards the packet to a router rather than trying to deliver it locally. Most hosts are configured with a **default gateway** parameter. The default gateway is the IP address of a router interface that the host can use to forward packets to other networks. The default gateway must be in the same IP network as the host.

Public and Private Addressing

To communicate on the Internet, a host must be configured with a unique **public IP address.** Public addresses are allocated to customer networks by ISPs. Relatively few companies can obtain sufficient public IPv4 addresses for all their computers to communicate over the Internet, however. There are various mechanisms to work around the shortage of available public addresses.

Private Address Ranges

The IPv4 address scheme defines certain ranges as reserved for **private** addressing, often called "RFC 1918" addresses after the document in which they were published. Hosts with IP addresses from these ranges are not allowed to route traffic over the public Internet. Use of the addresses is confined to private LANs. There are three private address ranges:

- 10.0.0.0 to 10.255.255.255 (Class A private address range).
- 172.16.0.0 to 172.31.255.255 (Class B private address range).
- 192.168.0.0 to 192.168.255.255 (Class C private address range).

Address Classes and Default Subnet Masks

The address classes (A, B, and C) derive from the earliest form of IP. When first defined, IP did not include the concept of subnet masks. Hosts would identify the network ID just by using the address class. The subnet masks that align precisely with octet boundaries mirror this functionality. They are often referred to as the "default masks":

Class	Dotted Decimal Mask	Network Prefix	Binary Mask
A	255.0.0.0	/8	11111111 00000000 00000000 00000000
B	255.255.0.0	/16	11111111 11111111 00000000 00000000
C	255.255.255.0	/24	11111111 11111111 11111111 00000000

Internet Access Using Private Addressing

As a host configured with a private address cannot access the Internet directly, some mechanism must be used to allow it to forward packets. Internet access can be facilitated for hosts using a private addressing scheme in two ways:

- Through a router configured with a single or block of valid public addresses; the router uses **network address translation (NAT)** to convert between the private and public addresses.

- Through a proxy server that fulfills requests for Internet resources on behalf of clients.

IPv4 Host Address Configuration

Each host must be configured with an IP address and subnet mask at a minimum to communicate on an IPv4 network. This minimum configuration will not prove very usable, however. Several other parameters must be configured for a host to make full use of a modern network or the Internet. There are also different ways to supply this configuration information to hosts.

An IPv4 address and subnet mask can be set manually in a static configuration:

- The IPv4 address is entered as four decimal numbers separated by periods, such as `192.168.0.100`.

- The subnet mask is entered in dotted decimal notation, such as `255.255.255.0`. When used with the IP address `192.168.0.100`, this mask identifies `192.168.0.0` as the network ID and means that the last octet (`.100`) is the host ID. Alternatively, this parameter might be entered as the mask length in bits.

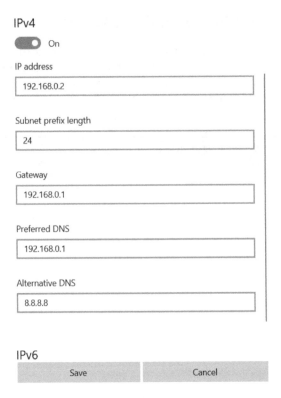

Configuring a Windows 10 host to use a static IP address configuration. Note that this dialog uses a prefix length parameter rather than requiring the subnet mask in dotted decimal format. (Screenshot courtesy of Microsoft.)

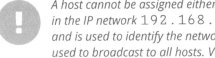 *A host cannot be assigned either the first or last address in an IP network. For example, in the IP network 192.168.0.0/24, 192.168.0.0 is the first address and is used to identify the network itself. The last address 192.168.0.255 is used to broadcast to all hosts. Valid host addresses range from 192.168.0.1 to 192.168.0.254.*

Two other parameters are typically configured to make the host fully functional:

- The default **gateway** parameter is the IPv4 address of a router, such as 192.168.0.1. This is the IP address to which packets destined for a remote network should be sent by default. This setting is not compulsory, but failure to enter a gateway would limit the host to communication on the local network only.

- One or more **Domain Name System (DNS)** server IPv4 addresses. These servers provide resolution of host and domain names to their IP addresses and are essential for locating resources on the Internet. Most local networks also use DNS for name resolution. Typically, the primary DNS server address would be configured as the same as the gateway address. The router would be configured to forward DNS queries to a secure resolver. Often two DNS server addresses (preferred and alternate) are specified for redundancy.

Static Versus Dynamic Host Address Configuration

Using **static** addressing requires an administrator to visit each computer to manually enter the configuration information for that host. If the host is moved to a different IP network or subnet, the administrator must manually reconfigure it. The administrator must keep track of which IP addresses have been allocated to avoid issuing duplicates. In a large network, configuring IP statically on each node can be very time consuming and prone to errors that can potentially disrupt communication on the network.

Static addresses are typically only assigned to systems with a dedicated functionality, such as router interfaces or application servers that need to use a fixed IP address.

Dynamic Host Configuration Protocol

As an alternative to static configuration, a host can receive its IP address, subnet mask, default gateway, and DNS server addresses from a **dynamic host configuration protocol (DHCP)** server.

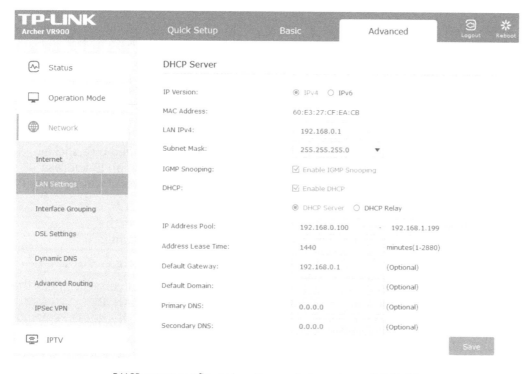

DHCP server configuration. (Screenshot courtesy of TP-Link.)

Automatic Private IP Addressing

Hosts have a failover mechanism for when the IP configuration specifies use of a DHCP server but the host cannot contact one. In this scenario, the computer selects an address at random from the range 169.254.0.1 to 169.254.255.254. Microsoft calls this **automatic private IP addressing (APIPA)**. When a host is using an APIPA address, it can communicate with other hosts on the same network that are using APIPA but cannot reach other networks or communicate with hosts that have managed to obtain a valid DHCP lease.

Other vendors and open-source products use the term "link local" rather than APIPA. Not all hosts use link-local addressing. Some may just leave IP unconfigured or use the IP address 0.0.0.0 to indicate that the IPv4 address of the interface is not known.

SOHO Router Configuration

Unlike end system host computers, a router has multiple interfaces. For example, a SOHO router has a public digital modem interface to connect to the ISP and a private Ethernet interface on the LAN. Both interfaces must be configured with an IP address and subnet mask. The LAN interface is the address used by hosts as the default gateway parameter. It is also the address used to access the router's web management interface, such as `https://192.168.0.1` or `https://192.168.1.1`.

The router's public interface IP address is determined by the ISP. This must be an address from a valid public range, such as `203.0.113.1`. Some Internet access packages assign a static IP or offer an option to pay for a static address. Otherwise, the public interface is dynamically configured using the ISP's DHCP server.

In fact, `203.0.113.1` is not actually a valid public address. It is from a small range reserved for use as documentation and examples. However, in general terms, you can identify a public IPv4 address because it is not from a private range (10.x.y.z, 172.16-32.x.y, or 192.168.0-255.x), does not start with a zero, and is not a value of 224.x.y.z or above (the upper range of IP addresses is reserved for other types of addressing schemes).

To configure a SOHO router, first connect a computer to one of the device's RJ45 ports or join its wireless network using the default name (identified by a sticker on the back of the unit). Make sure the computer is set to obtain an IP address automatically. Wait for the DHCP server running on the router to allocate a valid IP address to the computer.

Use a browser to open the device's management URL, as listed in the documentation. This could be an IP address or a host/domain name:

`http://192.168.0.1 http://www.routerlogin.com`

It might use HTTPS rather than unencrypted HTTP. If you cannot connect, check that the computer's IP address is in the same range as the router's LAN IP.

Enter the default administrator username and password as listed in the documentation or printed on a sticker accompanying the router. The management software will prompt you to choose a new administrator password. Choose a strong password of at least 12 characters.

Most appliances use a wizard-based setup to connect to the Internet. The public IP address and DSL/cable link parameters are normally self-configuring. If manual configuration is required, obtain the settings from your ISP.

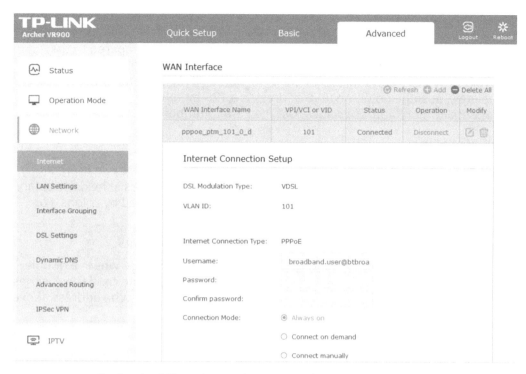

Configuring DSL modem settings. (Screenshot courtesy of TP-Link.)

You can also use the management console to view line status and the system log. These might be required by the ISP to troubleshoot any issues with the connection.

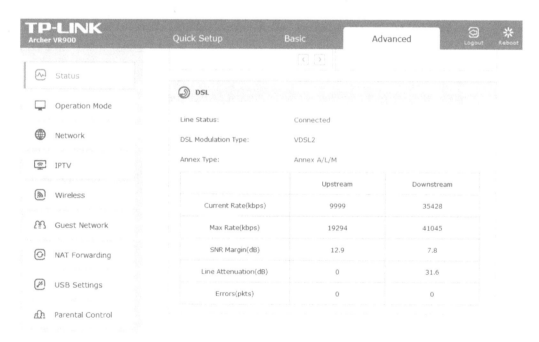

Viewing DSL line status. (Screenshot courtesy of TP-Link.)

IPv6 Addressing

The pool of available IPv4 public addresses is not very large, compared to the number of devices that need to connect to the Internet. While private addressing and NAT provides a workable solution, IP version 6 (IPv6) is intended to replace IPv4 completely, at some point. An **IPv6** address is a 128-bit number and so can express exponentially more address values that the 32-bit number used in IPv4.

IPv6 Notation

IPv6 addresses are written in hexadecimal notation. One hex digit can represent a four-bit binary value (a nibble). To express a 128-bit IPv6 address in hex, the binary address is divided into eight double-byte (16-bit) values delimited by colons. For example:

```
2001:0db8:0000:0000:0abc:0000:def0:1234
```

To shorten how this is written and typed in configuration dialogs, where a double byte contains leading zeros, they can be ignored. In addition, one contiguous series of zeroes can be replaced by a double colon place marker. Thus, the address above would become

```
2001:db8::abc:0:def0:1234
```

IPv6 Network Prefixes

An IPv6 address is divided into two main parts: the first 64 bits are used as a network ID, while the second 64 bits designate a specific interface.

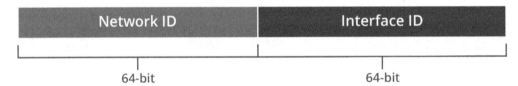

In IPv6, the interface identifier is always the last 64 bits; the first 64 bits are used for network addressing.

As the network and host portions are fixed size, there is no need for a subnet mask. Network addresses are written using prefix notation, where /nn is the length of the routing prefix in bits. Within the 64-bit network ID, the length of any given network prefix is used to determine whether two addresses belong to the same IP network.

 For example, most ISPs receive allocations of /32 blocks and issue each customer with a /48 prefix for use on a private network. A /48 block allows the private network to be configured with up to 65,346 subnets.

Global and Link-Local Addressing

In IPv4, hosts generally have a single IP address per interface. IPv6 interfaces are more likely to be configured with multiple addresses. The main types are global and link-local:

- A global address is one that is unique on the Internet (equivalent to public addresses in IPv4). In hex notation, a global address starts with a `2` or with a `3`.

- Link-local addresses are used on the local segment to communicate with neighbor hosts. In hex notation, link-local addresses start with `fe80::`

While it is possible to configure IPv6 addresses statically, most hosts obtain a global and link-local address via the local router. This process is referred to as StateLess Address Auto Configuration (SLAAC). IPv6 hosts do not need to be configured with a default gateway. IPv6 uses a protocol called Neighbor Discovery (ND). ND is used to implement SLAAC, allows a host to discover a router, and performs the interface address querying functions performed by ARP in IPv4.

Dual Stack

While IPv6 is designed to replace IPv4, transitioning from IPv4 has proved enormously difficult. Consequently, most hosts and routers can operate both IPv4 and IPv6 at the same time. This is referred to as "dual stack." Typically, a host will default to attempting to establish an IPv6 connection and fall back to IPv4 if the destination host does not support IPv6.

Review Activity:

Basic TCP/IP Concepts

Answer the following questions:

1. A host is configured with the IP address 172.16.1.100 in the 172.16.1.0/16 IP network. What value should be entered as the subnet mask?

2. You are setting up a printer to use static IPv4 addressing. What type of value is expected in the default gateway field?

3. Another technician has scribbled some notes about IPv4 addresses used in various networks associated with support tickets. One of them is assigned to the WAN interface of a SOHO router that requires troubleshooting. Which of these addresses must it be?

   - 52.165.16.254

   - 192.168.100.52

   - 169.254.1.121

   - 172.30.100.32

   - 224.100.100.1

4. True or false? A SOHO router can be configured to provide an IPv4 address configuration to hosts without further administrator attention.

5. True or false? A valid IPv6 configuration does not require a subnet mask.

Topic 5C

Compare Protocols and Ports

CORE 1 EXAM OBJECTIVES COVERED
2.1 Compare and contrast Transmission Control Protocol (TCP) and User Datagram Protocol (UDP) ports, protocols, and their purposes.

Network hardware and addressing/forwarding protocols establish basic connectivity. Hosts use this connectivity to serve and consume multiple network applications. When you understand how a TCP/IP host manages simultaneous sessions for these different applications, you will be able to provide more effective support and security solutions for your customers.

Protocols and Ports

The network hardware and protocols that we have covered to this point are primarily concerned with moving frames and packets between hosts and networks. At the Link layer, Ethernet allows hosts to send one another frames of data using MAC addresses. These frames would typically be transporting IP packets. At the Internet layer, IP provides addressing and routing functionality for a network of networks. The next layer up in the TCP/IP protocol stack is the Transport layer.

Any given host will be communicating with many other hosts using many different types of networking data. One of the functions of the Transport layer is to identify each type of network application. It does this by assigning each application a port number between 0 and 65535. For example, data addressed to the HTTP web browsing application can be identified as port 80, while data requesting an email transmission service can be identified as port 25. The host could be transmitting multiple HTTP and email segments at the same time. These are multiplexed using the port numbers onto the same network link.

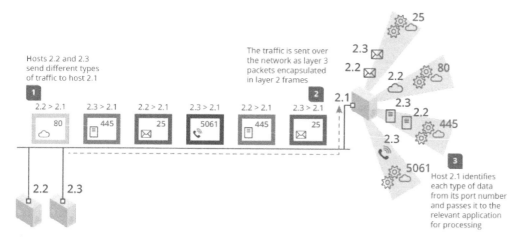

Communications at the transport layer. (Images © 123RF.com)

In fact, each host assigns two port numbers. On the client, the destination port number is mapped to the service that the client is requesting (HTTP on port 80, for instance). The client also assigns a random source port number (47747, for instance). The server uses this client-assigned port number (47747) as the destination port number for its replies and its application port number (80 for HTTP) as its source port. This allows the hosts to track multiple "conversations" for the same application protocol.

In the TCP/IP suite, two different protocols implement this port assignment function: TCP and UDP.

Transmission Control Protocol

IP transmits a stream of application data as a series of packets. Any given packet could be damaged or fail to arrive due to faults or network congestion. TCP provides several mechanisms to overcome this lack of reliability. It is described as a "**connection-oriented**" protocol because it performs the following functions:

- Establishes a connection between the sender and recipient using a handshake sequence of SYN, SYN/ACK, and ACK packets.

- Assigns each packet a sequence number so that it can be tracked.

- Allows the receiver to acknowledge (ACK) that a packet has been received.

- Allows the receiver to send a negative acknowledgement (NACK) to force retransmission of a missing or damaged packet.

- Allows the graceful termination of a session using a FIN handshake.

The main drawback is that this connection information requires multiple header fields. Using TCP can add 20 bytes or more to the size of each packet.

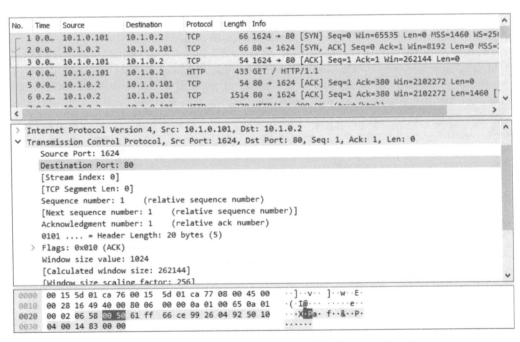

Observing the TCP handshake with the Wireshark protocol analyzer.
(Screenshot courtesy of Wireshark.)

TCP is used when the application protocol cannot tolerate missing or damaged information. For example, the following application protocols must use TCP:

- **HyperText Transfer Protocol (HTTP)/HyperText Transfer Protocol Secure (HTTPS)**—This protocol is used to deliver web pages and other resources. The secure version uses encryption to authenticate the server and protect the information that is being transmitted. A single missing packet would cause this process to fail completely.

- **Secure Shell (SSH)**—This protocol is used to access the command-line interface of a computer from across the network. It uses encryption to authenticate the server and user and protect the information that is being transmitted. This process would also fail if a data packet is not received.

User Datagram Protocol

Sometimes it is more important that communications be faster than they are reliable. The connection-oriented process of TCP adds lots of header bytes to each packet. The **User Datagram Protocol (UDP)** is a **connectionless**, non-guaranteed method of communication with no sequencing or acknowledgements. There is no guarantee regarding the delivery of messages or the sequence in which packets are received.

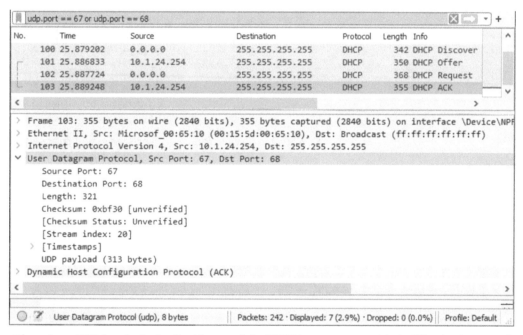

Observing a UDP header in the final frame of the DHCP lease process with the Wireshark protocol analyzer. (Screenshot courtesy of Wireshark.)

UDP is suitable for applications that do not require acknowledgement of receipt and can tolerate missing or out-of-order packets. It is often used by applications that transfer time-sensitive data but do not require complete reliability, such as voice or video, because missing data manifests as glitches rather than application errors or complete connection failures. The reduced overhead means that delivery is faster. If necessary, the application layer can be used to control delivery reliability.

Two other examples of protocols that use UDP are DHCP and TFTP:

- **Dynamic Host Configuration Protocol (DHCP)**—This protocol is used by clients to request IP configuration information from a server. It uses broadcast transmissions, which are not supported by TCP, so it must use UDP. The protocol is quite simple, so if a response packet is not received, the client just restarts the process and tries again repeatedly, until timing out.

- **Trivial File Transfer Protocol (TFTP)**—This protocol is typically used by network devices to obtain a configuration file. The application protocol uses its own acknowledgement messaging, so it does not require TCP.

Well-Known Ports

Server port numbers are assigned by the Internet Assigned Numbers Authority (IANA). Some of the "well-known" port numbers and the functions of the application protocols they represent are listed in the following table.

Port#	TCP/UDP	Protocol	Purpose
20	TCP	File Transfer Protocol (FTP)—Data connection	Make files available for download across a network (data connection port)
21	TCP	File Transfer Protocol (FTP)—Control connection	Make files available for download across a network (control connection port)
22	TCP	Secure Shell (SSH)	Make a secure connection to the command-line interface of a server
23	TCP	Telnet	Make an unsecure connection to the command-line interface of a server
25	TCP	Simple Mail Transfer Protocol (SMTP)	Transfer email messages across a network
53	TCP/UDP	Domain Name System (DNS)	Facilitate identification of hosts by name alongside IP addressing
67	UDP	Dynamic Host Configuration Protocol (DHCP) Server	Provision an IP address configuration to clients
68	UDP	DHCP Client	Request a dynamic IP address configuration from a server
80	TCP	HyperText Transfer Protocol (HTTP)	Provision unsecure websites and web services
110	TCP	Post Office Protocol (POP)	Retrieve email messages from a server mailbox
137–139	UDP/TCP	NetBIOS over TCP/IP	Support networking features of legacy Windows versions
143	TCP	Internet Mail Access Protocol (IMAP)	Read and manage mail messages on a server mailbox

Port#	TCP/UDP	Protocol	Purpose
161	UDP	Simple Network Management Protocol (SNMP)	Query status information from network devices
162	UDP	SNMP trap operation	Report status information to a management server
389	TCP	Lightweight Directory Access Protocol (LDAP)	Query information about network users and resources
443	TCP	HTTP Secure (HTTPS)	Provision secure websites and services
445	TCP	Server Message Block (SMB)	Implement Windows-compatible file and printer sharing services on a local network (also sometimes referred to as Common Internet File System [CIFS])
3389	TCP	Remote Desktop Protocol (RDP)	Make a secure connection to the graphical desktop of a computer

These application protocols will be covered in more detail over the course of the next topic and the next lesson.

Review Activity:

Protocols and Ports

Answer the following questions:

1. True or false? At the Transport layer, connections between hosts to exchange application data are established over a single port number.

2. What feature of DCHP means that it must use UDP at the transport layer?

3. Another technician has scribbled some notes about a firewall configuration. The technician has listed only the port numbers 25 and 3389. What is the purpose of the protocols that use these ports by default?

4. The technician has made a note to check that port 445 is blocked by the firewall. What is the purpose of the protocol that uses this port by default, and why should it be blocked?

Topic 5D

Compare Network Configuration Concepts

 CORE 1 EXAM OBJECTIVES COVERED
2.6 Compare and contrast common network configuration concepts.

The low-level addressing implemented by IP uses long and difficult-to-remember numeric values. DHCP and DNS are commonly deployed to provide an autoconfiguration mechanism and simpler name-based addressing of network hosts and resources. As a CompTIA A+ technician, understanding the configuration parameters for these services will enable you to better support and troubleshoot your networks.

Additionally, corporate networks have performance and security requirements that are different to SOHO LANs. This topic will explain why corporate networks use virtual LAN (VLAN) and virtual private network (VPN) network configurations.

Dynamic Host Configuration Protocol

When an interface is assigned a static configuration manually, the installer may make a mistake with the address information—perhaps duplicating an existing IP address or entering the wrong subnet mask—or the configuration of the network may change, requiring the host to be manually configured with a new static address. To avoid these problems, a **DHCP** server can be used to allocate an appropriate IP address and subnet mask (plus other settings) to any host that connects to the network and requests address information.

DHCP Scope

A **scope** is the range of addresses that a DHCP server can offer to client hosts in a particular subnet. The scope should exclude any addresses that have been configured statically. For example, the LAN address of a SOHO router is typically `192.168.0.1`. This is also the address used by the DHCP server running on the router. The scope must exclude this address. If the scope is defined as `192.168.0.100` to `192.168.0.199`, that allows for 100 dynamically addressed hosts on the local network.

DHCP Leases

A host is configured to use DHCP by specifying in its TCP/IP configuration that it should automatically obtain an IP address. When a DHCP client initializes, it broadcasts a DHCPDISCOVER packet to find a DHCP server. All communications are sent using UDP, with the server listening on port 67 and the client on port 68.

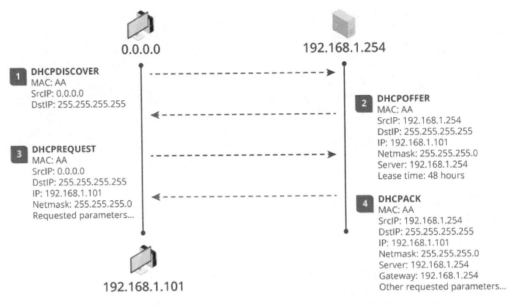

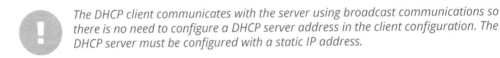

DHCP Discover, Offer, Request, Ack process. (Images © 123RF.com.)

> The DHCP client communicates with the server using broadcast communications so there is no need to configure a DHCP server address in the client configuration. The DHCP server must be configured with a static IP address.

Presuming it has an IP address available, the DHCP server responds to the client with a DHCPOFFER packet, containing the address and other configuration information, such as default gateway and DNS server addresses. The client may choose to accept the offer using a DHCPREQUEST packet that is also broadcast onto the network.

Assuming the offer is still available, the server will respond with a DHCPACK packet. The client broadcasts an ARP message to check that the address is unused. If so, it will start to use the address and options; if not, it declines the address and requests a new one.

The IP address is leased by the server for a limited period only. A client can attempt to renew or rebind the **lease** before it expires. If the lease cannot be renewed, the client must release the IP address and start the discovery process again.

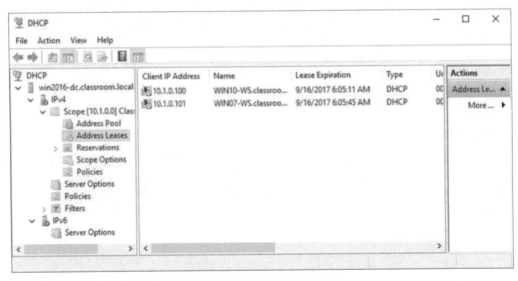

Windows DHCP server showing address leases. (Screenshot courtesy of Microsoft.)

If the address information needs to change, this can be done on the DHCP server, and clients will update themselves automatically when they seek a new lease (or a new lease can be requested manually).

DHCP Reservations

It is often useful for a host to use the same IP address. Servers, routers, printers, and other network infrastructure can be easier to manage if their IP addresses are known. One option is to use static addressing for these appliances, but this is difficult to implement. Another option is to configure the DHCP server to **reserve** a particular IP address for each device. The DHCP server is configured with a list of the MAC addresses of hosts that should receive the same IP address. When it is contacted by a host with one of the listed MAC addresses, it issues a lease for the reserved IP address.

 Some operating systems send a different unique identifier than a MAC address by default. The identification method should be configured appropriately on the client so that the server has the correct information.

Domain Name System

IP uses a binary address value to locate a host on an internetwork. The dotted decimal (IPv4) or hex (IPv6) representation of this IP address is used for configuration purposes, but it is not easy for people to remember or input correctly. For this reason, a "friendly" **host name** is also typically assigned to each host. The host name is configured when the OS is installed. The host name must be unique on the local network.

To avoid the possibility of duplicate host names on the Internet, the host name can be combined with a domain name and suffix. This is referred to as a **fully qualified domain name (FQDN)**. An example of an FQDN might be `nut.widget.example`. The host name is `nut`, and the domain suffix is `widget.example`. This domain suffix consists of the domain name `widget` within the top-level domain (TLD) `.example`. A domain suffix could also contain subdomains between the host and domain name.

FQDNs are assigned and managed using **DNS**. DNS is a global hierarchy of distributed name server databases that contain information about each domain and the hosts within those domains. At the top of the DNS hierarchy is the root, which is represented by the null label, consisting of just a period (.). There are 13 root-level servers (A to M).

Immediately below the root lie the top-level domains (TLDs). There are several types of TLDs, but the most prevalent are generic (such as .com, .org, .net, .info, .biz), sponsored (such as .gov, .edu), and country code (such as .uk, .ca, .de). DNS is operated by ICANN (icann.org), which also manages the generic TLDs. Country codes are generally managed by an organization appointed by the relevant government.

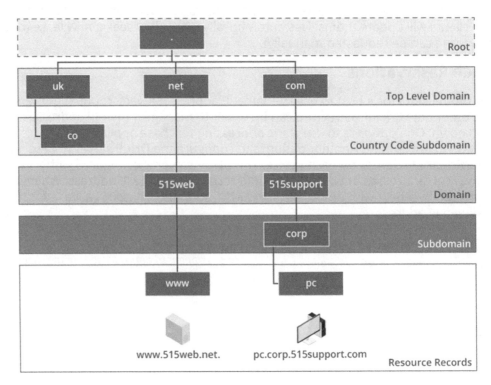

DNS hierarchy. (Images © 123RF.com.)

Each FQDN reflects this hierarchy, from most specific on the left (the host name) to least specific on the right (the TLD followed by the root). For example: `pc.corp.515support.com.`

DNS Queries

To resolve a host name or FQDN to an IP address, the client must obtain the appropriate record from a DNS server. For example, a user might type an FQDN into the address bar of a web browser client application. The client app, referred to as a "stub resolver," checks its local cache for the mapping. If no mapping is found, it forwards the query to its local DNS server. The IP addresses of one or more DNS servers that can act as resolvers are usually set in the TCP/IP configuration. The client communicates with a DNS server over **port 53**. The resolution process then takes place as follows:

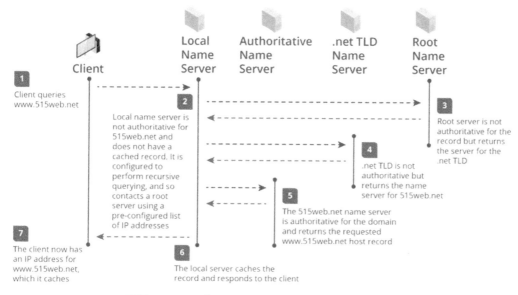

DNS name resolution process. (Images © 123RF.com.)

DNS Record Types

The DNS server IP addresses configured on a client machine are used to resolve the client's queries for hosts and domains across the Internet. At least one DNS server also needs to be configured to act as an authoritative store of information about each domain. These name servers are normally installed separately to the ones used as client resolvers.

The DNS server responsible for managing a zone will contain numerous **resource records**. These records allow the name server to resolve queries for names and services hosted in the domain into IP addresses. Resource records can be created and updated manually (statically), or they can be generated dynamically from information received from client and server computers on the network.

Address (A) and Address (AAAA) Resource Records

An **address (A)** record is used to resolve a host name to an IPv4 address. An **AAAA** record resolves a host name to an IPv6 address.

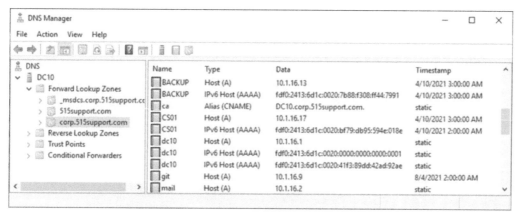

Both types of host records (A and AAAA) in Windows Server DNS.
(Screenshot courtesy of Microsoft.)

Mail Exchanger (MX) Resource Records

A **Mail Exchange (MX)** record is used to identify an email server for the domain so that other servers can send messages to it. In a typical network, multiple servers are installed to provide redundancy, and each one will be represented by an **MX record**. Each MX record is given a preference value, with the lowest numbered entry preferred. The host name identified in an MX record must have an associated A or AAAA record.

DNS Spam Management Records

A **TXT record** is used to store any free-form text that may be needed to support other network services. A single domain name may have many TXT records, but they are most commonly used to verify email services and block the transmission of spoofed and unwanted messages, referred to as **spam**.

Sender Policy Framework

Sender Policy Framework (SPF) uses a TXT resource record published via DNS by an organization hosting email service. The SPF record—there must be only one per domain—identifies the hosts authorized to send email from that domain. An SPF can also indicate what to do with mail from servers not on the list, such as rejecting them (`-all`), flagging them (`~all`), or accepting them (`+all`).

DomainKeys Identified Mail

DomainKeys Identified Mail (DKIM) uses cryptography to validate the source server for a given email message. This can replace or supplement SPF. To configure DKIM, the organization uploads a public encryption key as a TXT record in the DNS server. Organizations receiving messages can use this key to verify that a message derives from an authentic server.

Domain-Based Message Authentication, Reporting, and Conformance

The **Domain-Based Message Authentication, Reporting, and Conformance (DMARC)** framework ensures that SPF and DKIM are being utilized effectively. A DMARC policy is published as a DNS TXT record. DMARC can use SPF or DKIM or both. DMARC specifies a more robust policy mechanism for senders to specify how DMARC authentication failures should be treated (flag, quarantine, or reject), plus mechanisms for recipients to report DMARC authentication failures to the sender.

Virtual LANs

All hosts connected to the same unmanaged switch are said to be in the same broadcast domain. This does not present any problem on a small network. However, the switching fabric on an enterprise network can provide thousands of ports. Placing hundreds or thousands of hosts in the same broadcast domain reduces performance. To mitigate this, the ports can be divided into groups using a feature of managed switches called **virtual LAN (VLAN)**.

The simplest means of assigning a node to a VLAN is by configuring the port interface on the switch with a VLAN ID in the range 2 to 4094. For example, switch ports 1 through 10 could be configured as a VLAN with the ID 10 and ports 11 through 20 could be assigned to VLAN 20. Host A connected to port 2 would be in VLAN 10, and host B connected to port 12 would be in VLAN 20.

```
interface swp5
    bridge-access 100

interface swp6
    bridge-access 100

interface swp7
    bridge-access 100

interface swp8
    bridge-access 100

interface swp9
    bridge-access 200

interface swp10
    bridge-access 200

interface swp11
    bridge-access 200

interface swp12
    bridge-access 200

interface bridge
    bridge-ports swp5 swp6 swp7 swp8 swp9 swp10 swp11 swp12
    bridge-vids 10 100 200
    bridge-vlan-aware yes
```

Cumulus VX switch output showing switch ports swp 5–8 configured in VLAN 100 and ports 9–12 in VLAN 200.

 The VLAN with ID 1 is referred to as the "default VLAN." Unless configured differently, all ports on a managed switch default to being in VLAN 1.

When hosts are placed in separate VLANs, they can no longer communicate with one another directly, even though they might be connected to the same switch. Each VLAN must be configured with its own subnet address and IP address range. Communications between VLANs must go through an IP router. Each VLAN must also be provisioned with its own DHCP and DNS services.

As well as reducing the impact of excessive broadcast traffic, from a security point of view, each VLAN can represent a separate zone. Traffic passing between VLANs can easily be filtered and monitored to ensure it meets security policies. VLANs are also used to separate nodes based on traffic type, such as isolating devices used for VoIP so that they can more easily be prioritized over data passing over other VLANs.

Virtual Private Networks

A **virtual private network (VPN)** enables hosts to connect to the LAN without being physically installed at the site. Rather than attach to a switch or AP, the host connects to the local network via a remote access server that accepts connections from the Internet. Because the Internet is a public network, it is important for the VPN connection to be secure.

A secure VPN configures a protected tunnel through the Internet. It uses special connection protocols and encryption technology to ensure that the tunnel is protected against snooping and that the user is properly authenticated. Once the connection has been established, to all intents and purposes, the remote computer becomes part of the local network, though it is still restricted by the bandwidth available over the Internet connection.

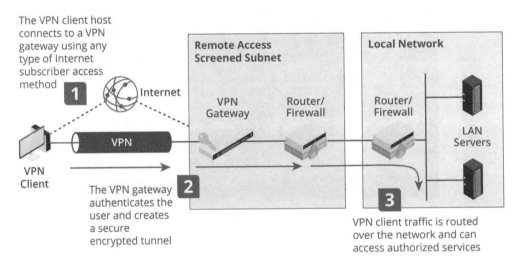

A typical remote access VPN configuration. (Image © 123RF.com.)

 The VPN described above is for remote access to the LAN by teleworkers and roaming users. VPNs can also be used to connect sites over public networks, such as linking branch offices to a head office, or within a local network as an additional security mechanism.

Review Activity:

Network Configuration Concepts

Answer the following questions:

1. You need to ensure that a print device receives the same IP address when connecting to the network. What value do you need to configure on the DHCP server to enable a reservation?

2. True or false? A top-level domain such as .com represents the top of the DNS hierarchy.

3. You are advising another technician about typical DNS configuration. The technician thinks that the name server hosting the 515 support domain resource records on the Internet should be configured as the primary DNS server entry in the IP configuration of local clients. Why is this unlikely to be the case?

4. What type of value would you expect a query for an AAAA resource record to return?

5. What type of TXT record uses cryptography to help recipient servers reject spoofed messages and spam?

6. Which network configuration technology can be configured on switches to divide a local network into multiple broadcast domain segments?

Lesson 5

Summary

You should be able to compare Internet connection types, TCP/IP protocols, and common network configuration concepts and to configure SOHO routers and clients.

Guidelines for Installing and Configuring SOHO Networks

Follow these guidelines to install and configure a SOHO network:

- Identify the most suitable Internet connection type from those available, considering ADSL, cable, FTTC/VDSL, FTTP/full fiber, WISP, satellite, or cellular (4G/5G).

- Either use the ISP-provided SOHO router or provision a router and/or modem to work with the Internet connection type and check that the WAN interface is cabled or connected correctly to the service provider network.

- Use a computer to connect to the router interface over a LAN port or Wi-Fi and verify the status of the Internet connection.

- Optionally, adjust DHCP settings to customize the address scope or configure reservations.

- If configuring one or more hosts with static addresses, ensure each has an IPv4 address and subnet mask that is consistent with the DHCP private address range scope and address scope. Configure the router IP address as the default gateway and optionally as the primary DNS server. If using IPv6, configure an address and network prefix that is consistent with the settings on the router.

- Verify that the router is configured to use trusted DNS resolvers, such as those of the ISP.

- If allowing Internet connections through the firewall, identify the TCP and UDP protocols and ports that need to be opened.

- If allowing Internet connections and maintaining a domain name, consider which services need to be published as address, MX, and TXT records to allow Internet hosts to connect to web and email servers in the domain.

- If expanding the network, consider requirements to use managed switches, VLANs, and IP subnets to divide the LAN into multiple broadcast domains and to allow remote access via a VPN.

Lesson 6
Supporting Network Services

LESSON INTRODUCTION

Application protocols implement services such as web browsing, email, and file sharing. As well as computer server roles, modern networks use a variety of Internet security appliances and smart devices. Some networks are integrated with embedded system devices that underpin industrial technologies. While you will not have responsibility for configuring the devices and servers that run these applications, being able to summarize the functions and purposes of server roles will help you to assist other technicians.

Being able to summarize the function of protocols all the way up the network stack is also a prerequisite for troubleshooting network issues. When you are diagnosing connectivity problems with a host, you need to determine whether the issue is with a cable or adapter that you can resolve or whether there is a wider network or application server issue that you will need to escalate to senior support staff.

Lesson Objectives

In this lesson, you will:

- Summarize services provided by networked hosts.

- Compare Internet and embedded appliances.

- Troubleshoot networks.

Topic 6A

Summarize Services Provided by Networked Hosts

CORE 1 EXAM OBJECTIVES COVERED
2.4 Summarize services provided by networked hosts.

IP, TCP/UDP, DHCP, and DNS establish the basic addressing and forwarding functions necessary to implement network connectivity. Network applications use these underlying network and transport functions to run user-level services, such as web browsing or file sharing. In this topic, you will learn to summarize the server roles that are used to implement network applications.

File/Print Servers

One of the core network functions is to provide shared access to disk and print resources. Like many network protocols, resource sharing is implemented using a client/server architecture. The machine hosting the disk or printer is the **server**. A server disk configured to allow clients to access it over the network is a **fileshare**. Machines accessing those resources are the clients.

The fileshare and print server roles may be implemented on a local network using proprietary protocols, such as File and Print Services for Windows Networks. A **file server** could also be implemented using TCP/IP protocols, such as File Transfer Protocol (FTP).

Server Message Block

Server Message Block (SMB) is the application protocol underpinning file and printer sharing on Windows networks. SMB usually runs directly over the TCP/445 port.

SMB has gone through several updates, with SMB3 as the current version. SMB1 has very serious security vulnerabilities and is now disabled by default on current Windows versions (docs.microsoft.com/en-us/windows-server/storage/file-server/troubleshoot/detect-enable-and-disable-smbv1-v2-v3).

Support for SMB in UNIX- or Linux-based machines and network attached storage (NAS) appliances is provided by using the Samba software suite (samba.org/samba/what_is_samba.html), which allows a Windows client to access a Linux host as though it were a Windows file or print server.

*SMB is sometimes referred to as the **Common Internet File System (CIFS)**, though technically that should only be used to refer to a specific dialect of SMB version 1.*

Network Basic Input/Output System

The earliest Windows networks used a protocol stack called the **Network Basic Input/Output System (NetBIOS)** rather than TCP/IP. NetBIOS allowed computers to address one another by name and establish sessions for other protocols, such as SMB. As the TCP/IP suite became the standard for local networks, NetBIOS was re-engineered to work over the TCP and UDP protocols, referred to as NetBIOS over TCP/IP (NetBT). NetBT uses UDP/137 for name services and TCP/139 for session services.

Modern networks use IP, TCP/UDP, and DNS for these functions, so NetBT is obsolete. NetBT should be disabled on most networks, as it poses a significant risk to security. It is only required if the network must support file sharing for Windows versions earlier than Windows 2000.

File Transfer Protocol

The **File Transfer Protocol (FTP)** allows a client to upload and download files from a network server. It is often used to upload files to websites.

FTP is associated with the use of port TCP/21 to establish a connection and either port TCP/20 to transfer data in "active" mode or a server-assigned port in "passive" mode.

 Plain FTP is unencrypted and so poses a high security risk. Passwords for sites are submitted in plaintext. There are ways of encrypting FTP sessions, such as FTP-Secure (FTPS) and FTP over Secure Shell (SFTP), and it is the encrypted services that are most widely used now.

Web Servers

A **web server** is one that provides client access using HTTP or its secure version (HTTPS). Websites and web applications are perhaps the most useful and ubiquitous of network services. Web technology can be deployed for a huge range of functions and applications, in no way limited to the static pages of information that characterized the first websites.

HyperText Transfer Protocol

HTTP enables clients (typically web browsers) to request resources from an HTTP server. A client connects to the HTTP server using port **TCP/80** (by default) and submits a request for a resource (GET). The server either returns the data requested data if it is available or responds with an error code.

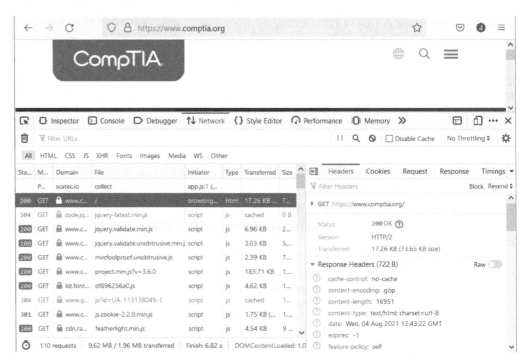

Using Firefox's web developer tools to inspect the HTTP requests and response headers involved in serving a typical modern web page. (Screenshot courtesy of Mozilla.)

HyperText Markup Language, Forms, and Web Applications

HTTP is usually used to serve HTML web pages, which are plain text files with coded tags describing how the document should be formatted. A web browser can interpret the tags and display the text and other resources associated with the page (such as picture or sound files). Another powerful feature is the ability to provide hyperlinks to other related documents. HTTP also features forms mechanisms (POST) whereby a user can submit data from the client to the server.

The functionality of HTTP servers is often extended by support for scripting and programmable features (web applications).

Uniform Resource Locators

Resources on the Internet are accessed using an addressing scheme known as a **uniform resource locator (URL)**. A URL contains all the information necessary to identify and access an item. For example, a URL for an HTTP resource might contain the following elements:

- The protocol describes the access method or service type being used.

- The host location is usually represented by a FQDN. The FQDN is not case sensitive. The host location can also be an IP address; an IPv6 address must be enclosed in square brackets.

- The file path specifies the directory and file name location of the resource (if required). The file path may or may not be case sensitive, depending on how the server is configured.

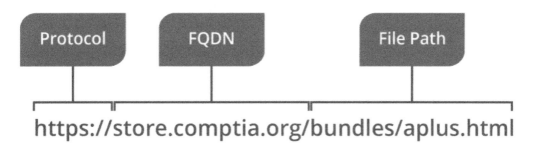

URL for an HTTPS website. The site is identified by the FQDN store.comptia.org and the requested resource is in the file path /bundles/aplus.html from the site root.

Web Server Deployment

Typically, an organization will lease a web server or space on a server from an ISP. Larger organizations with Internet-connected datacenters may host websites themselves. Web servers are not only used on the public Internet, however. Private networks using web technologies are described as "intranets" (if they permit only local access) or "extranets" (if they permit remote access).

Hypertext Transfer Protocol Secure

One of the critical problems for the provision of early websites was the lack of security in HTTP. Under HTTP, all data is sent unencrypted, and there is no authentication of client or server. Secure Sockets Layer (SSL) was developed by Netscape in the 1990s to address these problems. SSL proved very popular with the industry. **Transport Layer Security (TLS)** was developed from SSL and ratified as a standard by the IETF.

When TLS is used with the HTTP application, it is referred to as **HTTPS**. Encrypted traffic between the client and server is sent over port **TCP/443** (by default), rather than the open and unencrypted port 80. TLS can also be used to secure other TCP application protocols, such as FTP, POP3/IMAP, SMTP, and LDAP.

 TLS can also be used with UDP, referred to as Datagram Transport Layer Security (DTLS), most often in virtual private networking (VPN) solutions.

To implement HTTPS, the web server is installed with a digital **certificate** issued by some trusted **certificate authority (CA)**. The certificate uses encrypted data to prove the identity of the server to the client, assuming that the client also trusts the CA. The system uses a public/private encryption key pair. The private key is kept a secret known only to the server; the public key is given to clients via the digital certificate.

The server and client use the key pair in the digital certificate and a chosen cipher suite within the TLS protocol to set up an encrypted tunnel. Even though someone else might know the public key, they cannot decrypt the contents of the tunnel without obtaining the server's private key. This means that the communications cannot be read or changed by a third party.

A web browser will open a secure session to an HTTPS server by using a URL starting with https:// and it will also show a padlock icon in the address bar to indicate that the server's certificate is trusted and that the connection is secure. A website can be configured to require a secure session and reject or redirect plain HTTP requests.

HTTPS padlock icon. (Screenshot courtesy of Microsoft.)

Mail Servers

Electronic mail enables a person to compose a message and send it to another user on their own network (intranet) or anywhere in the world via the Internet. Two types of **mail servers** and protocols are used to process **email**: mail transfer and mailbox access protocols:

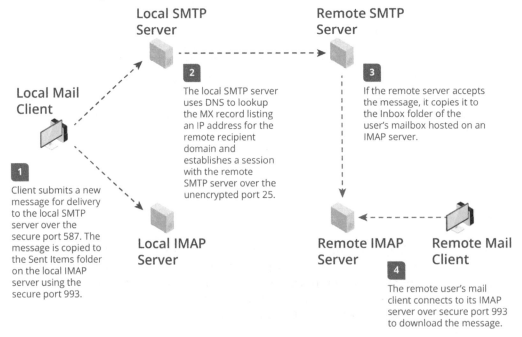

Operation of delivery and mailbox email protocols. (Images © 123RF.com.)

Internet email addresses follow the mailto URL scheme. An Internet email address comprises two parts—the username (local part) and the domain name, separated by an @ symbol. The domain name may refer to a company or an ISP; for example, `david.martin@comptia.org` or `david.martin@aol.com`.

The **Simple Mail Transfer Protocol (SMTP)** specifies how email is delivered from one mail domain to another. The SMTP server of the sender discovers the IP address of the recipient SMTP server by using the domain name part of the recipient's email address. The SMTP servers for the domain are registered in DNS using Mail Exchange (MX) and host (A/AAAA) records.

Typical SMTP configurations use the following ports and secure services:

- **Port TCP/25** is used for message relay between SMTP servers, or message transfer agents (MTAs). Transmissions over port 25 are usually unsecure.

- **Port TCP/587** is used by mail clients—message submission agents (MSAs)—to submit messages for delivery by an SMTP server. Servers configured to support port 587 should use encryption and authentication to protect the service.

Mailbox Servers

SMTP is used only to deliver mail to server hosts that are permanently available. When an email is received by an SMTP server, it delivers the message to a mailbox server. The mailbox server could be a separate machine or a separate process running on the same computer. A mailbox access protocol allows the user's client email software to retrieve messages from the mailbox.

Post Office Protocol 3

The **Post Office Protocol (POP)** is an early example of a mailbox access protocol. POP is often referred to as POP3 because the active version of the protocol is version 3. A POP client application, such as Microsoft Outlook® or Mozilla Thunderbird®, establishes a connection to the POP server on port TCP/110 or over the secure port TCP/995. The user is authenticated (by username and password), and the contents of the mailbox are downloaded for processing on the local PC. With POP3, the messages are typically deleted from the mailbox server when they are downloaded, though some clients have the option to leave messages on the server.

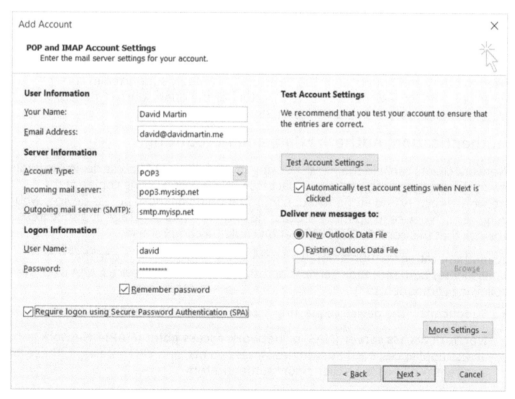

Configuring an email account. The incoming server is either POP3 or IMAP while the outgoing server is SMTP. (Screenshot courtesy of Microsoft.)

Internet Message Access Protocol

The **Internet Message Access Protocol (IMAP)** addresses some of the limitations of POP. IMAP is a mail retrieval protocol, but its mailbox management features lack POP. IMAP supports permanent connections to a server and connecting multiple clients to the same mailbox simultaneously. It also allows a client to manage the mailbox on the server (to organize messages in folders and to control when they are deleted, for instance) and to create multiple mailboxes.

A client connects to an IMAP server over port TCP/143, but this port is unsecure. Connection security can be established using TLS. The default port for IMAP-Secure (IMAPS) is TCP/993.

Directory and Authentication Servers

DHCP allows a network client to request an IP configuration, and DNS allows it to request resources using plain names. Most networks must also authenticate and authorize clients before allowing them to connect to fileshares and mail servers.

This security requirement is met by configuring an access control system to prevent unauthorized users (and devices) from connecting. In a Windows workgroup, for example, the access control method is a simple password, shared with all authorized users. Enterprise networks use directory servers to maintain a centralized database of user accounts and authenticate the subjects trying to use those accounts. These protocols allow a user to authenticate once to access the network and gain authorization for all the compatible application servers running on it. This is referred to as single sign-on (SSO).

Lightweight Directory Access Protocol

Network resources can be recorded as objects within a directory. A directory is a type of database, where an object is like a record and things that you know about the object (attributes) are like fields. Most directories are based on the X.500 standard. The **Lightweight Directory Access Protocol (LDAP)** is a TCP/IP protocol used to query and update an X.500 directory. It is widely supported in current directory products—Windows Active Directory or the open source OpenLDAP, for instance. LDAP uses TCP and UDP port 389 by default.

Authentication, Authorization, and Accounting

Network clients can join the network using multiple types of access device, including switches, access points, and remote access VPN servers. Storing copies of the network directory and authentication information on all these access devices would require each device to do more processing and have more storage. It also increases the risk that this confidential information could be compromised.

An authentication, authorization, and accounting (AAA) server is one that consolidates authentication services across multiple access devices. AAA uses the following components:

- **Supplicant**—The device requesting access, such as a user's PC or laptop.

- **Network access server (NAS) or network access point (NAP)**—Network access appliances, such as switches, access points, and VPN gateways. These are also referred to as "AAA clients" or "authenticators."

- **AAA server**—The authentication server, positioned within the local network.

With AAA, the network access appliances do not have to store any authentication credentials. They simply act as a transit to forward this data between the AAA server and the supplicant. AAA is often implemented using a protocol called **Remote Authentication Dial-in User Service (RADIUS)**.

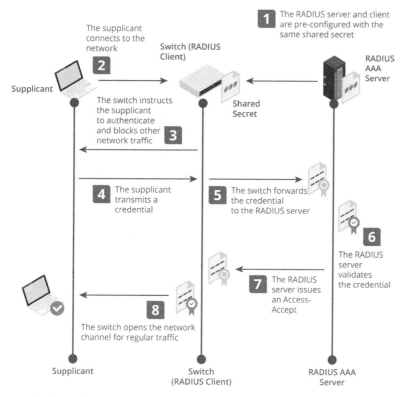

Communications between RADIUS server, client, and supplicant in AAA architecture.
(Images © 123RF.com.)

Remote Terminal Access Servers

A remote terminal server allows a host to accept connections to its command shell or graphical desktop from across the network. The name "terminal" comes from the early days of computing where configuration was performed by a teletype (TTY) device. The TTY is the terminal or endpoint for communication between the computer and the user. It handles text input and output between the user and the shell, or command environment. Where the terminal accepts input and displays output, the shell performs the actual processing.

A **terminal emulator** is any kind of software that replicates this TTY input/output function. A given terminal emulator application might support connections to multiple types of shell. A remote terminal emulator allows you to connect to the shell of a different host over the network.

Secure Shell

Secure Shell (SSH) is the principal means of obtaining secure remote access to UNIX and Linux servers and to most types of network appliances (switches, routers, and firewalls). As well as encrypted terminal emulation, SSH can be used for SFTP and to achieve many other network configurations. Numerous commercial and open source SSH servers and terminal emulation clients are available for all the major NOS platforms (UNIX®, Linux®, Windows®, and macOS®). The most widely used is OpenSSH (openssh.com). An SSH server listens on port TCP/22 by default.

Telnet

Telnet is both a protocol and a terminal emulation software tool that transmits shell commands and output between a client and the remote host. A Telnet server listens on port TCP/23 by default.

PuTTY Telnet client. (Screenshot courtesy of PuTTY.)

A Telnet interface can be password protected, but the password and other communications are not encrypted and therefore could be vulnerable to packet sniffing and replay. Historically, Telnet provided a simple means to configure switch and router equipment, but only secure access methods should be used for these tasks now.

Remote Desktop Protocol

Telnet and SSH provide terminal emulation for command-line shells. This is sufficient for most administrative tasks, but where users want to connect to a desktop, they usually prefer to work with a graphical interface. A GUI remote administration tool sends screen and audio data from the remote host to the client and transfers mouse and keyboard input from the client to the remote host. **Remote Desktop Protocol (RDP)** is Microsoft's protocol for operating remote GUI connections to a Windows machine. RDP uses port TCP/3389. The administrator can specify permissions to connect to the server via RDP and can configure encryption on the connection.

RDP clients are available for other OSs, including Linux, macOS, iOS, and Android so you can connect to a Windows desktop remotely using a non-Windows device. There are also open-source RDP server products, such as xrdp (xrdp.org).

Network Monitoring Servers

SSH and RDP allow administrators to log on and manage hosts and switches/routers/firewalls remotely. For a network to run smoothly, it is also important to gather information regularly from these systems. This type of remote monitoring can identify an actual or possible fault more quickly.

Simple Network Management Protocol

The **Simple Network Management Protocol (SNMP)** is a framework for management and monitoring network devices. SNMP consists of a management system and agents.

The agent is a process running on a switch, router, server, or other SNMP-compatible network device. This agent maintains a database called a management information base (MIB) that holds statistics relating to the activity of the device. An example of such a statistic is the number of frames per second handled by a switch. The agent is also capable of initiating a trap operation where it informs the management system of a notable event (port failure, for instance). The threshold for triggering traps can be set for each value.

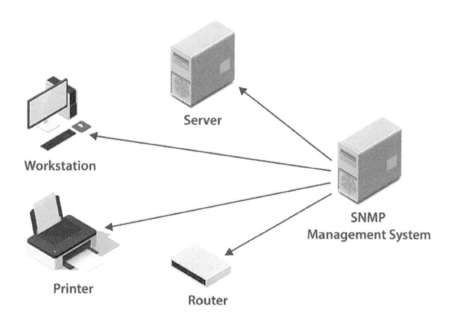

SNMP agents and management system. (Image © 123RF.com.)

The management system monitors all agents by polling them at regular intervals for information from their MIBs and displays the information for review. It also displays any trap operations as alerts for the network administrator to assess and act upon as necessary.

SNMP device queries take place over port UDP/161; traps are communicated over port UDP/162.

Syslog

Effective network management often entails capturing logs from different devices. It is more efficient to review logs and respond to alerts if the logs are consolidated on a single system. A log collector aggregates event messages from numerous devices to a single storage location. As well as aggregating logs, the system can be configured to run one or more status and alerting dashboards.

Syslog is an example of a protocol and supporting software that facilitates log collection. It has become a de facto standard for logging events from distributed systems. For example, syslog messages can be generated by routers and switches, as well as UNIX or Linux servers and workstations. A syslog collector usually listens on port UDP/514.

Configuring an OPNsense security appliance to transmit logs to a remote syslog server. (Screenshot courtesy of OPNsense.)

As well as a protocol for forwarding messages to a remote log collector, syslog provides an open format for event data. A syslog message comprises a PRI code, a header containing a timestamp and host name, and a message part. The PRI code is calculated from the facility and a severity level. The message part contains a tag showing the source process plus content. The format of the content is application dependent.

Review Activity:

Services Provided by Networked Hosts

Answer the following questions:

1. **True or false? An HTTP application secured using the SSL/TLS protocol should use a different port to unencrypted HTTP.**

2. **A firewall filters applications based on their port number. If you want to configure a firewall on a mail server to allow clients to download email messages, which port(s) might you have to open?**

3. **You are configuring a network attached storage (NAS) appliance. What file sharing protocol(s) could you use to allow access to Windows, Linux, and Apple macOS clients?**

4. **True or false? AAA allows switches and access points to hold directory information so that they can authenticate clients as they connect to the network.**

5. **You are advising a company on configuring systems to provide better information about network device status. Why would you recommend the use of both SNMP and syslog?**

Topic 6B

Compare Internet and Embedded Appliances

CORE 1 EXAM OBJECTIVES COVERED
2.4 Summarize services provided by networked hosts.

As well as the roles fulfilled by computer servers, most networks also require dedicated Internet security appliances and must manage embedded systems and legacy systems. Internet security appliances are installed to the network border to filter content and improve performance. Embedded devices might be present on the network as features of industrial or building control systems or as Internet of Things devices installed to office workspaces. As an A+ technician, it is important that you can compare and contrast the functions of these types of appliances and embedded devices so that you can support and troubleshoot networks more effectively.

Proxy Servers

On a SOHO network, devices on the LAN access the Internet via the router using a type of NAT, specifically port-based or overloaded NAT. This type of NAT device translates between the private IP addresses used on the LAN and the publicly addressable IP address configured on the router's WAN interface.

Many enterprise networks also use some sort of NAT, but another option is to deploy a **proxy server**. A proxy server does not just translate IP addresses. It takes a whole HTTP request from a client, checks it, then forwards it to the destination server on the Internet. When the reply comes back, it checks it and then shuttles it back to the LAN computer. A proxy can be used for other types of traffic, too (email, for instance).

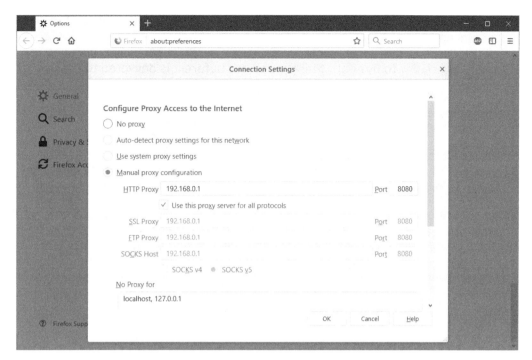

Configuring the Firefox web browser to use a proxy server at 192.168.0.1 to connect to the Internet. (Screenshot courtesy of Mozilla.)

A proxy server can usually operate either as a transparent service, in which case, the client requires no special configuration, or as nontransparent. For a nontransparent proxy, the client must be configured with the IP address and service port (often 8080 by convention) of the proxy server.

A proxy can perform a security function by acting as a content filter to block access to sites deemed inappropriate. It can also apply rules to access requests, such as restricting overall time limits or imposing time-of-day restrictions. As well as managing and filtering outgoing access requests, a proxy can be configured to cache content to improve performance and reduce bandwidth consumption.

Spam Gateways and Unified Threat Management

Networks connected to the Internet need to be protected against malicious threats by various types of security scanner. These services can be implemented as software running on PC servers, but enterprise networks are more likely to use purpose-built Internet security appliances. The range of security functions performed by these appliances includes the following:

- Firewalls allow or block traffic based on a network access control list specifying source and destination IP addresses and application ports.

- Intrusion detection systems (IDS) are programmed with scripts that can identify known malicious traffic patterns. An IDS can raise an alert when a match is made. An intrusion prevention system (IPS) can additionally take some action to block the source of the malicious packets.

- Antivirus/antimalware solutions scan files being transferred over the network to detect any matches for known malware signatures in binary data.

- **Spam gateways** use SPF, DKIM, and DMARC to verify the authenticity of mail servers and are configured with filters that can identify spoofed, misleading, malicious, or otherwise unwanted messages. The spam gateway is installed as a network server to filter out these messages before it is delivered to the user's inbox.

- Content filters are used to block outgoing access to unauthorized websites and services.

- Data leak/loss prevention (DLP) systems scan outgoing traffic for information that is marked as confidential or personal. The DLP system can verify whether the transfer is authorized and block it if it is not.

These security functions could be deployed as separate appliances or server applications, each with its own configuration and logging/reporting system. A **unified threat management (UTM)** appliance is one that enforces a variety of security policies and controls, combining the work of multiple security functions. A UTM centralizes the threat management service, providing simpler configuration and reporting compared to isolated applications spread across several servers or devices.

Load Balancers

A **load balancer** can be deployed to distribute client requests across server nodes in a farm or pool. You can use a load balancer in any situation where you have multiple servers providing the same function. Examples include web servers, email servers, web conferencing servers, and streaming media servers. The load balancer is placed in front of the server network and distributes requests from the client network or Internet to the application servers. The service address is advertised to clients as a virtual server. This is used to provision high availability services that can scale from light to heavy loads.

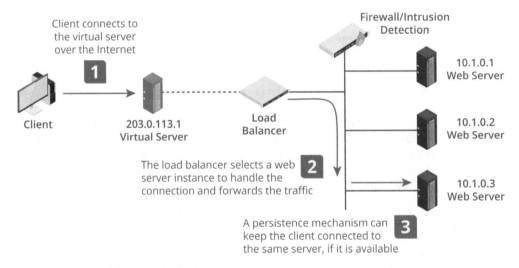

Topology of basic load balancing architecture. (Images © 123RF.com.)

Legacy Systems

A **legacy system** is one that is no longer directly supported by its vendor. This might be because the vendor has gone out of business or formally deprecated use of the product. A product that is no longer supported is referred to as **end of life (EOL)**. Networks often need to retain hosts running legacy OSs and applications software or old-style mainframe computers to run services that are too complex or expensive to migrate to a more modern platform.

Legacy systems usually work well for what they do—which is why they don't get prioritized for replacement—but they represent severe risks in terms of security vulnerabilities. If attackers discover faulty code that they can use to try to exploit the device, the vendor will not be available to develop a software patch to block the exploit. It is important to isolate them as far as possible from the rest of the network and to ensure that any network channels linking them are carefully protected and monitored.

Embedded Systems and SCADA

An **embedded system** is an electronic device that is designed to perform a specific, dedicated function. These systems can be as small and simple as a microcontroller in an intravenous drip-rate meter or as large and complex as an industrial control system managing a water treatment plant. Embedded systems might typically have been designed to operate within a closed network, where the elements of the network are all known to the system vendor and there is no connectivity to wider computer data networks. Where embedded systems need to interact within a computer data network, there are special considerations to make in terms of the network design and support, especially regarding security.

Workflow and Process Automation Systems

An industrial control system (ICS) provides mechanisms for workflow and process automation. An ICS controls machinery used in critical infrastructure, such as power suppliers, water suppliers, health services, telecommunications, and national security services.

An ICS comprises plant devices and equipment with embedded programmable logic controllers (PLCs). The PLCs are linked by a cabled network to actuators that operate valves, motors, circuit breakers, and other mechanical components, plus sensors that monitor some local state, such as temperature. An embedded system network is usually referred to as an **operational technology (OT)** network to distinguish it from an IT network. Output and configuration of a PLC is performed by a human–machine interface (HMI). An HMI might be a local control panel or software running on a computing host. PLCs are connected within a control loop, and the whole process automation system can be governed by a control server. Another important concept is the data historian, which is a database of all the information generated by the control loop.

Supervisory Control and Data Acquisition

A **supervisory control and data acquisition (SCADA)** system takes the place of a control server in large-scale, multiple-site ICSs. SCADAs typically run as software on ordinary computers, gathering data from and managing plant devices and equipment with embedded PLCs, referred to as "field devices." These embedded systems typically use WAN communications, such as cellular or satellite, to link the SCADA server to field devices.

Both legacy and embedded systems represent a risk in terms of maintenance and troubleshooting as well as security, because they tend to require more specialized knowledge than modern, off-the-shelf, computing systems. Consultants with expertise in such systems can become highly sought after.

Internet of Things Devices

The term **Internet of Things (IoT)** is used to describe the global network of wearable technology, home appliances, home control systems, vehicles, and other items that have been equipped with sensors, software, and network connectivity. These features allow these types of objects to communicate and pass data between themselves and other traditional systems, such as computer servers. Smart devices are used to implement home automation systems. An IoT smart device network will generally use the following types of components:

- **Hub/control system**—IoT devices usually require a communications hub to facilitate wireless networking. There must also be a control system, as many IoT devices are headless, meaning they cannot be operated directly using input and output devices. A hub could be implemented as a smart speaker operated by voice control or use a smartphone/PC app for configuration.

- **Smart devices**—IoT endpoints implement the function, such as a smart lightbulb, refrigerator, thermostat/heating control, or doorbell/video entry phone that you can operate and monitor remotely. These devices are capable of compute, storage, and network functions that are all potentially vulnerable to malicious code. Most smart devices use a Linux or Android kernel. Because they're effectively running mini-computers, smart devices are vulnerable to some of the standard attacks associated with web applications and network functions. Integrated peripherals, such as cameras or microphones, could be compromised to facilitate surveillance.

While the control system is typically joined to the Wi-Fi network, smart devices may use other wireless technologies, such as Z-Wave or Zigbee, to exchange data via the hub. These protocols are designed for operation on low-power devices without substantial CPU or storage resource.

Review Activity:

Internet and Embedded Appliances

Answer the following questions:

1. You are advising a customer about replacing the basic network address translation (NAT) function performed by a SOHO router with a device that can work as a proxy. The customer understands the security advantages of this configuration. What other benefit can it have?

2. You are recommending that a small business owner replace separate firewall and antimalware appliances with a UTM. What is the principal advantage of doing this?

3. A network owner has configured three web servers to host a website. What device can be deployed to allow them to work together to service client requests more quickly?

4. You are writing an advisory to identify training requirements for support staff and have included OT networks as one area not currently covered. Another technician thinks you should have written IT. Are they correct?

5. You are auditing your network for the presence of legacy systems. Should you focus exclusively on identifying devices and software whose vendor has gone out of business?

Topic 6C

Troubleshoot Networks

CORE 1 EXAM OBJECTIVES COVERED
5.7 Given a scenario, troubleshoot problems with wired and wireless networks.

As a CompTIA A+ technician, you often assist users with basic network connectivity issues. At this support level, you will be focusing on client issues. As you have learned, networks are complex and involve many different hardware devices, protocols, and applications, meaning that there are lots of things that can go wrong! In this topic, you will learn how to identify and diagnose the causes of some common wired and wireless network issues.

Troubleshoot Wired Connectivity

A client wired connectivity issue means that either the network adapter does not establish a network link at all (no connectivity) or the connection is unstable or intermittent. Assuming that you can establish that the problem affects a single host only, you need to isolate the precise location of the physical issue.

Troubleshoot Cable and Network Adapter Issues

A typical Ethernet link for an office workstation includes the following components:

- NIC port on the host.

- RJ45 terminated patch cord between the host and a wall port.

- Structured cable between the wall port and a patch panel, terminated to insulation displacement connector (IDC) blocks (the permanent link).

- RJ45 terminated patch cord between the patch panel port and a switch port.

- Network transceiver in the switch port.

The link LEDs on network adapter and switch ports will indicate whether the link is active and possibly at what speed the link is working. The LEDs typically flicker to show network activity.

1. The first step in resolving a no or intermittent connectivity issue is to check that the patch cords are properly terminated and connected to the network ports. If you suspect a fault, substitute the patch cord with a known good cable. You can verify patch cords using a cable tester.

2. If you cannot isolate the problem to the patch cords, test the transceivers. You can use a loopback tool to test for a bad port.

3. If you don't have a loopback tool available, another approach is to substitute known working hosts (connect a different computer to the link or swap ports at the switch). This method may have adverse impacts on the rest of the network, however, and issues such as port security may make it unreliable.

4. If you can discount faulty patch cords and bad network ports/NICs, use a cable tester to verify the structured cabling. The solution may involve installing a new permanent link, but there could also be a termination or external interference problem. An advanced type of cable tester called a "certifier" can report detailed information about cable performance and interference.

5. If there is no issue in the structured cabling, verify the Ethernet speed/duplex configuration on the switch interface and NIC. This should usually be set to autonegotiate. You might also try updating the NIC's device driver software.

Troubleshoot Port Flapping Issues

Intermittent connectivity might manifest as **port flapping**, which means that the NIC or switch interface transitions continually between up and down states. This is often caused by bad cabling or external interference or a faulty NIC at the host end. You can use the switch configuration interface to report how long a port remains in the up state.

Troubleshoot Network Speed Issues

The transfer speed of a cabled link could be reduced by mismatched duplex settings on the network adapter and switch port. With Gigabit Ethernet, both should be set to autonegotiate. Check the configuration of the network adapter driver on the client OS and the setting for the switch port via the switch's management software.

If there is no configuration issue, **slow network speeds** can be caused by a variety of other problems and difficult to diagnose. Apply a structured process to investigate possible causes:

1. If a user reports slow speed, establish exactly what network activity they are performing (web browsing, file transfer, authentication, and so on). Establish that there is a link speed problem by checking the nominal link speed and using a utility to measure transfer rate independent of specific apps or network services.

2. If you can isolate the speed issue to a single cable segment, the cabling could be affected by interference. **External interference** is typically caused by nearby power lines, fluorescent lighting, motors, and generators. Poorly installed cabling and connector termination can also cause a type of interference called "crosstalk." Check the ends of cables for excessive untwisting of the wire pairs or improper termination. If you have access to a network tap, the analyzer software is likely to report high numbers of damaged frames. You can also view error rates from the switch interface configuration utility.

3. If the cabling is not the issue, there could be a problem with the network adapter driver. Install an update if available. If the latest driver is installed, check whether the issue affects other hosts using the same NIC and driver version.

4. Consider the possibility that the computer could be infected with malware or have faulty software installed. Consider removing the host from the network for scanning. If you can install a different host to the same network port and that solves the issue, identify what is different about the original host.

5. Establish the scope of the problem: are network speeds an issue for a single user, for all users connected to the same switch, or for all users connecting to the Internet, for instance? There may be congestion at a switch or router or some other network-wide problem. This might be caused by a fault or by user behavior, such as transferring a very large amount of data over the network.

Troubleshoot Wireless Issues

When troubleshooting wireless networks, as with cabled links, you need to consider problems with the physical media, such as interference, and configuration issues.

The radio frequency (RF) signal from radio-based devices weakens considerably as the distance between the devices increases. If you experience **intermittent wireless connectivity**, slow transfer speeds, or inability to establish a connection, as a first step, try moving the devices closer together. If you still cannot obtain a connection, check that the security and authentication parameters are correctly configured on both devices.

Troubleshooting Wireless Configuration Issues

If a user is looking for a network name that is not shown in the list of available wireless networks (SSID not found), the user could be out of range or the SSID name broadcast might be suppressed. In the latter scenario, the connection to the network name must be configured manually on the client.

Another factor to consider is standards mismatch. If an access point is not operating in compatibility mode, it will not be able to communicate with devices that only support older standards. Also, when an older device joins the network, the performance of the whole network can be affected. To support 802.11b clients, an 802.11b/g/n access point must transmit legacy frame preamble and collision avoidance frames, adding overhead. If possible, upgrade 802.11b devices rather than letting them join the WLAN. Both 802.11g and 802.11n/ac/ax are more compatible in terms of negotiating collision avoidance.

Also consider that not all clients supporting 802.11n have dual-band radios. If a client cannot connect to a network operating on the 5 GHz band, check whether its radio is 2.4 GHz-capable only.

Received Signal Strength Indicator

A wireless adapter will reduce the connection speed if the **received signal strength indicator (RSSI)** is not at a minimum required level. The RSSI is an index level calculated from the signal strength level. For example, an 802.11n adapter might be capable of a 144 Mbps data rate with an optimum signal, but if the signal is weak, it might reduce to a 54 Mbps or 11 Mbps rate to make the connection more reliable. If the RSSI is too low, the adapter will drop the connection entirely and try to use a different network. If there are two weak networks, the adapter might "flap" between them. Try moving to a location with better reception.

Troubleshooting Wireless Signal Issues

If a device is within the supported range but the signal is weak or you can only get an **intermittent connection**, there is likely to be interference from another radio source broadcasting at the same frequency. If this is the case, try adjusting the channel that the devices use. Another possibility is interference from a powerful electromagnetic source, such as a motor, or a microwave oven. Finally, there might be something blocking the signal. Radio waves do not pass easily through metal or dense objects. Construction materials, such as wire mesh, foil-backed plasterboard, concrete, and mirrors, can block or degrade signals. Try angling or repositioning the device or antenna to try to get better reception.

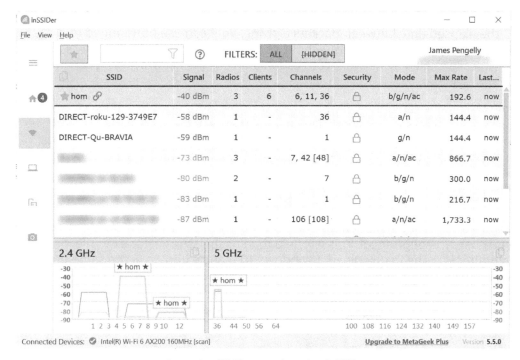

Surveying Wi-Fi networks using inSSIDer.
(Screenshot courtesy of MetaGeek, LLC. © Copyright 2005-2021.)

Wi-Fi analyzer software is designed to identify the signal strength of nearby networks on each channel. It shows the signal strength, measured in dBm, and expressed as a negative value, where values close to zero represent a stronger signal. The analyzer will show how many networks are utilizing each channel. Setting the network to use a less congested channel can improve performance.

Troubleshoot VoIP Issues

While slow network speeds are a problem for all types of network traffic, there are other performance characteristics that affect real-time network protocols and devices. "Real time" refers to services such as voice and video. One example is **Voice over Internet Protocol (VoIP)** protocols. These use data networks to implement voice calling. The symptoms of poor VoIP service quality are dropouts, echo, or other glitches in the call.

With "ordinary" data, it might be beneficial to transfer a file as quickly as possible, but the sequence in which the packets are delivered and variable intervals between packets arriving do not materially affect the application. This type of data transfer is described as "bursty." Network protocols, such as HTTP, FTP, or email, are sensitive to packet loss but tolerant of delays in delivery. The reverse is applicable to real-time applications. These can compensate for some amount of packet loss but are very sensitive to delays in data delivery or packets arriving out of sequence.

Problems with the timing and sequence of packet delivery are defined as latency and jitter:

- **Latency** is the time it takes for a signal to reach the recipient, measured in milliseconds (ms). Latency increases with distance and can be made worse by processing delays at intermediate systems, such as routers. VoIP can support a maximum one-way latency of about 150 ms. Round trip time (RTT) or two-way latency is the time taken for a host to receive a response to a probe.

- **Jitter** is the amount of variation in delay over time and is measured by sampling the elapsed time between packets arriving. VoIP can use buffering to tolerate jitter of up to around 30 ms without severe impact on call quality. Jitter is typically caused by network congestion affecting packet processing on routers and switches.

VoIP call quality can only really be established by using a **quality of service (QoS)** mechanism across the network. QoS means that switches, access points, and routers are all configured to identify VoIP data and prioritize it over bursty data. Enterprise networks can deploy sophisticated QoS and traffic engineering protocols on managed switches and routers. However, it is difficult to guarantee QoS over a public network, such as the Internet.

On a SOHO network, you may be able to configure a QoS or bandwidth control feature on the router/modem to prioritize the port used by a VoIP application over any other type of protocol. This will help to mitigate issues if, for example, one computer is trying to download a Windows 10 feature update at the same time as another set of computers are trying to host a video conference.

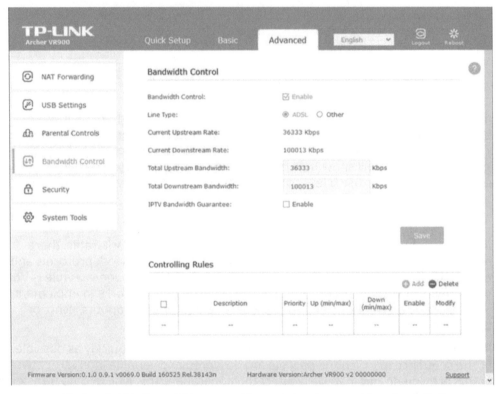

The Bandwidth Control feature on this router/modem provides a basic QoS mechanism. (Screenshot courtesy of TP-Link.)

You should also be able to use the management interface to report connection latency and possibly jitter too. If not, you can use a speed test site to measure latency and bandwidth. If latency is persistently higher than an agreed service level, contact your ISP to resolve the issue.

Troubleshoot Limited Connectivity

In Windows, a **limited connectivity** message specifically means that the host can establish a physical connection to the network but has not received a lease for an IP configuration from a DHCP server. The host will be configured with an address in the automatic IP addressing (APIPA) 169.254.x.y range. A Linux host might also use APIPA, set the IP address to unknown (0.0.0.0), or just leave IP unconfigured.

- **Establish the scope of the issue**—If the issue affects multiple users, the problem is likely to be the DHCP server itself. Remember that DHCP leases take time to expire, so a problem with the DHCP server might take a few hours to manifest as different clients try to renew their leases over time. The DHCP server could be offline, it could have run out of available leases, or forwarding between the server and clients could be improperly configured.

- **Check the configuration of patch cords**—Verify that the wall port is connected to an appropriate port on a switch via the patch panel. If the computer is not connected to an appropriate switch port, it is unlikely to connect to the expected services, such as its default gateway, DHCP, and DNS.

- **Check the VLAN configuration**—If the switch port is not configured with the correct VLAN ID, it can have the same effect as connecting the host to the wrong switch port.

Windows may also report that a network adapter has no Internet access. This means that the adapter has obtained an IP configuration (or is configured statically) but cannot reach msftncsi.com to download a test file. This error indicates that there is an issue with either Internet access at the gateway router or name resolution. On a SOHO network, access the router management interface and verify the Internet connection via a status update page. If the link is down, contact your ISP. The router may also have tools to test connectivity. Verify that it can connect to the servers configured for DNS.

Review Activity:

Networks

Answer the following questions:

1. You are updating a support knowledge base article to help technicians identify port flapping. How can port flapping be identified?

2. A user reports that the Internet is slow. What first step should you take to identify the problem?

3. You are trying to add a computer to a wireless network but cannot detect the network name. What possible causes should you consider?

4. What readings would you expect to gather with a Wi-Fi analyzer?

5. A probe reports that the Internet connection has RTT latency of 200 ms. What is the likely impact on VoIP call quality?

6. A user reports that a "Limited connectivity" desktop notification is displayed on their computer, and they cannot connect to the Internet. Will you need to replace the NIC in the computer?

Lesson 6

Summary

You should be able to summarize services provided by networked hosts and troubleshoot common problems with wired and wireless links.

Guidelines for Supporting Networks

Follow these guidelines to support network services and troubleshoot common problems:

- Document the server roles, such as the following:

  - File/print services based on SMB over port TCP/445 or over legacy NetBIOS over TCP/IP ports UDP/137 and TCP/139.

  - FTP over port TCP/21 and TCP/20.

  - Web services over HTTP port TCP/80 and HTTP Secure over port TCP/443.

  - SMTP over port TCP/25 for server-to-server transport or TCP/587 for clients to submit messages for delivery.

  - Mailbox services such as POP3 over TCP/110 and TCP/995 (secure) and IMAP over TCP/143 and TCP/993 (secure).

  - DHCP network addressing over UDP/67+68 and DNS name resolution over UDP/53.

  - LDAP directory services over port 389.

  - Remote terminal access over SSH (TCP/22), Telnet (TCP/23), or RDP (TCP/3389).

  - SNMP-based network monitoring over UDP/161+162 and syslog-based log collection over UDP/514.

- Document Internet security and authentication architecture, such as the following:

  - Use of AAA servers and protocols to authenticate clients as they connect to the network.

  - Use of proxy servers to manage and optimize outgoing access to websites and services.

  - Use of UTM appliances to implement firewall, malware and intrusion detection, spam and content filtering, and DLP at the network edge.

  - Use of load balancers to provision highly available services.

- Document use of legacy systems, embedded/SCADA systems, and IoT devices to identify special support and security procedures.

- Use network documentation and configuration information plus test tools to identify the scope of lost or intermittent wired or wireless connectivity, speed/latency/jitter issues, and limited connectivity issues.

Lesson 7
Summarizing Virtualization and Cloud Concepts

LESSON INTRODUCTION

The use of virtualization to run multiple OS and application environments on a single hardware platform has huge impacts on modern computing. Delivering environments for testing and training is made much more straightforward, and there are security and management benefits of provisioning servers and desktops as virtual machines.

Virtualization is also the technology underpinning cloud computing. Cloud is one of the most dominant trends in networking and service provision. Many organizations are outsourcing parts of their IT infrastructure, platforms, storage, or services to cloud solutions providers. Virtualization is at the core of cloud service provider networks. If you can compare and contrast the delivery and service models for cloud, your customers will benefit from your advice and support when deploying cloud resources.

Lesson Objectives

In this lesson, you will:

- Summarize client-side virtualization.

- Summarize cloud concepts.

Topic 7A

Summarize Client-Side Virtualization

 CORE 1 EXAM OBJECTIVES COVERED
4.2 Summarize aspects of client-side virtualization.

Virtualization separates multiple software environments—OS, drivers, and applications—from each other and from the physical hardware by using an additional software layer to mediate access. Virtualization can provide flexibility in terms of deploying OS versions for testing and training. It can increase resource utilization by allowing resources to be pooled and leveraged as part of a virtual infrastructure, and it can provide for centralized administration and management of all the resources being used throughout the organization.

As a CompTIA A+ technician, you will often be called upon to deploy, configure, and support virtual machines (VMs). You need to know about the types, capabilities, and uses of different virtualization technologies.

Hypervisors

In a basic configuration, a single computer is designed to run a single OS at any one time. This makes multiple applications available on that computer—whether it be a workstation or server—but the applications must all share a common OS environment. Improvements in CPU and system memory technology mean that all but budget and entry-level computers are now capable of virtualization. **Virtualization** means that multiple OSs can be installed and run simultaneously on one computer.

The software facilitating this is called a "hypervisor." The OSs installed under the hypervisor are called **virtual machines (VMs)** or guest OSs. Any OS expects exclusive access to resources such as the CPU, system memory, storage devices, and peripherals. The hypervisor emulates these resources and mediates access to the actual system hardware to avoid conflicts between the guest OSs. The VMs must be provided with drivers for the emulated hardware components. The hypervisor might be limited in terms of the different types of guest OSs it can support.

There are two basic ways of implementing a hypervisor:

- In a guest OS (or host-based) system, the hypervisor application is itself installed onto a host OS. Examples of these Type 2 hypervisors include VMware Workstation™, Oracle® Virtual Box, and Parallels® Workstation. The hypervisor software must support the host OS, and the computer must have resources to run the host OS, the hypervisor, and the guest operating systems.

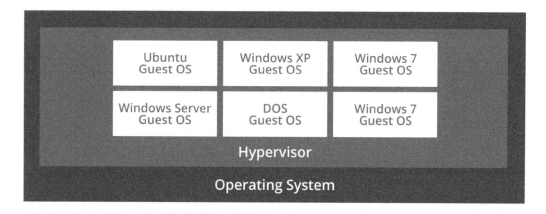

Guest OS virtualization (Type II hypervisor). The hypervisor is an application running within a native OS, and guest OSes are installed within the hypervisor.

- A bare metal virtual platform means that a Type 1 hypervisor is installed directly onto the computer and manages access to the host hardware without going through a host OS. Examples include VMware ESXi® Server, Microsoft's Hyper-V®, and Citrix's XEN Server. The hardware needs to support only the base system requirements for the hypervisor plus resources for the type and number of guest OSs that will be installed.

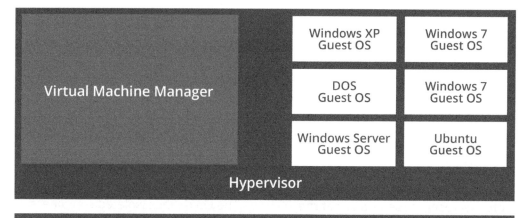

Type I bare metal hypervisor. The hypervisor is installed directly on the host hardware along with a management application, then VMs are installed within the hypervisor.

Uses for Virtualization

There are many different **purposes** for deploying virtualization.

Client-Side Virtualization

Client-side virtualization refers to any solution designed to run on "ordinary" desktops or workstations. Each user will be interacting with the virtualization host directly. Desktop virtual platforms, usually based on some sort of guest OS hypervisor, are typically used for **testing and development**:

- **Sandbox**—Create an isolated environment in which to analyze viruses, worms, and Trojans. As the malware is contained within the guest OS, it cannot infect the researcher's computer or network.

- Support **legacy software applications and OSs**—If the host computers have been upgraded, software apps may not work well with the new OS. In this scenario, the old OS can be installed as a VM, and the application software accessed using the VM.

- **Cross-platform virtualization**—Test software applications under different OSs and/or resource constraints.

- Training—Lab environments can be set up so that students can practice using a live OS and software without impacting the production environment. At the end of the lab, changes to the VM can be discarded so that the original environment is available again for the next student to use.

Server-Side Virtualization

Server-side virtualization means deploying a server role as a virtual machine. For server computers and applications, the main use of virtualization is better hardware utilization through server consolidation. A typical hardware server may have resource utilization of about 10%. This implies that you could pack the server computer with another 8–9 server software instances and obtain the same performance.

Application Virtualization

Application virtualization means that the client either accesses a particular application hosted on a server or streams the application from the server for local processing. This enables programmers and application administrators to ensure that the application used by clients is always updated with the latest code.

Most application virtualization solutions are based on Citrix XenApp. Microsoft has developed an App-V product within its Windows Server range. VMware has the ThinApp product.

Container Virtualization

Container virtualization dispenses with the idea of a hypervisor and instead enforces resource separation at the OS level. The OS defines isolated containers for each user instance to run in. Each container is allocated CPU and memory resources, but the processes all run through the native OS kernel.

These containers may run slightly different OS distributions but cannot run guest OSs of different types (you could not run Windows or Ubuntu in a RedHat Linux container, for instance). Alternatively, the containers might run separate application processes, in which case, the variables and libraries required by the application process are added to the container.

One of the best-known container virtualization products is Docker (docker.com). **Containerization** is also being widely used to implement corporate workspaces on mobile devices.

Container vs. VMs

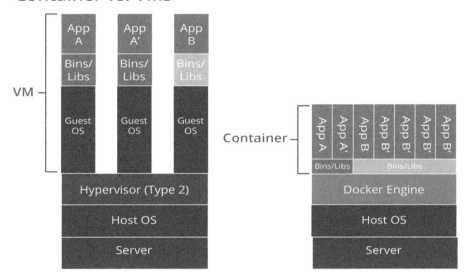

Comparison of virtual machines versus containers.

Virtualization Resource Requirements

To deploy a client-side virtualization workstation, you must identify the **resource requirements** of the hypervisor and of each guest that you plan to install.

CPU and Virtualization Extensions

CPU vendors have built special instruction sets to improve virtualization performance. The Intel technology for this is called "VT-x" (Virtualization Technology), while AMD calls it "AMD-V." Most virtualization products also benefit from a processor feature called "Second Level Address Translations" (SLAT), which improves the performance of virtual memory when multiple VMs are installed. Intel implements SLAT as a feature called "Extended Page Table" (EPT), and AMD calls it "Rapid Virtualization Indexing" (RVI).

Most virtualization software requires a CPU with virtualization support enabled, and even if there is no formal requirement, performance of the VMs will be impaired if hardware-assisted virtualization is not available. Some cheaper CPU models ship without the feature, and it may be disabled in the system firmware. If specifying a computer that will be used for virtualization, check the CPU specification carefully to confirm that it supports Intel VT-x or AMD-V and SLAT and verify that these features are enabled via system setup.

Apart from virtualization extensions, multiple CPU resources—whether through multiple physical processors, multi-core, or HyperThreading—will greatly benefit performance, especially if more than one guest OS is run concurrently.

 If the hypervisor is running in a 64-bit environment, 32-bit guest OSs can still be installed, providing the hypervisor supports them. However, 32-bit hypervisors will not support 64-bit guest OSs.

System Memory

Each guest OS requires sufficient system memory over and above what is required by the host OS/hypervisor. For example, it is recommended that Windows 10 be installed on a computer with at least 2 GB memory. This means that the virtualization workstation must have at least 4 GB RAM to run the host and a single Windows 10 guest OS. If you want to run multiple guest OSs concurrently, the resource demands can quickly add up. If the VMs are only used for development and testing, then performance might not be critical, and you may be able to specify less memory.

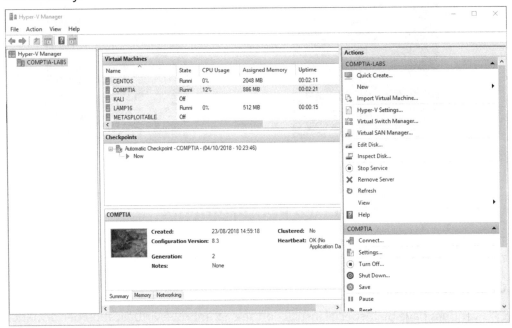

Microsoft Hyper-V hypervisor software. This machine is running several Windows and Linux guest OSs. You can see each is allocated a portion of system memory to use. (Screenshot used with permission from Microsoft.)

Mass Storage

Each guest OS also takes up a substantial amount of disk space. The VM's "hard disk" is stored as an image file on the host. Most hypervisors use a dynamically expanding image format that only takes up space on the host as files are added to the guest OS. Even so, a typical Windows installation might require 20 GB. More space is required if you want to preserve snapshots (the state of a disk at a particular point in time). This is useful if you want to be able to roll back changes you make to the VM during a session.

In an enterprise environment, you need not be constrained by the local disk resources on the host. Disk images could be stored in a high-speed storage area network (SAN).

Networking

A hypervisor will be able to create a virtual network environment through which all the VMs can communicate and a network shared by the host and by VMs on the same host and on other hosts. Enterprise virtual platforms allow the configuration of virtual switches and routers.

Virtualization Security Requirements

Like any computing technology, deploying a virtualization solution comes with **security requirements** and challenges.

Guest OS Security

Each guest OS must be patched and protected against malware like any other OS. Patching each VM individually has performance implications, so in most environments, a new template **image** would be patched and tested then deployed to the production environment. Running security software (antivirus and intrusion prevention) on each guest OS can cause performance problems. Virtualization-specific solutions for running security applications through the host or hypervisor are available.

Ordinary antivirus software installed on the host will NOT detect viruses infecting the guest OS. Scanning the virtual disks of a guest OS from the host could cause serious performance problems.

The process of developing, testing, and deploying VM template images brings about the first major security concern with the virtual platform itself: rogue VMs (one that has been installed without authorization). The uncontrolled deployment of more and more VMs is referred to as **virtual machine sprawl (VM sprawl)**.

System management software can be deployed to detect rogue builds. More generally, the management procedures for developing and deploying machine images need to be tightly drafted and monitored. VMs should conform to an application-specific template with the minimum configuration needed to run that application (that is, not running unnecessary services). Images should not be developed or stored in any sort of environment where they could be infected by malware or have any sort of malicious code inserted. One of the biggest concerns here is of rogue developers or contractors installing backdoors or "logic bombs" within a machine image.

Host Security

Another key security vulnerability in a virtual platform is that the host represents a single point of failure for multiple guest OS instances. For example, if the host loses power, three or four guest VMs and the application services they are running will suddenly go offline.

Hypervisor Security

Apart from ensuring the security of each guest OS and the host machine itself, the hypervisor must also be monitored for security vulnerabilities and exploits. Another issue is **virtual machine escaping (VM escaping)**. This refers to malware running on a guest OS jumping to another guest or to the host. As with any other type of software, it is vital to keep the hypervisor code up to date with patches for critical vulnerabilities.

Review Activity:

Client-Side Virtualization

Answer the following questions:

1. What is a Type 2 hypervisor?

2. You need to provision a virtualization workstation to run four guest OSs simultaneously. Each VM requires 2 GB system RAM. Is an 8 GB workstation sufficient to meet this requirement?

3. What is the main security requirement of a virtualization workstation configured to operate VMs within a sandbox?

Topic 7B

Summarize Cloud Concepts

CORE 1 EXAM OBJECTIVES COVERED
2.2 Compare and contrast common networking hardware. (SDN only)
4.1 Summarize cloud-computing concepts.

The cloud makes almost any type of IT infrastructure available for use over the Internet with pay-per-use billing. Most companies make use of at least one cloud service, and many have moved all of what used to be on-premises server roles to the cloud. In this topic, you will learn to summarize cloud deployment and service models. This will help you to support cloud-connected networks and provide informed advice and support to your users.

Cloud Characteristics

Cloud characteristics are the features that distinguish a cloud provisioning model from on-premises or hosted client/server network architecture.

From the consumer point of view, **cloud computing** is a service that provides on-demand resources—server instances, file storage, databases, or applications—over a network, typically the Internet. The service is a cloud because the end user is not aware of or responsible for any details of the procurement, implementation, or management of the infrastructure that underpins those resources. The end user is interested in and pays for only the services provided by the cloud. The per-use billing for resources consumed by the cloud is referred to as **metered utilization**. The metering measurement is based on the type of resource such as storage, processing, bandwidth, or active users. The metering mechanism should be accessible to the customer via a reporting dashboard, providing complete transparency in usage and billing.

From the provider point of view, provisioning a cloud is like provisioning any other type of large-scale datacenter. Cloud computing almost always uses one or more methods of virtualization to ensure that resources are reliably and quickly provisioned to the client who requires them.

Among other benefits, the cloud provides high availability, scalability, and **elasticity**:

- **High availability (HA)** means that the service experiences very little downtime. For example, a service with "Five Nines" or 99.999% availability experiences only 5 minutes and 15 seconds annual downtime. Downtime can occur as a result of scheduled maintenance and unexpected outages.

- **Scalability** means that the costs involved in supplying the service to more users are linear. For example, if the number of users doubles in a scalable system, the costs to maintain the same level of service would also double (or less than double). If costs more than double, the system is less scalable. Scalability can be achieved by adding nodes (horizontal/scaling out) or by adding resources to each node (vertical/scaling up).

- **Rapid elasticity** refers to the system's ability to handle changes to demand in real time. A system with high elasticity will not experience loss of service or performance if demand suddenly doubles (or triples, or quadruples). Conversely, it may be important for the system to be able to reduce costs when demand is low.

To meet availability, scalability, and elasticity requirements, cloud providers must be able to provision and deprovision resources automatically. This is achieved through pooling of **shared resources** and virtualization. Pooling of shared resources means that the hardware making up the cloud provider's datacenter is not dedicated or reserved to a single customer account. The layers of virtualization used in the cloud architecture allow the provider to provision more CPU, memory, disk, or network resource using management software, rather than (for instance) having to go to the datacenter floor, unplug a server, add a memory module, and reboot.

Common Cloud Deployment Models

A cloud can be provisioned using various ownership and access arrangements. These cloud deployment models can be broadly categorized as follows:

- **Public (or multitenant)** is a service offered over the Internet by **cloud service providers (CSPs)** to cloud consumers, often referred to as tenants. With this model, a CSP can offer subscriptions or pay-as-you-go financing or even provide lower-tier services free of charge. As a shared resource, there are risks regarding performance and security. Multicloud architectures are where the consumer organization uses services from more than one CSP.

- **Private** is cloud infrastructure that is completely private to and owned by the organization. In this case, there is likely to be one business unit dedicated to managing the cloud, while other business units make use of it. With private cloud computing, organizations can exercise greater control over the privacy and security of their services. This type of delivery method is geared more toward banking and governmental services that require strict access control in their operations.

- **Community** is where several organizations share the costs of either a hosted private or fully private cloud. This is usually done to pool resources for a common concern, such as standardization and security policies.

- **Hybrid** is a cloud computing solution that implements some sort of hybrid public/ private/community. For example, a travel organization may run a sales website for most of the year using a private cloud but "break out" the solution to a public cloud at times when much higher utilization is forecast. As another example, a hybrid deployment may be used to provide some functions via a public cloud but keep sensitive or regulated infrastructure, applications, and data on-premises.

Common Cloud Service Models

As well as the deployment model—public, private, hybrid, or community— **cloud service models** are often differentiated on the level of complexity and preconfiguration provided. Some of the most common models are infrastructure, software, platform, and desktop.

Infrastructure as a Service

Infrastructure as a service (IaaS) is a means of provisioning IT resources, such as servers, load balancers, and storage area network (SAN) components, quickly. Rather than purchase these components and the Internet links they require, you deploy them as needed from the service provider's datacenter. Examples include Amazon Elastic Compute Cloud (aws.amazon.com/ec2), Microsoft® Azure® Virtual Machines (azure.microsoft.com/services/virtual-machines), and OpenStack® (openstack.org).

Software as a Service

Software as a service (SaaS) is a different model of provisioning software applications. Rather than purchasing software licenses for a given number of seats, a business would access software hosted on a supplier's servers on a pay-as-you-go arrangement. Virtual infrastructure allows developers to provision on-demand applications much more quickly than previously. The applications can be developed and tested in the cloud without the need to test and deploy on client computers. Examples include Microsoft Office 365® (support.office.com), Salesforce® (salesforce.com), and Google Workspace™ (workspace.google.com).

Platform as a Service

Platform as a service (PaaS) provides resources somewhere between SaaS and IaaS. A typical PaaS solution would deploy servers and storage network infrastructure (as per IaaS) but also provide a multi-tier web application/database platform on top. This platform could be based on Oracle® or MS SQL or PHP and MySQL™. Examples include Oracle Database (cloud.oracle.com/paas), Microsoft Azure SQL Database (azure.microsoft.com/services/sql-database), and Google App Engine™ (cloud.google.com/appengine).

As distinct from SaaS though, this platform would not be configured to run an application. Your own developers would have to create the software (the sales contact or e-commerce application) that runs using the platform. The service provider would be responsible for the integrity and availability of the platform components, but you would be responsible for the security of the application you created on the platform.

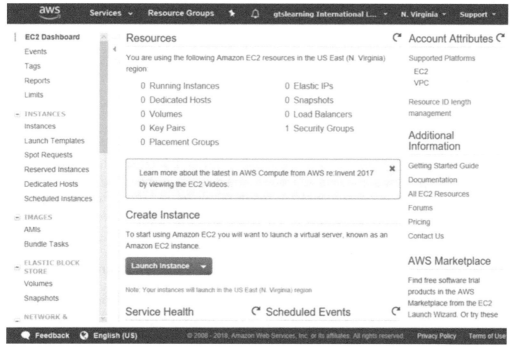

Dashboard for Amazon Web Services Elastic Compute Cloud (EC2) IaaS/PaaS. (Screenshot courtesy of Amazon.)

Desktop Virtualization

Virtual desktop infrastructure (VDI) refers to using VMs as a means of provisioning corporate desktops. In a typical **desktop virtualization** solution, desktop computers are replaced by low-spec thin client computers.

When the thin client starts, it boots a minimal OS, allowing the user to log on to a VM stored on the company server or cloud infrastructure. The user makes a connection to the VM using some sort of remote desktop protocol, such as Microsoft Remote Desktop or Citrix ICA. The thin client must locate the correct image and use an appropriate authentication mechanism. There may be a 1:1 mapping based on machine name or IP address, or the process of finding an image may be handled by a connection broker.

All application processing and data storage in the virtual desktop environment (VDE) or workspace is performed by the server. The thin client computer need only be powerful enough to display the screen image, play audio, and transfer mouse, key commands and video, and audio information over the network.

The virtualization server hosting the virtual desktops can be provisioned either as an **on-premises server** (on the same local network as the clients) or in the **cloud**. This centralization of data makes it easier to back up. The desktop VMs are easier to support and troubleshoot. They are better locked against unsecure user practices because any changes to the VM can easily be overwritten from the template image. With VDI, it is also easier for a company to completely offload their IT infrastructure to a third-party services company.

The main disadvantage is that during a failure in the server and network infrastructure, users have no local processing ability. This can mean that downtime events may be more costly in terms of lost productivity.

 *Provisioning VDI as a cloud service is often referred to as **desktop as a service (DaaS)**.*

Cloud File Storage

Cloud storage is a particular type of software as a service. Most Office productivity suites are backed by some level of free and paid storage. The cloud storage app OneDrive is closely integrated with Microsoft Windows and the Office 365 suite, for instance. Dropbox is another file storage service that can be accessed similarly. Other cloud file storage services that can be synchronized between all of a user's devices include iCloud from Apple and Google Drive.

One of the advantages of cloud storage is automated **file synchronization** between different devices, such as a PC and smartphone. Cloud storage also allows file sharing. Multiple users can simultaneously access the content to work collaboratively, or they can access it at different times. Edits by each user can be tracked, and review features allow users to comment on and highlight parts of the document.

As well as supporting storage apps for customers, file synchronization is also important within the cloud. Files are often replicated between the datacenters underpinning the cloud to improve access times. For example, content delivery networks (CDNs) specialize in provisioning media and resources for websites to multiple Internet exchange points (IXPs) where they are close to ISP networks and can be downloaded more quickly by customers.

It is also important to replicate data within the datacenter to ensure that it can be provisioned reliably. Storage backing the various XaaS models is offered in cost tiers that represent how quickly it can be replicated to datacenter availability zones and between different geographical areas.

Software-Defined Networking

Cloud services require the rapid provisioning and deprovisioning of server instances and networks. This means that these components must be fully accessible to scripting. **Software-defined networking (SDN)** is a model for how these processes can be used to provision and deprovision networks.

In the SDN model defined by IETF (datatracker.ietf.org/doc/html/rfc7426), network functions are divided into three layers. The top and bottom layers are application and infrastructure:

- The application layer applies business logic to make decisions about how traffic should be prioritized and secured and where it should be switched.

- The infrastructure layer contains the devices (physical or virtual) that handle the actual forwarding (switching and routing) of traffic.

The principal innovation of SDN is to insert a control layer between the application and infrastructure layers. The functions of the control plane are implemented by a virtual device referred to as the "SDN controller." Each layer exposes an **application programming interface (API)** that can be automated by scripts that call functions in the layer above or below. The interface between SDN applications and the SDN controller is described as the service interface or as the "northbound" API, while that between the SDN controller and infrastructure devices is the "southbound" API.

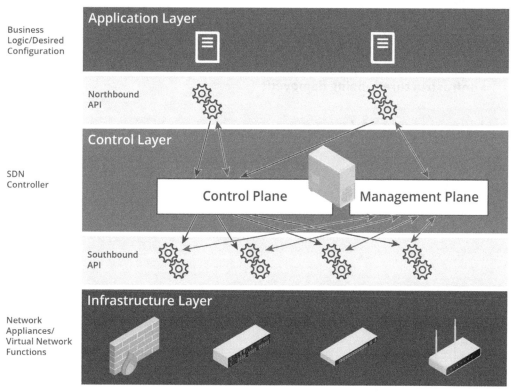

Layers and components in a typical software defined networking architecture.
(Images © 123RF.com.)

Review Activity:

Cloud Concepts

Answer the following questions:

1. A cloud service provides a billing dashboard that reports the uptime, disk usage, and network bandwidth consumption of a virtual machine. What type of cloud characteristic does this demonstrate?

2. A company has contracted the use of a remote datacenter to offer exclusive access to platform as a service resources to its internal business users. How would such a cloud solution be classed?

3. A technician provisions a network of virtual machines running web server, scripting environment, and database software for use by programmers working for the sales and marketing department. What type of cloud model has been deployed?

4. When users connect to the network, they use a basic hardware terminal to access a desktop hosted on a virtualization server. What type of infrastructure is being deployed?

Lesson 7

Summary

You should be able to summarize aspects of client-side virtualization and cloud computing.

Guidelines for Supporting Virtualization and Cloud Computing

Follow these guidelines to support the use of virtualization and cloud services in your networks:

- Identify user requirements to run client-side virtualization for a given purpose (sandbox, test development, legacy software/OS, cross-platform support).

- Identify CPU, system RAM, mass storage, and networking resource requirements for the host OS and/or hypervisor plus intended guest machines. Ensure that computers provisioned as virtualization workstations have hardware-assisted virtualization CPU extensions enabled.

- Document use of hypervisors and VMs and establish a plan to manage and monitor security requirements, such as patching, blocking rogue VM sprawl, and preventing VM escaping.

- Given security requirements and costs, determine the best cloud deployment model from public, private, community, and hybrid.

- Evaluate cloud service providers to ensure that they meet criteria for reliable and responsive cloud delivery characteristics, such as metered utilization, rapid elasticity, high availability, and file synchronization.

- Assess requirements for cloud service models, such as IaaS, SaaS, PaaS, and VDI.

Lesson 8
Supporting Mobile Devices

LESSON INTRODUCTION

This lesson focuses on mobile devices and how they differ from desktop systems in terms of features, upgrade/repair procedures, and troubleshooting. As a certified CompTIA® A+® technician, you will be expected to configure, maintain, and troubleshoot laptops, smartphones, and tablets. With the proper information and the right skills, you will be ready to support these devices as efficiently as you support their desktop counterparts.

Lesson Objectives

In this lesson, you will:

- Set up mobile devices and peripherals.

- Configure mobile device apps.

- Install and configure laptop hardware.

- Troubleshoot mobile device issues.

Topic 8A

Set Up Mobile Devices and Peripherals

CORE 1 EXAM OBJECTIVES COVERED
1.2 Compare and contrast the display components of mobile devices.
1.3 Given a scenario, set up and configure accessories and ports of mobile devices.

The design of laptops, smartphones, and tablets makes them portable and easy to use on the move. At the same time, mobile devices can be connected to peripherals and used comfortably for an extended period while sitting at a desk. In this topic, you will examine the portability features, connection types, and accessories used for mobiles. Being able to compare and contrast these features will make you better able to advise and support your users in their selection and use of portable computing devices.

Mobile Display Types

For a device to be considered mobile, its form factor must closely integrate both the system components and peripheral devices for video, sound, and input control. Smartphone, tablet, and hybrid tablet/laptop form factors solve this design issue by using a **touch screen** as output and input device and as part of the system case to hold the CPU, RAM, mass storage, networking, and power components.

Liquid Crystal Displays

Most mobile devices use a flat-panel screen technology based on a type of **liquid crystal display (LCD)**. A liquid crystal is a compound whose properties change with the application of voltage. Each picture element (pixel) in a color LCD comprises subpixels with filters to generate the primary red, green, and blue (RGB) colors. Each pixel is addressed by a transistor to vary the intensity of each cell, therefore creating the gamut (range of colors shades) that the display can generate.

In the types of flat panel used for computer and mobile device displays, the liquid crystal elements and transistors are placed on a **thin film transistor (TFT),** and such LCD panels are often just referred to as "TFTs." There are three main types of TFT technology:

- **Twisted nematic (TN)** crystals twist or untwist in response to the voltage level. This is the earliest type of TFT technology and might still be found in budget displays. This type of display supports faster response times than other TFT technologies. Fast response time helps to reduce ghosting and motion trail artifacts when the input source uses a high frame rate.

You need to distinguish between refresh rate and response time when evaluating displays. Refresh rate is the speed at which the whole image is redrawn, measured in Hz. The refresh rate should be a multiple of the video source frame rate. Response time is the time taken for a pixel to change color, measured in milliseconds (ms).

- **In-plane switching (IPS)** uses crystals that rotate rather than twist. The main benefit is to deliver better color reproduction at a wider range of viewing angles. Most IPS panels support 178/178 degree horizontal and vertical viewing angles. The main drawback of early and cheaper IPS screens is slightly worse response times. A high-quality IPS display will usually be the best TFT option for both gaming and graphics/design work, however, as it will be capable of similar response times to TN while retaining better color reproduction and viewing angles.

- **Vertical alignment (VA)** uses crystals that tilt rather than twist or rotate. This technology supports a wide color gamut and the best contrast-ratio performance. Contrast ratio is the difference in shade between a pixel set to black and one set to white. For example, where a high-end IPS panel might support a 1200:1 contrast ratio, a VA panel would be 2000:1 or 3000:1. However, viewing angles are generally not quite as good as IPS, and response times are worse than TN, making a VA panel more prone to motion blur and ghosting.

LED Backlit Displays

An LCD must be illuminated to produce a clear image. In a TFT, the illumination is provided by an array of **light-emitting diodes (LED)**. Most smartphone and tablet screens use edge lighting where the LEDs are arranged at the top or bottom of the screen, and a diffuser makes the light evenly bright across the whole of the screen.

*Early types of laptop display used a cold cathode fluorescent (CCFL) bulb as a backlight. The bulb requires AC power, so an **inverter** component is used to convert from the DC power supplied by the motherboard to the AC power for the bulb. This type of panel is no longer in mainstream production, but you might come across older laptop models that use it.*

Organic LED Displays

In an **organic LED (OLED)** display, or technically an advanced matrix OLED (AMOLED), each pixel is generated by a separate LED. This means that the panel does not require a separate **backlight**. This allows much better contrast ratios and allows the display to be thinner, lighter, and consume less power. Also, OLEDs can be made from plastic with no requirement for a layer of glass. This means that the display can be curved to different shapes. Manufacturers are even experimenting with flexible, roll-up displays.

OLED has two main drawbacks. One is is that the maximum brightness may be lower than with LCDs, making the display less clear when used in bright sunlight. An OLED display is also more susceptible to burn-in, where displaying the same static image for many hours causes the LEDs to retain the image persistently.

Mobile Display Components

The display panel is only a single layer within the screen assembly for a mobile device. Several other **display components** make up the whole screen.

Digitizer Functions

A touch screen can also be referred to as a **digitizer** because of the way it converts analog touch input to digital software instructions. The digitizer is sandwiched between a layer of protective glass and the display panel. Analog signals are detected by a grid of sensors when you tap or swipe the surface of the screen. The information from the sensors is sent through the digitizer cable to a circuit that converts the analog signal to a digital signal.

Modern mobile devices use capacitive digitizers. These capacitive displays support multitouch, meaning that gestures such as "sweeping" or "pinching" the screen can be interpreted as events and responded to by software in a particular way. Newer devices are also starting to provide haptic feedback, or touch responsiveness, making virtual key presses or gestures feel more real to the user.

The touchscreen itself is covered by a thin layer of scratch-resistant, shock-resistant tempered glass, such as Corning's Gorilla Glass. Some users may also apply an additional screen protector. If so, these need to be applied carefully (without bubbling) so as not to interfere with the touch capabilities of the screen.

Typical smartphone form factor. (Image © 123RF.com)

Rotating and Removable Screens

Most mobile devices can be used either in portrait or landscape orientation. Components called *accelerometers* and *gyroscopes* can detect when the device changes position and adjust the screen orientation appropriately. As well as switching screen orientation, this can be used as a control mechanism (for example, a driving game could allow the tablet itself to function as a steering wheel).

Some laptops are based on tablet hybrid form factors where the touch screen display can be fully flipped or rotated between portrait and landscape orientations. Another approach, used on Microsoft's Surface tablet/laptop hybrids, is for the keyboard portion of the laptop to be detachable and for the screen to work independently as a tablet.

Mobile Device Accessories

Some popular accessories and peripheral options for mobile devices include the following:

Touchpads, Trackpads, and Drawing Pads

The digitizer touch and gesture support built into touchscreens can be deployed in a variety of other form factors:

- Touchpad usually refers to the embedded panel on a laptop computer that is used for pointer control. Most touchpads now support multitouch and gestures.

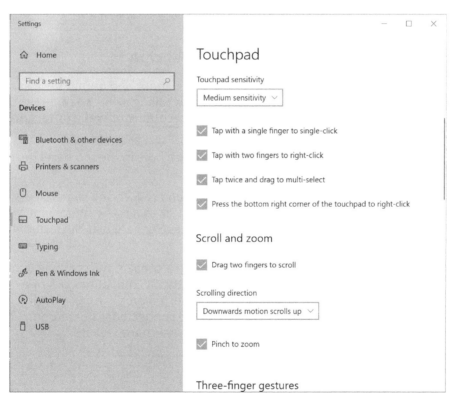

Use the Settings app in Windows 10 to configure touchpad settings, such as sensitivity, tap events, and gestures. (Screenshot courtesy of Microsoft.)

- **Trackpad** can be used to mean the same thing as *touchpad*, but it is often used to mean a larger-format device attached as a peripheral.

- Drawing pad also refers to a large-format touch device attached as a peripheral. These are also called graphics tablets as they are most widely used for sketching and painting in a digital art application.

A touch device can require careful configuration to set up gesture support, calibrate to the screen area, and adjust sensitivity. This might be performed via OS settings or by installing a driver or app for the device.

Touch Pens

Most drawing pads and some touchscreens can be used with a **touch pen** or stylus rather than fingers. A stylus allows for more precise control and can be used for handwriting and drawing. This functionality is often referred to as natural input. Touch pens are available in a wide range of sizes, from small styluses designed for use with smartphones to full-size pens designed for use with tablet touchscreens and dedicated graphics pads. Touch pens designed for use with drawing pads have removable and changeable nibs for use as different pen/brush types with digital art applications.

A digitizer may only be compatible with a specific touch pen model or range. Capacitive touch pens should work with most touch screen types. Drawing pads often use more sophisticated active pens with better support for pressure sensitivity, nib angles, palm rejection (ignoring the user's palm if it is resting on the pad), and additional input controls, such as switching between drawing and eraser functions.

Microphone, Speakers, and Camera/Webcam

Mobile devices also feature integrated audio/video input and output devices. A **microphone** is used to record audio and for voice calling, while **speakers** produce audio output. A **digital camera** allows for video recording or **web conferencing** and can also be used to take still pictures.

On a laptop, the **microphone** is exposed by a small hole in the top bezel next to the camera lens and an LED to illuminate the subject.

Smartphones and tablets have both front-facing and rear-facing camera lenses, both of which can function either as a still camera or as a **webcam** for video recording and streaming. The microphone and speakers are usually positioned on the bottom edge of the device.

An external **headset** or ear bud set provides both a speaker microphone and headphone speakers. Wired headsets use either the 3.5 mm audio jack or a USB/Lightning connector. If no audio jack is supported on the mobile device, an adapter cable can be used. Wireless headsets are connected via Bluetooth. These connections can also be used for more powerful external speakers.

Wi-Fi Networking

Every laptop, smartphone, and tablet supports a Wi-Fi radio. On a smartphone or tablet, the indicator on the status bar at the top of the screen shows the data link in use as the current Internet connection method. A device will usually default to Wi-Fi if present and show a signal strength icon.

Enabling and Disabling Wi-Fi

Each type of wireless radio link can be toggled on or off individually using the Control Center (swipe up from the bottom in iOS) or notification shade (swipe down from the top in Android). For example, you could disable the cellular data network while leaving Wi-Fi enabled to avoid incurring charges for data use over the cellular network. You can use the Settings menu to choose which network to connect to or to configure a manual connection to a hidden SSID.

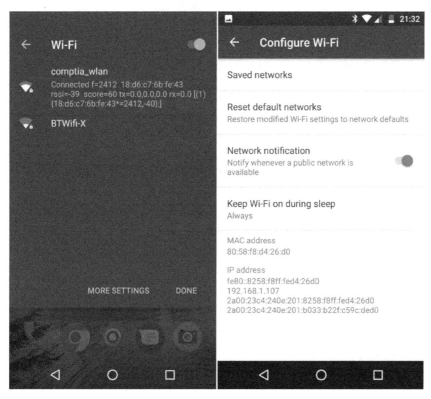

Using Android to join a Wi-Fi network (left). The device's network address can be checked using the Advanced Settings page (right). (Screenshot courtesy of Android platform, a trademark of Google LLC.)

Airplane Mode

Most airlines prohibit passengers from using radio-based devices while on board a plane. A device can be put into **airplane mode** to comply with these restrictions, though some carriers insist that devices must be switched off completely at times, such as during take-off and landing. Airplane mode disables some or all of the wireless features (cellular data, Wi-Fi, GPS, Bluetooth, and NFC), depending on the device type and model. On some devices, some services can selectively be re-enabled while still in airplane mode.

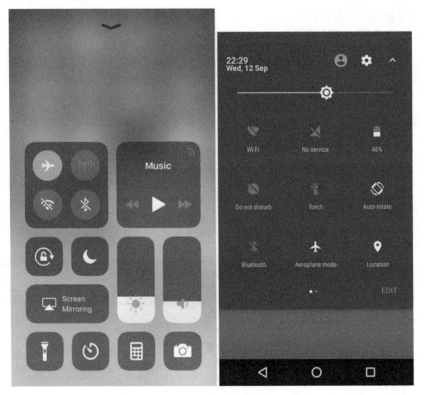

iOS iPhone (left) and Android phone (right) with Airplane (Aeroplane) mode enabled.
(Screenshots reprinted with permission from Apple Inc., and Android platform,
a trademark of Google LLC.)

Wi-Fi Antenna Connector/Placement

Another important point to note about the display screen is that the antenna wires for the Wi-Fi and cellular radios are run around it. The antenna wires are connected to the adapter via internal wiring.

Cellular Data Networking

Cellular data networking means connecting to the Internet via the device's cellular radio and the handset's network provider. The data rate depends on the technology supported by both the phone and the cell tower (3G or 4G, for instance). When a mobile device uses the cellular provider's network, there are likely to be charges based on the amount of data downloaded. These charges can be particularly high when the phone is used abroad (referred to as *international roaming*), so it is often useful to be able to disable mobile data access.

Global System for Mobile Communications vs. Code-Division Multiple Access

There are two competing 2G and 3G cellular network types, established in different markets:

- **Global System for Mobile Communication (GSM)** allows subscribers to use a removable subscriber identity module (SIM) card to use an unlocked handset with their chosen network provider. GSM is adopted internationally and by AT&T and T-Mobile in the United States.

- **Code Division Multiple Access (CDMA)** means that the handset is directly managed by the provider and there is no removable SIM card. CDMA adoption is largely restricted to the telecom providers Sprint and Verizon. Information that the cellular radio needs to connect to the network is provided as a **preferred roaming list (PRL)** update. A PRL update can be triggered from the device's Settings menu or by dialing a special code, such as ***228**.

- **Long Term Evolution (LTE)** 4G and 5G standards have removed this distinction. All 4G and 5G cellular data connections require a SIM card. Devices with SIM cards do not require the PRL to be updated manually.

Cellular Networking Data Indicators

When the cellular radio is enabled, the icon on the status bar shows which generation of data connection has been established:

- G/E or 1X—the icons G or E (for GSM) or 1X (for CDMA) represent minimal **2G** service levels, with connection speeds of 50–400 Kb/s only.

- **3G**—Universal Mobile Telecommunications Service (UMTS) on a GSM handset or Evolution-Data Optimized (EV-DO) on CDMA networks, working at up to around 3 Mb/s.

- H/H+—High Speed Packet Access (HSPA) provides improved "3.75G" data rates on GSM networks. Nominally, HSPA+ can work at up to 42 Mb/s, but real-world performance is likely to be lower.

- **4G**/4G+—LTE-Advanced has a maximum downlink of 300 Mb/s in theory, but no provider networks can deliver that sort of speed at the time of writing, with around 20–90 Mb/s typical of real-word performance.

- **5G**—Real-world speeds are nowhere near the hoped-for 1 Gb/s rate, ranging from about 50 Mb/s to 300 Mb/s at the time of writing.

Enabling and Disabling Cellular Data

The cellular data connection can usually be enabled or disabled via the notification shade, but there will also be additional configuration options via the Settings menu. You can usually set usage warnings and caps and prevent selected apps from using cellular data connections. Some handsets support the use of two SIMs, and you can choose which one to use for data networking.

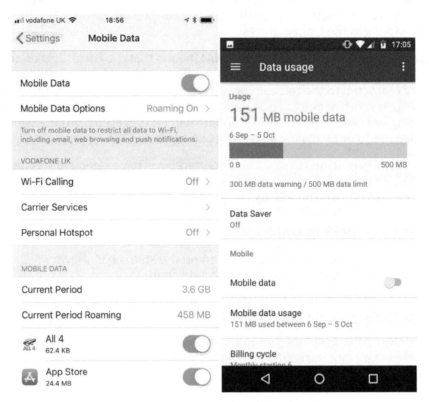

Configuring cellular data options in iOS (left) and Android (right).
(Screenshots reprinted with permission from Apple Inc., and
Android platform, a trademark of Google LLC.)

Mobile Hotspots and Tethering

A smartphone or tablet can be configured as a personal hotspot to share its cellular data connection with other computer devices. To enable a mobile **hotspot**, configure the device with the usual settings for an access point (network name, security type, and passphrase), and then other devices can connect to it as they would with any other Wi-Fi access points.

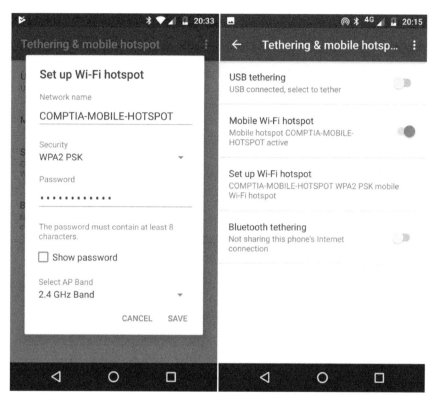

Configuring mobile hotspot settings (left), then enabling it (right). In this figure, hosts can connect to the "hippo" network and use the device's cellular data plan to get Internet access. (Screenshot courtesy of Android platform, a trademark of Google LLC.)

Tethering means connecting another device to a smartphone or tablet via USB or Bluetooth so that it can share its cellular data connection. Not all carriers allow tethering, and some only allow it as a chargeable service add-on. Connect the device to the PC via USB or Bluetooth, then configure tethering settings through the **Settings > Network** menu.

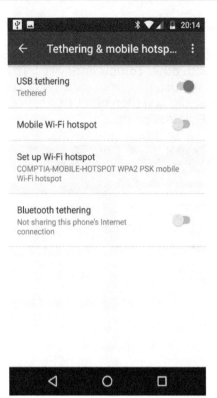

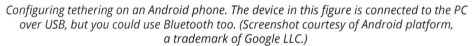

Configuring tethering on an Android phone. The device in this figure is connected to the PC over USB, but you could use Bluetooth too. (Screenshot courtesy of Android platform, a trademark of Google LLC.)

Mobile Device Wired Connection Methods

Although mobile devices are designed to be self-contained, they still need to support a variety of connection methods. These cabled and wireless interfaces allow the user to attach peripheral devices, share data with a PC, or attach a charging cable.

Laptop Ports

Laptops ship with standard wired ports for connectivity. The ports are usually arranged on the left and right edges. Older laptops might have ports at the back of the chassis. There will be at least one video port for an external display device, typically HDMI or DisplayPort/Thunderbolt, but possibly VGA or DVI on older laptops. There will also be a few USB Type A ports and one or more USB Type C ports on a modern laptop, some of which may also function as Thunderbolt ports.

Other standard ports include microphone and speaker jacks and RJ45 (Ethernet) for networking. Finally, a laptop might come with a memory card reader.

Smartphone and Tablet Connectors

Modern Android-based smartphones and tablets use the **USB-C** connector for wired peripherals and charging. The **Micro-B** USB and **Mini-B** connector form factors are only found on old devices.

Most iPhone and iPad Apple devices use the proprietary **Lightning** connector. Some of the latest iPad models, such as the iPad Pro, use USB-C.

Serial Interfaces

Serial is one of the oldest and simplest computer interfaces. While not many mobile devices have hardware serial ports, the software serial port is often used for programming and connectivity with some types of peripheral device. The serial software interface is called a **universal asynchronous receiver transmitter (UART)** port. On Android, UART interface data can be transferred over a USB hardware port or over Bluetooth. Apple devices do not allow direct connections to UART over the Lightning connector, except through enrollment in the developer program.

 Another use for a serial interface is to connect a laptop to the serial port of a managed switch or router. As most laptops no longer have 9-pin RS-232 hardware ports, these connections use special adapter cables that connect to a USB or RJ45 port on the laptop.

Bluetooth Wireless Connections

A **wireless connection for accessories** is often a better option for mobile devices than a cable. A **Bluetooth** wireless radio creates a short-range personal area network (PAN) to share data with a PC, connect to a printer, use a wireless headset, and so on.

Enabling Bluetooth

Bluetooth needs to be **enabled** for use via device settings. You may also want to change the device name—remember that this is displayed publicly.

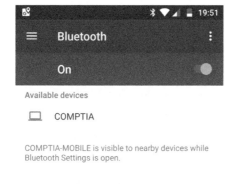

Enabling Bluetooth on an Android device. In this figure, the Android device is named "COMPTIA-MOBILE." "COMPTIA" is a nearby Windows PC with Bluetooth enabled. (Screenshot courtesy of Android platform, a trademark of Google LLC.)

Enable Pairing

To connect via Bluetooth, the Bluetooth radio on each device must be put into discoverable or **pairing** mode. Opening the settings page makes the device discoverable. In iOS, Bluetooth devices are configured via **Settings > General > Bluetooth** (or **Settings > Bluetooth**, depending on the iOS version). In Android, you can access Bluetooth settings via the notification shade. In Windows, you can manage Bluetooth Devices using the applet in Control Panel or Windows Settings and the Bluetooth icon in the notification area.

The settings page will show a list of nearby Bluetooth-enabled devices that are also in discoverable mode. Select a device to proceed. The pairing system should automatically generate a passkey or **PIN code** when a connection request is received. Input or confirm the key on the destination device, and accept the connection.

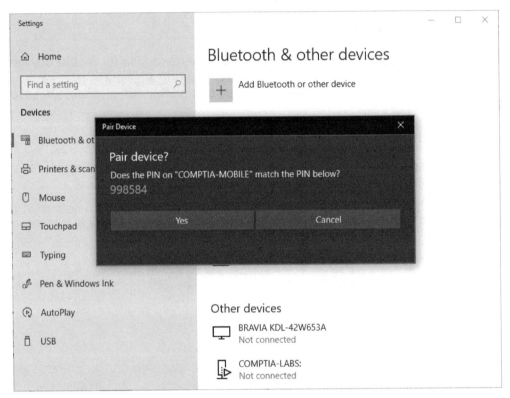

Pairing a Windows 10 computer with a smartphone. (Screenshot courtesy of Microsoft.)

Test Bluetooth Connection

To **test** the connection, you can simply try using the device—check that music plays through Bluetooth headphones, for example. If you are connecting a device and a PC, you can use the Bluetooth icon to try to send a file.

If you cannot connect a device, check that both have been made discoverable. If you make a computer or mobile device discoverable, check the pairing list regularly to confirm that the devices listed are valid.

Near-Field Communication Wireless Connections

An increasing range of mobile devices have **near-field communication (NFC)** chips built in. NFC allows for very short-range data transmission (up to about 20 cm/8 in) to activate a receiver chip in the contactless reader. The data rates achievable are very low, but these transactions do not require exchanging large amounts of information.

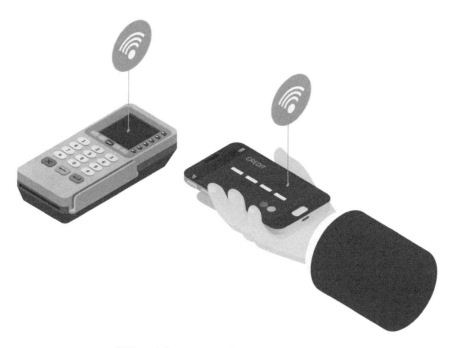

NFC mobile payment. (Image © 123RF.com)

NFC allows a mobile device to make payments via contactless point-of-sale (PoS) machines. To configure a payment service, the user enters their credit card information into a wallet app on the device. The wallet app does not transmit the original credit card information, but a one-time token that is interpreted by the card merchant and linked back to the relevant customer account. There are three major wallet apps: Apple Pay, Google Pay (formerly Android Pay), and Samsung Pay. Some PoS readers may only support a particular type of wallet app or apps.

On an Android device, NFC can be enabled or disabled via settings. With most wallets, the device must be unlocked to initiate a transaction over a certain amount.

NFC can also be used to configure other types of connection, such as pairing Bluetooth devices. For example, if a smartphone and headset both support NFC, tapping the headset will automatically negotiate a Bluetooth connection.

Port Replicators and Docking Stations

A laptop, tablet, or smartphone does not always provide sufficient connection methods. Port replicators and docking stations allow the connection of more peripheral devices so that a mobile can be used at a desk in a similar manner to a PC.

Port Replicator

A **port replicator** either attaches to a special connector on the back or underside of a laptop or is connected via USB. It provides a full complement of ports for devices such as keyboards, monitors, mice, and network connections. A replicator does not normally add any other functionality to the laptop.

A port replicator. (Image by Elnur Amikishiyev © 123RF.com)

Docking Station

A **docking station** is a sophisticated port replicator that may support add-in cards or drives via a media bay. When docked, a portable computer can function like a desktop machine or use additional features, such as a full-size expansion card.

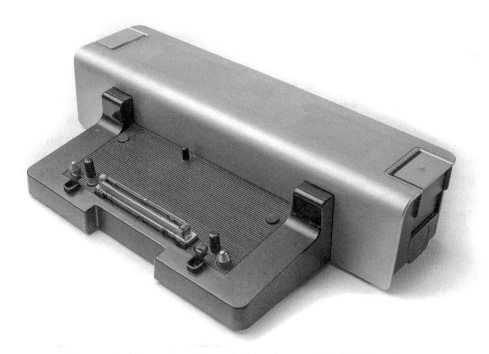

A laptop docking station. (Image by Luca Lorenzelli © 123RF.com)

Docking stations with media bays and adapter card support are no longer common. Often, the term "docking station" is just used to mean port replicator.

Smartphone and Tablet Docks

As modern smartphones develop, manufacturers have been able to include processing power to rival some desktops and sometimes even replace them altogether. A smartphone/tablet dock connects the device to a monitor, external speakers, and keyboard/mouse input devices via the mobile's USB or Lightning port.

Example of a smartphone dock. (Image © 123RF.com)

Review Activity:

Mobile Devices and Peripherals

Answer the following questions:

1. A company is ordering custom-built laptops to supply to its field sales staff for use predominantly as presentation devices. The company can specify the type of panel used and has ruled out IPS and OLED on cost grounds. Which of the remaining mainstream display technologies is best suited to the requirement?

2. You are writing a knowledge base article for remote sales staff who need to use their smartphones to facilitate Internet connectivity for their laptops from out-of-office locations. What distinguishes the hotspot and tethering means of accomplishing this?

3. What type of peripheral port would you expect to find on a current generation smartphone?

4. You are assisting a user with pairing a smartphone to a Bluetooth headset. What step must the user take to start the process?

5. You are identifying suitable smartphone models to issue to field sales staff. The models must be able to use digital payments. What type of sensor must the devices have?

Topic 8B

Configure Mobile Device Apps

 CORE 1 EXAM OBJECTIVES COVERED
1.4 Given a scenario, configure basic mobile-device network connectivity and application support.

Supporting mobile devices also involves supporting the apps that run on them. In this context, it is important to realize that the use of mobile devices within companies can raise support and security challenges. Some companies allow employees to use personal devices; others allow personal use of company-supplied devices. In these scenarios, policies and controls must be used to protect the confidentiality and integrity of workplace data and the privacy of a user's personal data.

Mobile Apps

An app is an installable program that extends the functionality of the mobile device. An app must be written and compiled for a particular mobile operating system. For example, an app written for Apple iOS cannot directly be installed on Android. The developer must make a version for each OS.

iOS Apps

In iOS, apps are distributed via Apple's **App Store**. Apps must be submitted to and approved by Apple before they are released to users. This is also referred to as the *walled garden model* and is designed to prevent the spread of malware or code that could cause faults or crashes. Apps can use a variety of commercial models, including free to use, free with in-app purchases, or paid-for.

Third-party developers can create apps for iOS using Xcode, which is Apple's integrated development environment (IDE), and the programming language Swift. Xcode can only be installed and run on a computer using macOS.

Apple's App Store and app permission settings. This app is already installed, but an update is available. (Screenshot reprinted with permission from Apple Inc., and WhatsApp.)

Android Apps

Android's app model is more relaxed, with apps available from both Google Play and third-party sites, such as Amazon's app store. The Java-based IDE, Android Studio, is available on Linux, Windows, and macOS.

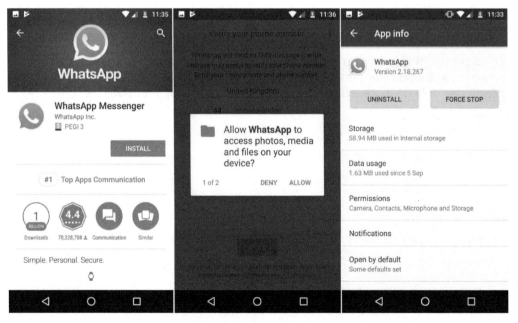

Use the Play Store to install an app (left), grant the app permissions (middle), and review permissions and other settings (right). (Screenshots courtesy of Android platform, a trademark of Google LLC., and WhatsApp.)

Permissions

On both iOS and Android, apps are suppose to run in a sandbox and have only the privileges granted by the user. An app will normally prompt when it needs to obtain permissions. If these are not granted, or if they need to be revoked later, you can do this via the app's Settings page.

Account Setup

Most mobile devices are designed to be used by a single user. The owner's user account is configured when the device is used for the first time (or re-initialized). This account is used to manage the apps installed on the device by representing the user on the app store. iOS requires an Apple ID, while an Android device requires either a Google Account or a similar vendor account, such as a Samsung Account. This type of account just requires you to select a unique ID (email address) and to configure your credentials (pattern lock, fingerprint, face ID, and so on). Accounts can also be linked to a cellphone number or alternative email address for verification and recovery functions.

As well as managing the app store, the owner account can be used to access various services, such as an email account and cloud storage. However, the device owner might want to use multiple other accounts or digital identities in conjunction with different apps. These accounts allow app settings and data to be **synchronized between multiple devices**. For example, a user can access his or her contacts list from both his or her mobile device and his or her laptop computer. Some examples of these services include:

- **Microsoft 365**—A Microsoft digital identity is used to access cloud subscriptions for the Office productivity software suite and the OneDrive cloud storage service. Microsoft identities use the @outlook.com domain by default but can be registered with a third-party address also.

- **Google Workspace**—A Google Account (@gmail.com) grants free access to Google's Workspace productivity software and the free storage tier on Google Drive.

- **iCloud**—An Apple ID (@icloud.com) grants free access to Apple's productivity software and the free storage tier on iCloud.

The device owner can set up sub-accounts for services not represented by their Apple ID or Google Account, such as a corporate email account. Each app can set up a subaccount too. For example, the device might have accounts for apps such as Facebook or LinkedIn.

Account settings allow you to choose which features of a particular account type are enabled to synchronize data with the device. You can also add and delete accounts from here.

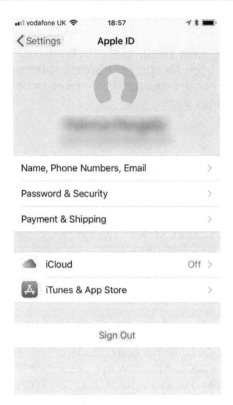

iOS supports a single Apple ID account per device. (Screenshot reprinted with permission from Apple Inc.)

Types of Data to Synchronize

Mobile device synchronization (sync) refers to copying data back and forth between different devices. This might mean between a PC and smartphone or between a smartphone, a tablet, and a PC. Many people have multiple devices and need to keep information up to date on all of them. If users edits contact records on a phone, they want the changes to appear when they next log into email on their PC.

There are many different types of information that users might synchronize and many issues you might face dealing with synchronization problems.

Contacts

A **contact** is a record with fields for name, address, email address(es), phone numbers, notes, and so on. One issue with contacts is that people tend to create them on different systems, and there can be issues matching fields or phone number formats when importing from one system to another using a file format such as comma separated values (CSV). vCard represents one standard format and is widely supported now. Maintaining a consistent, single set of contact records is challenging for most people, whatever the technology solutions available!

Calendar

A **calendar** item is a record with fields for appointment or task information, such as subject, date, location, and participants. Calendar records have the same sort of sync issues as contacts; people create appointments in different calendars and then have trouble managing them all. Calendar items can be exchanged between different services using the iCalendar format.

Mail

Most email systems store messages on the server, and the client device is used to manage them. There can often be sync issues, however, particularly with deletions, sent items, and draft compositions.

Pictures, Music, Video, and Documents

The main sync issue with media files such as **photos** tends to be the amount of space they take up. There might not be enough space on one device to sync all the files the user has stored. There can also be issues with file formats; not all devices can play or show all formats. Users editing a document on different devices may have trouble with version history, unless the changes are saved directly to the copy stored in the cloud.

Apps

An app will be available across all devices that the account holder signs in on, as long as they are the same platform. If you have a Windows PC and an Apple iPhone, you will find yourself managing two sets of apps. Most of them will share data seamlessly, however (the social media ones, for instance).

Passwords

Both iOS and Android will prompt you to save passwords when you sign in to apps and websites. These passwords are cached securely within the device file system and protected by the authentication and encryption mechanisms required to access the device via the lock screen.

These cached passwords can be synchronized across your devices using cloud services. You must remember that anyone compromising your device/cloud account will be able to access any service that you have cached the password for.

Email Configuration Options

One of the most important features of mobile devices is the ability to receive and compose email.

Commercial Provider Email Configuration

Most commercial email providers allow the OS to autodiscover connection settings. *Autodiscover* means that the mail service has published special DNS records that identify how the account for a particular domain should be configured. To connect an autodiscover-enabled account, simply choose the mail provider (Exchange, Gmail, Yahoo, Outlook.com, iCloud, and so on) then enter your email address and credentials.

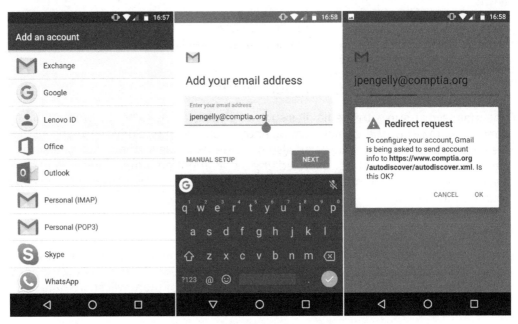

Configuring an autodiscover-enabled Exchange mail account in Android.
(Screenshot courtesy of Android platform, a trademark of Google LLC.)

Corporate and ISP Email Configuration

Many institutions use Microsoft's Exchange mail server for corporate email. Exchange is usually an integrated provider option and clients can autodiscover the correct settings. To manually configure an Exchange ActiveSync account, you need to enter the email address and username (usually the same thing) and a host address (obtain this from the Exchange administrator) as well as a password and the choice of whether to use Transport Layer Security (TLS). There is often also a field for domain, but this is usually left blank.

 If there is a single "Domain\Username" field, prefix the email address with a backslash: \me@company.com.

If you are connecting to an internet service provider (ISP) email host or **corporate mail gateway** that does not support autodiscovery of configuration settings, you can enter the server address manually by selecting **Other**, then inputting the appropriate server addresses:

- Incoming mail server—the FQDN or IP address of the Internet Mail Access Protocol (IMAP) or Post Office Protocol (POP3) server.

*Choose **IMAP** if you are viewing and accessing the mail from multiple devices. POP3 will download the mail to the device, removing it from the server mailbox. Note that Exchange doesn't use either POP3 or IMAP (though it can support them) but a proprietary protocol called Messaging Application Programming Interface (MAPI).*

- Outgoing mail server—the address of the Simple Mail Transfer Protocol (SMTP) server.

- Enable or disable Transport Layer Security (TLS).

TLS protects confidential information such as the account password and is necessary if you connect to mail over a public link (such as an open Wi-Fi "hotspot"). Note that you can only enable TLS if the mail provider supports it.

- Ports—the secure (TLS enabled) or unsecure ports used for IMAP, POP3, and SMTP would normally be left to the default. If the email provider uses custom port settings, you would need to obtain those and enter them in the manual configuration.

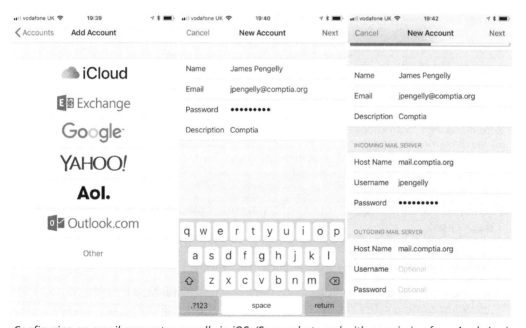

Configuring an email account manually in iOS. (Screenshot used with permission from Apple Inc.)

Synchronization Methods

Before cloud services became prevalent, data on a smartphone or tablet would typically be manually synchronized with a desktop PC. You might use the PC to back up data stored on the smartphone, for instance, or to sync calendar and contact records. Nowadays, it is much more likely for devices to be connected via cloud services. If given permission, the device OS and apps can back up data to the cloud service all the time. When you sign in to a new device, it syncs the data from the cloud seamlessly.

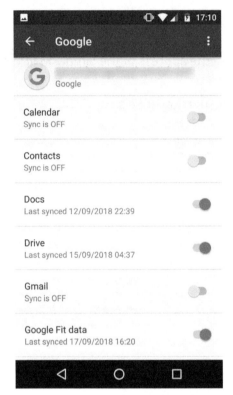

Account settings for the Google master account on an Android smartphone. This account is used for the Play Store and to sync data with other cloud services, but not email, contacts, or calendar. (Screenshot courtesy of Android platform, a trademark of Google LLC.)

When synchronizing large amounts of data, you should account for different types of **data caps**:

- The account will have an overall storage limit. Most accounts are issued with 5 GB of free tier storage. Additional storage needs to be purchased.

- If synchronizing over a cellular data network, there will be a monthly data allowance and a rate for any transfers exceeding the allowance. To avoid incurring unwanted charges, you can configure the device to warn and/or cap cellular data transfers. Most apps can be configured to sync over Wi-Fi only.

Synchronizing to PCs

If synchronizing via a cloud service is not an option, you can usually view an Android phone or tablet from Windows over USB or Bluetooth and use drag-and-drop for file transfer.

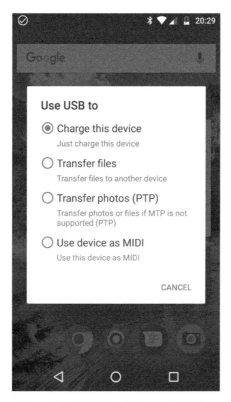

Connecting an Android smartphone to a Windows PC over USB. You can choose whether to allow some sort of data transfer as well as charge the battery. If you enable data transfer, the device's file system will be made available via File Explorer. (Screenshot courtesy of Android platform, a trademark of Google LLC.)

An iPad or iPhone can connect to a computer over a Lightning-to-USB adapter cable. Transferring files to a Windows PC requires the iTunes app to be installed on the computer.

Synchronizing to Automobiles

Most new automobiles come with in-vehicle entertainment and navigation systems. The main part of this system is referred to as the head unit. If supported, a smartphone can be used to "drive" the head unit so the navigation features from your smartphone will appear on the display (simplified for safe use while driving), or you could play songs stored on your tablet via the vehicle's entertainment system. The technologies underpinning this are Apple CarPlay and Android Auto.

Enterprise Mobility Management

Enterprise mobility management (EMM) is a class of management software designed to apply security policies to the use of mobile devices and apps in the enterprise. The challenge of identifying and managing all the devices attached to a network is often referred to as visibility.

 Enterprises use different deployment models to specify how mobile devices and apps are provisioned to employees. One example is bring your own device (BYOD), where employees are allowed to use a personally owned device to access corporate accounts, apps, and data.

There are two main functions of an EMM product suite:

- **Mobile device management (MDM)** sets device policies for authentication, feature use (camera and microphone), and connectivity. MDM can also allow device resets and remote wipes.

- **Mobile application management (MAM)** sets policies for apps that can process corporate data and prevents data transfer to personal apps. This type of solution configures an enterprise-managed container or workspace.

Examples of EMM solution providers include VMWare Workspace ONE (vmware.com/products/workspace-one.html), Microsoft Endpoint Manager/Intune (microsoft.com/en-us/security/business/microsoft-endpoint-manager), Symantec/Broadcom (broadcom.com/products/cyber-security/endpoint/end-user/protection-mobile), and Citrix Endpoint Management (citrix.com/products/citrix-endpoint-management).

When a device is enrolled with the MAM software, it can be configured into an enterprise workspace mode in which only a certain number of authorized **corporate applications** can run. For example, the app(s) used for corporate email, calendar, and contacts would store settings and data separately from the app used for personal email. Messages and attachments sent from the account might be subject to data loss prevention (DLP) controls to prevent unauthorized forwarding of confidential or privacy-sensitive data.

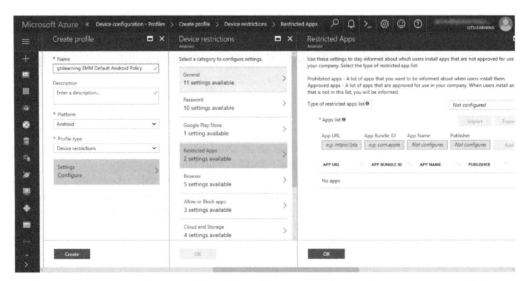

Endpoint management software such as Microsoft Intune can be used to approve or prohibit apps. (Screenshot courtesy of Microsoft.)

Apple operates enterprise developer and distribution programs to allow private app distribution via Apple Business Manager (developer.apple.com/business/distribute). Google's Play store has a private channel option called Managed Google Play. Both these options allow a MAM suite to push apps from the private channel to the device.

Two-factor Authentication

Most smartphones and tablets are single-user devices. Access control can be implemented by configuring a screen lock that can only be bypassed using the correct password, personal identification number (PIN), or swipe pattern. Many devices now support **biometric authentication**, usually as a fingerprint reader but sometimes using facial or voice recognition.

When enrolled with an enterprise management app, the user might have to re-authenticate to access the corporate workspace. The corporate policy might require stronger authentication methods, such as the use of **two-factor authentication (2FA)**. 2FA means that the user must submit two different kinds of credential to authenticate, such as both a fingerprint and a PIN. Alternatively, the account might be configured with an authenticator device or app, a trusted email account, or registered phone number. When the user uses a new device to access the account, or when the workspace policy requires 2FA, the user must first authenticate normally, using a fingerprint, for instance. If this is accepted, an email, text, or phone call is generated as a notification on the trusted authenticator app or device. The message may include a one-time password code for the user to input to confirm that the sign-in attempt is legitimate.

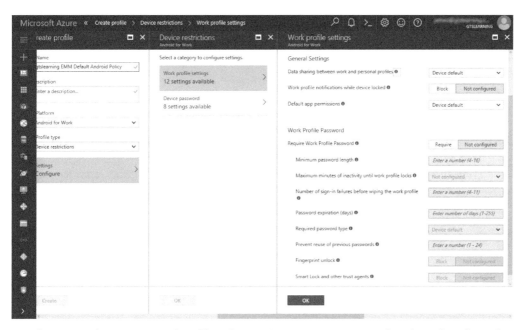

Configuring authentication and profile policies using Intune EMM. Note that the policy allows the user to have a different type of authentication to the workspace hosting corporate apps and data. (Screenshot courtesy of Microsoft.)

Location Services

Geolocation is the use of network attributes to identify (or estimate) the physical position of a device. A mobile device operates a **location service** to determine its current position. The location service can make use of two systems:

- **Global Positioning System (GPS)** is a means of determining the device's latitude and longitude based on information received from orbital satellites via a GPS sensor. Note that not all mobile devices are fitted with GPS sensors.

- **Indoor Positioning System (IPS)** works out a device's location by triangulating its proximity to other radio sources, such as cellular radio towers, Wi-Fi access points, and Bluetooth/RFID beacons.

As the location service stores highly personal data, it is only available to an app where the user has granted specific permission to use it.

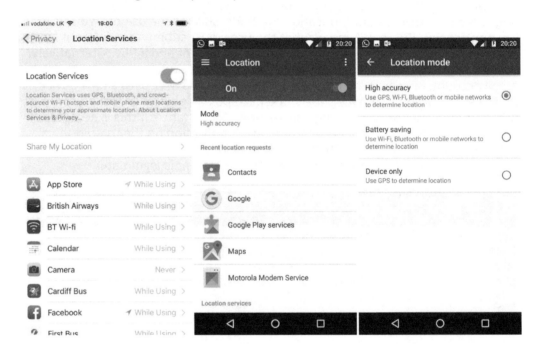

Configuring location services in iOS (left) and Android (right). (Screenshots reprinted with permission from Apple Inc., and Android platform, a trademark of Google LLC.)

 Some mobile devices are additionally fitted with a magnetometer sensor. This enables more accurate compass directions.

Review Activity:

Mobile Device Apps

Answer the following questions:

1. **Why must a vendor account usually be configured on a smartphone?**

2. **Which types of data might require mapping between fields when syncing between applications?**

3. **How do you configure an autodiscover-enabled email provider on a smartphone?**

4. **A company has discovered that an employee has been emailing product design documents to her smartphone and then saving the files to the smartphone's flash drive. Which technology can be deployed to prevent such policy breaches?**

Topic 8C

Install and Configure Laptop Hardware

 CORE 1 EXAM OBJECTIVES COVERED
1.1 Given a scenario, install and configure laptop hardware and components.

Laptops present fewer upgrade opportunities than desktop PCs, but there is still the chance of maximizing the lifetime of a device by adding RAM or replacing the battery or fixed disk. Also, as portable devices, laptops suffer more from wear and tear and with a stock of replacement parts, repairs to items such as the keyboard can be much more economical than buying a new laptop. In this topic, you will learn best practice procedures for installing, replacing, and upgrading laptop components

Laptop Disassembly Processes

Laptops have specialized hardware designed especially for use in a portable chassis and can run on battery or AC power. Laptops use the same sort of operating systems as desktop PCs, and unlike smartphones and tablets, typically have some upgradeable or replaceable components.

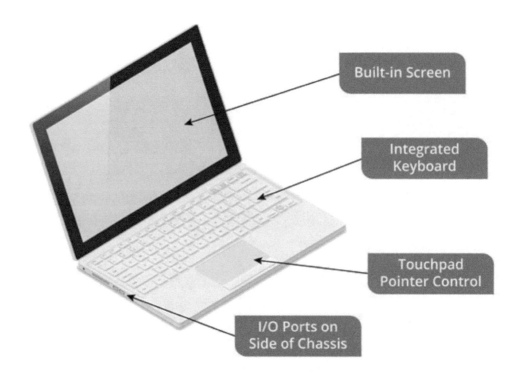

Distinctive features of a laptop computer, including the built-in screen, integrated keyboard, touchpad pointer control, and I/O ports (on both sides and rear of chassis). (Image © 123RF.com)

When it comes to performing upgrades or replacing parts, there are some issues specific to laptops that you should be aware of.

Hand Tools and Parts

Laptops use smaller screws than are found on desktops. You may find it useful to obtain a set of precision screwdrivers and other appropriate hand tools. It is also much easier to strip the screws—remove the notch for the screwdriver—take care and use an appropriately sized screwdriver!

You need to document the location of screws of a specific size and the location and orientation of ribbon cables and other connectors. It can be very easy to remove them quickly during disassembly and then to face a puzzle during reassembly.

 A useful tip is to take a photo of the underside of the laptop and print it out. As you remove screws, tape them to the relevant point in your picture. This ensures you will not lose any and will know which screw goes where. Photograph each stage of disassembly so you know where to re-fit cables and connectors.

As with a desktop, organize parts that you remove or have ready for installation carefully. Keep the parts away from your main work area so that you do not damage them by mistake. Keep static-sensitive parts, such as the SSDs, memory modules, and adapter cards, in anti-static packaging.

Form Factors and Plastics/Frames

The laptop chassis incorporates the motherboard, power supply, display screen, keyboard, and touchpad. The plastics or aluminum frames are the hard surfaces that cover the internal components of the laptop. They are secured using either small screws or pressure tabs. Note that screws may be covered by rubber or plastic tabs.

Make sure you obtain the manufacturer's service documentation before commencing any upgrade or replacement work. This should explain how to disassemble the chassis and remove tricky items, such as plastic bezels, without damaging them. You should only perform this work if a warranty option is not available.

Battery Replacement

Portable computers can work off both building power and battery operation.

AC Adapters

To operate from building power, the laptop needs a power supply to convert the AC supply from the power company to the DC voltages used by the laptop's components. The power supply is provided as an external AC adapter. AC adapters are normally universal (or auto-switching) and can operate from any 110–240 VAC 50/60 Hz supply, though do check the label to confirm.

A laptop AC adapter. (Image by Olga Popova © 123RF.com)

Plugging a fixed-input 220–240 V adapter into a 110–120 V supply won't cause any damage (though the laptop won't work), but plugging a fixed-input 110–120 V adapter into a 220–240 V supply will likely cause damage.

AC adapters are also rated for their power output (ranging from around 65–120 W). Again, this information will be printed on the adapter label. The AC adapter connects to the laptop via a DC jack or a USB port.

Battery Power

Laptop computers use removable, rechargeable Lithium ion (Li-ion) **battery** packs. Li-ion batteries are typically available in 6-, 9-, or 12-cell versions, with more cells providing for a longer charge. The connector and battery-pack form factor are typically specific to the laptop vendor and to a range/model.

Before inserting or removing the battery pack, you must turn the machine off and unplug it from the AC wall outlet. A portable battery is usually removed by releasing catches on the back or underside of the laptop.

A removable laptop battery pack. (Image by cristi180884 © 123RF.com)

The battery recharges when the laptop is connected to the AC adapter and is connected to power. When the laptop is in use, the battery is trickle charged. A laptop should come with a power management driver to ensure a proper charging regime and prevent repeated trickle charging from damaging it. Li-on battery life is affected by being fully drained of charge and by being held continually at 100% charge. Balanced power charging stops trickle charging at 80%. Li-ion batteries are also sensitive to heat. If storing a Li-ion battery, reduce the charge to 40% and store at below 20°C.

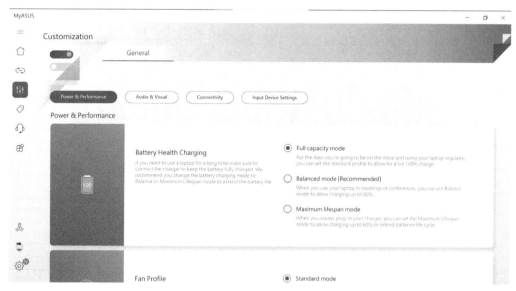

Customization in MyASUS V3.1.0.0. MyASUS laptop app with customizable power plans. Balanced mode prevents the battery from being continually trickle charged to 100%, which can reduce its operational life. (Screenshot used with permission from ASUSTek Computer Inc.)

Li-ion batteries hold less charge as they age and typically have a maximum usable life of around 2–3 years. If you charge a battery and the run time is substantially decreased, you may need to purchase a new battery.

RAM and Adapter Replacement

Laptops have fewer field-replaceable units (FRU) than desktops. That said, laptop components and designs have become better standardized. Using components sourced from the laptop vendor is still recommended, but basic upgrade options, such as system memory and fixed disks, have become much simpler.

Some FRUs can be accessed easily by removing a screw plate on the back cover (underside) of the laptop. This method generally provides access to the fixed disk, optical drive, memory modules, and possibly adapter card slots for components such as Wi-Fi cards and cellular radios.

Upgrading RAM Modules

Laptop DDRx SD**RAM** is packaged in small outline DIMMs (SODIMMs). As with DIMMs, a given SODIMM slot will only accept a specific type of DDR. For example, you cannot install a DDR4 SODIMM in a DDR3 slot. The slots are keyed to prevent incompatible modules from being installed.

Two SODIMM RAM modules. The modules stack one over the other. When the side catches are released, the modules pop up at an angle for easy removal. (Image courtesy of CompTIA.)

A SODIMM slot pops-up at a 45° angle to allow the chips to be inserted or removed. Sometimes one of the memory slots is easily accessible via a panel, but another requires more extensive disassembly of the chassis to access.

 There are a couple of other laptop memory module form factors, including Mini-DIMM and Micro-DIMM. These are smaller than SODIMM and used on some ultraportable models. Always check the vendor documentation before obtaining parts for upgrade or replacement.

Upgrading Adapter Cards

Depending on the design, adapters for modems, **wireless cards**, and SSD storage cards may be accessible and replaceable via screw-down panels. Note that there are several adapter formats, notably Mini PCIe, mSATA, and M.2, none of which are compatible with one another.

You can obtain mini PCIe or M.2 adapters for laptops that will provide some combination of Wi-Fi, Bluetooth, and/or cellular data connectivity. Remember that when upgrading this type of adapter, you need to re-connect the antenna wires used by the old adapter or install a new antenna kit. The antenna wires are usually routed around the screen in the laptop's lid. The antenna connections can be fiddly to connect and are quite delicate, so take care.

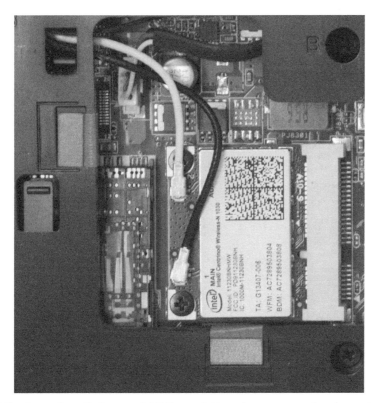

Wi-Fi adapter installed as a mini PCIe card. Note the antenna wire connections.
(Image courtesy of CompTIA.)

If installing an adapter with GSM or LTE cellular functionality, remember to insert the SIM card as well.

Disk Upgrades and Replacement

A laptop typically supports one internal mass storage device only, with extra storage attached to an external port. This means that to upgrade the fixed disk, there must be a plan for what to do with existing data:

- **Migration** means using backup software to create an image or clone of the old drive and store it on USB media. When the new drive has been installed, the system image can be restored to it. A system image is technology neutral, so an image of an HDD can be applied to an SSD. However, the new drive must be the same size or larger than the old one, unless using a cloning tool that can shrink the source image.

 As an alternative to using a third USB drive to store the image, a disk enclosure allows you to connect an internal drive temporarily as an external drive. You can then migrate the image directly to the SSD before removing the old drive and installing the new one.

- **Replacement** means that only data is backed up from the old drive. The new drive is then fitted to the laptop and an OS plus apps installed. User data can then be restored from backup.

The fixed disk can usually be accessed via a panel, but you may have to open the chassis on some models.

Laptop HDDs are usually 2.5" form factor, though sometimes the 1.8" form factor is used. Compared to 3.5" desktop versions, magnetic 2.5" HDDs tend to be slower (usually 5400 rpm models) and lower capacity. Within the 2.5" form factor, there are also reduced height units designed for ultraportable laptops. A standard 2.5" drive has a z-height of 9.5 mm; an ultraportable laptop might require a 7 mm (thin) or 5 mm (ultrathin) drive.

A laptop HDD with SATA interface. (Image © 123RF.com)

Magnetic drives use ordinary SATA data and power connectors, though the connectors on the drive mate directly to a port in the drive bay, without the use of a cable. Drive bays measuring 1.8" might require the use of the micro SATA (μSATA or uSATA) connector.

An SSD flash storage device can also use the SATA interface and connector form factors but is more likely to use an adapter card interface:

- mSATA—An SSD might be housed on a card with a Mini-SATA (mSATA) interface. These cards resemble Mini PCIe cards but are not physically compatible with Mini PCIe slots. mSATA uses the SATA bus, so the maximum transfer speed is 6 Gb/s.

- M.2—An M.2 SSD usually interfaces with the PCI Express bus, allowing much higher bus speeds than SATA. M.2 adapters can be different lengths (42 mm, 60 mm, 80 mm, or 110 mm), so you should check that any given adapter will fit within the laptop chassis. The most popular length for laptop SSDs is 80 mm (M.2 2280).

The specific M.2 form factor is written as xxyy, where xx is the card width and yy is the length. For example, 2280 means a card width of 22 mm and a length of 80 mm.

Keyboard and Security Component Replacement

As mechanical devices, components such as the keyboard, touch pad, and biometric sensors can easily be damaged. If parts can be obtained from the vendor, it can be more cost-effective to replace damaged components than buy a new laptop.

Keyboard and Touchpad Replacement

When you are replacing components such as the **keyboard** and **touchpad**, you will almost always need to use the same part as was fitted originally. Accessing the parts for removal and replacement might require complete disassembly of the chassis or might be relatively straightforward—check the service documentation.

Each part connects to the motherboard via a data cable, typically a flat ribbon type. The cable is held in place by a latch that must be released before trying to remove the cable and secured after insertion.

When replacing an input device, use the OS/driver settings utility or app to configure it. A keyboard should be set to the correct input region. Touchpads need to be configured to an appropriate sensitivity to be comfortable for the user.

Key Replacement

In some circumstances, it might be economical to lift a single key for cleaning or replacement. Carefully pry off the plastic key cap with a flat blade to expose the retainer clip. The retainer clip can also be removed for cleaning, but it is fragile so take care. To replace, line up each component carefully and then push to snap it back into place.

Biometric Security Components

A **biometric** sensor allows users to record a template of a feature of their body that is unique to them. On a laptop, this is typically implemented as a fingerprint scanner, though the camera can also be used to make facial scans or to scan an iris eye pattern. A fingerprint sensor might be installed as a separate component or might be a feature of the keyboard or touchpad.

A fingerprint reader board is attached to the motherboard by a flat ribbon cable in the same way as the keyboard and touchpad.

 If a laptop does not have an integrated fingerprint scanner, it is possible to obtain models that connect to a USB port.

A biometric sensor is configured in conjunction with an authenticator app, such as Windows Hello.

Near-field Scanner

A **near-field communication (NFC) scanner** on a laptop is primarily used to pair peripheral devices or to establish a connection to a smartphone. This is configured via the vendor's app.

NFC might be implemented as a feature of the keyboard, touchpad, or fingerprint reader. As well as the data connection to the motherboard, the NFC sensor must be connected to its antenna.

Review Activity:

Laptop Hardware

Answer the following questions:

1. Several laptops need to be replaced in the next fiscal cycle, but that doesn't begin for several months. You want to improve functionality as much as possible by upgrading or replacing components in some of the laptops that are having problems. Which items are most easily replaced in a laptop?

2. What is the process for installing memory in a laptop?

3. What type of standard adapter card might be used to connect internal FRU devices to the motherboard of a laptop?

4. A technician is performing a keyboard replacement and asks for your help. The data cable for the old keyboard will not pull out. How should it be removed?

Topic 8D

Troubleshoot Mobile Device Issues

CORE 1 EXAM OBJECTIVES COVERED
5.5 Given a scenario, troubleshoot common issues with mobile devices.

Part of your duties as a CompTIA A+ technician will be helping users when they encounter problems with their mobile devices. In this topic, you will troubleshoot mobile device hardware issues.

Power and Battery Issues

If you experience problems working from AC power, first test the outlet with a "known good" device (such as a lamp). Next, check that an LED on the AC adapter is green. If there is no LED, check the fuse on the plug, and if available, try testing with a known good adapter.

Sometimes AC adapters can get mixed up. If an underpowered adapter is used—for example, a 65 W adapter is plugged into a 90 W system—the laptop will display a warning at boot time.

If a mobile device will not power on when disconnected from building power, first check that the battery is seated properly in its compartment. Also check whether the battery contacts are dirty. You can clean them using swabs.

If the battery is properly inserted and the mobile device does not switch on or only remains on for a few seconds, it is most likely completely discharged. A battery exhibiting **poor health** will not hold a charge. This means that the battery is at the end of its useful life. You can test this by using a known good battery. If a known good battery does not work, then there is something wrong with the power circuitry on the motherboard.

While laptop batteries are replaceable, few smartphones or tablets come with removable battery packs. Most vendors try to design their devices so that they will support "typical" usage for a full day without charging. As the battery ages, it becomes less able to hold a full charge. If it is non-removable, the device will have to be returned to the vendor for battery replacement.

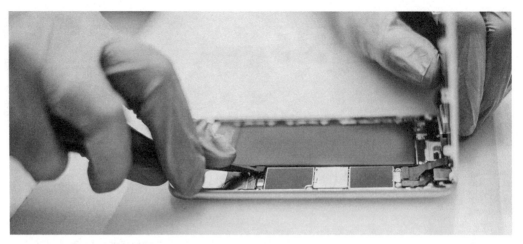

Mobile handset with cover removed—the battery is accessible but not designated as user-removable. (Image by guruxox © 123RF.com)

Improper Charging Symptoms

Properly caring for the battery not only prolongs battery life but also mitigates health and safety risks. Use the battery charger provided by the manufacturer or an approved replacement charger. Using an incorrect battery charging cable or exposing a battery to extreme heat carries risks of fire or even explosion.

 Exercise caution when leaving batteries to recharge unattended (for example, overnight). Do not leave a battery charger close to flammable material, and ensure there is plenty of ventilation around the unit.

An **improper charging** routine will reduce the usable life of a battery. Follow manufacturer instructions on the proper charging and discharging of the battery. Make use of power management features included with your device/OS to prolong battery life. A Li-ion battery should not be allowed to fully discharge regularly or be kept persistently at 100% charge, as this reduces battery life.

As batteries age, the maximum charge they can sustain decreases, so short battery life will usually indicate that the battery needs replacing. If the battery is not old or faulty, you could suspect that an app is putting excessive strain on the battery. You can use an app to check battery utilization.

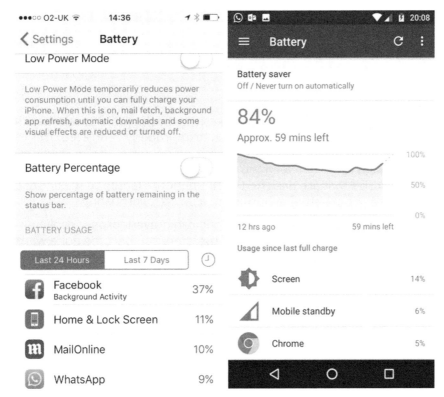

Battery status and notifications in iOS (left) and Android (right). (Screenshots reprinted with permission from Apple Inc., and Android platform, a trademark of Google LLC.)

Swollen Battery Symptoms

If you notice any **swelling** from the battery compartment, discontinue use of the mobile device immediately. Signs that the battery has swollen can include a device that wobbles when placed flat on a desk or a deformed touchpad or keyboard. A swollen battery indicates some sort of problem with the battery's charging circuit, which is supposed to prevent overcharging. If a device is exposed to liquid, this could also have damaged the battery.

Li-ion batteries are designed to swell to avoid bursting or exploding, but great care must be taken when handling a swollen battery to avoid further damage. A swollen battery is a fire hazard and could leak hazardous chemicals—do not allow these to come into contact with your skin or your eyes. If the battery cannot be released safely and easily from its compartment, contact the manufacturer for advice. You should also contact the manufacturer for specific disposal instructions. A swollen battery should not be discarded via standard recycling points unless the facility confirms it can accept batteries in a potentially hazardous state.

Manufacturing defects in batteries and AC adapters often occur in batches. Make sure you remain signed up to the vendor's alerting service so that you are informed about any product recalls or safety advisories.

Hardware Failure Issues

Mobile devices are more susceptible to mechanical problems than most desktop PCs, so you should be alert to the symptoms of hardware failure.

Overheating Symptoms

The compact design of mobile devices makes them vulnerable to **overheating**. The bottom surface of a laptop becomes hot when improperly ventilated. This can easily happen when laptops are put on soft surfaces, on people's laps, or in places where there is not enough room between the vents and a wall. Laptop cooling (or chiller) pads are accessories that are designed to sit under the laptop to maximize airflow and protect a user from getting a burn from a device overheating.

Dust trapped in vents acts as an insulator and can prevent proper cooling. Handheld devices use passive cooling and therefore can become quite warm when used intensively. High screen brightness and use of the flashlight function will rapidly increase heat. A mobile device will start to overheat quickly when exposed to direct sunlight. Devices have protective circuitry that will initiate a shut down if the internal temperature is at the maximum safe limit. You can also use an app to monitor the battery temperature, and then compare that to the operating limits. Generally speaking, approaching 40ºC is getting too warm.

Liquid Damage Symptoms

Some mobile-device cases provide a degree of waterproofing. Waterproofing is rated on the Ingress Protection (IP) scale. A case or device will have two numbers, such as IP67. The first (6) is a rating for repelling solids, with a 5 or 6 representing devices that are dust protected and dust proof, respectively. The second value (7) is for liquids, with a 7 being protected from immersion in up to 1 m and 8 being protected from immersion beyond 1 m.

 If dust protection is unrated, the IP value will be IPX7 or IPX8.

If a mobile device is exposed to **liquid damage**, there may be visible signs of water under the screen. The screen might display graphics artefacts or not show an image. Even if there is no visible sign, power off the device immediately if you suspect liquid damage. Dry as much excess liquid as possible. If you suspect that the internal components have been exposed, the device must be disassembled to fully dry. Once dry, clean the circuit boards and contacts. The battery will usually need to be replaced.

Physically Damaged Port Symptoms

Improper insertion and removal of connectors can easily **damage the external ports** of a mobile device. If a port is damaged, the connector may be loose or may no longer fit. There may be no data connection at all, or it might be intermittent. The device may fail to charge properly.

Educate users to remove a connector by holding the connector and pulling it straight. A connector should not be jiggled to remove it. USB-C and Lightning connectors are reversible. Make sure users take care to orient other connector types properly before plugging them in.

Screen and Calibration Issues

When you are troubleshooting a mobile display issue, you will often need to take into account the use of the integrated display and/or an external display and how to isolate a problem to a particular component, such as the graphics adapter, display panel, backlight, and digitizer.

If there is no image on the screen, check that the video card is good by using an external monitor. Alternatively, there should be a very dim image on the display if the graphics adapter is functioning, but the backlight has failed. Most screens use LED backlights. Older laptops might use an inverter component to power a fluorescent backlight.

As well as the display itself, it is common for the plastics around a laptop case to get cracked or broken and for the hinges on the lid to wear out. The plastics are mostly cosmetic (though a bad break might expose the laptop's internal components to greater risks), but if the hinges no longer hold up the screen, they will have to be replaced.

Broken Screen Issues

Mobile devices are very easy to drop, and while the glass is designed to be tough, impacts on a hard surface from over 1m in height will usually result in cracking or shattering. If only the glass layer is damaged, the digitizer and display may remain usable, to some extent. A **broken screen** is likely to require warranty or professional services to repair it, however.

If there are no visible cracks, the screen or digitizer circuitry may have been damaged by liquid.

Digitizer Issues

Symptoms such as the touch screen not responding to input indicate a problem with the digitizer. If you can discount shock and liquid damage, try the following tests:

• Verify that the touchscreen and the user's fingers are clean and dry.

• If a screen protector is fitted, check that it is securely adhered to the surface and that there are no bubbles or lifts.

• Check that there is not a transitory software problem by restarting the device. Holding the power button (Android) or Sleep and Home buttons (iPhone) for a few seconds will force the device to perform a soft reset.

• Try using the device in a different location in case some source of electromagnetic interference (EMI) is affecting the operation of the digitizer.

• If the device has just been serviced, check that the right wires are still connected in the right places for the digitizer to function. Remember to ask, "What has changed?"

Cursor Drift/Touch Calibration Issues

On a laptop, if touchpad sensitivity is too high, typing can cause vibrations that move the cursor. Examples include the pointer drifting across the screen without any input or a "ghost cursor" jumping about when typing. Install up-to-date drivers and configure input options to suit the user. Many laptops now come with a Fn key to disable the touchpad.

If you can rule out simple hardware causes, unresponsive or inaccurate touch input can be an indication of resources being inadequate (too many open apps) or badly written apps that hog memory or other resources. A soft reset will usually fix the problem in the short term. If the problem is persistent, either try to identify whether the problem is linked to running a particular app or try freeing space by removing data or apps. Windows devices and some versions of Android support re-calibration utilities, but if you cannot identify another cause, then you are likely to have to look at warranty repair.

Connectivity Issues

Wi-Fi and Bluetooth **connectivity** issues on a mobile can be approached in much the same way as on a PC. Problems can generally be categorized as either relating to "physical" issues, such as interference, or to "software" configuration problems.

Consider these guidelines when you are troubleshooting issues with communication and connectivity:

- Verify that the adapter is enabled. Check the status of function key toggles on a laptop, or use the notification shade toggles on a mobile device to check that airplane mode has not been enabled or that the specific radio is not disabled.

- If a laptop has been serviced recently and wireless functions have stopped working, check that the antenna connector has not been dislodged or wrongly connected.

- If a wireless peripheral such as a Bluetooth mouse or keyboard that has been working stops, it probably needs a new battery.

- If you experience problems restoring from hibernate or sleep mode, try cycling the power on the device or reconnecting it and checking for updated drivers for the wireless controller and the devices.

If you are experiencing intermittent connectivity issues:

- Try moving the two devices closer together.

- Try moving the devices from a side-to-side or up-and-down position to a different position or changing the way in which the device is held.

 The radio antenna wire for a mobile will be built into the case (normally around the screen). On some devices, certain hand positions can stop the antenna from functioning as well as it should.

- Consider using a Wi-Fi analyzer to measure the signal strength in different locations to try to identify the source of interference.

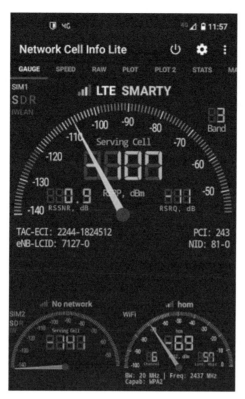

Network Cell Info Lite showing cell tower connection status in the top gauge and Wi-Fi in the lower gauge. (Screenshot used with permission from M2Catalyst, LLC).

A similar utility (Cell Tower Analyzer or GSM Signal Monitor) can be used to analyze cellular radio signals, which use different frequencies than Wi-Fi uses. An app might combine both functions.

Malware Issues

Whenever a device does not function as expected, you should assess whether it could be infected with malware. Consider the following scenarios:

- Malware or rogue apps are likely to try to collect data in the background. They can become unresponsive and might not shut down when closed. Such apps might cause excessive power drain and high resource utilization, potentially leading to overheating problems.

- Another tell-tale sign of a hacked device is reaching the data transmission overlimit unexpectedly. Most devices have an option to monitor data usage and have limit triggers to notify the user if the limit has been reached. This protects from large data bills but should also prompt the user to check the amount of data used by each application in order to monitor their legitimacy.

- Malware may try to use the camera or microphone to record activity. Check that the camera LED is not activated.

Review Activity:

Mobile Device Issues

Answer the following questions:

1. You are troubleshooting a laptop display. If the laptop can display an image on an external monitor but not on the built-in one, which component do you know is working, and can you definitively say which is faulty?

2. You received a user complaint about a laptop being extremely hot to the touch. What actions should you take in response to this issue?

3. A user complains that their Bluetooth keyboard, which has worked for the last year, has stopped functioning. What would you suggest is the problem?

4. A laptop user reports that they are only getting about two hours of use out of the battery compared to about three hours when the laptop was first supplied to them. What do you suggest?

5. A laptop user is complaining about typing on their new laptop. They claim that the cursor jumps randomly from place to place. What might be the cause of this?

Lesson 8

Summary

You should be able to set up and troubleshoot mobile-device accessories, connectivity, and applications.

Guidelines for Supporting Mobile Devices

Follow these guidelines to support the use of smartphones, tablets, and laptops by your users:

- Document supported display types (LCD IPS, LCD TN, LCD VA, OLED) and connection methods (USB, Lightning, Serial, Bluetooth, NFC, Wi-Fi, and Cellular) to facilitate issue identification and maintain a spare parts inventory.

- Educate users on procedures for enabling/disabling radios, using connector cables correctly, and pairing Bluetooth peripherals to reduce support calls.

- Identify support procedures to help users manage Microsoft 365, Google Workspace, and iCloud digital identities.

- Identify support procedures to assist users synchronizing mail, photos, calendar, and contacts between devices and cloud services and recognizing data caps.

- Create work instructions for enrolling devices in MDM/MAM suites and configuring corporate email, apps, and two-factor authentication.

- Create work instructions and prepare inventory to support laptop repair and upgrade tasks, such as battery, keyboard/keys, RAM, HDD/SSD migration, wireless cards, and biometric/NFC security components.

- Establish a knowledge base to document symptoms and solutions to common issues, such as poor battery health, swollen battery, broken screen, improper charging, poor/no connectivity, liquid damage, overheating, digitizer issues, physically damaged ports, malware, and cursor drift/touch calibration.

Lesson 9
Supporting Print Devices

LESSON INTRODUCTION

Despite predictions that computers would bring about a paperless office environment, the need to transfer digital information to paper or back again remains strong. As a CompTIA® A+® certified professional, you will often be called upon to set up, configure, and troubleshoot print and scan devices. Having a working knowledge of the many printer technologies and components will help you to support users' needs in any technical environment.

Lesson Objectives

In this lesson, you will:

- Deploy printer and multifunction devices.

- Replace print device consumables.

- Troubleshoot print device issues.

Topic 9A

Deploy Printer and Multifunction Devices

CORE 1 EXAM OBJECTIVES COVERED
3.6 Given a scenario, deploy and configure multifunction devices/printers and settings.

Although the different technologies used in various printer types affect maintenance and troubleshooting, the type of printer does not substantially affect the way it is installed and configured in an operating system, such as Windows, or shared on a network. The skills you will learn in this topic should prepare you to install, share, and configure a printer effectively and securely.

Printer Unboxing and Setup Location

A **printer** type or printer technology is the mechanism used to make images on the paper. The most common types for general home and office use are inkjet (or ink dispersion) and laser, though others are used for more specialist applications. Some of the major **print device** vendors include HP, Epson, Canon, Xerox, Brother, OKI, Konica/Minolta, Lexmark, Ricoh, and Samsung.

There is a distinction between the software components that represent the printer and the physical printer itself. The software representation of the printer may be described as the "printer object," "logical printer," or simply "printer." Terms relating to the printer hardware include "print device" or "physical printer." Be aware that "printer" could mean either the physical print device or the software representation of that device. Pay attention to the context in which these terms are used.

The following criteria are used to select the best type and model of printer:

- The basic speed of a printer is measured in pages per minute (ppm). You will see different speeds quoted for different types of output. For example, pages of monochrome text will print more quickly than color photos.

- The maximum supported resolution, measured in dots per inch (dpi), determines output quality. Printer dots and screen image pixels are not equivalent. It requires multiple dots to reproduce one pixel at acceptable quality. Pixel dimensions are typically quoted in pixels per inch (ppi) to avoid confusion. Vertical and horizontal resolution are often different, so you may see figures such as 2400x600 quoted. The horizontal resolution is determined by the print engine (that is, either the laser scanning unit or inkjet print head); vertical resolution is determined by the paper handling mechanism.

- Paper handling means the sizes and types of paper or media that can be loaded. It may be important that the printer can handle labels, envelopes, card stock, acetate/ transparencies, and so on. The amount of paper that can be loaded and output is also important in high-volume environments. Overloaded output trays will cause paper jams. If the output tray is low capacity, this could happen quite quickly in a busy office.

- Options add functionality. Examples include an automatic **duplex unit** for double-sided printing and a finisher unit for folding, stapling, and hole punching. These may be fitted by default or available for purchase as an add-on component.

Setup Location

When deploying a new print device, consider the following factors to select an optimum **setup location**:

- The print device must have a power outlet and potentially a network data port. Ensure that cables are run without being trip hazards and that the print device is placed on a stable, flat surface that can bear the device weight with no risk of toppling.

- As with a PC, ensure that the print device is not exposed to direct sunlight and that there is space around it for air to flow. The area should be well-ventilated to ensure dispersal of fumes such as ozone generated during printer operation. Printer paper and most consumables should be stored where there is no risk of high humidity or temperature extremes. Consult the material safety data sheet (MSDS) accompanying the print device to check for any other special installation considerations.

- The print device should be accessible to its users, but take account of noise and foot traffic that might be disruptive to employees working at nearby desks. If a print device is used to output confidential information, it may need to be installed in an access-controlled area.

Unboxing

When you have selected an installation location, follow the manufacturer's instructions to **unbox** and set up the printer. Be aware of the following general factors:

- Many print devices are heavy and may require two persons to lift safely. Make sure you use safe lifting techniques and bend at the knees to avoid damaging your back. Identify handle locations on the device, and use only those to grip and lift it. If carrying a bulky device, ensure the path is free from trip hazards.

- Printer parts will be secured using packing strips and supports. Ensure that these are all removed before the printer is switched on. Remember to check for strips on removable components that are concealed by panels.

- A print device should normally be left to acclimate after removing the packaging materials. Leave the device unboxed and powered off for a few hours to reduce risks from condensation forming within an appliance that has moved from a cold storage/transport environment to a warmer installation environment. Similarly, printer paper should be stored for a day or more before use to allow it to adjust to the temperature and humidity of the installation location.

Print Device Connectivity

Each print device supports a range of wired and wireless connection interfaces.

USB Print Device Connectivity

Install a printer with **USB connectivity**, connect the device plug (usually a Type B connector) to the printer's USB port and the Type A host plug to a free port on the computer. In most cases, the OS will detect the printer using Plug and Play and install the driver automatically. You can confirm that the printer is successfully installed and print a test page using the driver or OS utility.

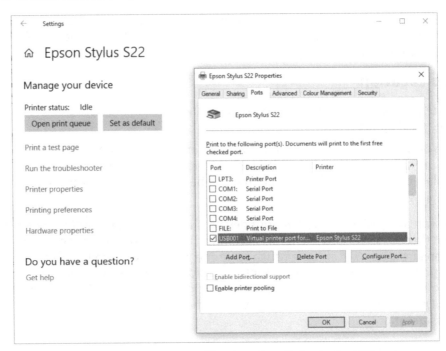

Using Windows Settings to verify printer installation to the USB port.
(Screenshot courtesy of Microsoft.)

Ethernet Print Device Connectivity

Most printers are fitted with an Ethernet network adapter and RJ45 port. The print device can be configured to obtain an Internet Protocol (IP) configuration from a Dynamic Host Configuration Protocol (DHCP) server or be manually configured. The print device's IP can also be registered as a host record on a Domain Name System (DNS) server to facilitate client connections via a fully qualified domain name (FQDN).

Most printers provide a mechanism for locally configuring the printer's network settings. Usually, this is by means of a menu system that you navigate by using an LCD display and adjacent buttons or a touchscreen on the front of the printer.

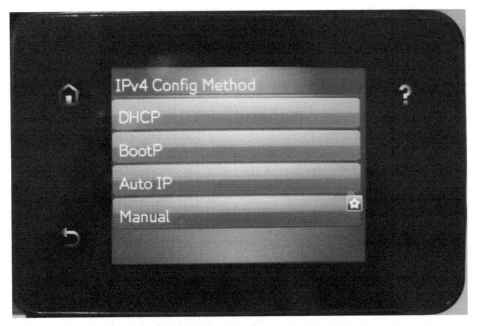

Setting the IP address configuration method via the printer's control panel.
(Image courtesy of CompTIA.)

This method is suitable for small office environments where you have few printers to manage. It is also useful in troubleshooting situations when the printer is inaccessible from the network. However, the printer vendor will usually supply a web-based utility to discover and manage its printers, whereas more advanced management suites are available for enterprise networks.

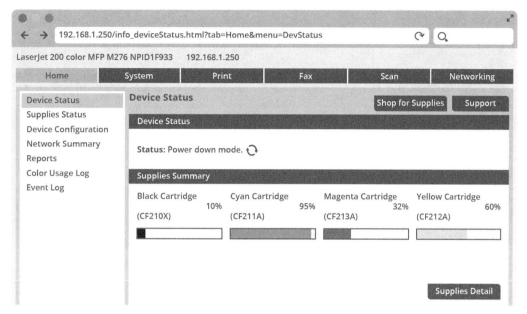

Managing a printer using a browser.

The printer will need to communicate with computers over one or more TCP or UDP network ports. If a network connection cannot be established, verify that these ports are not being blocked by a firewall or other security software.

Wireless Print Device Connectivity

The two principal **wireless** printer interfaces are Bluetooth and Wi-Fi.

To connect a Windows client to a printer via Bluetooth, use the print device control panel to make it discoverable, then use the **Bluetooth** page in Windows Settings to add the device.

Wi-Fi connectivity can be established in two different ways:

- **Infrastructure mode**—Connect the print device to an access point to make it available to clients on the network via an IP address or FQDN. The printer's wireless adapter must support an 802.11 standard available on the access point.

Using the printer control panel to verify Wi-Fi connection status in infrastructure mode.
(Image courtesy of CompTIA.)

- **Wi-Fi Direct**—Configure a software-implemented access point on the print device to facilitate connections to client devices.

Printer Drivers and Page Description Languages

Applications that support printing are typically what you see is what you get (WYSIWYG), which means that the screen and print output are supposed to be identical. To achieve this, the printer **driver** provides an interface between the print device and the operating system. If a networked print device is used by clients with different OSs, each client must be installed with a suitable driver. Note that if the client OS is 64-bit, a 64-bit driver is required.

 Many older print devices have become unusable as the vendor has not developed a 64-bit driver for them. If no up-to-date driver is available from Microsoft, download the driver from the printer vendor's website, extract it to a folder on your PC, then use the Have Disk option in the Add Printer Wizard to install it.

The appropriate print driver will normally be selected and installed when the print device connection is detected. This is referred to as Plug and Play (PnP). In some circumstances, you might need to add the driver manually or choose a driver version with support for a particular **page description language (PDL)**.

A PDL is used to create a raster file from the print commands sent by the software application. A raster file is a dot-by-dot description of where the printer should place ink. In general terms, a PDL supports the following features:

- **Scalable fonts**—originally, characters were printed as bitmaps. A bitmap font consists of dot-by-dot images of each character at a particular font size. This meant that the character could only be printed at sizes defined in the font. Scalable fonts are described by vectors. A vector font consists of a description of how each character should be drawn. This description can be scaled up or down to different font sizes. All Windows printers support scalable TrueType or OpenType fonts.

- **Vector graphics**—as with fonts, scalable images are built from vectors, which describe how a line should be drawn rather than provide a pixel-by-pixel description, as is the case with bitmap graphics.

- **Color printing**—computer displays use an additive red, green, blue color model. The subtractive model used by print devices uses the reflective properties of **cyan, magenta, yellow, and black (CMYK)** inks. A PDL's support for a particular color model provides an accurate translation between on-screen color and print output and ensures that different d evices produce identical output.

The "K" in CMYK is usually explained as standing for "key," as in a key plate used to align the other plates in the sort of offset print press used for professional color printing in high volumes. It might be more helpful to think of it as "blacK," though.

The choice of which PDL to use will largely be driven by compatibility with software applications. Adobe **PostScript** is a device independent PDL and often used for professional desktop publishing and graphical design output. HP's **Printer Control Language (PCL)** is more closely tied to individual features of printer models and can introduce some variation in output depending on the print device. PCL is usually a bit faster than PostScript, however. Many Windows print devices default to using Microsoft's XML paper specification (XPS) PDL.

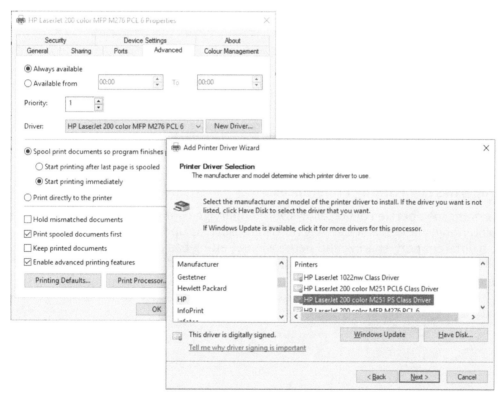

A print device might support more than one PDL—this HP printer supports both Printer Control Language (PCL) and PostScript (PS). (Screenshot courtesy of Microsoft.)

Printer Properties

Each logical printer object can be set up with default **configuration settings** via its driver or app.

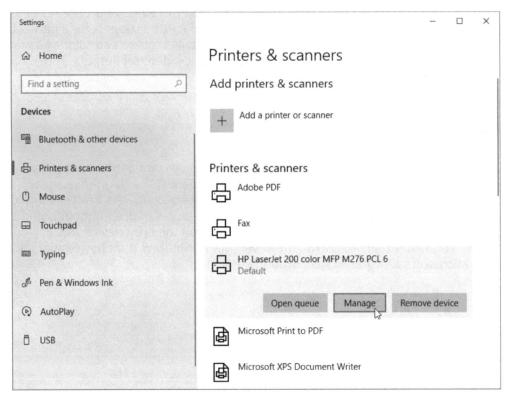

Viewing the print queue and configuring preferences through the Printers and Scanners Settings app page. (Screenshot courtesy of Microsoft.)

In Windows, there are two main configuration dialogs for a local printer: **Printer Properties** and **Printing Preferences**.

A printer's **Properties** dialog allows you to manage configuration settings for the printer object and the underlying hardware, such as updating the driver, printing to a different port, sharing and permissions, setting basic device options (such as whether a **duplex unit** or finisher unit is installed), and configuring default paper types for different feed **trays**.

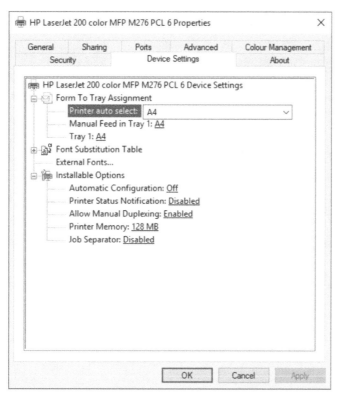

Printer properties—this HP printer allows defaults and installable options to be configured here. (Screenshot courtesy of Microsoft.)

The **About** tab contains information about the driver and the printer vendor and may include links to support and troubleshooting tips and utilities.

Printing Preferences

In contrast to the Properties dialog box, the Preferences dialog sets the default print job options, such as the type and **orientation** of paper or whether to print in color or black and white. These settings can also be changed on a per-job basis by selecting the Properties button in the application's Print dialog. Alternatively, the printer may come with management software that you can use to change settings.

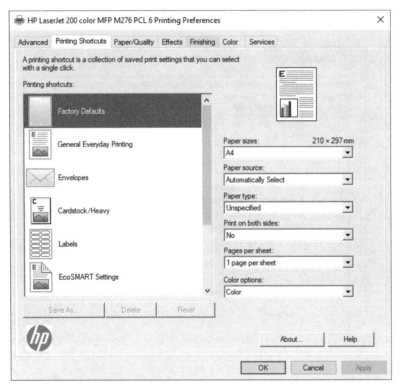

Printing Preferences dialog box—this shortcuts tab lets you select from preset option templates. (Screenshot courtesy of Microsoft.)

Paper/Quality

The **Paper/Quality** tab allows you to choose the type of paper stock (size and type) to use and whether to use an economy or draft mode to preserve ink/toner. You can also use the **Color** tab to select between color and grayscale printing.

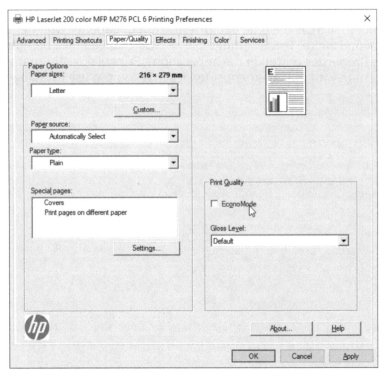

Use the Paper/Quality tab to configure the paper type and whether to use a reduced ink/toner economy mode. (Screenshot courtesy of Microsoft.)

Finishing

The **Finishing** tab lets you select output options such as whether to print on both sides of the paper (duplex), print multiple images per sheet, and/or print in portrait or landscape orientation.

Printer Sharing

The interfaces on a print device determine how it is connected to the network. The printer **sharing** model describes how multiple client devices access the printer.

Some printers come with integrated or embedded **print server** hardware and firmware, allowing client computers to connect to them directly over the network without having to go via a server computer.

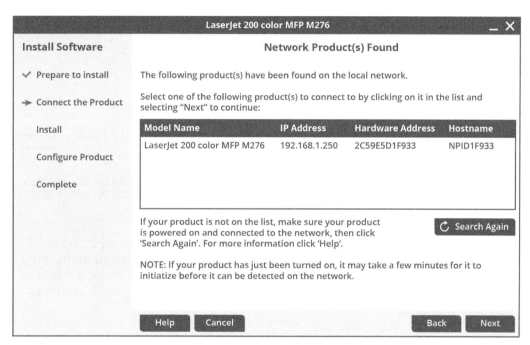

Installing a network printer using a vendor tool. The printer has been connected to the network via an Ethernet cable and been assigned an Internet Protocol (IP) address by a Dynamic Host Configuration Protocol (DHCP) server.

A **public** printer is configured with no access controls so any guest client may use it.

Windows Print Server Configuration

As an alternative to allowing clients to connect directly to the print device, any computer with a print device installed can share that printer object for use by other client computers. The print server could be connected to the print device via a local USB port or over the network. This sharing model allows more administrative control over which clients are allowed to connect. The printer object can be configured with permissions that allow only authenticated users to submit print jobs.

In Windows, a share is configured using the **Sharing** tab in the printer's **Properties** dialog. Drivers for different operating systems can also be made available so that clients can download and install the appropriate driver when they connect to the print share.

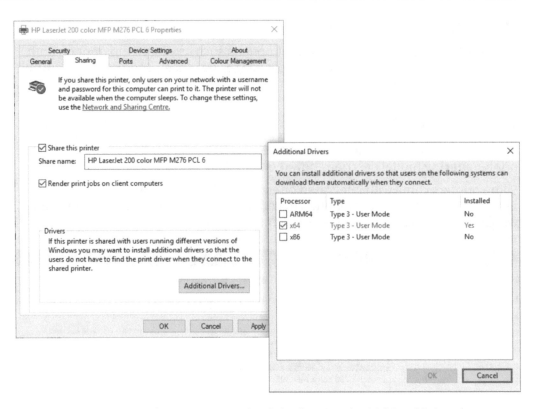

Sharing a printer via the Printer Properties dialog box. Use the Additional Drivers button from the Sharing page to install drivers for operating systems other than the host print server. (Screenshot courtesy of Microsoft.)

If the network has clients running a mix of different operating systems, you need to consider how to make a printer driver available for each supported client. If the printer supports a "Type 3" driver, you need only add x86 (32-bit Windows) and/or x64 (64-bit Windows) support. For earlier "Type 2" drivers, each specific Windows version requires its own driver.

Windows 10 adds support for Type 4 drivers. These are designed to move toward a print class driver framework, where a single driver will work with multiple devices. Where a specific print device driver is required, the client obtains it from Windows Update rather than the print server.

Shared Printer Connections

Ordinary users can connect to a network printer if the print server administrator has given them permissions to use it. One way of doing this is to browse through the network resources using the **Network** object in **File Explorer**. Open the server computer hosting the printer, then right-click the required printer and select **Connect**.

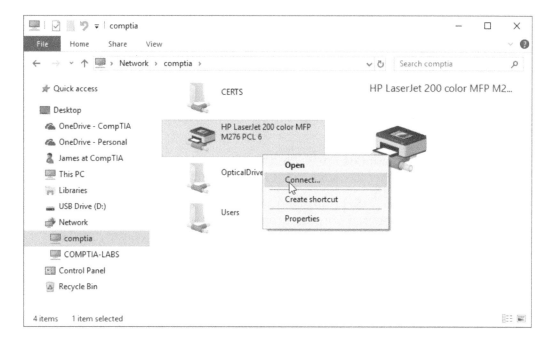

Connecting to a network printer via File Explorer. (Screenshot courtesy of Microsoft.)

Printer Security

Use of printers raises several security issues, including access to print services and risks to the confidentiality of printed output.

User Authentication

It may be necessary to prevent unauthorized use of a network printer. User authentication means that the printer sharing server or print device will only accept print jobs from authorized user accounts.

User authentication can be configured on a print share. For example, in Windows, the Sharing and Security tabs can be configured with a list of users or groups permitted to submit print jobs.

 Windows shares, permissions, and authentication are covered in more detail in the Core 2 course.

The print device might support user authentication options for clients who connect directly. A local authentication option means that a list of valid usernames and passwords is stored on the print device itself. A network option means that the print device can communicate with a directory server to authenticate and authorize users.

Secured Print and Badging

A **secured print** is held on the print device until the user authenticates directly with the print device. This mitigates the risk of confidential information being intercepted from the output tray before the user has had time to collect it. Authentication to release the print job might be supported using different formats:

- PIN entry requires the user to input the correct password or code via the device control panel.

- Badging means the print device is fitted with a smart card reader. The employee must present his or her ID badge to the reader to start the print job.

The secured print option may be selected as a default option or configured for a particular print job. Secured prints may only be cached for a limited time and deleted if not printed in time. The print device might require a memory card or other storage to cache encrypted print jobs.

Audit Logs

A printer share server or print device can be configured to **log** each job. This provides an **audit** record of documents that were sent to the printer by given user accounts and client devices. An audit log could be used to identify documents that were printed and have gone missing or to identify unauthorized release of information. If the log is generated on the print device, a log collector such as syslog can be configured to transmit the logs to a centralized log server.

Scanner Configuration

Many office printers are implemented as multi-function devices (MFDs). An MFD typically performs the functions of a printer, scanner/copier, and fax machine.

A **scanner** is a digital imaging device, designed to create computer file data from a real-life object. Typically, scanners handle flat objects, like documents, receipts, or photographs. **Optical Character Recognition (OCR)** software can be used to convert scanned text into digital documents, ready for editing.

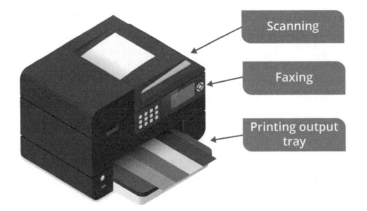

An MFD that can scan, print, and fax documents. (Image © 123RF.com)

Scanner Types

Scanners are available in two basic formats: A **flatbed scanner** works by shining a bright light at the object, which is placed on a protective glass surface. A system of mirrors reflects the illuminated image of the object onto a lens. The lens either uses a prism to split the image into its component RGB colors or focuses it onto imaging sensors coated with different color filters. This information is used to create a bitmap file of the object. An **automatic document feeder (ADF)** passes paper over a fixed scan head. This is a more efficient means of scanning multi-page documents.

Network Scan Services

An MFD or standalone scanner can be configured as a network device in the same way as a basic print device. When configured on the network, one or more services is used to direct the scan output to a particular media:

- **Scan to email** means that the scan is created as a file attachment to an email message. The MFD must be configured with the IP address of an SMTP server. The SMTP server would typically authenticate the user account before accepting the message for delivery.

- **Server Message Block (SMB) or scan to folder** means that the scan is created as a file on a shared network folder. The MFD must be configured with the path to a suitably configured file server and shared folder. Each user must have permission to write to the share.

- **Scan to cloud** services mean that the scan is uploaded as a file to a document storage and sharing account in the cloud. Cloud services such as OneDrive or Dropbox will generally be available as options on the MFD, or there may be the ability to configure a custom service via a template. The scan dialogs will allow the user to authenticate to a given cloud account.

Review Activity:

Printer and Multifunction Devices

Answer the following questions:

1. Following some past issues with faults arising in print devices because of improper setup procedures, you are updating the company's work instructions for printer installation. You have noted that technicians must refer to the product instructions, use safe lifting techniques, and ensure removal of packing strips. What additional guidance should you include?

2. You use three Windows 10 applications that need to print to a Canon inkjet printer. How many printer drivers must you install?

3. Users in the marketing department complain that a recently installed printer is not producing accurate color output. What step might resolve the problem?

4. True or false? To enable printer sharing via Windows, the print device must be connected to the Windows PC via an Ethernet or Wi-Fi link.

5. What configuration information does a user need to use a print device connected to the same local network?

6. To minimize paper costs, a department should use the duplex printing option on a shared printer by default. The print device is already configured with an automatic duplex finishing unit. What additional step should you take to try to ensure duplex printing?

Topic 9B

Replace Print Device Consumables

CORE 1 EXAM OBJECTIVES COVERED
3.7 Given a scenario, install and replace printer consumables.

Before you can provide the right level of support for print services, you must understand how the various components work within each type of print device to provide the desired outputs. In this topic, you will learn the components and maintenance procedures for laser, inkjet, thermal, impact, and 3-D print device types.

Laser Printer Imaging Process

Laser printers are one of the most popular printer technologies for office applications because they are inexpensive (both to buy and to run), quiet, and fast, and they produce high-quality output that does not smear or fade. There are both grayscale and color models.

The laser print process follows the steps detailed in the following sections.

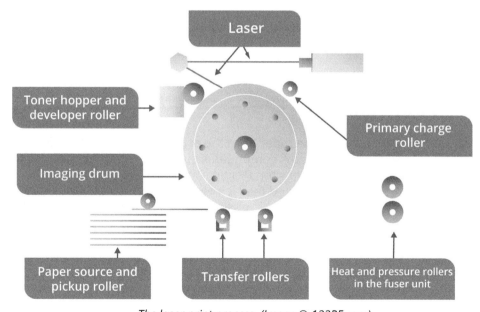

The laser print process. (Image © 123RF.com)

Processing Stage

Laser printers produce output as a series of dots. The OS driver encodes the page in a page description language and sends it to the print device. In the **processing** stage, the printer's formatter board processes the data to create a bitmap (or raster) of the page and stores it in the printer's RAM.

Charging Stage

In the **charging** stage, the **imaging drum** is conditioned by the primary charge roller (PCR). The PCR is a metal roller with a rubber coating powered by a high voltage power supply assembly. The PCR applies a uniform -600 V electrical charge across the drum's surface.

Exposing Stage

The surface coating of the photosensitive imaging drum loses its charge when exposed to light. In the **exposing** stage, as the laser receives the image information, it fires a short pulse of light for each dot in the raster to neutralize the charge that was applied by the PCR. The pulsing light beam is reflected by a polygonal mirror through a system of lenses onto the rotating photosensitive drum. The drum ends up with a series of raster lines with charge/no-charge dots that represent an electrostatic latent image of the image to be printed.

Developing Stage

Laser **toner** is composed of a fine compound of dyestuff and either wax or plastic particles. The toner is fed evenly onto a magnetized **developer roller** from a hopper.

The developer roller is located very close to the photosensitive drum. The toner carries the same negative charge polarity as the drum, which means that, under normal circumstances, there would be no interaction between the two parts. However, once areas of charge have been selectively removed from the photosensitive drum by the laser, the toner is attracted to them and sticks to those parts of its surface. The drum, now coated with toner in the image of the document, rotates until it reaches the paper.

 The imaging drum, PCR, developer roller, and toner hopper are provided as components within a toner cartridge.

Transferring Stage

The **transferring** stage moves the toner from the drum onto the print media. The paper transport mechanism includes components such as gears, pads, and rollers that move the paper through the printer. Pickup components lift a single sheet of paper from the selected input tray and feed it into the printer. To do this, a **pickup roller** turns once against the paper stack, pushing the paper into a **feed** and **separation roller** assembly. This assembly is designed to allow only one sheet to pass through.

Pickup, feed, and separation rollers on an HP 5Si laser printer. (Image courtesy of CompTIA.)

*A printer will have a number of automatic trays and a manual tray. The manual feed tray uses a **separation pad** rather than rollers.*

When the paper reaches the registration roller, a signal tells the printer to start the image development process. When the drum is ready, the paper is fed between the imaging drum and the high voltage **transfer roller**. The transfer roller applies a positive charge to the underside of the paper. This causes the toner on the drum to be attracted to the paper. As the paper leaves the transfer assembly, a static eliminator strip (or detac corona) removes any remaining charge from the paper. This is done to avoid the paper sticking to the drum or curling as it enters the **fuser** unit.

Fusing Stage

From the transfer assembly, the paper passes into the **fuser assembly**. The fuser unit squeezes the paper between a hot roller and a pressure roller so that the toner is melted onto the surface of the paper. The hot roller is a metal tube containing a heat lamp; the pressure roller is typically silicon rubber. The heat roller has a Teflon coating to prevent toner from sticking to it.

Cleaning Stage

To complete the printing cycle, the photosensitive drum is cleaned to remove any remaining toner particles using a cleaning blade, roller, or brush resting on the surface of the drum. Any residual electrical charge is removed, using either a discharge (or erase lamp) or the PCR.

The entire laser printer cycle takes place in one smooth sequence, but since the circumference of the drum that processes the image is smaller than a sheet of paper, the early stages must be repeated 2–4 times (according to size) to process a single page.

Duplex Printing and Paper Output Path

When the paper has passed through the fuser, if a **duplexing assembly** unit is installed, it is turned over and returned to the developer unit to print the second side. Otherwise, the paper is directed to the selected output bin using the exit rollers.

If there is no auto duplex unit, the user can manually flip the paper stack. When manual duplex mode is selected for the print job, the printer pauses after printing the first side of each sheet. The user must then take the printed pages and return them (without changing the orientation) to the same input paper tray. Once this is done, the user can resume the print job.

Color Laser Printers

Color laser print devices use separate toner cartridges for each additive CMYK color. Color laser printers can use different processes to create the image. Some may use four passes to put down each color in turn; others combine the colored toner on a **transfer belt** and print in one pass.

Laser Printer Maintenance

As devices with mechanical parts and consumable items that deplete quickly, printers need more maintenance than most other IT devices. Printers generate a lot of dirt—principally paper dust and ink/toner spills—and consequently require regular cleaning. Consumable items also require replacing frequently under heavy use. To keep a print device working in good condition requires a regular maintenance schedule and user training.

 When performing any type of maintenance other than loading paper, unplug the printer from the power supply. Open the panels, and allow all components to cool to room temperature.

Loading Paper

The printer will report when a tray runs out of paper. When loading new paper, remember the following guidelines:

- Use good quality paper designed for use with the model of printer that you have and the required output type (document versus photo, for instance).

- Position the media guides at the edges of the loaded stack. The printer uses sensors from the guides to detect the paper size. Different trays may support different types, sizes, and thicknesses of media. Do not add unsupported media to a tray or overload it.

- Do not use creased, dirty, or damp paper. Ensure that paper is stored in a climate-controlled location with no excessive humidity, temperature, or dust.

Replacing the Toner Cartridge

You will need to maintain a supply of the proper **toner cartridges** for your printer model. When toner is low, the printer will display a status message advising you of the fact. Frugal departments may continue printing until the actual output starts to dip in quality. Removing the cartridge and rocking gently from front-to-back can help to get the most out of it. Color lasers will usually have four cartridges for the different colors, which can be replaced separately.

To replace the toner cartridge, remove the old cartridge by opening the relevant service panel and pulling it out. Place the cartridge in a bag to avoid shedding toner.

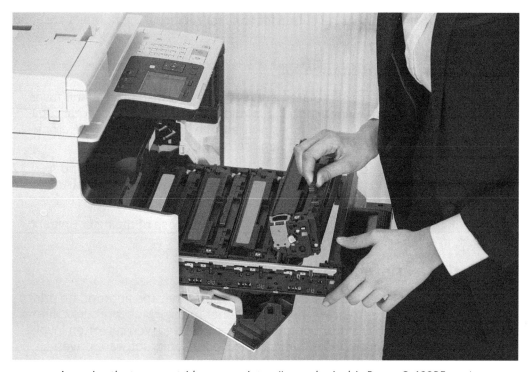

Accessing the toner cartridge on a printer. (Image by Andriy Popov © 123RF.com)

Take the new cartridge and remove the packing strips as indicated by the instructions. Rock the cartridge gently from front to back to distribute the toner evenly. Insert the cartridge, close the service panel, turn on, and print a test page.

 The drum in the toner cartridge is light-sensitive. Fit the cartridge in the print device immediately.

Toner cartridges are Waste from Electrical and Electronic Equipment (WEEE) and must be disposed of according to local regulations, such as by recycling them at an approved facility. Do not dispose of cartridges as general waste.

Cleaning the Printer

Consult and follow the manufacturer's specific recommendations for **cleaning** and maintenance. The following guidelines generally apply:

- Use a damp cloth to clean exterior surfaces.

- Wipe dust and toner away from the printer interior or exterior with a soft cloth, or use a toner-safe vacuum.

Do not use a compressed air blaster to clean a laser printer! You risk blowing toner dust into the room, creating a health hazard. Do not use an ordinary domestic vacuum cleaner. Toner is conductive and can damage the motor. Toner is also so fine that it will pass straight through the dust collection bag and back into the room.

- If toner is spilled on skin or clothes, wash it off with cold water. Using hot water is not recommended because heat can open the pores of your skin and allow toner particles to penetrate more easily.

- Use IPA (99% Isopropyl Alcohol solution) and non-scratch, lint-free swabs to clean rollers and electronic contacts. Take care not to scratch a roller.

- Follow the manufacturer's recommendations for replacing the printer's dust and ozone filters regularly.

Replacing the Maintenance Kit

A **maintenance kit** is a set of replacement feed rollers, transfer roller, and fuser unit. Replacement of the maintenance kit is guided by the printer's internal copy count of the number of pages that it has printed. The printer's status indicator will display the message "Maintenance Kit Replace" at this point.

Remove the old fuser and rollers and clean the printer. Install the fuser and new rollers—remembering to remove the packing strips and following the instructions carefully.

As with toner cartridges, use a recycling program to dispose of the fuser unit and old rollers in an environmentally responsible manner.

Calibrating a Printer

Calibration is the process by which the printer determines the appropriate print density or color balance (basically, how much toner to use). Most printers calibrate themselves automatically. If print output is not as expected, you can often invoke the calibration routine from the printer's control panel or its software driver.

Inkjet Printer Imaging Process

Inkjet printers are often used for good-quality color output, such as photo printing. Inkjets are typically cheap to buy but expensive to run, with costly consumables such as ink cartridges and high-grade paper. Compared to laser printers, they are slower and often noisier, making them less popular in office environments, except for low-volume, good-quality color printing.

Inkjet Printer Imaging Process

Inkjets work by firing microscopic droplets of ink at the paper. The process creates high-quality images, especially when specially treated paper is used, but they can be prone to smearing and fading.

There are two main types of inkjet **print head**. Epson printers use a charge (or piezoelectric) method. HP, Canon, and Lexmark use a thermal method. Each of these four vendors has licensed its inkjet technology to several other vendors to produce re-branded versions of its printers.

- With the thermal method, the ink at each nozzle in the print head is heated, creating a bubble. When the bubble bursts, it sprays ink through the nozzle and draws more ink from the reservoir. In general, thermal inkjet print heads are cheaper and simpler to produce, but the heating elements have a relatively short life. Most thermal printers use a combined print head and ink reservoir. When the ink runs out, the print head is also replaced.

- In the Epson design, the nozzle contains a piezoelectric element, which changes shape when a voltage is applied. This acts like a small pump, pushing ink through the nozzle and drawing ink from the reservoir.

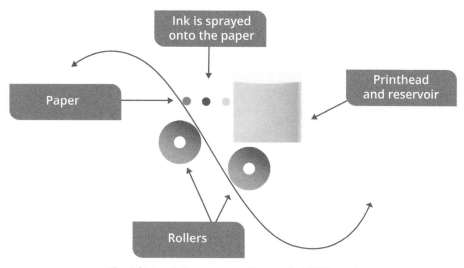

The inkjet printing process. (Image © 123RF.com)

Carriage System

Inkjet printers build up the image line by line. The print head is moved back and forth over the paper by a **carriage system**. On some types of printers, ink is applied when the print head moves in one direction only; bidirectional models apply ink on both the outward and return passes over the page. The carriage system uses a stepper motor, pulley, and **belt** to move the print head, a guide shaft to keep the print head stable, and sensors to detect the position of the print head. A flat ribbon data cable connects the print head to the printer's circuit board.

When a line has been completed, another stepper motor advances the page a little bit, and the next line or row is printed.

There may also be a lever used to set the platen gap or the printer may adjust this automatically depending on driver settings. The platen gap is the distance between the print head and the paper. Having an adjustable platen gap allows the printer to use thicker media.

The carriage mechanism in an inkjet printer. (Image by Erik Bobeldijk © 123RF.com)

Inkjet Printer Maintenance

Inkjets do not usually handle such high print volumes as laser printers, so maintenance focuses on paper stocking and replacing or refilling ink cartridges, which always seem to run down very quickly. Manufacturers recommend not trying to clean inside the case as you are likely to do harm for no real benefit. The outside of the printer can be cleaned using a soft, damp cloth.

Paper Handling and Duplexing Assembly

Most inkjets only support one paper path, with single input and output trays, though some have automatic duplexers, and some may have accessory trays. Printers are generally split between models that load from the top and output at the bottom and those that have both input and output bins at the bottom and turn the paper (an "up-and-over" path).

1. The paper pickup mechanism is similar to that of a laser printer. A load **roller** turns against the paper stack to move the top sheet while a separation **roller** prevents more than one sheet entering.

2. When the paper is sufficiently advanced, it is detected by a sensor. The stepper motor controlling the paper-feed mechanism advances the paper as the print head completes each pass until the print is complete.

3. The eject rollers then deliver the paper to the **duplexing assembly** (if installed and duplex printing has been selected) or the output bin. Some inkjets with a curved paper path may have a "straight-through" rear panel for bulkier media.

Inkjets tend to have smaller paper trays than laser printers and therefore can need restocking with paper more often. Most inkjets can use "regular" copier/laser printer paper, but better results can be obtained by using less absorbent, premium grades of paper stock, specifically designed for inkjet use. Often this type of paper is designed to be printed on one side only—make sure the paper is correctly oriented when loading the printer.

Replacing Inkjet Cartridges

Inkjet print heads are often considered consumable items. Often this is unavoidable because the print head is built into the **ink cartridge**, as is the case with most (but not all) thermal print heads. Epson piezoelectric print heads are non-removable and designed to last as long as the rest of the printer components.

The cartridge reservoir has sensors to detect the level of ink remaining. A color printer needs at least four reservoirs for each of the CMYK inks. These reservoirs may come in a single cartridge or there may be separate cartridges for black and colored ink, or each ink may come in its own cartridge. Some inkjets use light cyan and light magenta inks to support a wider color gamut.

Ink cartridges. (Image © 123RF.com)

When the inkjet's driver software determines that a cartridge is empty, it will prompt you to replace it. Check the printer's instruction manual for the correct procedure.

Other Inkjet Maintenance Operations

Two other maintenance operations may be required periodically.

- **Print head alignment**—If output is skewed, use the print head alignment function from the printer's property sheet to **calibrate** the printer. This is typically done automatically when you replace the ink cartridges.

- **Print head cleaning**—A blocked or dirty nozzle will show up on output as a missing line. Use the printer's cleaning cycle (accessed via the property sheet or control panel) to try to fix the problem. If it does not work, there are various inkjet cleaning products on the market.

Use the Maintenance or Tools tab on an inkjet printer's property sheet to access cleaning routines and calibration utilities. (Screenshot courtesy of Microsoft.)

Thermal Printer Maintenance

A **thermal printer** is a general term for any device that uses a heating element to create the image on the paper. There are several types of thermal printers that use significantly different technologies and are intended for different uses, but the most common type that you are likely to have to support is the direct thermal printer. Portable or small form factor direct thermal transfer printers are used for high-volume barcode and label printing and to print receipts. Such devices typically support 200–300 dpi, with some models able to print one or two colors. Print speeds are measured in inches per second.

A direct thermal receipt printer. (Image © 123RF.com)

Direct Thermal Printer Imaging Process

Most direct thermal print devices require special **thermal paper** that contains chemicals designed to react and change color as it is heated by the **heating element** within the printer to create images.

In the **feed assembly**, paper is friction-fed through the print mechanism by a stepper motor turning a rubber-coated roller. Paper and labels may be fanfold or roll format.

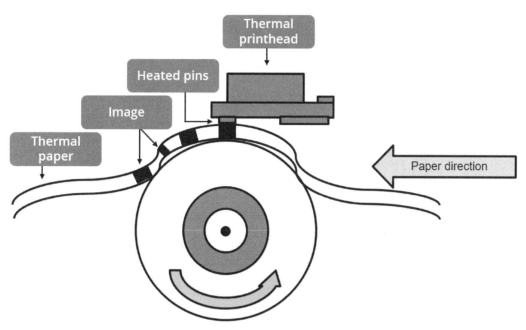

Direct thermal print process.

Direct Thermal Printer Maintenance Tips

When you are **replacing the paper roll**, you need to obtain the specific size and type for the brand and model of thermal printer you are using. The process is usually quite simple—just open the printer case, insert the roll, keeping the shiny, **heat-sensitive** print side facing outward, then ensure that the end of the paper is held in place by the print head when closing the case again.

Each receipt is separated by ripping the paper across serrated teeth. This can lead to a build-up of paper dust in the printer. It can also lead to bits of **paper debris** becoming lodged in the mechanism if a clean slice is not made and bits of leftover paper fall into the printer. Use a vacuum or soft brush to remove any paper debris.

Label printers can end up with sticky residue inside the printer. If labels are not loaded correctly, they can separate from the backing while being fed through the printer. You will need to ensure users know how to properly load the labels and how to clean up if labels get stuck inside the printer. Use a swab and appropriate cleaning fluid, such as isopropyl alcohol (IPA), to clean the print head or any sticky residue inhibiting the feed mechanism. Alternatively, you can often purchase cleaning cards to feed through the printer to clean the print head safely.

Impact Printer Maintenance

An **impact printer** strikes an inked ribbon against paper to leave marks. One common type is the dot matrix printer, which uses a column of pins in a print head to strike the ribbon. Desktop dot matrix devices are no longer very widely deployed for document printing, but they are still used for specialist functions such as printing invoices or pay slips on continuous, tractor-fed paper.

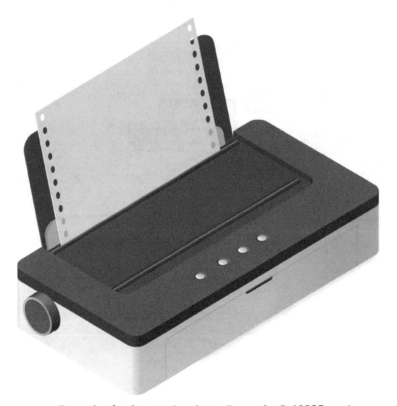

Example of a dot matrix printer. (Image by © 123RF.com)

Impact Printer Paper

Impact printers can be used with either plain, carbon, or tractor-fed paper:

- Plain paper is held firmly against the moving roller (the platen) and pulled through the mechanism by friction as the platen rotates. A cut sheet feeder may be added to some printers to automate the process of providing the next page.

- Carbon paper (or **impact paper**) is used to make multiple copies of a document in the same pass (hence carbon copy, or "cc"). A sheet of carbon paper is inserted between each sheet of plain paper, and when the print head strikes, the same mark is made on each sheet.

- **Tractor-fed** paper is fitted with removable, perforated side strips. The holes in these strips are secured over studded rollers at each end of the platen. This type of paper is more suitable for multi-part stationery as there is less chance of skewing or slippage since the end rollers fix the movement of the paper.

When you are **loading a tractor-fed impact printer with paper**, ensure that the holes in the paper are engaged in the sprockets and that the paper can enter the printer cleanly. Ensure that the lever is in the correct position for friction feed or tractor feed as appropriate for the media being used.

Impact Printer Components

An impact printer will also have some form of **replaceable ribbon**. Older-style printers used to have a two-spool ribbon. However, most units now have a cartridge device that slots over or around the carriage of the print head. These integrated ribbons simplify the design of the printer because they can be made as a complete loop moving in one direction only. The two-spool design requires a sensor and reversing mechanism to change the direction of the ribbon when it reaches the end.

When the ribbon on an impact printer fails to produce sufficiently good print quality, the ribbon-holder and contents are normally replaced as an integrated component. Some printers can use a re-usable cartridge.

Follow the manufacturer's instructions to **replace the print head**. Take care, as the print head may become very hot during use.

3-D Printer Maintenance

A **3-D print process** builds a solid object from successive layers of material. The material is typically some sort of plastic, but there are printer types that can work with rubber, carbon fiber, or metal alloys too.

3-D printing has very different use cases to printing to paper. It is most widely used in manufacturing, especially to create proof-of-concept working models from designs. The range of other applications is growing, however. For example, 3-D printing can be used in healthcare (dentistry and prosthetics), the clothing industry, and to make product samples and other marketing material.

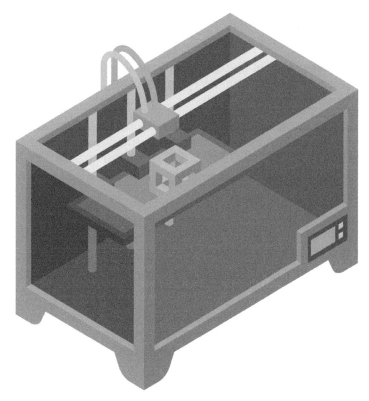

A 3-D printer. (Image by © 123RF.com)

3-D Printer Imaging Process

The **3-D printer** imaging process begins with either a scan of an existing object or by creating a design using 3-D modeling software. From either of these methods, you end up with a 3-D model created in software and saved to a 3-D model format.

The model is rendered into discrete horizontal layers or slices. The slicing software might be contained in the 3-D modeling software or within the 3-D printer. The result is a print job specifying how each layer in the finished object is to be deposited.

The sliced model is then fed to the 3-D printer over a USB or Wi-Fi connection or by inserting an SD card containing the file into the printer. The printer then melts a filament and extrudes it onto the build surface, creating layer upon layer based on the slices. The extruder (and sometimes the build bed) is moved as needed on X/Y/Z axes to create the build.

3-D Printer Components

There are several types of 3-D printers. Fused filament fabrication (FFF), also known as fused deposition modeling (FDM), lays down layers of filament at a high temperature. As layers are extruded, adjacent layers are allowed to cool and bond together before additional layers are added to the object. The main components in an FDM 3-D printer are:

- **Print bed**/**build plate**—a flat glass plate onto which the material is extruded. The bed is usually heated to prevent the material from warping. The bed must be leveled for each print job—this is usually automated, but cheaper printer models require manual calibration. It is very important that the printer frame be strong and rigid enough to keep the bed as stable as possible. Any vibration will result in poor-quality printing.

- **Bed/build surface**—a sheet placed onto the base plate to hold the object in position while printing but also allow its removal on completion. The bed surface material may need to be matched to the filament material for best results.

- **Extruder**—the equivalent of a print head in an inkjet. A motor in the extruder draws filament from the "cold end" through to the nozzle (or "hot end"), where it is melted and squirted onto the object. Different-size nozzles can be fitted to the extruder.

- **Gears/motors/motion control**—enable precise positioning of the extruder.

- **Fan**—cools the melted plastic where necessary to shape the object correctly.

The printer must be installed in a suitable environment. A stable, vibration-free floor and dust-free, humidity-controlled surroundings will ensure best results.

3-D printing involves several possible safety risks. Components work at high temperatures, and use of sharp tools such as scrapers and finishing knives is required. Ideally, the 3-D print facility should be accessible only to trained users.

Filament

The "ink" for a 3-D printer is supplied as a spool of **filament**. Filament is provided in a diameter of either 1.75 mm or 3 mm. There are various filament materials. The two most popular plastics are polylactic acid (PLA) and acrylonitrile butadiene styrene (ABS). Most printers can use a range of filament types, but it is best to check compatibility if a specific "exotic" is required for a project. Each material operates at different extruder and print-bed temperatures.

To change a filament, the extruder must be heated to the appropriate temperature. Pull as much of the old filament out as possible—taking care not to burn yourself— then push the new filament through. Do not start printing until all the old filament has been pushed out.

Filament spools require careful storage once opened. They should be kept free from heat and humidity.

Resin and Other 3-D Printer Types

There are two other common types of 3-D printer. These use different materials than filament:

- Stereolithography (SLA) uses liquid plastic **resin** or photopolymer to create objects which are cured using an ultraviolet laser. Excess photopolymer is stored in a tank under the print bed. The print bed lowers into the tank as the object is created. A liquid solvent removes uncured polymer after the model is finished.

- Selective laser sintering (SLS) fuses layers together using a pulse laser. The object is created from a powder and lowered into a tank as each layer is added. The powder can be plastic or metal.

Review Activity:

Print Device Consumables

Answer the following questions:

1. **What must you do before installing a new toner cartridge into a printer?**

2. **Which components are provided as part of a laser printer maintenance kit?**

3. **What types of paper/stationery can dot matrix printers use that laser and inkjet printers cannot?**

4. **You have been asked to perform basic maintenance on a printer in the Research and Development area. The dot matrix printer used to create shipping documents seems to be printing lighter than normal, and one of the pins seems to not be connecting near the center of the print head as there are blank areas in some letters and images. What maintenance should you perform?**

5. **A thermal printer used to create labels for parts bins, kits, and boxes is jammed due to a label coming loose during printing. How should you resolve this problem?**

6. **What considerations for locating a 3-D printer do you have to make?**

Topic 9C

Troubleshoot Print Device Issues

CORE 1 EXAM OBJECTIVES COVERED
5.6 Given a scenario, troubleshoot and resolve printer issues.

Users often need to print documents urgently. When the print process fails, it can cause a great deal of disruption. Users will look to you to identify and resolve their problems quickly, so you will need to recognize common issues and to correct them efficiently when they occur.

Printer Connectivity Issues

A printer connectivity issue might arise either because the device cannot be located when trying to install it or because the OS reports an installed device as offline or unavailable.

In many cases there will be an error message or code displayed on the print device's control panel. You may need to look the error code up in the printer documentation to confirm what it means. In the absence of any error code or descriptive error log, remember to test obvious things first:

- Verify that the printer is switched on and online. A printer can be taken offline quite easily by pressing the button on the control panel. Often this happens by accident. A printer may also go offline because it is waiting for user intervention, it has detected a network error, or because it has received corrupt print job data.

- Check that all components and cartridges are correctly installed, that all service panels are closed, and that at least one tray is loaded with paper.

- Print a test page using the printer's control panel. If this works, the issue lies with the connection to the computer/network.

- Cycle the power on the print device. If this does not solve the issue, consider performing a factory reset.

- Inspect the USB/Ethernet cable and connectors. Consider replacing with a known good cable to test for a cable or connector problem. If possible, attempt a different connection type. For example, if a wireless printer is not detected, try connecting to a computer via USB or using an Ethernet cable.

Remember to ask: "What has changed?" It is important to establish whether something has never worked or has just stopped working. If something never worked, then there has been an installation error; if something has stopped working, look for a configuration change or maintenance issue.

Print Feed Issues

If there is connectivity with the print device but multiple jobs do not print, there is likely to be a mechanical problem with the printer.

Paper Jam Issues

A **paper jam** is where a sheet of paper becomes lodged somewhere in the paper path. Fixing a paper jam is usually quite straightforward. The key point is to gain proper access to the stuck page. Do not use force to try to remove a sheet as you may cause further damage. Most sheets will pull free from most parts of the printer, but if a page is stuck in the fuser unit of a laser printer, you must use the release levers to get it out. Pulling the paper forcibly through the fuser can damage the rollers and, if the paper rips, leave paper debris on them.

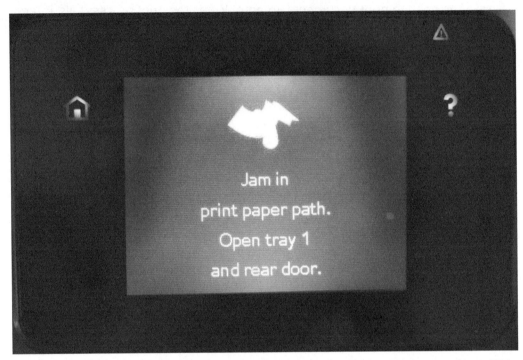

The printer control panel should identify the location of the paper jam. (Image courtesy of CompTIA.)

If paper jams are frequent, you need to diagnose the problem rather than simply fix the symptom each time. Most paper jams arise because the media (paper or labels) are not suitable for the printer or because a sheet is creased, folded, or not loaded properly in the tray. There could be a problem with a roller too. Identify whether or not the jam occurs in the same place each time, and take appropriate preventive maintenance (clean or replace the part).

 If the media and pickup rollers are good and if the jam occurs within the drum assembly but before the image is fused, the cause could be a faulty static eliminator. Normally, this part removes the high static charge from the paper as it leaves the transfer unit. If the strip fails, the paper may stick to the drum or curl as it enters the fuser unit.

With an inkjet, it is usually easy to see exactly where the paper has jammed. If the sheet will not come out easily, do not just try to pull it harder—check the instruction manual to find out how to release any components that might prevent you from removing the paper.

Paper Feed Issues

If paper is **not feeding** into the printer or if the printer is **feeding multiple sheets** at the same time, make the following checks:

- Verify that the **paper size and weight is compatible** with the options allowed for the print tray and that it is loaded in the tray properly with the media guides set properly.

- Check that the paper is not creased, damp, or dirty.

 Fan the edge of a paper stack with your thumb to separate the sheets before loading the tray. Do not overdo this, however—you can generate a static charge that will hold the sheets together.

- If you can discount a media problem, try changing the pickup rollers. In a laser printer, these are part of the maintenance kit.

Grinding Noise Issues

On a laser printer, a **grinding noise** indicates a problem with the toner cartridge, fuser, or other gears/rollers. Try to identify the specific source of the noise. Check all components to ensure they are seated correctly. Check the paper path carefully for jams and debris. If this does not solve the issue, replace either the printer cartridge or maintenance kit (or both).

On an inkjet, a grinding noise typically indicates a fault in the carriage mechanism. Check the vendor documentation for tips on re-engaging the clutch mechanism with the gear that moves the cartridge.

Print Quality Issues

If a job prints but the output is smudged, faded, or arrives with unusual marks (print defects), the problem is likely to be a printer hardware or media fault. The causes of print defects tend to be specific to the technology used by the imaging process. Always consult the manufacturer's documentation and troubleshooting notes.

Laser Printer Print Defects

The following defects are common in laser printers:

- **Faded or faint prints**—If a simple cause such as the user choosing an option for low density (draft output) can be discounted, this is most likely to indicate that the toner cartridge needs replacing.

- **Blank pages**—This is usually an application or driver problem, but it could indicate that a toner cartridge has been installed without removing its packing seals. Alternatively, if these simple causes can be discounted, this could also be a sign that the transfer roller is damaged (the image transfer stage fails).

- **White stripes**—This indicates either that the toner is poorly distributed (give the cartridge a gentle shake) or that the transfer roller is dirty or damaged.

- **Black stripes or whole page black**—This indicates that the primary charge roller is dirty or damaged or that the high voltage power supply to the developer unit is malfunctioning. Try printing with a known good toner cartridge.

- **Speckling on output**—Loose toner may be getting onto the paper. Clean the inside of the printer using an approved toner vacuum.

- **Vertical or horizontal lines**—Marks that appear in the same place (referred to as repetitive defects) are often due to dirty feed rollers (note that there are rollers in the toner cartridge and fuser unit too) or a damaged or dirty photosensitive drum.

- **Toner not fused to paper**—Output that smudges easily indicates that the fuser needs replacing.

- **Double/echo images**—This is a sign that the photosensitive drum has not been cleaned properly. The drum is smaller than the size of a sheet of paper, so if the latent image is not completely cleared, it will repeat as a light "ghost" or dark "shadow" image farther down the page. Images may also appear from previous prints. Try printing a series of different images, and see if the problem resolves itself. If not, replace the drum/toner cartridge.

- **Incorrect chroma display**—If prints come out in the wrong color (for example, if the whole print has a magenta tint), ensure that the toner cartridges have been installed in the correct location (for instance, that a magenta cartridge hasn't been installed in the cyan slot). Also ensure that there is sufficient toner in each cartridge. If there is a cast or shadow-like effect, the transfer belt or one or all of the cartridges or rollers are probably misaligned. Try reseating them, and then run the printer calibration utility and print a test page to verify the problem is solved.

- **Color missing**—If a color is completely missing, try replacing the cartridge. If this does not solve the issue, clean the contacts between the printer and cartridge.

Inkjet Print Defects

Lines running through printouts indicate a dirty print head or blocked ink nozzle, which can usually be fixed by running a cleaning cycle. Most other print quality problems (output that smears easily, wavy or wrinkled output, or blurry output) is likely to be a media problem. As with laser printers, persistent marks on output probably indicate a dirty feed roller. If the print head jams, the printer will probably display a status message or show a flashing LED. Try turning the printer off and unplugging it, then turning it back on. Inconsistent color output indicates that one of the ink reservoirs is running low (or that a print head for one of the color cartridges is completely blocked). If a document does not print in color, check that color printing has been selected.

Dot Matrix Print Defects

Lines in dot matrix printer output indicate a stuck pin in the print head. Output can also be affected by the platen position. The platen adjusts the gap between the paper and the print head to accommodate different paper types. Incorrect adjustment of the platen gap can cause faint printing (gap too wide) or smudging (too narrow).

Finishing Issues

A **finisher unit** can be installed on laser printers and MFDs to perform various functions, including stapling the pages of a print job or punching holes in the sheets so that they can be placed in a binder. The printer settings must be configured to select the finisher as an installed output option.

- **Incorrect page orientation**—The paper size and orientation must be set correctly for the print job or the finishing/binding will be aligned to the wrong edge. It can be tricky for users to paginate the source document and select the correct output options, especially when using a booklet print option to apply staples to the middle of the sheet. The icon in the printing preferences dialog will show which edge is selected for binding. Test settings on a short document first.

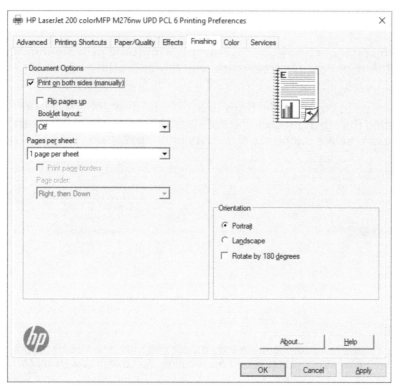

The Finishing tab in Printing Preferences allows you to select orientation and duplex output (this printer allows only manual duplex, where the stack must be flipped by the user and reinserted into the paper tray manually). You can also configure booklet layout. Note the icon showing which edge is used for binding. (Screenshot courtesy of Microsoft.)

- **Hole punch**—The main issue with hole punching is exceeding the maximum number of sheets. This can cause the finishing unit to jam. Make sure print jobs are sent in batches of less than the maximum permissible sheet count for the finisher unit. Be aware that the maximum number of sheets may depend on the paper weight (sheet thickness).

- **Staple jam**—An excessive number of sheets is also the primary cause of staple jams. One staple will become bent and stuck within the punch mechanism. Remove the staple cartridge, and release the catch at the end to allow removal of stuck staples.

Print Job Issues

If there is no hardware or media issue, investigate the OS print queue and driver settings.

Print Monitors

In Windows, display and print functions for compatible applications are usually handled by the Windows Presentation Foundation (WPF) subsystem. A WPF print job is formatted using the PDL and spooled in the logical printer's spool folder within %SystemRoot%\System32\Spool\Printers\.

The **print monitor** transmits the print job to the printer and provides status information. If a problem is encountered during printing, the print device sends a status message back to the print monitor, which displays a desktop notification.

If the print device is accessed over the network, a redirector service on the local computer passes the print job from the locally spooled file to the spooler on the print server. The print server then transmits it to the print device.

Print Queue and Spooler Troubleshooting

A backed-up print queue means that there are **multiple prints pending** but not printing. This might occur because the print device is offline or out of paper or ink/toner. It could also occur because of an error processing a particular print job.

In Windows, go to Windows **Settings** to access the printer and open its print queue. Try restarting the job (right-click the document name and select **Restart**). If that does not work, delete the print job, and try printing it again.

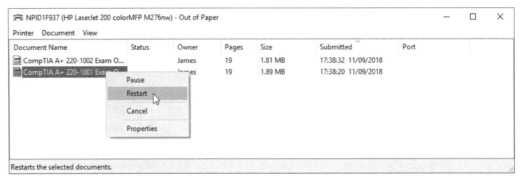

Use the print queue to manage jobs—in this instance, you should be loading the printer with some paper rather than trying to restart the print job. (Screenshot courtesy of Microsoft.)

If you cannot delete a job (if the print queue is backed up or stalled), you will need to stop and restart the Print **Spooler** service.

 The same steps apply to a shared printer. The server's print queue will hold jobs from multiple users.

Garbled Print Issues

A **garbled print** is one where the print device emits many pages with a few characters on each or many blank pages. This typically occurs because of a fault in rendering the print job somewhere in the path between the application, printer driver, page description language, and print device. To discount a transitory error, cancel the print job, clear the print queue, cycle the power on the printer (leaving it off for 30 seconds to clear the memory), and try to print again.

Use the OS to print a test page. If the test page prints successfully, then the problem is related to the print function of a particular application. Try printing a different file from the same application; if this works, then you know that the problem is specific to a particular file. If the test page does not print, try using the printer's control panel to print a test page directly from the device. If this works, there is some sort of communication problem between the print device and Windows.

If the problem persists, update the printer driver, and check that the printer is set to use a PDL (PCL or PostScript) that is supported by the source application.

If the characters in a document are different from those expected or if strange characters appear in an otherwise normal print, check that fonts specified in the document are available on the PC and/or printer. The software application should indicate whether the specified font is available or whether it is substituting it for the nearest match.

Review Activity:

Print Device Issues

Answer the following questions:

1. A user reports that the printed output is not up to the usual standards for her printer. You will need to resolve this issue so she can print her report. What is the overall process for troubleshooting this issue?

2. How would you track down the source of a paper jam?

3. Paper is repeatedly jamming in an inkjet printer. What could be causing this?

4. A laser printer is producing white stripes on the paper. What could be causing this?

5. What effect does a dirty primary charge roller have on laser printing?

6. You have been asked to perform basic maintenance on an inkjet printer. One of the users noticed that the colors are not printing correctly and that the bottom of some letters are not printing. What would you do?

7. If print jobs do not appear at the printer and the queue is clear, what could you try first to solve the problem?

Lesson 9

Summary

You should be able to deploy, maintain, and troubleshoot printers and multifunction devices.

Guidelines for Supporting Print Devices

Follow these guidelines to support the use of print and scan services in your organization:

- Ensure that operational procedures account for selection of an appropriate printer type, setup location, and unboxing to meet end-user and print application requirements.

- Identify an appropriate printer networking model (direct to print device versus sharing via print server), make drivers available to the range of clients, configure appropriate defaults for printer properties and printing preferences, and ensure that appropriate options are applied to protect the security and privacy of output (such as authentication to use the printer and use of secured print options).

- Create work instructions and prepare inventory for tasks relating to supported printer types:

  - Laser imaging drum, pickup rollers, separation pads, transfer roller/belt, fuser assembly, duplexing assembly, toner and maintenance kit replacement, calibration, and cleaning.

  - Inkjet cartridge, print head, roller, feeder, duplexing assembly, carriage belt, cleaning, cartridge replacement, and calibration.

  - Direct thermal feed assembly, heating element, special thermal paper, and cleaning.

  - Impact printer print head, ribbon, tractor feed and impact paper, and ribbon and print head replacement.

  - 3-D printer print bed and filament versus resin types.

- Establish a knowledge base to document common issues, such as lines down the printed pages, garbled print, toner not fusing to paper, paper jams, faded print, incorrect paper size, paper not feeding, multipage misfeed, multiple prints pending in queue, speckling on printed pages, double/echo images on the print, incorrect chroma display, grinding noise, finishing issues, and incorrect page orientation.

Appendix A

Mapping Course Content to CompTIA® A+® Core 1 (Exam 220-1101)

Achieving CompTIA A+ certification requires candidates to pass Exams 220-1101 and 220-1102. This table describes where the exam objectives for Exam 220-1101 are covered in this course.

1.0 Mobile Devices	
1.1 Given a scenario, install and configure laptop hardware and components.	**Covered in**
Hardware/device replacement	Lesson 8, Topic C
Battery	
Keyboard/keys	
Random-access memory (RAM)	
Hard disk drive (HDD)/solid-state drive (SSD) migration	
HDD/SSD Replacement	
Physical privacy and security components	Lesson 8, Topic C
Biometrics	
Near-field scanner features	

1.2 Compare and contrast the display components of mobile devices.	**Covered in**
Types	Lesson 8, Topic A
Liquid crystal display (LCD)	
In-plane switching (IPS)	
Twisted nematic (TN)	
Vertical alignment (VA)	
Organic light-emitting diode (OLED)	
Mobile display components	Lesson 8, Topic A
Wi-Fi antenna connector/placement	Lesson 8, Topic A
Camera/webcam	Lesson 8, Topic A
Microphone	Lesson 8, Topic A
Touch screen/digitizer	Lesson 8, Topic A
Inverter	Lesson 8, Topic A

1.3 Given a scenario, set up and configure accessories and ports of mobile devices.	Covered in
Connection methods	Lesson 8, Topic A
Universal Serial Bus (USB)/USB-C/microUSB/miniUSB	
Lightning	
Serial interfaces	
Near-field communication (NFC)	
Bluetooth	
Hotspot	
Accessories	Lesson 8, Topic A
Touch pens	
Headsets	
Speakers	
Webcam	
Docking station	Lesson 8, Topic A
Port replicator	Lesson 8, Topic A
Trackpad/drawing pad	Lesson 8, Topic A

1.4 Given a scenario, configure basic mobile-device network connectivity and application support.	Covered in
Wireless/cellular data network (enable/disable)	Lesson 8, Topic B
2G/3G/4G/5G	
Hotspot	
Global System for Mobile Communications (GSM) vs. code-division multiple access (CDMA)	
Preferred Roaming List (PRL) updates	
Bluetooth	Lesson 8, Topic B
Enable Bluetooth	
Enable pairing	
Find a device for pairing	
Enter the appropriate PIN code	
Test connectivity	
Location services	Lesson 8, Topic B
Global Positioning System (GPS) services	
Cellular location services	
Mobile device management (MDM)/mobile application management (MAM)	Lesson 8, Topic B
Corporate email configuration	
Two-factor authentication	
Corporate applications	

1.4 Given a scenario, configure basic mobile-device network connectivity and application support.	Covered in
Mobile device synchronization	Lesson 8, Topic B

Account setup

    Microsoft 365

    Google Workspace

    iCloud

Data to synchronize

    Mail

    Photos

    Calendar

    Contacts

    Recognizing data caps

2.0 Networking

2.1 Compare and contrast Transmission Control Protocol (TCP) and User Datagram Protocol (UDP) ports, protocols, and their purposes.	Covered in
Ports and protocols	Lesson 5, Topic C

20/21 - File Transfer Protocol (FTP)

22 - Secure Shell (SSH)

23 - Telnet

25 - Simple Mail Transfer Protocol (SMTP)

53 - Domain Name System (DNS)

67/68 - Dynamic Host Configuration Protocol (DHCP)

80 - Hypertext Transfer Protocol (HTTP)

110 - Post Office Protocol 3 (POP3)

137/139 - Network Basic Input/Output System (NetBIOS)/NetBIOS over TCP/IP (NetBT)

143 - Internet Mail Access Protocol (IMAP)

161/162 - Simple Network Management Protocol (SNMP)

389 - Lightweight Directory Access Protocol (LDAP)

443 - Hypertext Transfer Protocol Secure (HTTPS)

445 - Server Message Block (SMB)/Common Internet File System (CIFS)

3389 - Remote Desktop Protocol (RDP)

TCP vs. UDP	Lesson 5, Topic C

Connectionless

    DHCP

    Trivial File Transfer Protocol (TFTP)

Connection-oriented

    HTTPS

    SSH

2.2 Compare and contrast common networking hardware.	Covered in
Routers	Lesson 5, Topic A
Switches	Lesson 4, Topic B
Managed	
Unmanaged	
Access points	Lesson 4, Topic D
Patch panel	Lesson 4, Topic B
Firewall	Lesson 5, Topic A
Power over Ethernet (PoE)	Lesson 4, Topic B
Injectors	
Switch	
PoE standards	
Hub	Lesson 4, Topic B
Cable modem	Lesson 5, Topic A
Digital subscriber line (DSL)	Lesson 5, Topic A
Optical network terminal (ONT)	Lesson 5, Topic A
Network interface card (NIC)	Lesson 4, Topic B
Software-defined networking (SDN)	Lesson 7, Topic B

2.3 Compare and contrast protocols for wireless networking.	Covered in
Frequencies	Lesson 4, Topic D
2.4GHz	
5GHz	
Channels	Lesson 4, Topic D
Regulations	
2.4GHz vs. 5GHz	
Bluetooth	Lesson 4, Topic D
802.11	Lesson 4, Topic D
a	
b	
g	
n	
ac (Wi-Fi 5)	
ax (Wi-Fi 6)	
Long-range fixed wireless	Lesson 4, Topic D
Licensed	
Unlicensed	
Power	
Regulatory requirements for wireless power	
NFC	Lesson 4, Topic D
Radio-frequency identification (RFID)	Lesson 4, Topic D

2.4 Summarize services provided by networked hosts.	Covered in
Server roles	Lesson 5, Topic D
DNS	Lesson 6, Topic A
DHCP	
Fileshare	
Print servers	
Mail servers	
Syslog	
Web servers	
Authentication, authorization, and accounting (AAA)	
Internet appliances	Lesson 6, Topic B
Spam gateways	
Unified threat management (UTM)	
Load balancers	
Proxy servers	
Legacy/embedded systems	Lesson 6, Topic B
Supervisory control and data acquisition (SCADA)	
Internet of Things (IoT) devices	Lesson 6, Topic B

2.5 Given a scenario, install and configure basic wired/ wireless small office/home office (SOHO) networks.	Covered in
Internet Protocol (IP) addressing	Lesson 5, Topic B
IPv4	
Private addresses	
Public addresses	
IPv6	
Automatic Private IP Addressing (APIPA)	
Static	
Dynamic	
Gateway	

2.6 Compare and contrast common network configuration concepts.	Covered in
DNS	Lesson 5, Topic D
Address	
A	
AAAA	
Mail exchanger (MX)	
Text (TXT)	
Spam management	
DomainKeys Identified Mail (DKIM)	
Sender Policy Framework (SPF)	
Domain-based Message Authentication, Reporting, and Conformance (DMARC)	

2.6 Compare and contrast common network configuration concepts.	Covered in
DHCP	Lesson 5, Topic D
Leases	
Reservations	
Scope	
Virtual LAN (VLAN)	
Virtual private network (VPN)	

2.7 Compare and contrast Internet connection types, network types, and their features.	Covered in
Internet connection types	Lesson 5, Topic A
Satellite	
Fiber	
Cable	
DSL	
Cellular	
Wireless Internet service provider (WISP)	
Network types	Lesson 4, Topic A
Local area network (LAN)	
Wide area network (WAN)	
Personal area network (PAN)	
Metropolitan area network (MAN)	
Storage area network (SAN)	
Wireless local area network (WLAN)	

2.8 Given a scenario, use networking tools.	Covered in
Crimper	Lesson 4, Topic C
Cable stripper	Lesson 4, Topic C
Wi-Fi analyzer	Lesson 4, Topic D
Toner probe	Lesson 4, Topic C
Punchdown tool	Lesson 4, Topic C
Cable tester	Lesson 4, Topic C
Loopback plug	Lesson 4, Topic C
Network tap	Lesson 4, Topic C

3.0 Hardware

3.1 Explain basic cable types and their connectors, features, and purposes.	Covered in
Network cables	Lesson 4, Topic C

Network cables

Copper

    Cat 5

    Cat 5e

    Cat 6

    Cat 6a

    Coaxial

    Shielded twisted pair

        Direct burial

    Unshielded twisted pair

Plenum

Optical

    Fiber

T568A/T568B

Peripheral cables   Lesson 1, Topic C

USB 2.0

USB 3.0

Serial

Thunderbolt

Video cables   Lesson 1, Topic C

High-Definition Multimedia Interface (HDMI)

DisplayPort

Digital Visual Interface (DVI)

Video Graphics Array (VGA)

Hard drive cables   Lesson 1, Topic C

Serial Advanced Technology Attachment (SATA)

Small Computer System Interface (SCSI)

External SATA (eSATA)

Integrated Drive Electronics (IDE)

Adapters   Lesson 1, Topic A

Connector types   Lesson 1, Topic A

RJ11

RJ45

F type

Straight tip (ST)

Subscriber connector (SC)

Lucent connector (LC)

Punchdown block

microUSB

miniUSB

USB-C

Molex

Lightning port

DB9

3.2 Given a scenario, install the appropriate RAM.	Covered in
RAM types	Lesson 2, Topic C
Virtual RAM	
Small outline dual inline memory module (SODIMM)	
Double Data Rate 3 (DDR3)	
Double Data Rate 4 (DDR4)	
Double Data Rate 5 (DDR5)	
Error correction code (ECC) RAM	
Single-channel	Lesson 2, Topic C
Dual-channel	Lesson 2, Topic C
Triple-channel	Lesson 2, Topic C
Quad-channel	Lesson 2, Topic C

3.3 Given a scenario, select and install storage devices.	Covered in
Hard drives	Lesson 2, Topic B
Speeds	
5,400 rpm	
7,200 rpm	
10,000 rpm	
15,000 rpm	
Form factor	
2.5	
3.5	
SSDs	Lesson 2, Topic B
Communications interfaces	
Non-volatile Memory Express (NVMe)	
SATA	
Peripheral Component Interconnect Express (PCIe)	
Form factors	
M.2	
mSATA	
Drive configurations	Lesson 2, Topic B
Redundant Array of Independent (or Inexpensive) Disks (RAID) 0, 1, 5, 10	
Removable storage	Lesson 2, Topic B
Flash drives	
Memory cards	
Optical drives	

3.4 Given a scenario, install and configure motherboards, central processing units (CPUs), and add-on cards.	Covered in
Motherboard form factor	Lesson 1, Topic B
Advanced Technology eXtended (ATX)	
Information Technology eXtended (ITX)	
Motherboard connector types	Lesson 1, Topic B
Peripheral Component Interconnect (PCI)	
PCI Express (PCIe)	
Power connectors	
SATA	
eSATA	
Headers	
M.2	
Motherboard compatibility	Lesson 2, Topic D
CPU sockets	
Advanced Micro Devices, Inc. (AMD)	
Intel	
Server	
Multisocket	
Desktop	
Mobile	
Basic Input/Output System (BIOS)/Unified Extensible Firmware Interface (UEFI) settings	Lesson 3, Topic B
Boot options	
USB permissions	
Trusted Platform Module (TPM) security features	
Fan considerations	
Secure Boot	
Boot password	
Hardware security module (HSM)	
Encryption	Lesson 3, Topic B
TPM	
Hardware security module (HSM)	
CPU architecture	Lesson 2, Topic D
x64/x86	
Advanced RISC Machine (ARM)	
Single-core	
Multicore	
Multithreading	
Virtualization support	

3.4 Given a scenario, install and configure motherboards, central processing units (CPUs), and add-on cards.	Covered in
Expansion cards	Lesson 1, Topic B
Sound card	
Video card	
Capture card	
NIC	
Cooling	Lesson 2, Topic A
Fans	
Heat sink	
Thermal paste/pads	
Liquid	

3.5 Given a scenario, install or replace the appropriate power supply.	Covered in
Input 110–120 VAC vs. 220–240 VAC	Lesson 2, Topic A
Output 3.3V vs. 5V vs. 12V	Lesson 2, Topic A
20-pin to 24-pin motherboard adapter	Lesson 2, Topic A
Redundant power supply	Lesson 2, Topic A
Modular power supply	Lesson 2, Topic A
Wattage rating	Lesson 2, Topic A

3.6 Given a scenario, deploy and configure multifunction devices/printers and settings.	Covered in
Properly unboxing a device - setup location considerations	Lesson 9, Topic A
Use appropriate drivers for a given OS	Lesson 9, Topic A
Printer Control Language (PCL) vs. PostScript	
Device connectivity	Lesson 9, Topic A
USB	
Ethernet	
Wireless	
Public/shared devices	Lesson 9, Topic A
Printer share	
Print server	
Configuration settings	Lesson 9, Topic A
Duplex	
Orientation	
Tray settings	
Quality	

3.6 Given a scenario, deploy and configure multifunction devices/printers and settings.	Covered in
Security	Lesson 9, Topic A
User authentication	
Badging	
Audit logs	
Secured prints	
Network scan services	Lesson 9, Topic A
Email	
SMB	
Cloud services	
Automatic document feeder (ADF)/flatbed scanner	Lesson 9, Topic A

3.7 Given a scenario, install and replace printer consumables.	Covered in
Laser	Lesson 9, Topic B
Imaging drum, fuser assembly, transfer belt, transfer roller, pickup rollers, separation pads, duplexing assembly	
Imaging process: processing, charging, exposing, developing, transferring, fusing, and cleaning	
Maintenance: Replace toner, apply maintenance kit, calibrate, clean	
Inkjet	Lesson 9, Topic B
Ink cartridge, print head, roller, feeder, duplexing assembly, carriage belt calibration	
Maintenance: Clean heads, replace cartridges, calibrate, clear jams	
Thermal	Lesson 9, Topic B
Feed assembly, heating element	
Special thermal paper	
Maintenance: Replace paper, clean heating element, remove debris	
Heat sensitivity	
Impact	Lesson 9, Topic B
Print head, ribbon, tractor feed	
Impact paper	
Maintenance: Replace ribbon, replace print head, replace paper	
3-D printer	Lesson 9, Topic B
Filament	
Resin	
Print bed	

4.0 Virtualization and Cloud Computing	
4.1 Summarize cloud-computing concepts.	**Covered in**
Common cloud models	Lesson 7, Topic B
Private cloud	
Public cloud	
Hybrid cloud	
Community cloud	
Infrastructure as a service (IaaS)	
Software as a service (SaaS)	
Platform as a service (PaaS)	
Cloud characteristics	Lesson 7, Topic B
Shared resources	
Metered utilization	
Rapid elasticity	
High availability	
File synchronization	
Desktop virtualization	Lesson 7, Topic B
Virtual desktop infrastructure (VDI) on premises	
VDI in the cloud	

4.2 Summarize aspects of client-side virtualization.	**Covered in**
Purpose of virtual machines	Lesson 7, Topic A
Sandbox	
Test development	
Application virtualization	
Legacy software/OS	
Cross-platform virtualization	
Resource requirements	Lesson 7, Topic A
Security requirements	Lesson 7, Topic A

5.0 Hardware and Network Troubleshooting

5.1 Given a scenario, apply the best practice methodology to resolve problems.	Covered in
Always consider corporate policies, procedures, and impacts before implementing changes.	Lesson 3, Topic A

1. Identify the problem.

    Gather information from the user, identify user changes, and, if applicable, perform backups before making changes.

    Inquire regarding environmental or infrastructure changes.

2. Establish a theory of probable cause (question the obvious).

    If necessary, conduct external or internal research based on symptoms.

3. Test the theory to determine the cause.

    Once the theory is confirmed, determine the next steps to resolve the problem.

    If the theory is not confirmed, re-establish a new theory or escalate.

4. Establish a plan of action to resolve the problem and implement the solution.

    Refer to the vendor's instructions for guidance.

5. Verify full system functionality and, if applicable, implement preventive measures.

6. Document the findings, actions, and outcomes.

5.2 Given a scenario, troubleshoot problems related to motherboards, RAM, CPU, and power.	Covered in
Common symptoms	Lesson 3, Topic C
Power-on self-test (POST) beeps	
Proprietary crash screens (blue screen of death [BSOD]/pinwheel)	
Black screen	
No power	
Sluggish performance	Lesson 3, Topic D
Overheating	
Burning smell	
Intermittent shutdown	
Application crashes	
Grinding noise	Lesson 3, Topic C
Capacitor swelling	Lesson 3, Topic D
Inaccurate system date/time	

5.3 Given a scenario, troubleshoot and diagnose problems with storage drives and RAID arrays.

Covered in

Common symptoms

Lesson 3, Topic C

Light-emitting diode (LED) status indicators

Grinding noises

Clicking sounds

Bootable device not found

Data loss/corruption

RAID failure

Self-monitoring, Analysis, and Reporting Technology (S.M.A.R.T.) failure

Extended read/write times

Input/output operations per second (IOPS)

Missing drives in OS

5.4 Given a scenario, troubleshoot video, projector, and display issues.

Covered in

Common symptoms

Lesson 3, Topic D

Incorrect data source

Physical cabling issues

Burned-out bulb

Fuzzy image

Display burn-in

Dead pixels

Flashing screen

Incorrect color display

Audio issues

Dim image

Intermittent projector shutdown

5.5 Given a scenario, troubleshoot common issues with mobile devices.

Covered in

Common symptoms

Lesson 8, Topic D

Poor battery health

Swollen battery

Broken screen

Improper charging

Poor/no connectivity

Liquid damage

Overheating

Digitizer issues

Physically damaged ports

Malware

Cursor drift/touch calibration

5.6 Given a scenario, troubleshoot and resolve printer issues.	Covered in

Common symptoms   Lesson 9, Topic C

    Lines down the printed pages

    Garbled print

    Toner not fusing to paper

    Paper jams

    Faded print

    Incorrect paper size

    Paper not feeding

    Multipage misfeed

    Multiple prints pending in queue

    Speckling on printed pages

    Double/echo images on the print

    Incorrect chroma display

    Grinding noise

    Finishing issues

        Staple jams

        Hole punch

    Incorrect page orientation

5.7 Given a scenario, troubleshoot problems with wired and wireless networks.	Covered in

Common symptoms   Lesson 6, Topic C

    Intermittent wireless connectivity

    Slow network speeds

    Limited connectivity

    Jitter

    Poor Voice over Internet Protocol (VoIP) quality

    Port flapping

    High latency

    External interference

Solutions

Review Activity: Cable Types and Connectors

1. **A technician has removed an adapter card from a PC. Should the technician obtain and install a blanking plate to complete the service operation?**

Yes. The fan system is designed to draw cool air across the motherboard and blow out warm air. Large holes in the chassis disrupt this air flow. Also, dust will be able to settle on the system components more easily. A blanking plate covers the empty slot in the case.

2. **You are labelling spare parts for inventory. What type of USB connector is shown in the exhibit?**

USB 2.0 Type B micro.

3. **What is the nominal data rate of a USB port supporting Gen 3.2 2x1?**

10 Gbps.

4. **True or false? USB-C ports and connectors are compatible with Apple Lightning connectors and ports.**

False. An adapter cable is required.

5. **A technician connects a single port on a graphics card to two monitors using two cables. What type of interface is being used?**

Both DisplayPort and Thunderbolt interfaces support this type of daisy-chaining.

6. **A technician is completing a storage upgrade on an older computer. Examining the power supply, the technician notices that only two of the five plugs of the type shown in the exhibit are connected to devices. What is the purpose of these plugs, and can some be left unconnected?**

A Molex cable is a power cable used for storage devices that require more power than can be supplied over most internal bus types. Unused connectors do not pose any problem (though they should be secured with cable ties to minimize disruption to air flow). Note that Molex is a legacy connector format. Most drives use SATA power connectors these days.

Review Activity: Motherboards

1. **What type of motherboard socket is used to install system memory?**

Dual inline memory module (DIMM).

2. **How many storage devices can be attached to a single SATA port?**

One.

3. **What is the bandwidth of a PCIe v2.0 x16 graphics adapter?**

8 GBps in each direction (full-duplex). PCIe v2 supports 500 MBps per lane.

4. **You have a x8 PCIe storage adapter card—can you fit this in a x16 slot?**

Yes—this is referred to as up-plugging. On some motherboards it may only function as a x1 device though.

5. **You are labelling spare parts for inventory. What type of motherboard is displayed here?**

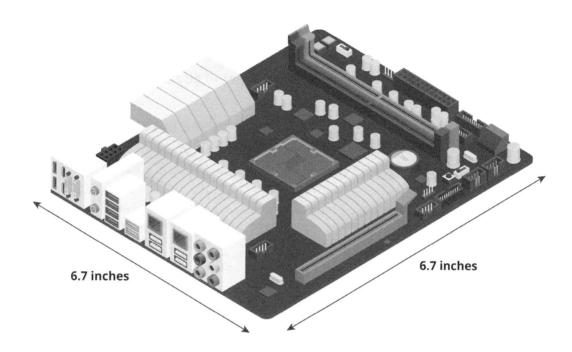

Both Micro-ATX and Mini-ITX are square form factors, but Mini-ITX is 6.7 inches square, while Micro-ATX is 9.6 inches x 9.6 inches.

6. **You have another part to label for inventory. What category of adapter card is shown in the exhibit?**

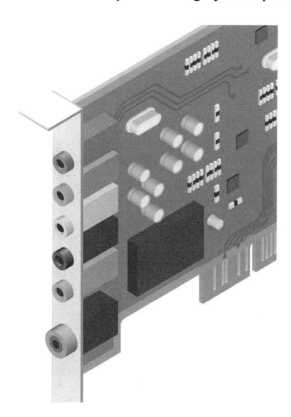

This is a sound card. It can be identified by the distinctive 3.5 mm audio jacks for connecting microphones and speakers.

Review Activity: Legacy Cable Types

1. **You are labelling systems for inventory. What two types of display cabling can be connected to this laptop?**

The image shows a 15-pin D-shell type video graphics array (VGA) port and a beveled high-definition multimedia interface (HDMI) port. The port in between them is an RJ45 network port, and the two ports on the right are USB Type A ports.

2. **Which ports are present on the graphics card shown below?**

The port on the left is digital visual interface (DVI). The pattern of pins identifies it specifically as dual link DVI-I, which supports both digital and analog signaling. The port on the right is a DisplayPort interface.

3. **Which interfaces does the adapter cable shown below support?**

DVI-I (left) and HDMI.

Review Activity: Power Supplies and Cooling

1.   What is the significance of a PSU's wattage rating when you are designing a custom-build PC?

It determines the CPU model and number and type of memory modules, expansion cards, and storage devices that can be installed. The PSU's wattage rating must be higher than the sum of the power requirements of all the PC's components.

2.   Your company has recently closed a foreign branch office, and you are repurposing some PCs that were shipped from the old location. What feature of the PSUs must you check before powering the systems on?

You must check that the voltage selector is set to the correct voltage or, if there is no selector, that the PSU is suitable for the voltage used by the building power circuit.

3.   One of the PCs has a faulty CPU, and one has a faulty power supply. You can use the CPU from one machine in the other. You have opened the case and taken antistatic precautions. What steps must you perform to access the CPU?

You will have to remove the fan and heat-sink assembly, disconnect the fan's power connector, release the pins or screws that attach the assembly to the motherboard, and remove the assembly (a gentle twisting motion may be required if the thermal paste has stuck the heat sink firmly to the CPU).

4.   The repurposed PC is put into service, but later that day the PC's user contacts you to say that the system has been displaying numerous alerts about high temperature. What do you think might be the cause?

You would need to open the case to investigate the problem. Perhaps when the upgrade was performed, one of the fan power connectors was not attached properly, or there could be a fault in the fan on the PSU.

Review Activity: Storage Devices

1.   True or false? A solid-state drive (SSD) attached to an M.2 port must be using the non-volatile memory host controller interface specification (NVMHCI) or NVM Express (NVMe).

False. M.2 is a physical form factor and can support both SATA and NVMe interfaces.

2.   What basic factor might you look at in selecting a high-performance hard disk drive?

Revolutions per minute (RPM)—the speed at which it spins. The top-performing drives are 15,000 (15K) or 10,000 (10K).

3.   If you have a computer with three hard disks, what type of RAID fault-tolerant configuration will make best use of them?

RAID 5 (striping with parity). RAID 0 is not fault tolerant. RAID 1 and RAID 10 require an even number of disks.

4.   You are configuring four 120 GB drives in a RAID 5 array. How much space will be available?

360 GB.

5. **What is the minimum number of disks required to implement RAID 10, and how much of the disks' total capacity will be available for the volume?**

RAID 10 requires at least four disks (two mirrored pairs) and comes with a 50% capacity overhead, so the volume will only be half the total disk capacity.

6. **True or false? A memory card reader is needed to attach a thumb drive to a PC.**

False—a thumb or pen drive will plug into a USB port.

Review Activity: System Memory

1. **What type of memory technology supports paging?**

Virtual RAM or virtual memory. The operating system creates a virtual address space for each process. This address space can use physical system random-access memory (RAM) modules and swap space or paging files stored on fixed disks (hard drives and SSDs). Paging moves data between system RAM and the swap space as required.

2. **You need to upgrade the system RAM on a PC. The motherboard has two 8 GB modules of DDR3 RAM installed and two free slots. You have two spare 16 GB DDR4 modules in your stores. Can these be used for this upgrade?**

No. The DDR generation of the motherboard slot and modules must match. You can only use DDR3 modules.

3. **You are configuring a different workstation with dual-channel memory. You have two modules and there are four slots. How would you determine which slots to use?**

Check the vendor's setup/service manual. Many systems will use the slots marked A1 and B1, but it's best not to proceed without consulting the vendor's documentation.

4. **Consulting the vendor documentation, you find that this system uses DDR4 error-correcting code (ECC) RDIMMs. The spares you have are DDR4 ECC UDIMMs. Can they be used for the upgrade?**

No. If the vendor documentation specifies registered memory (RDIMMs), you must use RDIMM modules. Unbuffered DIMMs (UDIMMs) will not be compatible even if they are ECC.

Review Activity: CPUs

1. **Why can cache improve performance?**

A CPU tends to repeat the same routines and access the same data over and over again. If these routines are stored in fast cache RAM, they can be accessed more quickly than instructions and data stored in system memory.

2. **A workstation has a multi-socket motherboard but only a single LGA 1150 socket is populated. The installed CPU is a Xeon E3-1220. You have a Xeon E3-1231 CPU in store that also uses the LGA 1150. Should this be used to enable symmetric multiprocessing and upgrade system performance?**

No. The CPU models must be identical. If the CPUs are not identical, the system is unlikely to boot. Even if the system boots, it is not likely to operate reliably.

3. **You are specifying a computer for use as a software development workstation. This will be required to run multiple virtual machines (VMs). Can any x64-compatible CPU with sufficient clock speed be used?**

No. You must verify that the CPU model supports virtualization extensions.

4. **What must you check when inserting a PGA form factor CPU?**

You must check that pin 1 is aligned properly and that the pins on the package are aligned with the holes in the socket. Otherwise, you risk damaging the pins when the locking lever is secured.

Review Activity: Troubleshooting Methodology

1. **You are dealing with a support request and think that you have identified the probable cause of the reported problem. What should be your next troubleshooting step?**

Test the theory to determine the cause.

2. **If you must open the system case to troubleshoot a computer, what should you check before proceeding?**

You should check that data on the PC has been backed up. You should always verify that you have a backup before beginning any troubleshooting activities.

3. **What should you do if you cannot determine the cause of a problem?**

You could consult a colleague, refer to product documentation, or search the web. It might also be appropriate to escalate the problem to more senior support staff.

4. **You think you have discovered the solution to a problem in a product Knowledge Base, and the solution involves installing a software patch. What should be your next troubleshooting step?**

You should identify any negative consequences in applying the software patch, then devise an implementation plan to install the file. You need to schedule the work so as to minimize disruption. You should also make a plan to roll back the installation, should that prove necessary.

5. **After applying a troubleshooting repair, replacement, or upgrade, what should you do next?**

You should test that the fix works and that the system as a whole is functional. You might also implement preventative measures to reduce the risk of the problem occurring again.

Review Activity: BIOS/UEFI

1. **Name three keys commonly used to run a PC's BIOS/UEFI system setup program.**

Esc, Del, F1, F2, F10, or F12.

2. **What widely supported boot method is missing from the following list? HDD, Optical, USB.**

Network/PXE (Pre-eXecution Environment)—obtaining boot information from a specially configured server over the network.

3. **When you are configuring firmware-enforced security, what is the difference between a supervisor password and a user password?**

The user password allows the boot sequence to continue, while a supervisor password controls access to the firmware setup program.

4. **True or false? A TPM provides secure removable storage so that encryption keys can be used with different computers.**

False. A trusted platform module (TPM) provides secure storage for a single computer as it is an embedded function of the CPU or motherboard chipset. The term hardware security module (HSM) is sometimes used to describe a secure USB thumb drive for storing encryption keys on portable media.

Review Activity: Power and Disk Issues

1. **You have been servicing a computer, but when you have finished you find that it will not turn on. There was no power problem before, and you have verified that the computer is connected to a working electrical outlet. What is the most likely explanation?**

It is most likely that one or more power connectors have not been reconnected. Check the P1 motherboard connector, a 4-pin CPU connector, and all necessary SATA or Molex device connectors. Also, the cable connecting the power button to a motherboard header could have been disconnected.

2. **Additional memory was installed in a user's system, and now it will not boot. What steps would you take to resolve this job ticket?**

Use the vendor's system setup guide to verify that the correct memory type was installed on the system and in the correct configuration (consider whether dual-channel memory was installed in the correct slots). Check that the new memory module is seated properly in its slot. Try swapping memory around in the memory slots.

3. **You are trying to install Windows from the setup disc, but the computer will not boot from the DVD. What should you do?**

Check that the boot order in system setup is set correctly. If the boot order is correct, check that the disc is not dirty or scratched. If the disc loads in another computer, check that the optical drive data and power cables are connected.

4. **Following a power cut, a user reports that their computer will not boot. The message "BCD missing" is shown on the screen. The computer does not store data that needs to be backed up. What is the best first step to try to resolve the issue?**

Use a system recovery disk to try to repair the disk drive's boot information.

5. **A user reports that there is a loud clicking noise when she tries to save a file. What should be your first troubleshooting step?**

Determine whether a data backup has been made. If not, try to make one.

6. **You receive a support call from a user of one of the company's computer-aided design (CAD) workstations. The user reports that a notification "RAID utility reports that the volume is degraded" is being displayed. A recent backup has been made. What should you do to try to restore the array?**

A degraded volume is still working but has lost one of its disks. In most RAID configurations, another disk failure would cause the volume to fail, so you should add a new disk as soon as possible (though do note that rebuilding the array will reduce performance).

7. **A user reports hearing noises from the hard disk—does this indicate it is failing and should be replaced?**

Not necessarily. Hard disks do make noises, but they are not all indicators of a problem. Question the user to find out what sort of noises are occurring or inspect the system yourself.

Review Activity: System and Display Issues

1. **What cause might you suspect if a PC experiences intermittent lockups?**

Assuming the cause is not related to software or device drivers, then thermal or power problems are most likely. Loose connections, faulty system components (motherboard, CPU, and memory), and corruption of OS files due to bad sectors/blocks are also possibilities.

2. **True or false? Running the fans continually at maximum speed is the best way to prevent overheating.**

False. This is likely to damage the fans and draw more dust into the case. It will also cause a lot of excess noise. To prevent overheating, the PC should be installed to a suitable location (away from direct sunlight and radiators) and cleaned and maintained to a schedule.

3. **You receive a support call from a lecturer. A projector is only displaying a very dim image. Which component should you prioritize for investigation?**

A dim image is likely to be caused by a blow bulb (or one that is about to blow). If there is no visible sign of damage to the bulb, you should rule out a simple configuration issue, such as the brightness control being turned all the way down.

4. **A user has been supplied with a monitor from stores as a temporary replacement. However, the user reports that the device is unusable because of a thick green band across the middle of the screen. What technique could you use to diagnose the cause?**

Replace the cable with a known good one. If this does not solve the problem, suspect an issue with the monitor. As the PC was used with no issues with another monitor, there is not likely to be an issue with the video card.

Review Activity: Network Types

1. **A network uses an IEEE 802.11 standard to establish connections. What type of network is this?**

A wireless local area network (WLAN).

2. **What type of network has no specific geographical restrictions?**

A wide area network (WAN) can span any geographical distance.

3. **A network uses Fiber Channel adapters to implement connections. What type of network is this?**

A storage area network (SAN).

Review Activity: Networking Hardware

1. **True or false? A MAC address identifies the network to which a NIC is attached.**

False. A media access control (MAC) address is a unique hardware identifier for an interface port. It does not convey any information about logical network addresses.

2. **A workstation must be provisioned with a 4 Gbps network link. Is it possible to specify a single NIC to meet this requirement?**

Yes. On an NIC with 4 gigabit Ethernet ports, the ports can be bonded to establish a 4 Gbps link.

3. **You are completing a network installation as part of a team. Another group has cabled wall ports to a patch panel. Is any additional infrastructure required?**

Yes. The patch panel terminates cabling, but it does not establish any connections between the cable segments. You must install a networking appliance to act as a concentrator and connect the cable segments. On modern networks, this means installing a switch and cabling it to the patch panel ports using RJ45 patch cords.

4. **You are planning to install a network of wireless access points with power supplied over data cabling. Each access point requires a 20W power supply. What version of PoE must the switch support to fulfill this requirement?**

PoE+ (802.3at) or PoE++/4PPoE (802.3bt).

Review Activity: Network Cable Types

1. **You are performing a wiring job, but the company wants to purchase the media and components from another preferred supplier. The plan is to install a network using copper cabling that will support Gigabit Ethernet. The customer is about to purchase Cat 5e cable spools. What factors should they consider before committing to this decision?**

Cat5e will meet the requirement and will cost the least. Cat 6 offers better performance without adding too much cost. Cat 6A would be the best choice for supporting future requirements, but it is likely to cost more than the customer is budgeting for.

2. **A network consultant is recommending the use of S/FTP to extend a cable segment through a factory. Is this likely to be an appropriate cable choice?**

Yes. Shielded/foiled twisted pair (S/FTP) will provide the best protection from the external interference sources likely to be generated by factory machinery.

3. **You are reviewing network inventory and come across an undocumented cable reel with "CMP/MMP" marked on the jacket. What installation type is this cable most suitable for?**

The cable is plenum cable, rated for use in plenum spaces (building voids used with HVAC systems).

4. **You need to connect permanent cable to the back of a patch panel. Which networking tool might help you?**

A cable stripper to remove the jacket insulation and a punchdown tool to terminate the wire pairs into insulation displacement connector (IDC) blocks.

5.   **Which fiber optic connector uses a small form factor design?**

The Lucent Connector (LC).

Review Activity: Wireless Networking Types

1.   **You are assessing standards compatibility for a Wi-Fi network. Most employees have mobile devices with single-band 2.4 GHz radios. Which Wi-Fi standards work in this band?**

Wi-Fi 6 (802.11ax), Wi-Fi 4 (802.11n), and the legacy standards 802.11g and 802.11b.

2.   **You are explaining your plan to use the 5 GHz band predominantly for an open plan office network. The business owner has heard that this is shorter range, so what are its advantages over the 2.4 GHz band?**

Each numbered channel in a 2.4 GHz network is only 5 MHz wide, while Wi-Fi requires about 20 MHz. Consequently, there is not much space for separate networks, and the chances of overlap are high. Numerous other product types of work in the 2.4 GHz band, increasing the risk of interference. Using 5 GHz will present a better opportunity to use channel bonding to increase bandwidth. As an open plan office does not have solid walls or other building features to block signals, the slightly reduced range of 5 GHz signaling should not be a significant drawback.

3.   **Can 802.11ac achieve higher throughput to a single client by multiplexing the signals from both 2.4 and 5 GHz frequency bands? Why or why not?**

No. First, a client can only use one radio at a time and so cannot connect simultaneously to the 2.4 GHZ and 5 GHz bands. Secondl, 802.11ac works only at 5 GHz; 802.11ac access points use the 2.4 GHz band to support 802.11b/g/n clients. The 802.11ac standard can increase bandwidth by using multiple input output (MIMO) antenna configurations to allocate more streams, such as 2x2 or 3x3.

4.   **You are setting up a Wi-Fi network. Do you need to configure the BSSID?**

No. You need to configure the service set identifier (SSID), unless you want to rely on the default value. The SSID is a name for users to recognize the network by. The basic SSID (BSSID) is the MAC address of the access point's radio. As this is coded into the device firmware, it does not need to be configured. Stations use the BSSID to send frames to the access point.

5.   **True or false? Only a single network name can be configured on a single access point.**

False. Each band can be assigned a different service set identifier (SSID) or network name. Access points also allow the configuration of multiple SSIDs per radio, such as configuring a secure network for known clients and an open network for guests.

6.   **True or false? A long-range fixed wireless installation operating without a license is always illegal.**

False. These installations may use unlicensed spectrum but must not exceed the effective isotropic radiated power (EIRP) defined for the frequency band by regulations.

Review Activity: Internet Connection Types

1.   **You are setting up an ADSL router/modem for a client; unfortunately, the contents of the box have become scattered. What type of cable do you need to locate to connect the router's WAN interface?**

Asymmetrical Digital Subscriber Line (DSL) connects to the phone line via a filter. You need an RJ11-terminated patch cord to make the connection.

2. **You are assisting another customer with a full fiber connection terminated to an optical network terminal (ONT). The customer's router was disconnected while some building work was being completed, and the patch cable is now missing. The customer thinks that the cable should be a fiber optic one because the service is "full fiber." What type of cable do you need to locate?**

An RJ45 unshielded twisted pair (UTP) patch cable. The ONT converts the optical signal over the external fiber optic cable to an electrical one to connect to the local router.

3. **True or false? Both 4G and 5G cellular can be used for fixed access broadband as well as in mobile devices.**

True. These can work as an alternative to wired broadband or as a backup/failover Internet connection type. Many router models now come with a cellular radio. A subscribed identity module (SIM) card from the service provider must also be installed.

4. **True or false? A SOHO router uses an embedded modem and Ethernet adapter to forward traffic between public and private network segments over a single hardware port.**

False. The modem and Ethernet interfaces use separate ports.

Review Activity: Basic TCP/IP Concepts

1. **A host is configured with the IP address 172.16.1.100 in the 172.16.1.0/16 IP network. What value should be entered as the subnet mask?**

A subnet mask field uses dotted decimal format. The /16 network prefix means that the first 16 bits in the mask are set to one: 11111111 11111111 00000000 00000000. A whole octet of ones converts to 255 in decimal. Therefore, the dotted decimal mask is 255.255.0.0.

2. **You are setting up a printer to use static IPv4 addressing. What type of value is expected in the default gateway field?**

The IPv4 address of the local router interface, entered in dotted decimal format.

3. **Another technician has scribbled some notes about IPv4 addresses used in various networks associated with support tickets. One of them is assigned to the WAN interface of a SOHO router that requires troubleshooting. Which of these addresses must it be?**

   - **52.165.16.254**

   - **192.168.100.52**

   - **169.254.1.121**

   - **172.30.100.32**

   - **224.100.100.1**

The WAN interface of the router must use an IPv4 address from a valid public range, so 52.165.16.254 is the only one it could be: 172.30.100.32 and 192.168.100.52 are in the class B and class C private ranges, 169.254.1.121 is in the range reserved for APIPA, and 224.100.100.1 is outside the range of valid public addresses (it is part of class D, which is used for a type of addressing called "multicasting").

4. **True or false? A SOHO router can be configured to provide an IPv4 address configuration to hosts without further administrator attention.**

True. This service is implemented by the Dynamic Host Configuration Protocol (DHCP).

5. **True or false? A valid IPv6 configuration does not require a subnet mask.**

True. In IPv6, the host ID portion of the address is always the last 64 bits. The network prefix length is used to determine which network a host is on, but a mask is not required.

Review Activity: Protocols and Ports

1. **True or false? At the Transport layer, connections between hosts to exchange application data are established over a single port number.**

False. The server application is identified by one port, but the client must also assign its own port to track the connection.

2. **What feature of DCHP means that it must use UDP at the transport layer?**

The Dynamic Host Configuration Protocol (DHCP) uses broadcast addressing, which is not supported by the connection-oriented Transport Control Protocol (TCP). Consequently, DHCP uses the connectionless User Datagram Protocol (UDP).

3. **Another technician has scribbled some notes about a firewall configuration. The technician has listed only the port numbers 25 and 3389. What is the purpose of the protocols that use these ports by default?**

Port TCP/25 is used by the Simple Mail Transfer Protocol (SMTP) to send and receive email messages. Port TCP/3389 is used by Remote Desktop Protocol (RDP) to connect to a computer's graphical shell over the network.

4. **The technician has made a note to check that port 445 is blocked by the firewall. What is the purpose of the protocol that uses this port by default, and why should it be blocked?**

Port TCP/445 is used by the Server Message Block (SMB) protocol that implements Windows File/Printer Sharing. SMB is designed for use on local networks only. Allowing access from the Internet would be a security risk.

Review Activity: Network Configuration Concepts

1. **You need to ensure that a print device receives the same IP address when connecting to the network. What value do you need to configure on the DHCP server to enable a reservation?**

The reservation should be configured with the media access control (MAC) address of the print device (plus the IP address to assign).

2. **True or false? A top-level domain such as .com represents the top of the DNS hierarchy.**

False. The Domain Name System (DNS) uses root servers at the top of the hierarchy. The root is represented by a trailing dot at the end of a fully qualified domain name (FQDN), though this can very commonly be omitted in ordinary usage.

3. **You are advising another technician about typical DNS configuration. The technician thinks that the name server hosting the 515 support domain resource records on the Internet should be configured as the primary DNS server entry in the IP configuration of local clients. Why is this unlikely to be the case?**

The role of a name server is to respond to queries for the resource records of the specific domain(s) that it is responsible for. The role of the DNS server types listed in a client's IP configuration is to resolve requests for records in any valid domain. To do this, the resolver must take on the task of querying multiple name servers on behalf of the client. Mixing these roles on the same server machine is possible in theory, but for performance and security reasons, they are more commonly performed by separate servers.

4. **What type of value would you expect a query for an AAAA resource record to return?**

An IPv6 address.

5. **What type of TXT record uses cryptography to help recipient servers reject spoofed messages and spam?**

DomainKeys Identified Mail (DKIM).

6. **Which network configuration technology can be configured on switches to divide a local network into multiple broadcast domain segments?**

Virtual LAN (VLAN).

Review Activity: Services Provided by Networked Hosts

1. **True or false? An HTTP application secured using the SSL/TLS protocol should use a different port to unencrypted HTTP.**

True. By default, HTTPS uses port TCP/443. It is possible in theory to apply SSL/TLS to port TCP/80, but most browsers would not support this configuration.

2. **A firewall filters applications based on their port number. If you want to configure a firewall on a mail server to allow clients to download email messages, which port(s) might you have to open?**

Either TCP port 993 (IMAPS) or 995 (POP3S), depending on the mail access protocol in use (IMAP or POP). These are the default ports for secure connections. Unsecure default ports are TCP port 143 and TCP port 110. Port 25 (SMTP) is used to send mail between servers and not to access messages stored on a server. Port 587 is often used by a client to submit messages for delivery by an SMTP server.

3. **You are configuring a network attached storage (NAS) appliance. What file sharing protocol(s) could you use to allow access to Windows, Linux, and Apple macOS clients?**

Most clients should support Server Message Block (SMB). Another option is to configure File Transfer Protocol (FTP).

4. **True or false? AAA allows switches and access points to hold directory information so that they can authenticate clients as they connect to the network.**

False. One of the purposes of authentication, authorization, and accounting (AAA) is to authenticate clients as they connect to the network, but the directory information and credentials are not stored on or verified by switches and access points. These devices are configured as clients of an AAA server and act only to transit authentication data between the end user device (the supplicant) and the AAA server.

5. **You are advising a company on configuring systems to provide better information about network device status. Why would you recommend the use of both SNMP and syslog?**

The Simple Network Management Protocol (SNMP) provides a means for devices to report operational statistics to a management server and to send a trap if a threshold for some critical value is exceeded. Syslog provides a means for devices to send log entries to a remote server. Both of these types of information are required for effective monitoring.

Review Activity: Internet and Embedded Appliances

1. **You are advising a customer about replacing the basic network address translation (NAT) function performed by a SOHO router with a device that can work as a proxy. The customer understands the security advantages of this configuration. What other benefit can it have?**

The proxy can be configured to cache data that is commonly requested by multiple clients, reducing bandwidth consumption and speeding up requests.

2. **You are recommending that a small business owner replace separate firewall and antimalware appliances with a UTM. What is the principal advantage of doing this?**

A unified threat management (UTM) appliance consolidates the configuration, monitoring, and reporting of multiple security functions to a single console or dashboard. You might also mention that the UTM might provide additional functionality not currently available, such as intrusion detection, spam filtering, or data loss prevention.

3. **A network owner has configured three web servers to host a website. What device can be deployed to allow them to work together to service client requests more quickly?**

A load balancer.

4. **You are writing an advisory to identify training requirements for support staff and have included OT networks as one area not currently covered. Another technician thinks you should have written IT. Are they correct?**

No. Operational technology (OT) refers to networks that connect embedded systems in industrial and process automation systems.

5. **You are auditing your network for the presence of legacy systems. Should you focus exclusively on identifying devices and software whose vendor has gone out of business?**

No. While this can be one reason for products becoming unsupported, vendors can also deprecate use of products that they will no longer support by classifying them as end of life (EOL).

Review Activity: Networks

1. **You are updating a support knowledge base article to help technicians identify port flapping. How can port flapping be identified?**

Use the switch configuration interface to observe how long the port remains in an up state. Port flapping means that the port transitions rapidly between up and down states.

2.   A user reports that the Internet is slow. What first step should you take to identify the problem?

Verify the link speed independently of user apps, such as web browsing, to determine if there is a cable or port problem.

3.   You are trying to add a computer to a wireless network but cannot detect the network name. What possible causes should you consider?

The network name is configured as nonbroadcast and must be entered manually, the wireless standard supported by the adapter is not supported by the access point, the station is not in range, or there is some sort of interference.

4.   What readings would you expect to gather with a Wi-Fi analyzer?

The signal strength of different Wi-Fi networks and their channels that are operating within range of the analyzer.

5.   A probe reports that the Internet connection has RTT latency of 200 ms. What is the likely impact on VoIP call quality?

Most vendors recommend that one-way latency should not exceed 150 ms. Round trip time (RTT) measures two-way latency, so 200 ms is within the recommended 300 ms tolerance. Call quality should not be severely impacted, but if latency is persistently that high, it might be worth investigating the cause.

6.   A user reports that a "Limited connectivity" desktop notification is displayed on their computer, and they cannot connect to the Internet. Will you need to replace the NIC in the computer?

No. Limited connectivity reported by the OS means that the link has been established, but the host has not been able to contact a DHCP server to obtain a lease for a valid configuration.

Review Activity: Client-Side Virtualization

1.   What is a Type 2 hypervisor?

Hypervisor software that must be installed as an application running on a host OS. A Type 1 (or bare metal) hypervisor is installed directly to the host hardware.

2.   You need to provision a virtualization workstation to run four guest OSs simultaneously. Each VM requires 2 GB system RAM. Is an 8 GB workstation sufficient to meet this requirement?

No. The host OS and/or hypervisor also requires system memory. If the host also a 2 GB requirement, you would only be able to launch three of the VMs simultaneously.

3.   What is the main security requirement of a virtualization workstation configured to operate VMs within a sandbox?

A sandbox means that the VM environment should be isolated from the host and from other VM environments. A sandbox is often used to investigate malware. If the sandbox is secure, the malware can be executed and observed without the risk of it spreading to other systems (VM escaping).

Review Activity: Cloud Concepts

1. **A cloud service provides a billing dashboard that reports the uptime, disk usage, and network bandwidth consumption of a virtual machine. What type of cloud characteristic does this demonstrate?**

Metered utilization.

2. **A company has contracted the use of a remote datacenter to offer exclusive access to platform as a service resources to its internal business users. How would such a cloud solution be classed?**

As a private deployment model.

3. **A technician provisions a network of virtual machines running web server, scripting environment, and database software for use by programmers working for the sales and marketing department. What type of cloud model has been deployed?**

This is a platform as a service (PaaS) model. Infrastructure as a service (IaaS) would only provision the VMs and network without the software. It is not software as a service (SaaS) because the web server and database are unconfigured.

4. **When users connect to the network, they use a basic hardware terminal to access a desktop hosted on a virtualization server. What type of infrastructure is being deployed?**

Virtual desktop infrastructure (VDI).

Review Activity: Mobile Devices and Peripherals

1. **A company is ordering custom-built laptops to supply to its field sales staff for use predominantly as presentation devices. The company can specify the type of panel used and has ruled out IPS and OLED on cost grounds. Which of the remaining mainstream display technologies is best suited to the requirement?**

Vertical alignment (VA) displays support good viewing angles and high-contrast ratios, which makes them well-suited to displaying slides to an audience. The twisted nematic (TN) type is cheap but does not support wide-angle viewing.

2. **You are writing a knowledge base article for remote sales staff who need to use their smartphones to facilitate Internet connectivity for their laptops from out-of-office locations. What distinguishes the hotspot and tethering means of accomplishing this?**

Configuring a hotspot allows the laptop to connect to the smartphone over Wi-Fi. Tethering means connecting the laptop via USB or Bluetooth.

3. **What type of peripheral port would you expect to find on a current generation smartphone?**

For Apple devices, the Lightning port. For Android, it will be USB-C.

4. **You are assisting a user with pairing a smartphone to a Bluetooth headset. What step must the user take to start the process?**

On the smartphone, open the Bluetooth page under Settings. This will make the phone discoverable and enable the user to find nearby devices. If the headset is not found automatically, check if there is a button on the headset to make it discoverable.

5. **You are identifying suitable smartphone models to issue to field sales staff. The models must be able to use digital payments. What type of sensor must the devices have?**

Near-field communications (NFC) allow the user to touch the phone to a point-of-sale terminal to authorize payment in conjunction with a wallet app.

Review Activity: Mobile Device Apps

1. **Why must a vendor account usually be configured on a smartphone?**

A vendor account, such as an Apple, Google, or Samsung account, is required to use the app store.

2. **Which types of data might require mapping between fields when syncing between applications?**

Contacts and calendar items.

3. **How do you configure an autodiscover-enabled email provider on a smartphone?**

Just select the provider then enter the email address. If the account is detected, you will be prompted for the password.

4. **A company has discovered that an employee has been emailing product design documents to her smartphone and then saving the files to the smartphone's flash drive. Which technology can be deployed to prevent such policy breaches?**

Mobile application management (MAM) allows an enterprise to create a protected container as a workspace for corporate apps and data and prevent copying to other storage areas.

Review Activity: Laptop Hardware

1. **Several laptops need to be replaced in the next fiscal cycle, but that doesn't begin for several months. You want to improve functionality as much as possible by upgrading or replacing components in some of the laptops that are having problems. Which items are most easily replaced in a laptop?**

The fixed drive, system memory (RAM), and plug-in wireless card will be the easiest upgradable components to install. If items need repairing, the battery, touchpad, and the keyboard should be straightforward to replace, if you can obtain compatible parts.

2. **What is the process for installing memory in a laptop?**

Verify that the DDR version of the upgrade module is supported by the motherboard. Take antistatic precautions. Locate the memory slot, which is usually accessed via a panel on the back cover. Move the connector up to 45° and insert the memory card, taking care to align it correctly. Push the card flat again.

3. **What type of standard adapter card might be used to connect internal FRU devices to the motherboard of a laptop?**

Mini-PCIe, mSATA, or M.2.

4. **A technician is performing a keyboard replacement and asks for your help. The data cable for the old keyboard will not pull out. How should it be removed?**

This type of flat data connector is secured by a latch. Pop the latch up before trying to remove the cable.

Review Activity: Mobile Device Issues

1. **You are troubleshooting a laptop display. If the laptop can display an image on an external monitor but not on the built-in one, which component do you know is working, and can you definitively say which is faulty?**

The graphics adapter is working. The problem must exist either in the cabling to the built-in screen or with a screen component, such as an inverter, backlight, or the display panel itself. Further tests will be required to identify which.

2. **You received a user complaint about a laptop being extremely hot to the touch. What actions should you take in response to this issue?**

Overheating can be a sign that dust and dirt is restricting the necessary airflow within the device, so start by cleaning the ventilation duct with compressed air, and then make sure that the device is getting proper air circulation around the outside of the case, such as by supplying a chiller pad.

3. **A user complains that their Bluetooth keyboard, which has worked for the last year, has stopped functioning. What would you suggest is the problem?**

The batteries in the keyboard have run down—replace them.

4. **A laptop user reports that they are only getting about two hours of use out of the battery compared to about three hours when the laptop was first supplied to them. What do you suggest?**

Batteries lose maximum charge over time. It may be possible to recondition the battery or to use power-saving features, but the only real way to restore maximum battery life is to buy a new battery.

5. **A laptop user is complaining about typing on their new laptop. They claim that the cursor jumps randomly from place to place. What might be the cause of this?**

The user could be touching the touchpad while typing, or vibrations could be affecting the touchpad. Update the driver or reduce the sensitivity/disable touch and tap events.

Review Activity: Printer and Multifunction Devices

1. **Following some past issues with faults arising in print devices because of improper setup procedures, you are updating the company's work instructions for printer installation. You have noted that technicians must refer to the product instructions, use safe lifting techniques, and ensure removal of packing strips. What additional guidance should you include?**

Allow the print device to acclimate for a few hours after unboxing to avoid risks from condensation.

2. **You use three Windows 10 applications that need to print to a Canon inkjet printer. How many printer drivers must you install?**

One. Applications rely on the operating system to mediate access to devices. They do not need their own drivers.

3. **Users in the marketing department complain that a recently installed printer is not producing accurate color output. What step might resolve the problem?**

Switch to a PostScript (PS) driver. This is likely to have better support for accurate color models. You might also suggest running a calibration utility.

4. **True or false? To enable printer sharing via Windows, the print device must be connected to the Windows PC via an Ethernet or Wi-Fi link.**

False—any print device can be shared via printer properties. The print device can be connected to the Windows print server over USB, Bluetooth, Ethernet, or Wi-Fi. Other clients connect to the printer via the share, however, so the Windows PC must be kept on to facilitate printing.

5. **What configuration information does a user need to use a print device connected to the same local network?**

The print device's IP address or host name. You might note that vendor utilities can search for a connected device on the local network, so "None" could also be a correct answer.

6. **To minimize paper costs, a department should use the duplex printing option on a shared printer by default. The print device is already configured with an automatic duplex finishing unit. What additional step should you take to try to ensure duplex printing?**

Set duplex mode as the default under Printing Preferences.

Review Activity: Print Device Consumables

1. **What must you do before installing a new toner cartridge into a printer?**

Remove the packing strips. The printer should also be turned off, and the old cartridge should be removed and placed into a sealed bag for recycling.

2. **Which components are provided as part of a laser printer maintenance kit?**

The main component is a new fuser assembly. The kit will also usually contain a transfer/secondary charge roller plus paper transport rollers for each tray (pickup rollers and a new separation pad).

3. **What types of paper/stationery can dot matrix printers use that laser and inkjet printers cannot?**

Multi-part or continuous tractor-fed stationery and carbon copy paper.

4. **You have been asked to perform basic maintenance on a printer in the Research and Development area. The dot matrix printer used to create shipping documents seems to be printing lighter than normal, and one of the pins seems to not be connecting near the center of the print head as there are blank areas in some letters and images. What maintenance should you perform?**

Using the steps in the printer documentation, replace the ribbon in the printer and clean the print head. If this does not fix the problem, replace the print head.

5. **A thermal printer used to create labels for parts bins, kits, and boxes is jammed due to a label coming loose during printing. How should you resolve this problem?**

Open the printer and locate the label that came off the backing. Remove the label, and if there is any sticky residue, clean it with isopropyl alcohol (IPA) applied to a swab. Ensure the roll of labels is properly loaded and that there are no loose labels that might come loose again.

6. **What considerations for locating a 3-D printer do you have to make?**

The 3-D print process is sensitive to movement and vibration, so the printer must be located on a firm and stable surface. The process can also be affected by dust and the ambient temperature and humidity (especially variations and drafts). Finally, some printer types are fully exposed, so there is some risk of burns from the high-heat elements. Ideally, the printer should not be accessible to untrained staff.

Review Activity: Print Device Issues

1. **A user reports that the printed output is not up to the usual standards for her printer. You will need to resolve this issue so she can print her report. What is the overall process for troubleshooting this issue?**

Print out a test page to see if you can reproduce the problem the user reported. If you see the same problem as reported by the user, identify the print defect, based on the type of printer, to resolve the problem. Document the steps you took to resolve the problem.

2. **How would you track down the source of a paper jam?**

Check the error message reported by the printer (this may be shown on the printer's console). It may indicate the location of the stuck pages. Otherwise, visually inspect the various feed and output mechanisms.

3. **Paper is repeatedly jamming in an inkjet printer. What could be causing this?**

The paper might not be loaded squarely, there might be too much paper loaded into the tray, or the paper is creased or dirty.

4. **A laser printer is producing white stripes on the paper. What could be causing this?**

Poorly distributed toner or a damaged/worn transfer corona wire. If the secondary corona does not apply a charge evenly across the paper, less toner is attracted from the drum to the part of the sheet where charging failed. Note that if there are repetitive white or black marks (rather than stripes) that do not smudge, the issue is more likely to be dirt or grease on the drum.

5. **What effect does a dirty primary charge roller have on laser printing?**

It leaves black stripes on the paper. If the roller does not apply the correct charge evenly to the drum, toner is attracted to the place where the charging failed, creating a black stripe all the way down the page.

6. **You have been asked to perform basic maintenance on an inkjet printer. One of the users noticed that the colors are not printing correctly and that the bottom of some letters are not printing. What would you do?**

Try using the printer's built-in cleaning cycle and then replacing the ink cartridge. If these do not work, try using an aftermarket cleaning product. Try using the printer properties sheet to check for print head alignment, color settings, and other settings.

7. **If print jobs do not appear at the printer and the queue is clear, what could you try first to solve the problem?**

Cycle the power on the printer.

Glossary

Core 1

32-bit versus 64-bit Processing modes referring to the size of each instruction processed by the CPU. 32-bit CPUs replaced earlier 16-bit CPUs and were used through the 1990s to the present day, though most PC and laptop CPUs now work in 64-bit mode. The main 64-bit platform is called AMD64 or EM64T (by Intel). Software can be compiled as 32-bit or 64-bit. 64-bit CPUs can run most 32-bit software, but a 32-bit CPU cannot execute 64-bit software.

3-D Printer Hardware device capable of small-scale manufacturing. Most 3-D printers use either a variety of filament (typically plastic) or resin media with different properties.

802.11 standards Specifications developed by IEEE for wireless networking over microwave radio transmission in the 2.4 GHz, 5 GHz, and 6 GHz frequency bands. The Wi-Fi standards brand has six main iterations: a, b, g, Wi-Fi 4 (n), Wi-Fi 5 (ac), and Wi-Fi 6 (ax). These specify different modulation techniques, supported distances, and data rates, plus special features, such as channel bonding, MIMO, and MU-MIMO.

802.3 Ethernet Standards developed as the IEEE 802.3 series describing media types, access methods, data rates, and distance limitations at OSI layers 1 and 2 using xBASE-y designations.

access point (AP) Device that provides a connection between wireless devices and can connect to wired networks, implementing an infrastructure mode WLAN.

adapter cable Peripheral cable converting between connector form factors or between signaling types, such as DisplayPort to HDMI.

Advanced Micro Devices (AMD) CPU manufacturer providing healthy competition for Intel. AMD chips such as the K6 or Athlon 64 and latterly the Ryzen have been very popular with computer manufacturers and have often out-performed their Intel equivalents.

Advanced RISC Machines (ARM) Designer of CPU and chipset architectures widely used in mobile devices. RISC stands for reduced instruction set computing. RISC microarchitectures use a small number of simple instructions that can be performed as a single operation. This contrasts with complex (CISC) microarchitectures, which use a large set of more powerful instructions that can take more than one operation to complete.

advanced technology extended (ATX) Standard PC case, motherboard, and power supply specification. Mini-, Micro-, and Flex-ATX specify smaller board designs.

airplane mode A toggle found on mobile devices enabling the user to disable and enable wireless functionality quickly.

app store Feature of mobile computing that provides a managed interface for installing third-party software apps.

application programming interface (API) Library of programming utilities used, for example, to enable software developers to access functions of the TCP/IP network stack under a particular operating system.

application virtualization Software delivery model where the code runs on a server and is streamed to a client.

authentication, authorization, and accounting (AAA) Security concept where a centralized platform verifies subject identification, ensures the subject is assigned relevant permissions, and then logs these actions to create an audit trail.

automatic document feeder (ADF) Device that feeds media automatically into a scanner or printer.

automatic private IP addressing (APIPA) Mechanism for Windows hosts configured to obtain an address automatically that cannot contact a DHCP server to revert to using an address from the range 169.254.x.y. This is also called a link-local address.

backlight LED or fluorescent lamp that illuminates the image on a flat-panel (TFT) screen. If the backlight component fails, only a dim image will be shown.

basic input/output system (BIOS) Legacy 32-bit firmware type that initializes hardware and provides a system setup interface for configuring boot devices and other hardware settings.

basic service set ID (BSSID) MAC address of an access point supporting a basic service area.

battery Power source for a portable computer, typically a rechargeable Lithium-ion (Li-ion) type. A small coin cell battery is also used in a computer to power CMOS RAM.

beep codes During POST, errors in hardware or the system firmware data can be brought to the attention of the user by beep noises. Each beep code is able to draw attention to a particular fault with the hardware. It was once customary for a computer to beep once to indicate that POST has been successful, though most modern computers boot silently.

binary Notational system with two values per digit (zero and one). Computers process code in binary because the transistors in its CPU and memory components also have two states (off and on).

biometric authentication Authentication mechanism that allows a user to perform a biometric scan to operate an entry or access system. Physical characteristics stored as a digital data template can be used to authenticate a user. Typical features used include facial pattern, iris, retina, fingerprint pattern, and signature recognition.

blue screen of death (BSOD) Microsoft status screen that indicates an error from which the system cannot recover (also called a stop error). Blue screens are usually caused by bad driver software or hardware faults (memory or disk). Other operating systems use similar crash indicators, such as Apple's pinwheel and Linux's kernel panic message.

Bluetooth Short-range, wireless radio-network-transmission medium normally used to connect two personal devices, such as a mobile phone and a wireless headset.

Blu-ray Disc Latest generation of optical drive technology, with disc capacity of 25 GB per layer. Transfer rates are measured in multiples of 36 MB/s.

boot option Disk or network adapter device from which an operating system can be loaded.

boot password Feature of system setup that prevents the computer from booting until the correct user password is supplied. A supervisor password restricts access to the system setup program.

bus Connections between components on the motherboard and peripheral devices providing data pathways, memory addressing, power supply, timing, and connector/port form factor.

cable modem Cable-Internet-access digital modem that uses a coaxial connection to the service provider's fiber-optic core network.

cable stripper Tool for stripping cable jacket or wire insulation.

cable tester Two-part tool used to test successful termination of copper cable by attaching to each end of a cable and energizing each wire conductor in turn with an LED to indicate an end-to-end connection.

capture card Adapter card designed to record video from a source such as a TV tuner or games console.

carriage belt Inkjet print device component that moves the print head over the paper.

cellular radio Standards for implementing data access over cellular networks are implemented as successive generations. For 2G (up to about 48 Kb/s) and 3G (up to about 42 Mb/s), there are competing GSM and CDMA provider networks. Standards for 4G (up to about 90 Mb/s) and 5G (up to about 300 Mb/s) are developed under converged LTE standards.

central processing unit (CPU) Principal microprocessor in a PC or mobile device responsible for running firmware, operating system, and applications software.

certificate Issued by a Certificate Authority (CA) as a guarantee that a public key it has issued to an organization to encrypt messages sent to it genuinely belongs to that organization.

certificate authority (CA) Server that guarantees subject identities by issuing signed digital certificate wrappers for their public keys.

channel Subdivision of frequency bands used by Wi-Fi products into smaller channels to allow multiple networks to operate at the same location without interfering with one another.

channel bonding Capability to aggregate one or more adjacent wireless channels to increase bandwidth.

chipset Processors embedded on a motherboard to support the operation of the CPU and implementing various controllers (for memory, graphics, I/O, and so on).

clock System clock signal that synchronizes the operation of all of the components within a PC. It also provides the basic timing signal for the processor, bus, and memory. The CPU typically runs at many multiples of the basic clock speed.

cloud computing Computing architecture where on-demand resources provisioned with the attributes of high availability, scalability, and elasticity are billed to customers on the basis of metered utilization.

cloud service model Classifying the provision of cloud services and the limit of the cloud service provider's responsibility as software, platform, infrastructure, and so on.

cloud service provider (CSP) Organization providing infrastructure, application, and/or storage services via an "as a service" subscription-based, cloud-centric offering.

coaxial cable Media type using two separate conductors that share a common axis categorized using the Radio Grade (RG) specifications.

code division multiple access (CDMA) Method of multiplexing a communications channel using a code to key the modulation of a particular signal. CDMA is associated with Sprint and Verizon cellular phone networks.

collision domain Network segment where nodes are attached to the same shared access media, such as a bus network or Ethernet hub.

community cloud Cloud that is deployed for shared use by cooperating tenants.

Compact Disc (CD) Optical storage technology supporting up to 700 MB per disc with recordable and re-writable media also available.

containerization Type of virtualization applied by a host operating system to provision an isolated execution environment for an application.

crimper Tool to join a Registered Jack (RJ) form factor connector to the ends of twisted-pair patch cable.

cyan, magenta, yellow, black (CMYK) Subtractive color model used by print devices. CMYK printing involves use of halftone screens. Four screens (or layers) of dots printed in each of the colors are overlaid. The size and density of the dots on each layer produce different shades of color and is viewed as a continuous tone image.

data cap Feature of mobile computing that allows use of a network connection to be limited to avoid incurring additional carrier charges.

data loss (leak) prevention (DLP) Software solution that detects and prevents sensitive information from being stored on unauthorized systems or transmitted over unauthorized networks.

datacenter Facility dedicated to the provisioning of reliable power, environmental controls, and network fabric to server computers.

DDR SDRAM (Double Data Rate SDRAM) Series of high-bandwidth system-memory standards (DDR3/DDR4/DDR5) where data is transferred twice per clock cycle.

decibel (dB) Unit for representing the power of network signaling.

decibels per isotropic (dBi) Unit for representing the increase in power gained by the directional design of a wireless antenna.

default gateway IP configuration parameter that identifies the address of a router on the local subnet that the host can use to contact other networks.

desktop as a service (DaaS) Cloud service model that provisions desktop OS and applications software.

digital camera Version of a 35 mm film camera where the film is replaced by light-sensitive diodes and electronic storage media (typically a flash memory card). The sensitivity of the array determines the maximum resolution of the image, measured in megapixels. Most mobile devices are fitted with embedded cameras that can function as both still and video cameras.

digital subscriber line (DSL) Carrier technology to implement broadband Internet access for subscribers by transferring data over voice-grade telephone lines. There are various "flavors" of DSL, notably S(ymmetric) DSL, A(symmetric)DSL, and V(ery HIgh Bit Rate)DSL.

Digital Video Interface (DVI) Legacy video interface that supports digital only or digital and analog signaling.

Digital Video/Versatile Disk (DVD) Optical storage technology supporting up to 4.7 GB per layer per disc with recordable and re-writable media also available.

digitizer As part of a touch screen assembly, the digitizer is a touch-sensitive layer placed on top of the display panel. The digitizer converts analog touch and gesture events to digital signals that can be interpreted as different types of input.

direct burial A type of outside plant (OSP) installation where cable is laid directly into the ground with no protective conduit.

DisplayPort Digital audio/video interface developed by VESA. DisplayPort supports some cross-compatibility with DVI and HDMI devices.

docking station Advanced type of port replicator designed to provide additional ports (such as network or USB) and functionality (such as expansion slots and drives) to a portable computer when used at a desk.

domain name system (DNS) Service that maps fully qualified domain name labels to IP addresses on most TCP/IP networks, including the Internet.

Domain-Based Message Authentication, Reporting, and Conformance (DMARC) Framework for ensuring proper application of SPF and DKIM utilizing a policy published as a DNS record.

DomainKeys Identified Mail (DKIM) Cryptographic authentication mechanism for mail utilizing a public key published as a DNS record.

D-subminiature shell connector (DB-9) Legacy connector form factor used for serial (9-pin) and VGA (15-pin) interfaces.

dual inline memory module (DIMM) Standard form factor for system memory. There are different pin configurations for different DDR-SDRAM RAM types.

dual-channel System-memory controller configuration that provides two data pathways between the memory modules and a compatible CPU.

duplex unit Installable option that enables a print device or scanner to use both sides of a page automatically.

dynamic frequency selection (DFS) Regulatory feature of wireless access points that prevents use of certain 5 GHz channels when in range of a facility that uses radar.

dynamic host configuration protocol (DHCP) Protocol used to automatically assign IP addressing information to hosts that have not been configured manually.

effective isotropic radiated power (EIRP) Signal strength from a transmitter, measured as the sum of transmit power, antenna cable/connector loss, and antenna gain.

elasticity Property by which a computing environment can add or remove resources in response to increasing and decreasing demands in workload.

electrostatic discharge (ESD) Metal and plastic surfaces can allow a charge to build up. This can discharge if a potential difference is formed between the charged object and an oppositely charged conductive object. This electrical discharge can damage silicon chips and computer components if they are exposed to it.

email Electronic store and forward messaging system. Email supports text messages and binary file attachments. For Internet email, an SMTP (Simple Mail Transfer Protocol) server is used to forward mail to a host. A mail client then uses either POP3 (Post Office Protocol) or IMAP (Internet Mail Access Protocol) to access the mailbox on the server and download messages.

embedded system Electronic system that is designed to perform a specific, dedicated function, such as a microcontroller in a medical drip or components in a control system managing a water treatment plant.

enclosure Chassis for connecting an internal disk unit as an external peripheral device.

end of life (EOL) Product life cycle phase where mainstream vendor support is no longer available.

error correction code (ECC) System memory (RAM) with built-in error correction security. It is more expensive than normal memory and requires motherboard support. It is typically only used in servers.

escalation In the context of support procedures, incident response, and breach-reporting, escalation is the process of involving expert and senior staff to assist in problem management.

external serial advanced technology attachment (eSATA) Variant of SATA cabling designed for external connectivity.

fan Cooling device fitted to PC cases and components to improve air flow.

fiber optic cable Network cable type that uses light signals as the basis for data transmission. Infrared light pulses are transmitted down the glass core of the fiber. The cladding that surrounds this core reflects light back to ensure transmission efficiency. Two main categories of fiber are available; multi-mode, which uses cheaper, shorter wavelength LEDs or VCSEL diodes, or single-mode, which uses more expensive, longer wavelength laser diodes. At the receiving end of the cable, light-sensitive diodes re-convert the light pulse into an electrical signal. Fiber optic cable is immune to eavesdropping and EMI, has low attenuation, supports rates of 10 Gb/s+, and is light and compact.

fiber to premise (FTTP) Internet connection type that uses a fiber link between the subscriber premises and ISP network. Fiber to the premises (FTTP) uses a full fiber link, while fiber to the curb (FTTC) retains a short segment of copper wire between the subscriber premises and a street cabinet.

filament 3-D print device media type.

file server In file server–based networks, a central machine provides dedicated file and print services to workstations. Benefits of server-based networks include ease of administration through centralization.

file transfer protocol (FTP) Application protocol used to transfer files between network hosts. Variants include S(ecure) FTP, FTP with SSL (FTPS and FTPES) and T(rivial)FTP. FTP utilizes ports 20 and 21.

finisher unit Print device component used to automate document production, such as hole punching or stapling print jobs.

firewall Software or hardware device that protects a network segment or individual host by filtering packets to an access control list.

firmware Software instructions embedded on a hardware device such as a computer motherboard. Modern types of firmware are stored in flash memory and can be updated more easily than legacy programmable read-only memory (ROM) types.

flash drive Solid state flash memory provisioned as a peripheral device with a USB interface.

flatbed scanner Type of scanner where the object is placed on a glass faceplate and the scan head moves underneath it.

form factor Size and shape of a component, determining its compatibility. Form factor is most closely associated with PC motherboard, case, and power supply designs.

frequency band Portion of the microwave radio-frequency spectrum in which wireless products operate, such as 2.4 GHz band or 5 GHz band.

F-type connector Screw down connector used with coaxial cable.

fully qualified domain name (FQDN) Unique label specified in a DNS hierarchy to identify a particular host within a subdomain within a top-level domain.

fuser Assembly in a laser print device that fixes toner to media. This is typically a combination of a heat and pressure roller.

Global Positioning System (GPS) Means of determining a receiver's position on Earth based on information received from orbital satellites.

Global System for Mobile Communication (GSM) Standard for cellular radio communications and data transfer. GSM phones use a SIM card to identify the subscriber and network provider. 4G and later data standards are developed for GSM.

Google Workspace Mobile/cloud computing office productivity and data storage suite operated by Google.

hard disk drive (HDD) Mass storage device that uses mechanical platters with a magnetic coating that are spun under disk heads that can read and write to locations on each platter (sectors).

hardware security module (HSM) An appliance for generating and storing cryptographic keys. This sort of solution may be less susceptible to tampering and insider threats than software-based storage.

header (motherboard) Connector on the motherboard for internal cabling, such as fan power and front panel ports and buttons.

headset Peripheral device supporting audio input (microphone) and output (speaker headphones).

heat sink Cooling device fitted to PC components to optimize heat transfer.

high availability (HA) Metric that defines how closely systems approach the goal of providing data availability 100% of the time while maintaining a high level of system performance.

High-Definition Multimedia Interface (HDMI) Digital audio/video interface developed for use on both consumer electronics and computer equipment.

hostname A human-readable name that identifies a network host.

hotspot Using the cellular data plan of a mobile device to provide Internet access to a laptop or PC. The PC can be tethered to the mobile by USB, Bluetooth, or Wi-Fi (a mobile hotspot).

hub Layer 1 (Physical) network device used to implement a star network topology on legacy Ethernet networks, working as a multiport repeater.

hybrid cloud Cloud deployment that uses both private and public elements.

HyperText Transfer Protocol/HTTP Secure Application protocol used to provide web content to browsers. HTTP uses port 80. HTTPS(ecure) provides for encrypted transfers, using TLS and port 443.

iCloud Mobile/cloud computing office-productivity and data-storage suite operated by Apple and closely integrated with macOS and iOS.

image Clone copy of an operating system installation (including installed software, settings, and user data) stored as a file on disk. VMs use images to store persistent data, and the technology is also used to make system backups.

imaging drum Drum or belt in a laser printer that supports a high electric charge that can be selectively removed using a laser or LED light source.

impact printer Typically a dot matrix printer, this uses pressure to transfer ink from a ribbon onto paper in a particular pattern, similar to the mechanism of a typewriter.

indoor positioning system (IPS) Technology that can derive a device's location when indoors by triangulating its proximity to radio sources such as Bluetooth beacons or Wi-Fi access points.

information technology extended (ITX) Series of motherboard form factors designed for small form factor (SFF) computers and appliances.

infrastructure as a service (IaaS) Cloud service model that provisions virtual machines and network infrastructure.

injector A device that can supply Power over Ethernet (PoE) if the Ethernet switch ports do not support it.

inkjet printer Type of printer where colored ink is sprayed onto the paper using microscopic nozzles in the print head. There are two main types of ink dispersion system: thermal shock (heating the ink to form a bubble that bursts through the nozzles) and piezoelectric (using a tiny element that changes shape to act as a pump).

in-plane switching Type of TFT display with the best overall quality, including wide viewing angles, good contrast ratio, and good response times (on premium units).

input voltage Range of alternating current (AC) voltages that a PSU can accept when connected to grid power. Some PSUs are manually switched between low-line 110–120 VAC and high-line 220–240 VAC.

input/output operations per second (IOPS) Performance indicator that measures the time taken to complete read/write operations.

insulation displacement connector (IDC) Block used to terminate twisted pair cabling at a wall plate or patch panel available in different formats, such as 110, BIX, and Krone.

integrated drive electronics (IDE) Legacy mass storage bus, most commonly implemented as extended IDE (EIDE) and also referred to as parallel advanced technology attachment (PATA). Each IDE controller port supports two devices connected over ribbon cable with three connectors (controller, primary device, and secondary device).

Intel Intel processors were used in the first IBM PCs, and the company's CPUs and chipsets continue to dominate the PC and laptop market.

Internet Message Access Protocol (IMAP) Application protocol providing a means for a client to access and manage email messages stored in a mailbox on a remote server. IMAP4 utilizes TCP port number 143, while the secure version IMAPS uses TCP/993.

Internet of Things (IoT) Devices that can report state and configuration data and be remotely managed over IP networks.

Internet Protocol (IP) Network (Internet) layer protocol in the TCP/IP suite providing packet addressing and routing for all higher-level protocols in the suite.

Internet Service Provider (ISP) Provides Internet connectivity and web services to its customers.

intrusion detection system (IDS) Security appliance or software that analyzes data from a packet sniffer to identify traffic that violates policies or rules.

inverter Fluorescent lamp backlights require AC power. An inverter component converts DC power from the motherboard to AC. The inverter can fail separately to the backlight.

IPv4 Version of the Internet Protocol that uses 32-bit address values and subnet masks typically expressed in dotted decimal notation.

IPv6 Version of the Internet Protocol that uses 64-bit address values typically expressed in canonical hex notation with slash notation network prefixes.

jitter Variation in the time it takes for a signal to reach the recipient. Jitter manifests itself as an inconsistent rate of packet delivery. If packet loss or delay is excessive, then noticeable audio or video problems (artifacts) are experienced by users.

land grid array (LGA) CPU socket form factor used predominantly by Intel where connector pins are located on the socket.

laser printer Type of printer that develops an image on a drum by using electrical charges to attract special toner, then applying it to paper. The toner is then fixed to the paper using a high-heat and pressure roller (fuser). The process can be used with black toner only or CMYK toner cartridges to create full-color prints.

latency Time taken for a signal to reach the recipient, measured in milliseconds. Latency is a particular problem for two-way applications, such as VoIP (telephone) and online conferencing.

lease (DHCP) Address configuration assigned by a DHCP server to a client for a limited period.

legacy system Hardware or software product that is no longer supported by its vendor and therefore no longer provided with security updates and patches.

light emitting diode (LED) Small, low-power lamps used both as diagnostic indicators, the backlight for a TFT display, and (as an organic LED array) in high-quality flat panels.

Lightning Proprietary connector and interface used by Apple iPhone and iPad devices.

Lightweight Directory Access Protocol (LDAP) Protocol used to access network directory databases, which store information about authorized users and their privileges, as well as other organizational information.

liquid cooling Cooling system that uses system of pipes, water blocks, and pumps to transfer heat away from components.

liquid crystal display (LCD) Flat-panel display technology where the image is made up of liquid crystal cells with color filters controlled using electrical charges. The display must be illuminated by a backlight.

load balancer Type of switch, router, or software that distributes client requests between different resources, such as communications links or similarly configured servers. This provides fault tolerance and improves throughput.

local area network (LAN) Network scope restricted to a single geographic location and owned/managed by a single organization.

local connector (LC) Small form factor push-pull fiber optic connector; available in simplex and duplex versions.

location service Feature of mobile computing that identifies or estimates the device's geographical position using GPS and/or network data.

Long Term Evolution (LTE) Packet data communications specification providing an upgrade path for both GSM and CDMA cellular networks. LTE Advanced is designed to provide 4G standard network access.

long-range fixed wireless Ground-based microwave transmission that supports long distances over precisely aligned directional antennas. These products can either make privileged use of licensed frequency bands or use public unlicensed radio-frequency spectrum.

loopback adapter Tool used to verify the integrity of a network interface port by checking that it can receive a signal generated by itself.

M.2 Hardware specification for internal adapter cards. M.2 is often used for PCIe-based SSDs.

maintenance kit On a laser printer, the fuser unit (the part that fuses toner onto the paper) needs replacing according to the maintenance kit schedule. A maintenance kit also includes new pickup, feed, and separation rollers. It may also include transfer components (roller or belt), or these may be replaced on a different schedule, depending on the printer model.

managed switch Ethernet switch that is configurable via a command-line interface or SDN controller.

mass storage Device with a persistent storage mechanism, such as hard drives, solid state drives, and optical drives.

media access control (MAC) Hardware address that uniquely identifies each network interface at layer 2 (Data Link). A MAC address is 48 bits long with the first half representing the manufacturer's organizationally unique identifier (OUI).

memory card Solid state flash memory provisioned as a peripheral device in a proprietary adapter card form factors, such as Secure Digital and microSD.

metered utilization Feature of cloud service models that allows customers to track and pay for precise compute, storage, and network resource units.

metropolitan area network (MAN) Network scope covers the area of a city (that is, no more than tens of kilometers).

Microsoft 365 Mobile/cloud computing office productivity and data storage suite operated by Microsoft.

mobile application management (MAM) Enterprise management function that enables control over apps and storage for mobile devices and other endpoints.

mobile device management (MDM) Process and supporting technologies for tracking, controlling, and securing the organization's mobile infrastructure.

modular power supply PSU design where power cables can be attached to ports on the unit as needed.

Molex connector Legacy power connector for internal devices such as hard drives and optical drives.

mSATA Connector form factor for internal solid state drives.

multicore CPU design that puts two chips onto the same package. Most CPUs are multicore (more than two cores).

multimode fiber (MMF) Fiber optic cable type using LED or vertical cavity surface emitting laser optics and graded using optical multimode types for core size and bandwidth.

multiple input multiple output (MIMO) Use of multiple reception and transmission antennas to boost wireless bandwidth via spatial multiplexing and to boost range and signal reliability via spatial diversity.

multisocket Motherboard configuration with multiple CPU sockets. The CPUs installed must be identical.

multithreading CPU architecture that exposes two or more logical processors to the OS, delivering performance benefits similar to multicore and multisocket to threaded applications.

multiuser MIMO (MU-MIMO) Use of spatial multiplexing to allow a wireless access point to support multiple client stations simultaneously.

MX record Type of DNS resource record used to identify the email servers used by a domain.

near-field communication (NFC) Standard for two-way radio communications over very short (around four inches) distances, facilitating contactless payment and similar technologies. NFC is based on RFID.

NetBIOS Session management protocol used to provide name registration and resolution services on legacy Microsoft networks.

network address translation (NAT) Routing mechanism that conceals internal addressing schemes from the public Internet by translating between a single public address on the external side of a router and private, non-routable addresses internally.

network attached storage (NAS) Storage device enclosure with network port and an embedded OS that supports typical network file access protocols (FTP and SMB for instance).

network interface card (NIC) Adapter card that provides one or more Ethernet ports for connecting hosts to a network so that they can exchange data over a link.

network mask Number of bits applied to an IP address to mask the network ID portion from the host/interface ID portion.

non-volatile memory express (NVMe) Internal interface for connecting flash memory devices, such as SSDs, directly to a PCI Express bus. NVMe allows much higher transfer rates than SATA/AHCI.

operational technology (OT) Communications network designed to implement an industrial control system rather than data networking.

optical character recognition (OCR) Software that can identify the shapes of characters and digits to convert them from printed images to electronic data files that can be modified in a word-processing program.

optical drive Mass storage device that supports CD, DVD, and/or Blu-ray media. Burner-type drives also support recording and rewriting.

optical network terminal (ONT) Device that converts between optical and electrical signaling deployed to facilitate full fiber Internet connection types.

organic LED (OLED) Type of flat panel display where each pixel is implemented as an LED, removing the need for a separate backlight.

orthogonal frequency division multiple access (OFDMA) Feature of Wi-Fi 6 allowing an access point to serve multiple client stations simultaneously.

output voltage Direct current (DC) 3.3 VDC, 5 VDC, and 12 VDC power supplied over PSU cables to computer components.

P1 connector Main power connector from the PSU to the motherboard.

page description language (PDL) Instructions that the print device can use to create an image on the page (for most printers, this means a raster describing the placement of dots on the paper).

pairing Feature of Bluetooth that establishes connectivity between two devices, often by entering a PIN.

patch cord Type of flexible network cable typically terminated with RJ45 connectors. Ethernet patch cords cannot be longer than five meters.

patch panel Type of distribution frame used with twisted pair cabling with IDCs to terminate fixed cabling on one side and modular jacks to make cross-connections to other equipment on the other.

PCI Express (PCIe) Internal expansion bus that uses serial point-to-point communications between devices. Each link can comprise one or more lanes (x1, x2, x4, x8, x12, x16, or x32). Each lane supports a full-duplex transfer rate of 500 MB/s (v1.0) up to about 4 GB/s (v5.0).

peripheral component interconnect (PCI) Legacy internal expansion bus supporting 32-bit parallel transfers working at 33 MHz.

permanent cable Type of solid network cable typically terminated to punchdown blocks that is run through wall and ceiling spaces.

personal area network (PAN) Network scope that uses close-range wireless technologies (usually based on Bluetooth or NFC) to establish communications between personal devices, such as smartphones, laptops, and printers/peripheral devices.

pickup rollers Print device components that feed paper between the input tray, print engine, and output tray.

pin grid array (PGA) CPU socket form factor used predominantly by AMD where connector pins are located on the CPU package.

plain old telephone system (POTS) Parts of a telephone network "local loop" that use voice-grade cabling. Analog data transfer over POTS using dial-up modems is slow (33.3 Kb/s).

platform as a service (PaaS) Cloud service model that provisions application and database services as a platform for development of apps.

Plenum Cable for use in building voids designed to be fire-resistant and to produce a minimal amount of smoke if burned.

port (TCP/UDP) In TCP and UDP applications, a unique number assigned to a particular application protocol. Server ports are typically assigned well-known or registered numbers, while client ports use dynamic or ephemeral numbering.

port flapping Network error where a port transitions rapidly between up and down states.

port replicator A simple device used to extend the range of ports (for example, USB, DVI, HDMI, Thunderbolt, network, and so on) available for a laptop computer when it is used on a desk.

Post Office Protocol (POP) Application protocol that enables a client to download email messages from a server mailbox to a client over port TCP/110 or secure port TCP/995.

PostScript (PS) Page description language developed by Adobe that is capable of creating accurate, device-independent output (this means that two different printer models will produce exactly the same output from the same print file).

Power over Ethernet (PoE) Specification allowing power to be supplied via switch ports and ordinary data cabling to devices such as VoIP handsets and wireless access points. Devices can draw up to about 13 W (or 25 W for PoE+).

power supply tester Type of meter designed to test that output voltages from PSU power connector cables are within expected tolerances.

power supply unit (PSU) Transformer that converts AC grid power into 3.3V, 5V, and 12V DC to power components on the motherboard. The type of PSU must match the case and motherboard form factor.

power-on self-test (POST) Test routine built into PC firmware to confirm that system components are available at boot or to signal an error condition via a beep code or on-screen status message.

preferred roaming list (PRL) Data that allows a CDMA-based handset to connect to nearby cell towers.

print bed 3-D print device component on which output is deposited.

print device Term used to describe the actual printer hardware that services a print job when submitted from an application.

print monitor In Windows, the print monitor is a process that checks the print queue (%SystemRoot%\System32\Spool\Printers\) for print jobs. When they arrive, they are processed, if necessary, then passed via a print port to the print device.

print server Computer configured to share a connected printer with other hosts. The client hosts connect to the printer share rather than directly to the print device.

printer "Printer" is often used to mean "print device" but also refers to a term used to describe the software components of a printing solution. The printer is the object that Windows sends output to. It consists of a spool directory, a printer driver, and configuration information.

Printer Control Language (PCL) Page description and printer control language developed by HP to implement printer driver functionality.

private cloud Cloud that is deployed for use by a single entity.

programmable logic controller (PLC) Type of processor designed for deployment in an industrial or outdoor setting that can automate and monitor mechanical systems.

proxy server Server that mediates the communications between a client and another server. It can filter and often modify communications as well as provide caching services to improve performance.

public cloud (multitenant) Cloud that is deployed for shared use by multiple independent tenants.

public IP address Some IP address ranges are designated for use on private networks only. Packets with source IP addresses in public ranges are permitted to be forwarded over the Internet. Packets with source IP addresses from private ranges should be blocked at Internet gateways or forwarded using some type of translation mechanism.

public switched telephone network (PSTN) Global network connecting national telecommunications systems.

punchdown tool Tool used to terminate solid twisted-pair copper cable to an insulation displacement connector block.

quadruple-channel System-memory controller configuration that provides four data pathways between the memory modules and a compatible CPU.

quality of service (QoS) Systems that differentiate data passing over the network that can reserve bandwidth for particular applications. A system that cannot guarantee a level of available bandwidth is often described as Class of Service (CoS).

radio-frequency ID (RFID) Means of encoding information into passive tags, which can be energized and read by radio waves from a reader device.

RAID0 Striping drive configuration that provides no redundancy against device failure.

RAID1 Mirrored two-disk redundant drive configuration with 50% capacity utilization.

RAID10 Stripe of mirrored four-disk redundant drive configuration with 50% capacity utilization. A RAID10 volume can support the loss of one device in each mirror.

RAID5 Striping with parity-redundant drive configuration supporting a flexible number of devices and better than 50% capacity utilization.

random-access memory (RAM) Volatile storage devices that hold computer data and program instructions while the computer is turned on.

real-time clock (RTC) Part of the system chipset that keeps track of the date and time. The RTC is powered by a battery, so the PC keeps track of the time even when it is powered down. If the computer starts losing time, it is a sign that the battery is failing.

received signal strength indicator (RSSI) Signal strength as measured at the receiver, using either decibel units or an index value.

redundant array of independent/ inexpensive disks (RAID) Specifications that support redundancy and fault tolerance for different configurations of multiple-device storage systems.

redundant power supply System case configuration supporting two power units for fault tolerance.

registered-jack connector (RJ) Series of jack/plug types used with twisted-pair cabling, such as RJ45 and RJ11.

Remote Authentication Dial-in User Service (RADIUS) AAA protocol used to manage remote and wireless authentication infrastructures.

Remote Desktop Protocol (RDP) Application protocol for operating remote connections to a host using a graphical interface. The protocol sends screen data from the remote host to the client and transfers mouse and keyboard input from the client to the remote host. It uses TCP port 3389.

reservation (DHCP) DHCP configuration that assigns either a prereserved or persistent IP address to a given host, based on its hardware address or other ID.

resin 3-D print device media type.

resource record Data file storing information about a DNS zone. The main records are as follows: A (maps a host name to an IPv4 address), AAAA (maps to an IPv6 address), CNAME (an alias for a host name), MX (the IP address of a mail server), and PTR (allows a host name to be identified from an IP address).

router Intermediate system working at the Network layer capable of forwarding packets around logical networks of different layer 1 and layer 2 types.

sandbox Computing environment that is isolated from a host system to guarantee that the environment runs in a controlled, secure fashion. Communication links between the sandbox and the host are usually completely prohibited so that malware or faulty software can be analyzed in isolation and without risk to the host.

Satellite System of microwave transmissions where orbital satellites relay signals between terrestrial receivers or other orbital satellites. Satellite internet connectivity is enabled through a reception antenna connected to the PC or network through a DVB-S modem.

scalability Property by which a computing environment is able to gracefully fulfill its ever-increasing resource needs.

scan to cloud Feature of scanners and multifunction devices that directs output to a cloud storage account.

scan to email Using an SMTP server (and possibly an LDAP server to look up recipients) to send a scanned job to a mail recipient directly.

scan to folder Using Windows Networking (SMB) to output a scanned job directly to a shared folder on the network.

scanner Type of copier that can convert the image of a physical object into an electronic data file. The two main components of a scanner are the lamp, which illuminates the object, and the recording device, an array of charge coupled devices (CCDs).

scope (DHCP) Range of consecutive IP addresses in the same subnet that a DHCP server can lease to clients.

secure boot Feature of UEFI that prevents unauthorized processes from executing during the boot operation.

Secure Shell (SSH) Application protocol supporting secure tunneling and remote terminal emulation and file copy. SSH runs over TCP port 22.

secured print Feature that holds print jobs until the user authenticates directly with the print device using a PIN or smart badge.

self-monitoring analysis and reporting technology (SMART) Technology designed to alert the user to an error condition in a mass-storage device before the disk becomes unusable.

Sender Policy Framework (SPF) DNS record identifying hosts authorized to send mail for the domain.

separation pad Print device component that ensures only a single sheet at a time is fed into the paper path.

serial ATA (SATA) Serial ATA is the most widely used interface for hard disks on desktop and laptop computers. It uses a 7-pin data connector with one device per port. There are three SATA standards specifying bandwidths of 1.5 Gb/s, 3 Gb/s, and 6 Gb/s respectively. SATA drives also use a new 15-pin power connector, though adapters for the old style 4-pin Molex connectors are available. External drives are also supported via the eSATA interface.

serial cable (RS-232) Legacy bus type using low bandwidth asynchronous serial transmission (RS-232).

Server Message Block (SMB) Application protocol used for requesting files from Windows servers and delivering them to clients. SMB allows machines to share files and printers, thus making them available for other machines to use. SMB client software is available for UNIX-based systems. Samba software allows UNIX and Linux servers or NAS appliances to run SMB services for Windows clients.

service set identifier (SSID) Character string that identifies a particular wireless LAN (WLAN).

shielded twisted pair (STP) Copper twisted-pair cabling with screening and shielding elements for individual wire pairs and/or the whole cable to reduce interference.

signal-to-noise ratio (SNR) Measurement of a wireless signal level in relation to any background noise.

Simple Mail Transfer Protocol (SMTP) Application protocol used to send mail between hosts on the Internet. Messages are sent between servers over TCP port 25 or submitted by a mail client over secure port TCP/587.

Simple Network Management Protocol (SNMP) Application protocol used for monitoring and managing network devices. SNMP works over UDP ports 161 and 162 by default.

single-channel System-memory controller configuration that provides one data pathway between the memory modules and the CPU.

single-mode fiber (SMF) Fiber optic cable type that uses laser diodes and narrow core construction to support high bandwidths over distances of more than five kilometers.

small computer systems interface (SCSI) Legacy expansion bus standard allowing for the connection of internal and external devices. Each device on a SCSI bus must be allocated a unique ID. The bus must also be terminated at both ends.

small office, home office (SOHO) Category of network type and products that are used to implement small-scale LANs and off-the-shelf Internet connection types.

smart device Device or appliance (such as a TV, refrigerator, thermostat, video entry phone, or lightbulb) that can be configured and monitored over an IoT network.

SODIMM System-memory form factor designed for use in laptops.

software as a service (SaaS) Cloud service model that provisions fully developed application services to users.

software-defined networking (SDN) APIs and compatible hardware/virtual appliances allowing for programmable network appliances and systems.

solid state drive (SSD) Persistent mass-storage device implemented using flash memory.

sound card Adapter card providing sound playback and recording functionality. A number of different audio ports exist on modern computer motherboards or on specialist sound cards. Commonly, audio ports may be marked as: audio out, audio in, speaker out, microphone input/mic, and headphones.

spam Junk, fraudulent, and malicious messaging sent over email (or instant messaging, which is called spim). Spam can also be spread via social networking.

spool Generic term describing how a print output stream is passed from a client application and stored temporarily at a print server until the print monitor can route the job to the print device.

storage area network (SAN) Network dedicated to provisioning storage resources, typically consisting of storage devices and servers connected to switches via host bus adapters.

straight-tip connector (ST) Bayonet-style twist-and-lock connector for fiber optic cabling.

subscriber connector (SC) Push/pull connector used with fiber optic cabling.

supervisory control and data acquisition (SCADA) Type of industrial control system that manages large-scale, multiple-site devices and equipment spread over geographically large areas from a host computer.

switch Intermediate system used to establish contention-free network segments at OSI layer 2 (Data Link). An unmanaged switch does not support any sort of configuration.

switched port analyzer (SPAN) Copying ingress and/or egress communications from one or more switch ports to another port. This is used to monitor communications passing over the switch.

syslog Application protocol and event-logging format enabling different appliances and software applications to transmit logs or event records to a central server. Syslog works over UDP port 514 by default.

T568A/T568B Twisted-pair termination pinouts defined in the ANSI/TIA/ EIA 568 Commercial Building Telecommunications Standards.

telnet Application protocol supporting unsecure terminal emulation for remote host management. Telnet runs over TCP port 23.

test access port (TAP) Hardware device inserted into a cable run to copy frames for analysis.

thermal paste/pad Cooling substance applied between a component and heat sink to optimize heat transfer.

thermal printer Type of printer that uses a heated print head and specially treated paper to form the image. Most direct thermal printers are handheld devices used for printing labels or receipts.

thin film transistor (TFT) Specific display technology used to implement modern flat-panel LCD displays.

Thunderbolt Thunderbolt can be used as a display interface (like DisplayPort) and as a general peripheral interface (like USB 3). The latest version uses USB-C connectors.

tone generator Two-part tool used to identify one cable within a bundle by applying an audible signal.

toner Specially formulated compound to impart dye to paper through an electrographic process (used by laser printers and photocopiers). The key properties of toner are the colorant (dye), ability to fuse (wax or plastic), and ability to hold a charge. There are three main types of toner, distinguished by the mechanism of applying the toner to the developer roller: dual component (where the toner is mixed with a separate magnetic developer), mono-component (where the toner itself is magnetic), and non-magnetic mono-component (where the toner is transferred using static properties).

touch pen Input device that can be used with a compatible digitizer/track pad/drawing tablet for natural input, such as handwriting and sketching.

touch screen A display screen combined with a digitizer that is responsive to touch input.

trackpad Sometimes synonymous with touch pad, but also a touch interface provisioned as a peripheral device, often dedicated to use with digital art applications.

transfer roller/belt Roller, corona wire, or belt assembly on a laser print device that applies a charge to the media (paper) so that it attracts toner from the photoconductor. A detac strip then removes the charge to prevent paper curl. On a color laser printer, the transfer unit is usually a belt.

Transmission Control Protocol (TCP) Protocol in the TCP/IP suite operating at the transport layer to provide connection-oriented, guaranteed delivery of packets.

Transmission Control Protocol/ Internet Protocol (TCP/IP) Network protocol suite used to implement the Internet and most WANs and LANs. It uses a four-layer network model that corresponds roughly to the OSI model as follows: Network Interface (Physical/ Data Link), Internet (Network), Transport (Transport), Application (Session, Presentation, Application).

Transport Layer Security (TLS) Security protocol that uses certificates for authentication and encryption to protect web communications and other application protocols.

triple-channel System-memory controller configuration that provides three data pathways between the memory modules and a compatible CPU.

Trivial File Transfer Protocol (TFTP) Simplified form of FTP supporting only file copying. TFTP works over UDP port 69.

troubleshooting methodology Structured approach to problem-solving using identification, theory of cause, testing, planning, implementation, verification, and documentation steps.

trusted platform module (TPM) Specification for secure hardware-based storage of encryption keys, hashed passwords, and other user- and platform-identification information.

twisted nematic (TN) Type of low-cost TFT display with relatively poor viewing angles and contrast ratio, but good response times.

twisted pair cable Network cable construction with insulated copper wires twisted about each other. A pair of color-coded wires transmits a balanced electrical signal. The twisting of the wire pairs at different rates acts to reduce interference and crosstalk.

two-factor authentication (2FA) Strong authentication mechanism that requires a user to submit two different types of credential, such as a fingerprint scan plus PIN. Often, the second credential is transmitted via a second trusted device or account. This is also referred to as 2-step verification.

TXT record DNS resource record for storing free-form string values.

unboxing Operational procedure for ensuring that a new device is installed safely to an optimum environment.

unified extensible firmware interface (UEFI) Type of system firmware providing support for 64-bit CPU operation at boot, full GUI and mouse operation at boot, and better boot security.

unified threat management (UTM) All-in-one security appliances and agents that combine the functions of a firewall, malware scanner, intrusion detection, vulnerability scanner, data-loss prevention, content filtering, and so on.

uniform resource locator (URL) Application-level addressing scheme for TCP/IP, allowing for human-readable resource addressing. For example: protocol://server/file, where "protocol" is the type of resource (HTTP, FTP), "server" is the name of the computer (www.microsoft.com), and "file" is the name of the resource you wish to access.

universal asynchronous receiver transmitter (UART) Controller that can send and receive data in an asynchronous serial format.

Universal Serial Bus (USB) USB is the main type of connection interface used on PCs. A larger Type A connector attaches to a port on the host; Type B and Mini- or Micro-Type B connectors are used for devices. USB 1.1 supports 12 Mb/s, while USB 2.0 supports

480 Mb/s and is backward compatible with 1.1 devices (which run at the slower speed). USB devices are hot swappable. A device can draw up to 2.5 W power. USB 3.0 and 3.1 define 5 Gb/s (SuperSpeed) and 10 Gb/s (SuperSpeed+) rates and can deliver 4.5 W power.

unshielded twisted pair Media type that uses copper conductors arranged in pairs that are twisted to reduce interference. Typically, cables are 4-pair or 2-pair.

USB permission Feature of system setup allowing USB ports to be disabled.

User Datagram Protocol (UDP) Protocol in the TCP/IP suite operating at the transport layer to provide connectionless, non-guaranteed communication.

vertical alignment (VA) Type of TFT display with good viewing angles and excellent contrast ratio.

video card Adapter that handles graphics processing and output to a display device over one or more video interface ports.

video graphics array (VGA) Legacy video interface supporting analog-only signaling over a 15-pin D-shell connector.

virtual desktop infrastructure (VDI) A virtualization implementation that separates the personal computing environment from a user's physical computer.

virtual local area network (VLAN) Logical network segment comprising a broadcast domain established using a feature of managed switches to assign each port a VLAN ID. Even though hosts on two VLANs may be physically connected to the same switch, local traffic is isolated to each VLAN, so they must use a router to communicate.

virtual machine (VM) Guest operating system installed on a host computer using virtualization software (a hypervisor).

virtual machine escaping (VM escaping) Attack against a virtualization platform where malware running in a

VM is able to interact directly with the hypervisor or host kernel.

virtual machine sprawl (VM sprawl) Configuration vulnerability where provisioning and deprovisioning of virtual assets are not properly authorized and monitored.

virtual private network (VPN) Secure tunnel created between two endpoints connected via an unsecure transport network (typically the Internet).

virtual RAM An OS mediates access to random-access memory (RAM) devices by assigning a virtual address space to each process. As well as protecting memory access, the memory capacity can be extended by configuring a swap space or pagefile on a mass-storage device (HDD or SSD).

virtualization Computing environment where multiple independent operating systems can be installed to a single hardware platform and run simultaneously.

virtualization support CPU extensions to allow better performance when a host runs multiple guest operating systems or VMs.

Voice over Internet Protocol (VoIP) Generic name for protocols that carry voice traffic over data networks.

wattage rating Measure of how much power can be supplied by a PSU.

webcam Type of digital camera used to stream and record video. There are many types, from devices built into laptops to standalone units. While early devices were only capable of low resolutions, most webcams are now HD-capable.

wide area network (WAN) Network scope that spans a large geographical area, incorporating more than one site and often a mix of different media types and protocols plus the use of public telecommunications networks.

Wi-Fi Brand name for the IEEE 802.11 standards that can be used to implement a wireless local area network (WLAN).

Wi-Fi analyzer Device or software that can report characteristics of a WLAN, such as signal strength and channel utilization.

Wireless Internet Service Provider (WISP) ISP offering Internet access over ground-based Line of Sight (LoS) microwave transmitters.

wireless local area network (WLAN) Network scope and type that uses wireless radio communications based on some variant of the 802.11 (Wi-Fi) standard series.

Index

Note: Page numbers with *Italics* represent charts, graphs, and diagrams.